CATCH-22
in the
Supreme Court

edited by

JOSHUA WARREN

This book is an original collection of public government works, compiled for the purpose of research and scholarly inquiry.

Persuant to Title 17 U.S. Code § 105: "Copyright protection under this title is not available for any work of the United States Government". Therefore, the court texts collected in this compilation are not protected by U.S. copyright.

Additionally, persuant to Title 17 U.S. Code § 107 the use "for purposes such as criticism, comment, news reporting, teaching (including multiple copies for classroom use), scholarship, or research, is not an infringement of copyright." Therefore, even if there was copyright protection in any of the works included in these government texts (and there isn't, persuant to § 105), the use in this compilation is a fair use persuant to § 107.

This book makes no claim to rights in the word "Catch-22" and this book is neither licensed by, nor affiliated with Joseph Heller, nor any subsequent publisher of the book of that title.

All other rights reserved.
Copyright © 2016   Joshua Warren
WARRBO.com, New York, NY
All rights reserved.
ISBN: 1539185176
ISBN-13: 978-1539185178

DEDICATION

to the empty chair

and

the 4-4

Published on the first Tuesday of October, 2016

Rest in peace dead justice.

Long live the Supreme Court of these United States.

Footnote 41 in Justice Stewart's dissent to Parker v. Levy (1974):

Cf. J. Heller, Catch-22, p. 395 (Dell ed. 1970):

"'We accuse you also of the commission of crimes and infractions we don't even know about yet. Guilty or innocent?'

"'I don't know, sir. How can I say if you don't tell me what they are?'

"'How can we tell you if we don't know?'"

EDITORS NOTE

These are the filed opinions from nine U.S. Supreme Court cases. Since these are all Supreme Court cases, these opinions are public domain and readily available on the internet. Full case citations are provided for each case. The court syllabi and references have been omitted. Use the internet to read more about these cases. Search for the case name and citation on any major search engine and you should be able to find full copies of the court filing and ample commentary. This book offers the opportunity to read full opinions from the Supreme Court collected around a single word. The term catch-22 has become part of the lexicon of law and can be found in many other federal cases at lower courts. These nine cases from America's highest court are each important in their own right and for different reasons. This book simply offers a view of how this term has appeared in the Supreme Court and does not claim to offer any definitive meaning beyond that.

FOREWORD

The idea of studying law by searching for a single phrase would usually be considered poor legal research. This book does not attempt to provide a complete picture of the law applicable to catch-22. It is merely a record of the mentions of "catch-22" in U.S. Supreme Court opinions.

This is both entertaining and informative. It can be amusing and humorous to read these references and this exposure to reading legal procedure will improve the readers' general understanding of American jurisprudence. Look up words you don't understand.

Some of these cases are old. Subsequent court action may have overruled these cases or limit their holdings. There is no guarantee that the law presented in this book is still good law. After you read a case, search the internet and find out more.

These are all serious legal texts each with a serious legal purpose about real people in real situations. These texts are also appreciable as the high art of American legal rhetoric. This collection is gathered with the hope of finding entertainment in scholarship and artistic interest in the written arts of jurisprudential work.

INTRODUCTION TO READING COURT OPINIONS FOR FUN (and learning)

THE ONLY RULE is PATIENCE

If you are reading this then, you already know how to read. Go somewhere with appropriate lighting and a comfortable chair and read patiently. Mark unusual words and move on, and later use a legal dictionary and internet search engines to amplify your understanding. With patience you will learn to read more.

As you begin to read a case, notice the year and notice what branch of the federal court the appeal to the Supreme Court came from. Identify the parties, what they are seeking, what prior legal actions have occurred. Or just jump right to any paragraph you want and start reading.

This book is designed to read cases. There is no over-reaching legal thesis and the cases are not individually summarized beyond the introductions. These real cases are simply arranged with hopes of sparking interest in reading law. The goal is merely to enjoy the reading.

Reading law will improve your ability to read law.

As you read you may consider yourself as a law clerk and try to summarize the arguments and holdings of each opinion. This is good practice and any attempt to write (and re-write) a case summary will promote your thinking. But if you prefer, just sit under a tree and enjoy the writings of the U.S. Supreme Court.

These are all serious legal texts each with a serious legal purpose but they are also appreciable as the high art of American legal civilization. This collection is gathered as a research and learning tool with the hope of finding some entertainment in scholarly works of jurisprudential art.

INTRODUCTION TO CATCH-22 IN THE SUPREME COURT

This book includes nine cases from the U.S. Supreme Court that include the term "catch-22." The spelling changes slightly throughout the cases, beginning as "Catch-22" with quotes and hyphen and becoming catch-22, lowercase. Along the way, one opinion uses catch 22 without hyphen or capitalization. The word moves from a book of fiction into the American legal lexicon.

This nine case collection begins with the case of Parker v. Levy in 1974. Incidentally this case was also published in another book of this series, "Creativity in the Supreme Court," because creativity is also mentioned. In this case, Justice Stewart dissents, thrice citing a Yale Law Journal note entitled: "Taps for the Real Catch-22." That note was published in 1972 as an note with no named author.

The title of the Yale note is a direct reference to Joseph Heller's book. Stewart also quotes a short passage from the book (see footnote 41). The Yale article makes specific commentary on the same case that is before the Court (the court martial of a doctor, Capt. Howard Levy). The court's majority decision, written by then Associate Justice William Rehnquist, upholds the court martial against this Vietnam-era doctor.

This Yale journal note, also appears in the prior decision on this same case at the 3rd Circuit, see Levy v. Parker, 478 F.2d 772 (3d Cir. 1973) and in a related case at the D.C. District Court, see Stolte v. Laird, 353 F. Supp. 1392 (1972). And it also appeared in a 2012 defense motion filed on behalf of Pfc. Bradley Manning (aka Chelsea Manning)[1].

The second case in this book is Helstoski v. Meanor. Five years after the Levy case, this dissent similarly accuses the majority of creating a legal catch-22. This case is not about military articles but is about

---

[1] See Defense Motion, U.S. v Manning, available at: https://archive.org/stream/usa-v-manning-appellate-exhibits-0-99/AE%2059%20Defense%20Article%20134%20Motion_djvu.txt

official government behaviors by a congressman. Justice Brennan, in the text of his dissenting opinion, specifically references Joseph Heller's book.

By the third case, Carey v. Brown, in 1980, the work no longer needs citation. Justice Rehnquist (writing as Associate Justice in dissent), maintains the capitalization and quotation marks, but there is no citation either to the book or to prior precedent. Here, again, this is a dissent accusing the majority of creating a bind, but this time the bound actor is a state. The state had legislated against residential picketing. The majority finds a first amendment violation. Justice Rehnquist has begun to co-opt the word.

In the fourth case, Aguilar v. Felton, Justice Rehnquist dissents again, and again placing "Catch-22" in quotes without citing the book. He does cite his own prior dissent from another case, Wallace v. Jaffree (an opinion which did not use the word and is therefore not included in this book collection). This is Justice Rehnquist putting a "Catch-22" pin onto his growing line of first amendment argument.

The fifth case, Bowen v. Kendrick, has the word in both the majority and the dissent. The court composition has changed. Justice Rehnquist is now Chief Justice and it is his majority opinion that includes the word, citing back to his dissenting opinion from Aguilar v. Felton (above). Justice Blackmun, in dissent, responds to the majority argument.

In the sixth case, Price Waterhouse v. Hopkins, the word appears without quotes, and without either capitalization or hyphenation (catch 22). Justice Brennan uses the phrase in his majority opinion, applying Title VII to employment discrimination based on gender. The case involves sex stereotyping and inconsistent treatment of female aggressiveness in employment that demands aggression.

It was almost two decades between the sixth and seventh case and the court composition has significantly changed. This seventh case, Boumediene v. Bush, returns to capitalization and hyphenation (Catch-22) but the quotes are gone, not to return in the later two cases. Here, Chief Justice Roberts, in dissent, revives the word as a slur against the majority reasoning. This case is particularly important case for the modern military and is about standing for enemy combatants. Incidentally, this case is also included in another book in this series, "Werewolf in the Federal Courts," because it refers to werewolves, as regarding enemy guerilla operations.

The eighth case is <u>Crawford v. Nashville</u>. Like Price Waterhouse v. Hopkins (above), this case is also about Title VII and gender discrimination but there is no citation back to Price Waterhouse because it is a different issue. The issue in this case is about the reporting of discrimination and whether one might be punished for speaking up but alternatively punished for not reporting. Justice Souter, writing for the majority calls this a catch-22.

Finally, the ninth case in this book is <u>Shelby County v. Holder</u>, an important case striking down portions of the Voting Rights act. Here, Justice Ginsburg takes up the word in her dissent, suggesting that the majority has put a bind on Congress preventing progress unless they also fail to achieve that progress.

Note that both the eighth and ninth cases retain the hyphen but use the word in lowercase (catch-22). Throughout these nine cases the reader sees catch-22 move from a proper noun, academic reference of a fictional text, to a generic term of legal art, a vague representation of bureaucratic binds.

<u>Parker v. Levy</u>, 417 U.S. 733 (1974)
<u>Helstoski v. Meanor</u>, 442 U.S. 500 (1979)
<u>Carey v. Brown</u>, 447 U.S. 455 (1980)
<u>Aguilar v. Felton</u>, 473 U.S. 402 (1985)
<u>Bowen v. Kendrick</u>, 487 U.S. 589 (1988)
<u>Price Waterhouse v. Hopkins</u>, 490 U.S. 228 (1989)
<u>Boumediene v. Bush</u>, 553 U.S. 723 (2007)
<u>Crawford v. Metro. Gov't of Nashville & Davidson</u>, 555 U.S. 271 (2009)
<u>Shelby County v. Holder</u>, 133 S. Ct. 2612 (2013)

TABLE OF CASES

1. *Parker v. Levy*, ... *page 20*
   417 U.S. 733 (1974)

    REHNQUIST, J., delivered the opinion of the Court, in which Burger, C.J., and White, Blackmun, and Powell, JJ., joined.
    BLACKMUN, J., filed a concurring statement, in which Burger, C.J., joined.
    DOUGLAS, J., filed a dissenting opinion.
    STEWART, J., filed a dissenting opinion, in which Douglas, J., and Brennan, J. joined.

2. *Helstoski v. Meanor*, ... *page 60*
   442 U.S. 500 (1979)

    BURGER, C. J., delivered the opinion of the Court, in which Stewart, White, Marshall, Blackmun, Rehnquist, and Stevens, JJ., joined.
    BRENNAN, J., filed a dissenting opinion.

3. *Carey v. Brown*, ... *page 68*
   447 U.S. 455 (1980)

    BRENNAN, J., delivered the opinion of the Court, in which Stewart, White, Marshall, Powell, and Stevens, JJ., joined.
    STEWART, J., filed a concurring opinion.
    REHNQUIST, J., filed a dissenting opinion, in which Burger, C.J., and Blackmun, J., joined.

4. *Aguilar v. Felton*, ... *page 95*
   473 U.S. 402 (1985)

    BRENNAN, J., delivered the opinion of the Court, in which Marshall, Blackmun, Powell, and Stevens, JJ., joined.
    POWELL, J., filed a concurring opinion.
    BURGER, C. J., filed a dissenting opinion.
    REHNQUIST, J., filed a dissenting opinion.
    O'CONNOR, J., filed a dissenting opinion, in which Rehnquist, J., joined as to Parts II and III.

5. *Bowen v. Kendrick*, ... page 120
   487 U.S. 589 (1988)

   REHNQUIST, C. J., delivered the opinion of the Court, in which White, O'Connor, Scalia, and Kennedy, JJ., joined.
   O'CONNOR, J., filed a concurring opinion.
   KENNEDY, J., filed a concurring opinion, in which Scalia, J., joined.
   BLACKMUN, J., filed a dissenting opinion, in which Brennan, Marshall, and Stevens, JJ., joined.

6. *Price Waterhouse v. Hopkins*, ... page 166
   490 U.S. 228 (1989)

   BRENNAN, J., announced the judgment of the Court and delivered an opinion, in which Marshall, Blackmun, and Stevens, JJ., joined.
   WHITE, J., filed an opinion concurring in the judgment.
   O'CONNOR, J., filed an opinion concurring in the judgment.
   KENNEDY, J., filed a dissenting opinion, in which Rehnquist, C. J., and Scalia, J., joined.

7. *Boumediene v. Bush*, ... page 215
   553 U.S. 723 (2007)

   KENNEDY, J., delivered the opinion of the Court, in which Stevens, Souter, Ginsburg, and Breyer, JJ., joined.
   SOUTER, J., filed a concurring opinion, in which Ginsburg and Breyer, JJ., joined.
   ROBERTS, C. J., filed a dissenting opinion, in which Scalia, Thomas, and Alito, JJ., joined.
   SCALIA, J., filed a dissenting opinion, in which Roberts, C. J., and Thomas and Alito, JJ., joined.

8. *Crawford v. Metro. Gov't of Nashville & Davidson County*,
   555 U.S. 271 (2009) ....*page 302*

   SOUTER, J., delivered the opinion of the Court, in which Roberts, C. J., and Stevens, Scalia, Kennedy, Ginsburg, and Breyer, JJ., joined.

   ALITO, J., filed an opinion concurring in the judgment, in which Thomas, J., joined.

9. *Shelby County v. Holder*, ...*page 312*
   133 S. Ct. 2612

   ROBERTS, C. J., delivered the opinion of the Court, in which Scalia, Kennedy, Thomas, and Alito, JJ., joined.

   THOMAS, J., filed a concurring opinion.

   GINSBURG, J., filed a dissenting opinion, in which Breyer, Sotomayor, and Kagan, JJ., joined.

CASE EXCERPTS

Parker v. Levy, 417 U.S. 733 (1974)
<u>Justice Stewart dissenting:</u>

FN2, FN11, & FN42:
Note, Taps for the Real *Catch-22*, 81 Yale L. J. 1518 n. 3.

FN41:
Cf. J. Heller, Catch-22, p. 395 (Dell ed. 1970): "'We accuse you also of the commission of crimes and infractions we don't even know about yet. Guilty or innocent?' 'I don't know, sir. How can I say if you don't tell me what they are?' 'How can we tell you if we don't know?'"

Helstoski v. Meanor, 442 U.S. 500 (1979)
<u>Justice Brennan dissenting:</u>

Mr. Helstoski may well be excused if he views the Court's holding as if it were a line out of Joseph Heller's "***Catch-22***." He cannot utilize mandamus because he should have sought a direct appeal.

Carey v. Brown, 447 U.S. 455 (1980)
<u>Justice Rehnquist dissenting:</u>

Here, where Illinois has drafted such a statute, avoiding an outright ban on all residential picketing, avoiding reliance on any vague or discretionary standards, and permitting categories of permissible picketing activity at residences where the State has determined the resident's own actions have substantially reduced his interest in privacy, the Court in response confronts the State with the "***Catch-22***' that the less restrictive categories are constitutionally infirm under principles of equal protection. Under the Court's approach today, the State would fare better by adopting *more* restrictive means, a judicial incentive I had thought this Court would hesitate to afford.

Either that, or uniform restrictions will be found invalid under the *First Amendment* and categorical exceptions found invalid under the *Equal Protection Clause*, with the result that speech and only speech will be entitled to protection. This can only mean that the hymns of praise in prior opinions celebrating carefully drawn statutes are no more than sympathetic clucking, and in fact the State is damned if it does and damned if it doesn't.

Aguilar v. Felton, 473 U.S. 402 (1985)
Justice Rehnquist dissenting:

I dissent for the reasons stated in my dissenting opinion in *Wallace v. Jaffree, 472 U.S. 38, 91, 86 L. Ed. 2d 29, 105 S. Ct. 2479 (1985)*. In this case the Court takes advantage of the "**Catch-22**" paradox of its own creation, see *Wallace, supra, at 109-110* (REHNQUIST, J., dissenting), whereby aid must be supervised to ensure no entanglement but the supervision itself is held to cause an entanglement.

Bowen v. Kendrick, 487 U.S. 589 (1988)
Justice Rehnquist majority opinion:

This, of course, brings us to the third prong of the *Lemon Establishment Clause* "test" -- the question whether the AFLA leads to "'an excessive government entanglement with religion.'" *Lemon, 403 U.S., at 613* (quoting *Walz v. Tax Comm'n, 397 U.S., at 674*). There is no doubt that the monitoring of AFLA grants is necessary if the Secretary is to ensure that public money is to be spent in the way that Congress intended and in a way that comports with the *Establishment Clause*. Accordingly, this litigation presents us with yet another "**Catch-22**" argument: the very supervision of the aid to assure that it does not further religion renders the statute invalid. See

Justice Blackmun dissenting:
The majority's brief discussion of *Lemon*'s "entanglement" prong is limited to (a) criticizing it as a "**Catch-22**," and (b) concluding that

because there is "no reason to assume that the religious organizations which may receive grants are 'pervasively sectarian' in the same sense as the Court has held parochial schools to be," there is no need to be concerned about the degree of monitoring which will be necessary to ensure compliance with the AFLA and the *Establishment Clause.*

Price Waterhouse v. Hopkins, 490 U.S. 228 (1989)
<u>Justice Brennan majority opinion:</u>

An employer who objects to aggressiveness in women but whose positions require this trait places women in an intolerable and impermissible ***catch 22***: out of a job if they behave aggressively and out of a job if they do not. Title VII lifts women out of this bind.

Boumediene v. Bush, 553 U.S. 723 (2007)
<u>Chief Justice Roberts dissenting:</u>

The basis for the Court's contrary conclusion is summed up in the following sentence near the end of its opinion: "To hold that the detainees at Guantanamo may, under the DTA, challenge the President's legal authority to detain them, contest the CSRT's findings of fact, supplement the record on review with exculpatory evidence, and request an order of release would come close to reinstating the § *2241* habeas corpus process Congress sought to deny them." *Ante, at 792, 171 L. Ed. 2d, at 94.* In other words, any interpretation of the statute that would make it an adequate substitute for habeas must be rejected, because Congress could not possibly have intended to enact an adequate substitute for habeas. The Court could have saved itself a lot of trouble if it had simply announced this ***Catch-22*** approach at the beginning rather than the end of its opinion.

Crawford v. Metro. Gov't of Nashville, 555 U.S. 271 (2009)
<u>Justice Souter majority opinion:</u>

The appeals court's rule would thus create a real dilemma for any knowledgeable employee in a hostile work environment if the boss took steps to assure a defense under our cases. If the employee reported discrimination in response to the enquiries, the employer might well be free to penalize her for speaking up. But if she kept quiet about the discrimination and later filed a Title VII claim, the employer might well escape liability, arguing that it "exercised reasonable care to prevent and correct [any discrimination] promptly" but "the plaintiff employee unreasonably failed to take advantage of . . . preventive or corrective opportunities provided by the employer." *Ellerth, supra,* at 765, 118 S. Ct. 2257, 141 L. Ed. 2d 633. Nothing in the statute's text or our precedent supports this **catch-22**.

Shelby County v. Holder, 133 S. Ct. 2612 (2013)
<u>Justice Ginsburg dissenting:</u>

Demand for a record of violations equivalent to the one earlier made would expose Congress to a **catch-22**. If the statute was working, there would be less evidence of discrimination, so opponents might argue that Congress should not be allowed to renew the statute. In contrast, if the statute was not working, there would be plenty of evidence of discrimination, but scant reason to renew a failed regulatory regime.

Catch-22 in the Supreme Court

Parker v. Levy

Supreme Court of the United States

February 20, 1974, Argued

June 19, 1974, Decided

No. 73-206

417 U.S. 733
94 S. Ct. 2547
41 L. Ed. 2d 439

PARKER, WARDEN, ET AL. v. LEVY

APPEAL FROM THE UNITED STATES COURT OF APPEALS FOR THE THIRD CIRCUIT.

Solicitor General Bork argued the cause for appellants. With him on the brief were Assistant Attorney General Petersen, Allan A. Tuttle, and Jerome M. Feit.

Charles Morgan, Jr., argued the cause for appellee. With him on the brief were Norman Siegel, Laughlin McDonald, Morris Brown, Neil Bradley, Reber F. Boult, Jr., Anthony G. Amsterdam, Alan H. Levine, Burt Neuborne, Melvin L. Wulf, and Henry W. Sawyer III.[*]

Rehnquist, J., delivered the opinion of the Court, in which Burger, C. J., and White, Blackmun, and Powell, JJ., joined.
Blackmun, J., filed a concurring statement, in which Burger, C. J., joined.
Douglas, J., filed a dissenting opinion.
Stewart, J., filed a dissenting opinion, in which Douglas, J., and Brennan, J. joined.
Marshall, J., took no part in the consideration or decision of the case.

---

[*] Briefs of amici curiae urging affirmance were filed by Marvin M. Karpatkin and Thomas M. Comerford for the Association of the Bar of the City of New York, and by Joseph H. Sharlitt and Neal E. Krucoff for Richard G. Augenblick.

JUSTICE REHNQUIST delivered the opinion of the Court.

Appellee Howard Levy, a physician, was a captain in the Army stationed at Fort Jackson, South Carolina. He had entered the Army under the so-called "Berry Plan," [1] under which he agreed to serve for two years in the Armed Forces if permitted first to complete his medical training. From the time he entered on active duty in July 1965 until his trial by court-martial, he was assigned as Chief of the Dermatological Service of the United States Army Hospital at Fort Jackson. On June 2, 1967, appellee was convicted by a general court-martial of violations of Arts. 90, 133, and 134 of the Uniform Code of Military Justice, and sentenced to dismissal from the service, forfeiture of all pay and allowances, and confinement for three years at hard labor.

The facts upon which his conviction rests are virtually undisputed. The evidence admitted at his court-martial trial showed that one of the functions of the hospital to which appellee was assigned was that of training Special Forces aide men. As Chief of the Dermatological Service, appellee was to conduct a clinic for those aide men. In the late summer of 1966, it came to the attention of the hospital commander that the dermatology training of the students was unsatisfactory. After investigating the program and determining that appellee had totally neglected his duties, the commander called appellee to his office and personally handed him a written order to conduct the training. Appellee read the order, said that he understood it, but declared that he would not obey it because of his medical ethics. Appellee persisted in his refusal to obey the order, and later reviews of the program established that the training was still not being carried out.

During the same period of time, appellee made several public statements to enlisted personnel at the post, of which the following is representative:

"The United States is wrong in being involved in the Viet Nam War. I would refuse to go to Viet Nam if ordered to do so. I don't see why any colored soldier would go to Viet Nam: they should refuse to go to Viet Nam and if sent should refuse to fight because they are discriminated against and denied their freedom in the United States, and they are sacrificed and discriminated against in Viet Nam by being given all the hazardous duty and they are suffering the majority of casualties. If I were a colored soldier I would refuse to go to Viet Nam and if I were a colored soldier and were sent I would refuse to fight. Special Forces personnel are liars and thieves and killers of peasants and murderers of women and children."

---

[1] See *50 U. S. C. App. § 454 (j)*.

Appellee's military superiors originally contemplated nonjudicial proceedings against him under Art. 15 of the Uniform Code of Military Justice, *10 U. S. C. § 815*, but later determined that court-martial proceedings were appropriate. The specification under Art. 90 alleged that appellee willfully disobeyed the hospital commandant's order to establish the training program, in violation of that article, which punishes anyone subject to the Uniform Code of Military Justice who "willfully disobeys a lawful command of his superior commissioned officer." [2] Statements to enlisted personnel were listed as specifications under the charges of violating Arts. 133 and 134 of the Code. Article 133 provides for the punishment of "conduct unbecoming an officer and a gentleman," [3] while Art. 134 proscribes, *inter alia*, "all disorders and neglects to the prejudice of good order and discipline in the armed forces." [4]

The specification under Art. 134 alleged that appellee "did, at Fort Jackson, South Carolina, . . . with design to promote disloyalty and disaffection among the troops, publicly utter [certain] statements to divers enlisted personnel at divers times . . . ."

---

[2] Article 90 of the Uniform Code of Military Justice, *10 U. S. C. § 890*, provides:

"Any person subject to this chapter who --

"(1) strikes his superior commissioned officer or draws or lifts up any weapon or offers any violence against him while he is in the execution of his office; or

"(2) willfully disobeys a lawful command of his superior commissioned officer;

"shall be punished, if the offense is committed in time of war, by death or such other punishment as a court-martial may direct, and if the offense is committed at any other time, by such punishment, other than death, as a court-martial may direct."

[3] Article 133 of the Uniform Code of Military Justice, *10 U. S. C. § 933*, provides:

"Any commissioned officer, cadet, or midshipman who is convicted of conduct unbecoming an officer and a gentleman shall be punished as a court-martial may direct."

[4] Article 134 of the Uniform Code of Military Justice, *10 U. S. C. § 934*, provides:

"Though not specifically mentioned in this chapter, all disorders and neglects to the prejudice of good order and discipline in the armed forces, all conduct of a nature to bring discredit upon the armed forces, and crimes and offenses not capital, of which persons subject to this chapter may be guilty, shall be taken cognizance of by a general, special, or summary court-martial, according to the nature and degree of the offense, and shall be punished at the discretion of that court."

⁵ The specification under Art. 133 alleged that appellee did "while in the performance of his duties at the United States Army Hospital . . . wrongfully and dishonorably" make statements variously described as intemperate, defamatory, provoking, disloyal, contemptuous, and disrespectful to Special Forces personnel and to enlisted personnel who were patients or under his supervision. ⁶

---

⁵ The specification under Art. 134 (Charge II) alleged in full:

"In that Captain Howard B. Levy, U.S. Army, Headquarters and Headquarters Company, United States Army Hospital, Fort Jackson, South Carolina, did, at Fort Jackson, South Carolina, on or about the period February 1966 to December 1966, with design to promote disloyalty and disaffection among the troops, publicly utter the following statements to divers enlisted personnel at divers times: 'The United States is wrong in being involved in the Viet Nam War. I would refuse to go to Viet Nam if ordered to do so. I don't see why any colored soldier would go to Viet Nam; they should refuse to go to Viet Nam and if sent should refuse to fight because they are discriminated against and denied their freedom in the United States, and they are sacrificed and discriminated against in Viet Nam by being given all the hazardous duty and they are suffering the majority of casualties. If I were a colored soldier I would refuse to go to Viet Nam and if I were a colored soldier and were sent I would refuse to fight. Special Forces personnel are liars and thieves and killers of peasants and murderers of women and children,' or words to that effect, which statements were disloyal to the United States, to the prejudice of good order and discipline in the armed forces."

⁶ The specification under Art. 133 (Additional Charge I) alleged that appellee

"did . . . at divers times during the period from on or about February 1966 to on or about December 1966 while in the performance of his duties at the United States Army Hospital, Fort Jackson, South Carolina, wrongfully and dishonorably make the following statements of the nature and to and in the presence and hearing of the persons as hereinafter more particularly described, to wit: (1) Intemperate, defamatory, provoking, and disloyal statements to special forces enlisted personnel present for training in the United States Army Hospital, Fort Jackson, South Carolina, and in the presence and hearing of other enlisted personnel, both patients and those performing duty under his immediate supervision and control and dependent patients as follows: 'I will not train special forces personnel because they are "liars and thieves," "killers of peasants," and "murderers of women and children,"' or words to that effect; (2) Intemperate and disloyal statements to enlisted personnel, both patients and those performing duty under his immediate supervision and control as follows: 'I would refuse to go to Vietnam if ordered to do so. I do not see why any colored soldier would go to Vietnam. They should refuse to go to Vietnam; and, if sent, they should refuse to fight because they are discriminated against and denied their freedom in the United States and they are sacrificed and discriminated against in Vietnam by being given all the hazardous duty, and they are suffering the majority of casualties. If I were a colored soldier, I would refuse to go to Vietnam; and, if I were a colored soldier and if I were sent to Vietnam, I would refuse to fight', or words to that effect; (3) Intemperate, contemptuous, and

Appellee was convicted by the court-martial, and his conviction was sustained on his appeals within the military.[7] After he had exhausted this avenue of relief, he sought federal habeas corpus in the United States District Court for the Middle District of Pennsylvania, challenging his court-martial conviction on a number of grounds. The District Court, on the basis of the voluminous record of the military proceedings and the argument of counsel, denied relief. It held that the "various articles of the Uniform Code of Military Justice are not unconstitutional for vagueness," citing several decisions of the United States Court of Military Appeals.[8] The court rejected the balance of appellee's claims without addressing them individually, noting that the military tribunals had given fair consideration to them and that the role of the federal courts in reviewing court-martial proceedings was a limited one.

The Court of Appeals reversed, holding in a lengthy opinion that Arts. 133 and 134 are void for vagueness. *478 F.2d 772 (CA3 1973)*. The court found little difficulty in concluding that "as measured by contemporary standards of vagueness applicable to statutes and ordinances governing civilians," the general articles "do not pass constitutional muster." It relied on such cases as *Grayned v. City of Rockford, 408 U.S. 104 (1972); Papachristou v. City of Jacksonville, 405 U.S. 156 (1972); Giaccio v. Pennsylvania, 382 U.S. 399 (1966); Coates v. City of Cincinnati, 402 U.S. 611 (1971)*, and *Gelling v. Texas, 343 U.S. 960 (1952)*. The Court of Appeals did not rule that

---

disrespectful statements to enlisted personnel performing duty under his immediate supervision and control, as follows: 'The Hospital Commander has given me an order to train special forces personnel, which order I have refused and will not obey,' or words to that effect; (4) Intemperate, defamatory, provoking, and disloyal statements to special forces personnel in the presence and hearing of enlisted personnel performing duty under his immediate supervision and control, as follows: 'I hope when you get to Vietnam something happens to you and you are injured,' or words to that effect; all of which statements were made to persons who knew that the said Howard B. Levy was a commissioned officer in the active service of the United States Army."

[7] *United States v. Levy, CM 416463, 39 C. M. R. 672 (1968)*, petition for review denied, *No. 21,641, 18 U. S. C. M. A. 627 (1969)*. Appellee also unsuccessfully sought relief in the civilian courts. *Levy v. Corcoran, 128 U. S. App. D. C. 388, 389 F.2d 929*, application for stay denied, *387 U.S. 915*, cert. denied, *389 U.S. 960 (1967); Levy v. Resor, 17 U. S. C. M. A. 135, 37 C. M. R. 399 (1967); Levy* v. Resor, Civ. No. 67-442 (SC July 5, 1967), aff'd *per curiam, 384 U.S. 689 (CA4 1967)*, cert. denied, *389 U.S. 1049 (1968); Levy v. Dillon, 286 F.Supp. 593 (Kan. 1968)*, aff'd, *415 F.2d 1263 (CA10 1969)*.

[8] *United States v. Howe, 17 U. S. C. M. A. 165, 37 C. M. R. 429 (1967); United States v. Sadinsky, 14 U. S. C. M. A. 563, 34 C. M. R. 343 (1964); United States v. Frantz, 2 U. S. C. M. A. 161, 7 C. M. R. 37 (1953)*.

appellee was punished for doing things he could not reasonably have known constituted conduct proscribed by Art. 133 or 134. Indeed, it recognized that his conduct fell within one of the examples of Art. 134 violations contained in the Manual for Courts-Martial, promulgated by the President by Executive Order. [9] Nonetheless, relying chiefly on *Gooding v. Wilson, 405 U.S. 518 (1972)*, the Court found the possibility that Arts. 133 and 134 would be applied to future conduct of others as to which there was insufficient warning, or which was within the area of protected *First Amendment* expression, was enough to give appellee standing to challenge both articles on their face. While it acknowledged that different standards might in some circumstances be applicable in considering vagueness challenges to provisions which govern the conduct of members of the Armed Forces, the Court saw in the case of Arts. 133 and 134 no "countervailing military considerations which justify the twisting of established standards of due process in order to hold inviolate these articles, so clearly repugnant under current constitutional values." Turning finally to appellee's conviction under Art. 90, the Court held that the joint consideration of Art. 90 charges with the charges under Arts. 133 and 134 gave rise to a "reasonable possibility" that appellee's right to a fair trial was prejudiced, so that a new trial was required.

Appellants appealed to this Court pursuant to *28 U. S. C. § 1252*. We set the case for oral argument, and postponed consideration of the question of our jurisdiction to the hearing on the merits. *414 U.S. 973 (1973)*.[10]

---

[9] Manual for Courts-Martial para. 213f (5) (1969).

[10] Title *28 U. S. C. § 1252* provides in pertinent part that "any party may appeal to the Supreme Court from an interlocutory or final judgment, decree or order of any court of the United States, . . . holding an Act of Congress unconstitutional in any civil action, suit, or proceeding to which the United States or any of its agencies, or any officer or employee thereof, as such officer or employee, is a party. . . ." In his motion to dismiss or affirm, appellee urged a lack of jurisdiction in this Court because the attorneys who filed and served the notice of appeal were not attorneys of record and because the attorney effecting service failed to comply with Rule 33.3 (c) of this Court requiring persons not admitted to the Bar of this Court to prove service by affidavit, rather than by certificate. Appellee alternatively contended that *28 U. S. C. § 1252* was not intended to permit appeals from the courts of appeals, but only from the district courts. We postponed consideration of the jurisdictional question to the hearing on the merits. Appellee now renews his contentions that the asserted defects in appellants' filing of their notice of appeal should be treated as a failure to file a timely notice of appeal, and that the appeal must accordingly be dismissed. See, *e. g., Territo v. United States, 358 U.S. 279 (1959); Department of Banking v. Pink, 317 U.S. 264, 268 (1942)*. He also urges that the question whether an appeal may be taken to this Court from the Court of Appeals under *28 U. S. C. § 1252* presents a question of first impression.

This Court has long recognized that the military is, by necessity, a specialized society separate from civilian society. We have also recognized that the military has, again by necessity, developed laws and traditions of its own during its long history. The differences between the military and civilian communities result from the fact that "it is the primary business of armies and navies to fight or be ready to fight wars should the occasion arise." *United States ex rel. Toth v. Quarles, 350 U.S. 11, 17 (1955).* In *In re Grimley, 137 U.S. 147, 153 (1890),* the Court observed: "An army is not a deliberative body. It is the executive arm. Its law is that of obedience. No question can be left open as to the right to command in the officer, or the duty of obedience in the soldier." More recently we noted that "the military constitutes a specialized community governed by a separate discipline from that of the civilian," *Orloff v. Willoughby, 345 U.S. 83, 94 (1953),* and that "the rights of men in the armed forces must perforce be conditioned to meet certain overriding demands of discipline and duty . . . ." *Burns v. Wilson, 346 U.S. 137, 140 (1953)* (plurality opinion). We have also recognized that a military officer holds a particular position of responsibility and command in the Armed Forces:

"The President's commission . . . recites that 'reposing special trust and confidence in the patriotism, valor, fidelity and abilities' of the appointee he is named to the specified rank during the pleasure of the President." *Orloff v. Willoughby, supra, at 91.*

Just as military society has been a society apart from civilian society, so "military law . . . is a jurisprudence which exists separate and apart from the law which governs in our federal judicial establishment." *Burns v. Wilson, supra, at 140.* And to maintain the discipline essential to perform its mission effectively, the military has developed what "may not unfitly be called the customary military law" or "general

---

We hold that "any court of the United States," as used in § 1252, includes the courts of appeals. The Reviser's Note for § 1252 states that the "term 'any court of the United States' includes the courts of appeals . . . ." The definitional section of Title 28, 28 U. S. C. § 451, provides: "As used in this title: The term 'court of the United States' includes the Supreme Court of the United States, courts of appeals, district courts . . . ." Our reading of § 1252 is further supported by that section's legislative history. *Section 1252* was originally enacted as § 2 of the Act of August 24, 1937, c. 754, 50 Stat. 751. Section 5 of that same Act defined "any court of the United States" to include any "circuit court of appeals." We also find no merit in appellee's contention that the asserted defects in appellants' notice of appeal deprive this Court of jurisdiction. As appellants note, appellee makes no claim that he did not have actual notice of the filing of the notice of appeal. Assuming that there was technical noncompliance with *Rule 33* of this Court for the reasons urged by appellee, that noncompliance does not deprive this Court of jurisdiction. Cf. *Taglianetti v. United States, 394 U.S. 316 n. 1 (1969); Heflin v. United States, 358 U.S. 415, 418 n. 7 (1959).*

usage of the military service." *Martin v. Mott, 12 Wheat. 19, 35 (1827)*. As the opinion in *Martin* v. *Mott* demonstrates, the Court has approved the enforcement of those military customs and usages by courts-martial from the early days of this Nation:

". . . Courts Martial, when duly organized, are bound to execute their duties, and regulate their modes of proceeding, in the absence of positive enactments. Upon any other principle, Courts Martial would be left without any adequate means to exercise the authority confided to them: for there could scarcely be framed a positive code to provide for the infinite variety of incidents applicable to them." *Id., at 35-36.*

An examination of the British antecedents of our military law shows that the military law of Britain had long contained the forebears of Arts. 133 and 134 in remarkably similar language. The Articles of the Earl of Essex (1642) provided that "all other faults, disorders and offenses, not mentioned in these Articles, shall be punished according to the general customs and laws of war." One of the British Articles of War of 1765 made punishable "all Disorders or Neglects . . . to the Prejudice of good Order and Military Discipline . . ." that were not mentioned in the other articles. [11] Another of those articles provided:

"Whatsoever Commissioned Officer shall be convicted before a General Court-martial, of behaving in a scandalous infamous Manner, such as is unbecoming the Character of an Officer and a Gentleman, shall be discharged from Our Service." [12]

In 1775 the Continental Congress adopted this last article, along with 68 others for the governance of its army. [13] The following year it was resolved by the Congress that "the committee on spies be directed to revise the rules and articles of war; this being a committee of five, consisting of John Adams, Thomas Jefferson, John Rutledge, James Wilson and R. R. Livingston . . . ." [14] The article was included in the new set of articles prepared by the Committee, which Congress adopted on

---

[11] Section XX, Art. III, of the British Articles of War of 1765; W. Winthrop, Military Law and Precedents 946 (2d ed. 1920).

[12] Section XV, Art. XXIII, of the British Articles of War of 1765; Winthrop, *supra*, at 945.

[13] Article XLVII of the American Articles of War of 1775; Winthrop, *supra*, at 957.

[14] *Id., at 22.*

September 20, 1776. [15] After being once more re-enacted without change in text in 1786, it was revised and expanded in 1806, omitting the terms "scandalous" and "infamous," so as to read:

"Any commissioned officer convicted before a general court-martial of conduct unbecoming an officer and a gentleman, shall be dismissed [from] the service." [16]

From 1806, it remained basically unchanged through numerous congressional re-enactments until it was enacted as Art. 133 of the Uniform Code of Military Justice in 1951.

The British article punishing "all Disorders and Neglects . . ." was also adopted by the Continental Congress in 1775 and re-enacted in 1776. [17] Except for a revision in 1916, which added the clause punishing "all conduct of a nature to bring discredit upon the military service," [18] substantially the same language was preserved throughout the various re-enactments of this article too, until in 1951 it was enacted as Art. 134 of the Uniform Code of Military Justice.

Decisions of this Court during the last century have recognized that the longstanding customs and usages of the services impart accepted meaning to the seemingly imprecise standards of Arts. 133 and 134. In *Dynes v. Hoover, 20 How. 65 (1857)*, this Court upheld the Navy's general article, which provided that "all crimes committed by persons belonging to the navy, which are not specified in the foregoing articles, shall be punished according to the laws and customs in such cases at sea." The Court reasoned:

"When offences and crimes are not given in terms or by definition, the want of it may be supplied by a comprehensive enactment, such as the 32d article of the rules for the government of the navy, which means that courts martial have jurisdiction of such crimes as are not specified, but which have been recognised to be crimes and offences by the usages in the navy of all nations, and that they shall be punished according to the laws and customs of the sea. Notwithstanding the

---

[15] Article 21 of Section XIV of the American Articles of War of 1776; Winthrop, *supra*, at 969.

[16] Article 83 of Section 1 of the American Articles of War of 1806; Winthrop, *supra*, at 983.

[17] Article L of the American Articles of War of 1775; Art. 5 of section XVIII of the American Articles of War of 1776; Winthrop, *supra*, at 957, 971.

[18] Act of Aug. 29, 1916, c. 418, 39 Stat. 619, 666.

apparent indeterminateness of such a provision, it is not liable to abuse; for what those crimes are, and how they are to be punished, is well known by practical men in the navy and army, and by those who have studied the law of courts martial, and the offences of which the different courts martial have cognizance." *Id., at 82.*

In *Smith v. Whitney, 116 U.S. 167 (1886)*, this Court refused to issue a writ of prohibition against Smith's court-martial trial on charges of "scandalous conduct tending to the destruction of good morals" and "culpable inefficiency in the performance of duty." The Court again recognized the role of "the usages and customs of war" and "old practice in the army" in the interpretation of military law by military tribunals. *Id., at 178-179.*

In *United States v. Fletcher, 148 U.S. 84 (1893)*, the Court considered a court-martial conviction under what is now Art. 133, rejecting Captain Fletcher's claim that the court-martial could not properly have held that his refusal to pay a just debt was "conduct unbecoming an officer and a gentleman." The Court of Claims decision which the Court affirmed in *Fletcher* stressed the military's "higher code termed honor, which holds its society to stricter accountability" [19] and with which those trained only in civilian law are unfamiliar. In *Swaim v. United States, 165 U.S. 553 (1897)*, the Court affirmed another Court of Claims decision, this time refusing to disturb a court-martial conviction for conduct "to the prejudice of good order and military discipline" in violation of the Articles of War. The Court recognized the role of "unwritten law or usage" in giving meaning to the language of what is now Art. 134. In rejecting Swaim's argument that the evidence failed to establish an offense under the article, the Court said:

"This is the very matter that falls within the province of courts-martial, and in respect to which their conclusions cannot be controlled or reviewed by the civil courts. As was said in *Smith v. Whitney, 116 U.S. 178*, 'of questions not depending upon the construction of the statutes, but upon unwritten military law or usage, within the jurisdiction of courts-martial, military or naval officers, from their training and experience in the service, are more competent judges than the courts of common law.'" *165 U.S., at 562.*

The Court of Claims had observed that cases involving "conduct to the prejudice of good order and military discipline," as opposed to conduct unbecoming an officer, "are still further beyond the bounds of ordinary judicial judgment, for they are not measurable by our innate sense of right and wrong, of honor and dishonor,

---

[19] *Fletcher v. United States, 26 Ct. Cl. 541, 563 (1891).*

but must be gauged by an actual knowledge and experience of military life, its usages and duties."[20]

II

The differences noted by this settled line of authority, first between the military community and the civilian community, and second between military law and civilian law, continue in the present day under the Uniform Code of Military Justice. That Code cannot be equated to a civilian criminal code. It, and the various versions of the Articles of War which have preceded it, regulate aspects of the conduct of members of the military which in the civilian sphere are left unregulated. While a civilian criminal code carves out a relatively small segment of potential conduct and declares it criminal, the Uniform Code of Military Justice essays more varied regulation of a much larger segment of the activities of the more tightly knit military community. In civilian life there is no legal sanction -- civil or criminal -- for failure to behave as an officer and a gentleman; in the military world, Art. 133 imposes such a sanction on a commissioned officer. The Code likewise imposes other sanctions for conduct that in civilian life is not subject to criminal penalties: disrespect toward superior commissioned officers, Art. 89, *10 U. S. C. § 889*; cruelty toward, or oppression or maltreatment of subordinates, Art. 93, *10 U. S. C. § 893*; negligent damaging, destruction, or wrongful disposition of military property of the United States, Art. 108, *10 U. S. C. § 908*; improper hazarding of a vessel, Art. 110, *10 U. S. C. § 910*; drunkenness on duty, Art. 112, *10 U. S. C. § 912*; and malingering, Art. 115, *10 U. S. C. § 915*.

But the other side of the coin is that the penalties provided in the Code vary from death and substantial penal confinement at one extreme to forms of administrative discipline which are below the threshold of what would normally be considered a criminal sanction at the other. Though all of the offenses described in the Code are punishable "as a court-martial may direct," and the accused may demand a trial by court-martial,[21] Art. 15 of the Code also provides for the imposition of nonjudicial "disciplinary punishments" for minor offenses without the intervention of a court-martial. *10 U. S. C. § 815*. The punishments imposable under that article are of a limited nature. With respect to officers, punishment may encompass suspension of duty, arrest in quarters for not more than 30 days, restriction for not more than 60 days, and forfeiture of pay for a limited period of time. In the case of enlisted men,

---

[20] *Swaim v. United States*, 28 Ct. Cl. 173, 228 (1893).

[21] Art. 15 (a), *10 U. S. C. § 815 (a)*.

such punishment may additionally include, among other things, reduction to the next inferior pay grade, extra fatigue duty, and correctional custody for not more than seven consecutive days. Thus, while legal proceedings actually brought before a court-martial are prosecuted in the name of the Government, and the accused has the right to demand that he be proceeded against in this manner before any sanctions may be imposed upon him, a range of minor sanctions for lesser infractions are often imposed administratively. Forfeiture of pay, reduction in rank, and even dismissal from the service bring to mind the law of labor-management relations as much as the civilian criminal law.

In short, the Uniform Code of Military Justice regulates a far broader range of the conduct of military personnel than a typical state criminal code regulates of the conduct of civilians; but at the same time the enforcement of that Code in the area of minor offenses is often by sanctions which are more akin to administrative or civil sanctions than to civilian criminal ones.

The availability of these lesser sanctions is not surprising in view of the different relationship of the Government to members of the military. It is not only that of lawgiver to citizen, but also that of employer to employee. Indeed, unlike the civilian situation, the Government is often employer, landlord, provisioner, and lawgiver rolled into one. That relationship also reflects the different purposes of the two communities. As we observed in *In re Grimley, 137 U.S., at 153*, the military "is the executive arm" whose "law is that of obedience." While members of the military community enjoy many of the same rights and bear many of the same burdens as do members of the civilian community, within the military community there is simply not the same autonomy as there is in the larger civilian community. The military establishment is subject to the control of the civilian Commander in Chief and the civilian departmental heads under him, and its function is to carry out the policies made by those civilian superiors.

Perhaps because of the broader sweep of the Uniform Code, the military makes an effort to advise its personnel of the contents of the Uniform Code, rather than depending on the ancient doctrine that everyone is presumed to know the law. Article 137 of the Uniform Code, *10 U. S. C. § 937*, requires that the provisions of the Code be "carefully explained to each enlisted member at the time of his entrance on active duty, or within six days thereafter" and that they be "explained again after he has completed six months of active duty . . . ." Thus the numerically largest component of the services, the enlisted personnel, who might be expected to be a good deal less familiar with the Uniform Code than commissioned officers, are required by its terms to receive instructions in its provisions. Article 137 further provides that a complete text of the Code and of the regulations prescribed by the

President "shall be made available to any person on active duty, upon his request, for his personal examination."

With these very significant differences between military law and civilian law and between the military community and the civilian community in mind, we turn to appellee's challenges to the constitutionality of Arts. 133 and 134.

III

Appellee urges that both Art. 133 and Art. 134 (the general article) are "void for vagueness" under the *Due Process Clause of the Fifth Amendment* and overbroad in violation of the *First Amendment*. We have recently said of the vagueness doctrine:

"The doctrine incorporates notions of fair notice or warning. Moreover, it requires legislatures to set reasonably clear guidelines for law enforcement officials and triers of fact in order to prevent 'arbitrary and discriminatory enforcement.' Where a statute's literal scope, unaided by a narrowing state court interpretation, is capable of reaching expression sheltered by the *First Amendment*, the doctrine demands a greater degree of specificity than in other contexts." *Smith v. Goguen, 415 U.S. 566, 572-573 (1974)*.

Each of these articles has been construed by the United States Court of Military Appeals or by other military authorities in such a manner as to at least partially narrow its otherwise broad scope.

The United States Court of Military Appeals has stated that Art. 134 must be judged "not in vacuo, but in the context in which the years have placed it," *United States v. Frantz, 2 U. S. C. M. A. 161, 163, 7 C. M. R. 37, 39 (1953)*. Article 134 does not make "every irregular, mischievous, or improper act a court-martial offense," *United States v. Sadinsky, 14 U. S. C. M. A. 563, 565, 34 C. M. R. 343, 345 (1964)*, but its reach is limited to conduct that is "'directly and palpably -- as distinguished from indirectly and remotely -- prejudicial to good order and discipline.'" *Ibid.; United States v. Holiday, 4 U. S. C. M. A. 454, 456, 16 C. M. R. 28, 30 (1954)*. It applies only to calls for active opposition to the military policy of the United States, *United States v. Priest, 21 U. S. C. M. A. 564, 45 C. M. R. 338 (1972)*, and does not reach all "disagreement with, or objection to, a policy of the Government." *United States v. Harvey, 19 U. S. C. M. A. 539, 544, 42 C. M. R. 141, 146 (1971)*.

The Manual for Courts-Martial restates these limitations on the scope of Art. 134. [22] It goes on to say that "certain disloyal statements by military personnel" may be

---

[22] Manual for Courts-Martial para. 213c (1969).

punishable under Art. 134. "Examples are utterances designed to promote disloyalty or disaffection among troops, as praising the enemy, attacking the war aims of the United States, or denouncing our form of government." [23] Extensive additional interpretative materials are contained in the portions of the Manual devoted to Art. 134, which describe more than sixty illustrative offenses.

The Court of Military Appeals has likewise limited the scope of Art. 133. Quoting from W. Winthrop, Military Law and Precedents 711-712 (2d ed. 1920), that court has stated:

"""... To constitute therefore the conduct here denounced, the act which forms the basis of the charge must have a double significance and effect. Though it need not amount to a crime, it must offend so seriously against law, justice, morality or decorum as to expose to disgrace, socially or as a man, the offender, and at the same time must be of such a nature or committed under such circumstances as to bring dishonor or disrepute upon the military profession which he represents.""" *United States v. Howe, 17 U. S. C. M. A. 165, 177-178, 37 C. M. R. 429, 441-442 (1967).*

The effect of these constructions of Arts. 133 and 134 by the Court of Military Appeals and by other military authorities has been twofold: It has narrowed the very broad reach of the literal language of the articles, and at the same time has supplied considerable specificity by way of examples of the conduct which they cover. It would be idle to pretend that there are not areas within the general confines of the articles' language which have been left vague despite these narrowing constructions. But even though sizable areas of uncertainty as to the coverage of the articles may remain after their official interpretation by authoritative military sources, further content may be supplied even in these areas by less formalized custom and usage. *Dynes v. Hoover, 20 How. 65 (1857).* And there also cannot be the slightest doubt under the military precedents that there is a substantial range of conduct to which both articles clearly apply without vagueness or imprecision. It is within that range that appellee's conduct squarely falls, as the Court of Appeals recognized:

"Neither are we unmindful that the *Manual for Courts-Martial* offers as an example of an offense under Article 134, 'praising the enemy, attacking the war aims of the United States, or denouncing our form of government.' With the possible exception of the statement that 'Special Forces personnel are liars and thieves and killers of peasants and murderers of women and children,' it would appear that

---

[23] *Id.*, para. 213f (5).

each statement for which [Levy] was court-martialed could fall within the example given in the *Manual*." *478 F.2d, at 794.*

The Court of Appeals went on to hold, however, that even though Levy's own conduct was clearly prohibited, the void-for-vagueness doctrine conferred standing upon him to challenge the imprecision of the language of the articles as they might be applied to hypothetical situations outside the considerable area within which their applicability was similarly clear.

We disagree with the Court of Appeals both in its approach to this question and in its resolution of it. This Court has on more than one occasion invalidated statutes under the *Due Process Clause of the Fifth* or *Fourteenth Amendment* because they contained no standard whatever by which criminality could be ascertained, and the doctrine of these cases has subsequently acquired the shorthand description of "void for vagueness." *Lanzetta v. New Jersey, 306 U.S. 451 (1939)*; *Winters v. New York, 333 U.S. 507 (1948)*. In these cases, the criminal provision is vague "not in the sense that it requires a person to conform his conduct to an imprecise but comprehensible normative standard, but rather in the sense that no standard of conduct is specified at all." *Coates v. City of Cincinnati, 402 U.S. 611, 614 (1971).*

But the Court of Appeals found in this case, and we agree, that Arts. 133 and 134 are subject to no such sweeping condemnation. Levy had fair notice from the language of each article that the particular conduct which he engaged in was punishable. This is a case, then, of the type adverted to in *Smith* v. *Goguen*, in which the statutes "by their terms or as authoritatively construed apply without question to certain activities, but whose application to other behavior is uncertain." *415 U.S., at 578.* The result of the Court of Appeals' conclusion that Levy had standing to challenge the vagueness of these articles as they might be hypothetically applied to the conduct of others, even though he was squarely within their prohibitions, may stem from a blending of the doctrine of vagueness with the doctrine of overbreadth, but we do not believe it is supported by prior decisions of this Court.

We have noted in *Smith* v. *Goguen, id., at 573*, that more precision in drafting may be required because of the vagueness doctrine in the case of regulation of expression. For the reasons which differentiate military society from civilian society, we think Congress is permitted to legislate both with greater breadth and with greater flexibility when prescribing the rules by which the former shall be governed than it is when prescribing rules for the latter. But each of these differentiations relates to how strict a test of vagueness shall be applied in judging a particular criminal statute. None of them suggests that one who has received fair warning of the criminality of his own conduct from the statute in question is nonetheless entitled to attack it because the language would not give similar fair warning with respect to other conduct which might be within its broad and literal ambit. One to whose conduct a statute clearly applies may not successfully challenge it for vagueness.

Because of the factors differentiating military society from civilian society, we hold that the proper standard of review for a vagueness challenge to the articles of the Code is the standard which applies to criminal statutes regulating economic affairs. Clearly, that standard is met here, for as the Court stated in *United States v. National Dairy Corp.*, 372 U.S. 29, 32-33 (1963):

"The strong presumptive validity that attaches to an Act of Congress has led this Court to hold many times that statutes are not automatically invalidated as vague simply because difficulty is found in determining whether certain marginal offenses fall within their language. E. g., *Jordan v. De George*, 341 U.S. 223, 231 (1951), and *United States v. Petrillo*, 332 U.S. 1, 7 (1947). Indeed, we have consistently sought an interpretation which supports the constitutionality of legislation. E. g., *United States v. Rumely*, 345 U.S. 41, 47 (1953); *Crowell v. Benson*, 285 U.S. 22, 62 (1932); see *Screws v. United States*, 325 U.S. 91 (1945).

"Void for vagueness simply means that criminal responsibility should not attach where one could not reasonably understand that his contemplated conduct is proscribed. *United States v. Harriss*, 347 U.S. 612, 617 (1954). In determining the sufficiency of the notice a statute must of necessity be examined in the light of the conduct with which a defendant is charged. *Robinson v. United States*, 324 U.S. 282 (1945)."

Since appellee could have had no reasonable doubt that his public statements urging Negro enlisted men not to go to Vietnam if ordered to do so were both "unbecoming an officer and a gentleman," and "to the prejudice of good order and discipline in the armed forces," in violation of the provisions of Arts. 133 and 134, respectively, his challenge to them as unconstitutionally vague under the *Due Process Clause of the Fifth Amendment* must fail.

We likewise reject appellee's contention that Arts. 133 and 134 are facially invalid because of their "overbreadth." In *Gooding v. Wilson*, 405 U.S., at 520-521, the Court said:

"It matters not that the words appellee used might have been constitutionally prohibited under a narrowly and precisely drawn statute. At least when statutes regulate or proscribe speech and when 'no readily apparent construction suggests itself as a vehicle for rehabilitating the statutes in a single prosecution,' *Dombrowski v. Pfister*, 380 U.S. 479, 491 (1965), the transcendent value to all society of constitutionally protected expression is deemed to justify allowing 'attacks on overly broad statutes with no requirement that the person making the attack demonstrate that his own conduct could not be regulated by a statute drawn with the requisite narrow specificity'. . . ."

While the members of the military are not excluded from the protection granted by the *First Amendment*, the different character of the military community and of the military mission requires a different application of those protections. The fundamental necessity for obedience, and the consequent necessity for imposition of discipline, may render permissible within the military that which would be constitutionally impermissible outside it. Doctrines of *First Amendment* overbreadth asserted in support of challenges to imprecise language like that contained in Arts. 133 and 134 are not exempt from the operation of these principles. The United States Court of Military Appeals has sensibly expounded the reason for this different application of *First Amendment* doctrines in its opinion in *United States v. Priest, 21 U. S. C. M. A., at 570, 45 C. M. R., at 344*:

"In the armed forces some restrictions exist for reasons that have no counterpart in the civilian community. Disrespectful and contemptuous speech, even advocacy of violent change, is tolerable in the civilian community, for it does not directly affect the capacity of the Government to discharge its responsibilities unless it both is directed to inciting imminent lawless action and is likely to produce such action. *Brandenburg v. Ohio, [395 U.S. 444 (1969)]*. In military life, however, other considerations must be weighed. The armed forces depend on a command structure that at times must commit men to combat, not only hazarding their lives but ultimately involving the security of the Nation itself. Speech that is protected in the civil population may nonetheless undermine the effectiveness of response to command. If it does, it is constitutionally unprotected. *United States v. Gray, [20 U. S. C. M. A. 63, 42 C. M. R. 255 (1970)]*."

In *Broadrick v. Oklahoma, 413 U.S. 601, 610 (1973)*, we said that "embedded in the traditional rules governing constitutional adjudication is the principle that a person to whom a statute may constitutionally be applied will not be heard to challenge that statute on the ground that it may conceivably be applied unconstitutionally to others, in other situations not before the Court." We further commented in that case that "in the past, the Court has recognized some limited exceptions to these principles, but only because of the most 'weighty countervailing policies.'" *Id., at 611*. One of those exceptions "has been carved out in the area of the *First Amendment*." *Ibid*. In the *First Amendment* context attacks have been permitted "on overly broad statutes with no requirement that the person making the attack demonstrate that his own conduct could not be regulated by a statute drawn with the requisite narrow specificity," *Dombrowski v. Pfister, 380 U.S. 479, 486 (1965)*.

This Court has, however, repeatedly expressed its reluctance to strike down a statute on its face where there were a substantial number of situations to which it might be validly applied. Thus, even if there are marginal applications in which a statute would infringe on *First Amendment* values, facial invalidation is inappropriate if the "remainder of the statute . . . covers a whole range of easily identifiable and constitutionally proscribable . . . conduct . . . ." *CSC v. Letter Carriers, 413 U.S. 548, 580-581 (1973)*. And the Court recognized in *Broadrick, supra*, that "where conduct and not merely speech is involved" the overbreadth must "not only be real, but substantial as well, judged in relation to the statute's plainly legitimate sweep." *413 U.S., at 615*. Here, as the Manual makes clear, both Art. 133 and Art. 134 do prohibit a "whole range of easily identifiable and constitutionally proscribable . . . conduct."

Both *Broadrick* and *Letter Carriers* involved basically noncriminal sanctions imposed on federal and state employees who were otherwise civilians. The Uniform Code of Military Justice applies a series of sanctions, varying from severe criminal penalties to administratively imposed minor sanctions, upon members of the military. However, for the reasons dictating a different application of *First Amendment* principles in the military context described above, we think that the "'weighty countervailing policies,'" *Broadrick, supra, at 611*, which permit the extension of standing in *First Amendment* cases involving civilian society, must be accorded a good deal less weight in the military context.

There is a wide range of the conduct of military personnel to which Arts. 133 and 134 may be applied without infringement of the *First Amendment*. While there may lurk at the fringes of the articles, even in the light of their narrowing construction by the United States Court of Military Appeals, some possibility that conduct which would be ultimately held to be protected by the *First Amendment* could be included within their prohibition, we deem this insufficient to invalidate either of them at the behest of appellee. His conduct, that of a commissioned officer publicly urging enlisted personnel to refuse to obey orders which might send them into combat, was unprotected under the most expansive notions of the *First Amendment*. Articles 133 and 134 may constitutionally prohibit that conduct, and a sufficiently large number of similar or related types of conduct so as to preclude their invalidation for overbreadth.

IV

Appellee urges that should we disagree with the Court of Appeals as to the constitutionality of Arts. 133 and 134, we should nonetheless affirm its judgment by invalidating his conviction under Art. 90. He contends that to carry out the hospital commandant's order to train aide men in dermatology would have constituted participation in a war crime, and that the commandant gave the order in question, knowing that it would be disobeyed, for the sole purpose of increasing the punishment which could be imposed upon appellee. The Court of Appeals observed that each of these defenses was recognized under the Uniform Code of Military Justice, but had been resolved against appellee on a factual basis by the court-martial which convicted him. The court went on to say that:

"In isolation, these factual determinations adverse to appellant under an admittedly valid article are not of constitutional significance and resultantly, are beyond our scope of review." *478 F.2d, at 797.*

See *Whelchel v. McDonald, 340 U.S. 122 (1950).* We agree with the Court of Appeals.

Appellee in his brief here mounts a number of alternative attacks on the sentence imposed by the court-martial, attacks which were not treated by the Court of Appeals in its opinion in this case. To the extent that these points were properly presented to the District Court and preserved on appeal to the Court of Appeals, and to the extent that they are open on federal habeas corpus review of court-martial convictions under *Burns v. Wilson, 346 U.S. 137 (1953)*, we believe they should be addressed by the Court of Appeals in the first instance.

Reversed.

MR. JUSTICE MARSHALL took no part in the consideration or decision of this case.

JUSTICE BLACKMUN, with whom CHIEF JUSTICE joins, concurring.

I wholly concur in the Court's opinion. I write only to state what for me is a crucial difference between the majority and dissenting views in this case. My Brother STEWART complains that men of common intelligence must necessarily speculate as to what "conduct unbecoming an officer and a gentleman" or conduct to the "prejudice of good order and discipline in the armed forces" or conduct "of a nature to bring discredit upon the armed forces" really means. He implies that the average soldier or sailor would not reasonably expect, under the general articles, to suffer military reprimand or punishment for engaging in sexual acts with a chicken, or window peeping in a trailer park, or cheating while calling bingo numbers. *Post*, at 779. He argues that "times have surely changed" and that the articles are "so vague and uncertain as to be incomprehensible to the servicemen who are to be governed by them." *Post*, at 781, 788.

These assertions are, of course, no less judicial fantasy than that which the dissent charges the majority of indulging. In actuality, what is at issue here are concepts of "right" and "wrong" and whether the civil law can accommodate, in special circumstances, a system of law which expects more of the individual in the context of a broader variety of relationships than one finds in civilian life.

In my judgment, times have not changed in the area of moral precepts. Fundamental concepts of right and wrong are the same now as they were under the Articles of the Earl of Essex (1642), or the British Articles of War of 1765, or the American Articles of War of 1775, or during the long line of precedents of this and other courts upholding the general articles. And, however unfortunate it may be, it is still necessary to maintain a disciplined and obedient fighting force.

A noted commentator, Professor Bishop of Yale, has recently stated that "almost all of the acts actually charged under [Articles 133 and 134], notably drug offenses, are of a sort which ordinary soldiers know, or should know, to be punishable." J. Bishop, Justice Under Fire 87-88 (1974). I agree. The subtle airs that govern the command relationship are not always capable of specification. The general articles are essential not only to punish patently criminal conduct, but also to foster an orderly and dutiful fighting force. One need only read the history of the permissive -- and short-lived -- regime of the Soviet Army in the early days of the Russian Revolution to know that command indulgence of an undisciplined rank and file can decimate a fighting force. Moreover, the fearful specter of arbitrary enforcement of the articles, the engine of the dissent, is disabled, in my view, by the elaborate system of military justice that Congress has provided to servicemen, and by the self-evident, and self-selective, factor that commanders who are arbitrary with their charges will not produce the efficient and effective military organization this country needs and demands for its defense.

In *Fletcher v. United States, 26 Ct. Cl. 541 (1891)*, the Court of Claims reviewed a court-martial finding that a Captain Fletcher was guilty of conduct unbecoming an officer in having, *"'with intent to defraud, failed, neglected, and refused to pay [one W.] the amount due him, though repeatedly requested to do so.'"* The court found this charged offense to come within the article. The sentiments expressed by Judge Nott, writing for the court in that case, are just as applicable to the case we decide today.

"It must be confessed that, in the affairs of civil life and under the rules and principles of municipal law, what we ordinarily know as fraud relates to the obtaining of a man's money, and not to refusing to pay it back. It is hard for the trained lawyer to conceive of an indictment or declaration which should allege that the defendant defrauded A or B by refusing to return to him the money which he had borrowed from him. Our legal training, the legal habit of mind, as it is termed, inclines us to dissociate punishment from acts which the law does not define as offenses. As one of our greatest writers of fiction puts it, with metaphysical fitness and accurate sarcasm, as she describes one of her legal characters, 'His moral horizon was limited by the civil code of Tennessee.' That it is a fraud to obtain a man's money by dishonest representations, but not a fraud to keep it afterwards by any amount of lying and deceit, is a distinction of statutory tracing. The gambler who throws away other people's money and the spendthrift who uses it in luxurious living instead of paying it back, cheat and defraud their creditors as effectually as the knaves and sharpers who drift within the meshes of the criminal law. We learnt as law students in Blackstone that there are things which are *malum in se* and, in addition to them, things which are merely *malum prohibitum*; but unhappily in the affairs of real life we find that there are many things which are *malum in se* without likewise being *malum prohibitum*. In military life there is a higher code termed honor, which holds its society to stricter accountability; and it is not desirable that the standard of the Army shall come down to the requirements of a criminal code." *Id., at 562-563.*

Relativistic notions of right and wrong, or situation ethics, as some call it, have achieved in recent times a disturbingly high level of prominence in this country, both in the guise of law reform, and as a justification of conduct that persons would normally eschew as immoral and even illegal. The truth is that the moral horizons of the American people are not footloose, or limited solely by "the civil code of Tennessee." The law should, in appropriate circumstances, be flexible enough to recognize the moral dimension of man and his instincts concerning that which is honorable, decent, and right. *

---

* My Brother DOUGLAS' rendition of Captain Levy's offense in this case would leave one to believe that Levy was punished for speaking against the Vietnam war at an Army wives' tea party. In fact, Levy was convicted under charges that he, while in the performance of his duties at the United States Army Hospital in Fort Jackson, South Carolina, told the enlisted personnel in his charge that he would not train Special Forces aide men "because they are 'liars and thieves,' 'killers of peasants,' and 'murderers of women and children.'" He also stated, in the presence of patients and those performing duty under his immediate supervision, that he would refuse to go to Vietnam if ordered to do so and they should refuse to do so. Moreover, after being ordered to give dermatological training to aide men, he announced to his students that "the Hospital Commander has given me an order to train special forces personnel, which order I have refused and will not obey." Unless one is to blind one's eyes in utter worship of the *First Amendment*, it needs no explication that these disloyal statements and actions undertaken by an officer in the course of duty, are subject to sanction.

JUSTICE DOUGLAS, dissenting.

Congress by Art. I, § 8, cl. 14, has power "To make Rules for the Government and Regulation of the land and naval Forces."

Articles 133 [1] and 134 [2] of the Uniform Code of Military Justice, *10 U. S. C. §§ 933 and 934*, at issue in this case, trace their legitimacy to that power.

So far as I can discover the only express exemption of a person in the Armed Services from the protection of the *Bill of Rights* is that contained in the *Fifth Amendment* which dispenses with the need for "a presentment or indictment" of a grand jury "in cases arising in the land or naval forces, or in the Militia, when in actual service in time of War or public danger."

By practice and by construction the words "all criminal prosecutions" in the *Sixth Amendment* do not necessarily cover all military trials. One result is that the guarantee of the *Sixth Amendment* of trial "by an impartial jury" is not applicable to military trials. [3] But Judge Ferguson in *United States v. Tempia, 16 U. S. C. M. A. 629, 37 C. M. R. 249*, properly said: [4]

---

[1] "Any commissioned officer, cadet, or midshipman who is convicted of conduct unbecoming an officer and a gentleman shall be punished as a court-martial may direct."

[2] "Though not specifically mentioned in this chapter, all disorders and neglects to the prejudice of good order and discipline in the armed forces, all conduct of a nature to bring discredit upon the armed forces, and crimes and offenses not capital, of which persons subject to this chapter may be guilty, shall be taken cognizance of by a general, special, or summary court-martial, according to the nature and degree of the offense, and shall be punished at the discretion of that court."

[3] *O'Callahan v. Parker, 395 U.S. 258, 262*, stated:

"If the case does not arise '*in the land or naval forces,*' then the accused gets *first*, the benefit of an indictment by a grand jury and *second*, a trial by jury before a civilian court as guaranteed by the *Sixth Amendment* and by Art. III, § 2, of the Constitution which provides in part:

"'The Trial of all Crimes, except in Cases of Impeachment, shall be by Jury; and such Trial shall be held in the State where the said Crimes shall have been committed; but when not committed within any State, the Trial shall be at such Place or Places as the Congress may by Law have directed.'"

[4] The Court of Military Appeals has held that the "probable cause" aspect of the *Fourth Amendment* is applicable to military trials. See, *e. g., United States v. Battista, 14 U. S. C. M. A.*

"Both the Supreme Court and this Court itself are satisfied as to the applicability of constitutional safeguards to military trials, except insofar as they are made inapplicable either expressly or by necessary implication. The Government, therefore, is correct in conceding the point, and the Judge Advocate General, United States Navy, as *amicus curiae*, is incorrect in his contrary conclusion. Indeed, as to the latter, it would appear from the authorities on which he relies that the military courts applied what we now know as the constitutional protection against self-incrimination in trials prior to and contemporaneous with the adoption of the Constitution. Hence, we find Major Andre being extended the privilege at his court-martial in 1780. Wigmore, Evidence, 3d ed, § 2251. The same reference was made in the trial of Commodore James Barron in 1808. Proceedings of the General Court Martial Convened for the Trial of Commodore James Barron (1822), page 98. And, the Articles of War of 1776, as amended May 31, 1786, provided for objection by the judge advocate to any question put to the accused, the answer to which might tend to incriminate him. See Winthrop's Military Law and Precedents, 2d ed, 1920 Reprint, pages 196, 972." *16 U. S. C. M. A., at 634, 37 C. M. R., at 254.*

But the cases we have had so far have concerned only the nature of the tribunal which may try a person and/or the procedure to be followed. [5] This is the first case that presents to us a question of what protection, if any, the *First Amendment* gives people in the Armed Services:

"Congress shall make no law . . . abridging the freedom of speech, or of the press."

On its face there are no exceptions -- no preferred classes for whose benefit the *First Amendment* extends, no exempt classes.

70, 33 C. M. R. 282; *United States v. Gebhart,* 10 U. S. C. M. A. 606, 28 C. M. R. 172; *United States v. Brown,* 10 U. S. C. M. A. 482, 28 C. M. R. 48.

It has been held that the right to counsel under the *Sixth Amendment* extends to military trials, see *United States v. Culp,* 14 U. S. C. M. A. 199, 216-217, 219, 33 C. M. R. 411, 428-429, 431 (opinions of Quinn, C. J., Ferguson, J.).

There are rulings also that freedom of speech protects, to some extent at least, those in the Armed Services. *United States v. Wysong,* 9 U. S. C. M. A. 249, 26 C. M. R. 29, and see *United States v. Gray,* 20 U. S. C. M. A. 63, 42 C. M. R. 255.

[5] See, e. g., *O'Callahan v. Parker,* 395 U.S. 258; *McElroy v. United States ex rel. Guagliardo,* 361 U.S. 281; *Grisham v. Hagan,* 361 U.S. 278; *Kinsella v. United States ex rel. Singleton,* 361 U.S. 234; *Reid v. Covert,* 354 U.S. 1; *United States ex rel. Toth v. Quarles,* 350 U.S. 11; *Ex parte Quirin,* 317 U.S. 1.

The military by tradition and by necessity demands discipline; and those necessities require obedience in training and in action. A command is speech brigaded with action, and permissible commands may not be disobeyed. There may be a borderland or penumbra that in time can be established by litigated cases.

I cannot imagine, however, that Congress would think it had the power to authorize the military to curtail the reading list of books, plays, poems, periodicals, papers, and the like which a person in the Armed Services may read. Nor can I believe Congress would assume authority to empower the military to suppress conversations at a bar, ban discussions of public affairs, prevent enlisted men or women or draftees from meeting in discussion groups at times and places and for such periods of time that do not interfere with the performance of military duties.

Congress has taken no such step here. By Art. 133 it has allowed punishment for "conduct unbecoming an officer and a gentleman." In our society where diversities are supposed to flourish it never could be "unbecoming" to express one's views, even on the most controversial public issue.

Article 134 covers only "all disorders and neglects to the prejudice of good order and discipline in the armed forces, all conduct of a nature to bring discredit upon the armed forces."

Captain Levy, the appellee in the present case, was not convicted under Arts. 133 and 134 for failure to give the required medical instructions. But as he walked through the facilities and did his work, or met with students, he spoke of his views of the "war" in Vietnam. Thus he said:

"The United States is wrong in being involved in the Viet Nam War. I would refuse to go to Viet Nam if ordered to do so. I don't see why any colored soldier would go to Viet Nam; they should refuse to go to Viet Nam and if sent should refuse to fight because they are discriminated against and denied their freedom in the United States, and they are sacrificed and discriminated against in Viet Nam by being given all the hazardous duty and they are suffering the majority of casualties. If I were a colored soldier I would refuse to go to Viet Nam and if I were a colored soldier and were sent I would refuse to fight. Special Forces personnel are liars and thieves and killers of peasants and murderers of women and children."

Those ideas affronted some of his superiors. The military, of course, tends to produce homogenized individuals who think -- as well as march -- in unison. In *United States v. Blevens, 5 U. S. C. M. A. 480, 18 C. M. R. 104*, the Court of Military Appeals upheld the court-martial conviction of a serviceman who had "affiliated" himself with a Communist organization in Germany. The serviceman argued that there was no allegation that he possessed any intent to overthrow the Government by force, so that the Smith Act, *18 U. S. C. § 2385*, would not reach his conduct. The Court of Military Appeals affirmed on the theory that his affiliation, nonetheless, brought "discredit" on the Armed Forces within the meaning of Art. 134:

"Most important to the case is the Government's contention that regardless of any deficiencies under the Smith Act, the specification properly alleges, and the evidence adequately establishes, conduct to the discredit of the armed forces, in violation of Article 134.

. . . .

"Membership by a school teacher in an organization advocating the violent disestablishment of the United States Government has been regarded as conduct requiring dismissal. *Adler v. Board of Education, 342 U.S. 485*. It seems to us that such membership is even more profoundly evil in the case of a person in the military establishment. True, affiliation implies something less than membership (*Bridges v. Wixon, 326 U.S. 135, 143)*, but the supreme duty of the military is the protection and security of the government and of the people. Hence, aside from a specific intent on the part of the accused to overthrow the government by violence, the conduct alleged is definitely discrediting to the armed forces." *5 U. S. C. M. A., at 483-484, 18 C. M. R., at 107-108.*

The limitations on expressions of opinion by members of the military continue to date. During the Vietnam war, a second lieutenant in the reserves, off duty, out of uniform, and off base near a local university, carried a placard in an antiwar demonstration which said "END JOHNSON'S FACIST [*sic*] AGGRESSION IN VIET NAM." He was convicted by a court-martial under Art. 88 for using "contemptuous words" against the President and under Art. 133 for "conduct unbecoming an officer." The Court of Military Appeals affirmed, theorizing that suppression of such speech was essential to prevent a military "man on a white horse" from challenging "civilian control of the military." *United States v. Howe, 17 U. S. C. M. A. 165, 175, 37 C. M. R. 429, 439.* The Court did not attempt to weigh the likelihood that Howe, a reserve second lieutenant engaging in a single off-base expression of opinion on the most burning political issue of the day, could ever be such a "man on a white horse." Indeed, such considerations were irrelevant:

"True, petitioner is a reserve officer, rather than a professional officer, but during the time he serves on active duty he is, and must be, controlled by the provisions of military law. In this instance, military restrictions fall upon a reluctant 'summer soldier'; but at another time, and differing circumstances, the ancient and wise provisions insuring civilian control of the military will restrict the 'man on a white horse.'" *Ibid.* See generally Sherman, The Military Courts And Servicemen's *First Amendment* Rights, 22 Hastings L. J. 325 (1971.)

The power to draft an army includes, of course, the power to curtail considerably the "liberty" of the people who make it up. But Congress in these articles has not undertaken to cross the forbidden *First Amendment* line. Making a speech or comment on one of the most important and controversial public issues of the past two decades cannot by any stretch of dictionary meaning be included in "disorders and neglects to the prejudice of good order and discipline in the armed forces." Nor can what Captain Levy said possibly be "conduct of a nature to bring discredit upon the armed forces." He was uttering his own belief -- an article of faith that he sincerely held. This was no mere ploy to perform a "subversive" act. Many others who loved their country shared his views. They were not saboteurs. Uttering one's beliefs is sacrosanct under the *First Amendment*. [6] Punishing the utterances is an "abridgment" of speech in the constitutional sense.

---

[6] The words of Mr. Justice Holmes written in dissent in *United States v. Schwimmer, 279 U.S. 644, 654-655,* need to be recalled:

"The whole examination of the applicant shows that she holds none of the now-dreaded creeds but thoroughly believes in organized government and prefers that of the United States to any other in the world. Surely it cannot show lack of attachment to the principles of the Constitution that she thinks that it can be improved. I suppose that most intelligent people think that it might be. Her particular improvement looking to the abolition of war seems to me not materially different in its bearing on this case from a wish to establish cabinet government as in England, or a single house, or one term of seven years for the President. To touch a more burning question, only a judge mad with partisanship would exclude because the applicant thought that the *Eighteenth Amendment* should be repealed.

"Of course the fear is that if a war came the applicant would exert activities such as were dealt with in *Schenck v. United States, 249 U.S. 47*. But that seems to me unfounded. Her position and motives are wholly different from those of Schenck. She is an optimist and states in strong and, I do not doubt, sincere words her belief that war will disappear and that the impending destiny of mankind is to unite in peaceful leagues. I do not share that optimism nor do I think that a philosophic view of the world would regard war as absurd. But most people who have known it regard it with horror, as a last resort, and even if not yet ready for cosmopolitan efforts, would welcome any practicable combinations that would increase the power on the side of peace. The notion that the applicant's optimistic anticipations would make her a worse citizen is sufficiently answered by her examination, which seems to me a better argument for her admission than any that I can offer. Some of her answers might excite popular prejudice, but if there is any principle of the Constitution that more imperatively calls for attachment than any other it is the principle of free thought -

JUSTICE STEWART, with whom JUSTICE DOUGLAS and JUSTICE BRENNAN join, dissenting.

Article 133 of the Uniform Code of Military Justice, *10 U. S. C. § 933*, makes it a criminal offense to engage in "conduct unbecoming an officer and a gentleman." [1] Article 134, *10 U. S. C. § 934*, makes criminal "all disorders and neglects to the prejudice of good order and discipline in the armed forces." and "all conduct of a nature to bring discredit upon the armed forces." [2] The Court today, reversing a

---

- not free thought for those who agree with us but freedom for the thought that we hate. I think that we should adhere to that principle with regard to admission into, as well as to life within this country. And recurring to the opinion that bars this applicant's way, I would suggest that the Quakers have done their share to make the country what it is, that many citizens agree with the applicant's belief and that I had not supposed hitherto that we regretted our inability to expel them because they believe more than some of us do in the teachings of the Sermon on the Mount."

That dissent by Holmes became the law when *Schwimmer, supra, United States v. Macintosh, 283 U.S. 605,* and *United States v. Bland, 283 U.S. 636,* were overruled by *Girouard v. United States, 328 U.S. 61.*

[1] Article 133 provides:

"Any commissioned officer, cadet, or midshipman who is convicted of conduct unbecoming an officer and a gentleman shall be punished as a court-martial may direct."

[2] Article 134 provides:

"Though not specifically mentioned in this chapter, all disorders and neglects to the prejudice of good order and discipline in the armed forces, all conduct of a nature to bring discredit upon the armed forces, and crimes and offenses not capital, of which persons subject to this chapter may be guilty, shall be taken cognizance of by a general, special, or summary court-martial, according to the nature and degree of the offense, and shall be punished at the discretion of that court."

The clause in Art. 134 prohibiting all "crimes and offenses not capital" applies only to crimes and offenses proscribed by Congress. See Manual for Courts-Martial para. 213 (e) (1969) (hereinafter sometimes referred to as Manual). Cf. *Grafton v. United States, 206 U.S. 333.* As such, this clause is simply assimilative, like *18 U. S. C. § 13*, and is not the subject of the vagueness attack mounted by appellee on the balance of Art. 134. See generally Wiener, Are the General Military Articles Unconstitutionally Vague?, 54 A. B. A. J. 357, 358; Note, Taps for the Real *Catch-22*, 81 Yale L. J. 1518 n. 3.

While only Art. 134 is expressly termed the "general article," Arts. 133 and 134 are commonly known as the "general articles" and will be so referred to herein.

unanimous judgment of the Court of Appeals, upholds the constitutionality of these statutes. I find it hard to imagine criminal statutes more patently unconstitutional than these vague and uncertain general articles, and I would, accordingly, affirm the judgment before us.

I

As many decisions of this Court make clear, vague statutes suffer from at least two fatal constitutional defects. First, by failing to provide fair notice of precisely what acts are forbidden, a vague statute "violates the first essential of due process of law." *Connally v. General Construction Co.*, 269 U.S. 385, 391. As the Court put the matter in *Lanzetta v. New Jersey*, 306 U.S. 451, 453: "No one may be required at peril of life, liberty or property to speculate as to the meaning of penal statutes. All are entitled to be informed as to what the State commands or forbids." "Words which are vague and fluid . . . may be as much of a trap for the innocent as the ancient laws of Caligula." *United States v. Cardiff*, 344 U.S. 174, 176. [3]

Secondly, vague statutes offend due process by failing to provide explicit standards for those who enforce them, thus allowing discriminatory and arbitrary enforcement. *Papachristou v. City of Jacksonville*, 405 U.S. 156, 165-171. "A vague law impermissibly delegates basic policy matters to policemen, judges, and juries for resolution on an *ad hoc* and subjective basis . . . ." *Grayned v. City of Rockford*, 408 U.S. 104, 108-109. [4] The absence of specificity in a criminal statute invites abuse on the part of prosecuting officials, who are left free to harass any individuals or groups who may be the object of official displeasure. [5]

---

[3] See also *United States v. Harriss*, 347 U.S. 612, 617:

"The constitutional requirement of definiteness is violated by a criminal statute that fails to give a person of ordinary intelligence fair notice that his contemplated conduct is forbidden by the statute. The underlying principle is that no man shall be held criminally responsible for conduct which he could not reasonably understand to be proscribed."

[4] See also *Smith v. Goguen*, 415 U.S. 566, 575:

"Statutory language of such a standardless sweep allows policemen, prosecutors, and juries to pursue their personal predilections. Legislatures may not so abdicate their responsibilities for setting the standards of the criminal law."

[5] This Court has repeatedly recognized that the dangers inherent in vague statutes are magnified where laws touch upon *First Amendment* freedoms. See, *e. g., id.*, at 573; *Grayned v. City of Rockford*, 408 U.S. 104, 109. In such areas, more precise statutory specificity is required, lest cautious citizens steer clear of protected conduct in order to be certain of not

It is plain that Arts. 133 and 134 are vague on their face; indeed, the opinion of the Court does not seriously contend to the contrary. [6] Men of common intelligence -- including judges of both military and civilian courts -- must necessarily speculate as to what such terms as "conduct unbecoming an officer and a gentleman" and "conduct of a nature to bring discredit upon the armed forces" really mean. In the past, this Court has held unconstitutional statutes penalizing "misconduct," [7] conduct that was "annoying," [8] "reprehensible," [9] or "prejudicial to the best interests" of a city, [10] and it is significant that military courts have resorted to several of these very terms in describing the sort of acts proscribed by Arts. 133 and 134. [11]

Facially vague statutes may, of course, be saved from unconstitutionality by narrowing judicial construction. But I cannot conclude, as does the Court, *ante*, at 752-755, that the facial vagueness of the general articles has been cured by the relevant opinions of either the Court of Military Appeals or any other military tribunal. In attempting to give meaning to the amorphous words of the statutes, the Court of Military Appeals has repeatedly turned to Winthrop's Military Law and

---

violating the law. See generally Note, The Void-for-Vagueness Doctrine in the Supreme Court, 109 U. Pa. L. Rev. 67, 75-85.

[6] Even one of the staunchest defenders of the general articles has recognized that:

"It cannot be denied that there is language in the void-for-vagueness cases broad enough to condemn as unduly indefinite the prohibition in Article 133 against 'conduct unbecoming an officer and a gentleman' and the prohibitions in Article 134 against 'all disorders and neglects to the prejudice of good order and discipline in the armed forces' and against 'all conduct of a nature to bring discredit upon the armed forces.'" Wiener, *supra*, n. 2, at 363.

[7] *Giaccio v. Pennsylvania, 382 U.S. 399.*

[8] *Coates v. Cincinnati, 402 U.S. 611.*

[9] *Giaccio v. Pennsylvania, supra.*

[10] *Gelling v. Texas,* 343 U.S. 960. Other federal courts have similarly held unconstitutional statutes containing language such as "reflect[s] discredit," *Flynn v. Giarrusso, 321 F.Supp. 1295* (ED La.); "offensive," *Pritikin v. Thurman, 311 F.Supp. 1400* (SD Fla.); and "immoral" or "demoralizing," *Oestreich v. Hale, 321 F.Supp. 445* (ED Wis.).

[11] See, *e. g., United States* v. *Lee,* 4 C. M. R. 185, 191 (ABR), petition for review denied, *1 U. S. C. M. A. 713, 4 C. M. R. 173* ("reprehensible conduct"); *United States* v. *Rio Poon,* 26 C. M. R. 830, 833 (CGBR) ("universally reprehended"). See also Note, Taps for the Real *Catch-22,* 81 Yale L. J. 1518, 1522.

Precedents, an 1886 treatise. That work describes "conduct unbecoming an officer and a gentleman" in the following manner:

"To constitute therefore the conduct here denounced, the act which forms the basis of the charge must have a double significance and effect. Though it need not amount to a crime, it must offend so seriously against law, justice, morality or decorum as to expose to disgrace, socially or as a man, the offender, and at the same time must be of such a nature or committed under such circumstances as to bring dishonor or disrepute upon the military profession which he represents." [12]

As to the predecessor statute of Art. 134, Col. Winthrop read it as applicable to conduct whose prejudice to good order and discipline was "*reasonably direct and palpable*," as opposed to that conduct which is simply "*indirectly or remotely*" prejudicial -- whatever that may mean. [13] These passages, and the decisions of the Court of Military Appeals that adopt them verbatim, scarcely add any substantive content to the language of the general articles. At best, the limiting constructions referred to by the Court represent a valiant but unavailing effort to read some specificity into hopelessly vague laws. Winthrop's definitions may be slightly

---

[12] W. Winthrop, Military Law and Precedents 711-712 (2d ed. 1920). The cited language is quoted in *United States v. Howe, 17 U. S. C. M. A. 165, 177-178, 37 C. M. R. 429, 441-442*, and in *United States v. Giordano, 15 U. S. C. M. A. 163, 168, 35 C. M. R. 135, 140.*

Such authoritative publications as The Officer's Guide do little better in defining "conduct unbecoming an officer and a gentleman":

"There are certain moral attributes which belong to the ideal officer and the gentleman, a lack of which is indicated by acts of dishonesty or unfair dealing, of indecency or indecorum, or of lawlessness, injustice, or cruelty. Not every one can be expected to meet ideal standards or to possess the attributes in the exact degree demanded by the standards of his own time; but there is a limit of tolerance below which the individual standards in these respects of an officer or cadet cannot fall without his being morally unfit to be an officer or cadet or to be considered a gentleman. This article contemplates such conduct by an officer or cadet which, taking all the circumstances into consideration, satisfactorily shows such moral unfitness." R. Reynolds, The Officer's Guide 435-436 (1969 rev.).

This language is substantially repeated in Manual para. 212.

[13] W. Winthrop, Military Law and Precedents 723 (2d ed. 1920). For cases embodying these definitions, see *United States v. Sadinsky, 14 U. S. C. M. A. 563, 34 C. M. R. 343; United States v. Holiday, 4 U. S. C. M. A. 454, 16 C. M. R. 28.* See also Manual para. 213 (b), containing identical language.

different in wording from Arts. 133 and 134, but they are not different in kind, for they suffer from the same vagueness as the statutes to which they refer.

If there be any doubt as to the absence of truly limiting constructions of the general articles, it is swiftly dispelled by even the most cursory review of convictions under them in the military courts. Article 133 has been recently employed to punish such widely disparate conduct as dishonorable failure to repay debts, [14] selling whiskey at an unconscionable price to an enlisted man, [15] cheating at cards, [16] and having an extramarital affair. [17] Article 134 has been given an even wider sweep, having been applied to sexual acts with a chicken, [18] window peeping in a trailer park, [19] and cheating while calling bingo numbers. [20] Convictions such as these leave little doubt that "an infinite variety of other conduct, limited only by the scope of a commander's creativity or spleen, can be made the subject of court-martial under these articles." Sherman, The Civilianization of Military Law, 22 Maine L. Rev. 3, 80.

In short, the general articles are in practice as well as theory "catch-alls," designed to allow prosecutions for practically any conduct that may offend the sensibilities of a military commander. [21] Not every prosecution of course, results in a

---

[14] *United States v. Journell,* 18 C. M. R. 752 (AFBR).

[15] *United States v. Kupfer,* 9 C. M. R. 283 (ABR), aff'd, *3 U. S. C. M. A. 478, 13 C. M. R. 34.*

[16] *United States v. West,* 16 C. M. R. 587 (AFBR), petition for review denied, *4 U. S. C. M. A. 744, 20 C. M. R. 398.*

[17] *United States v. Alcantara,* 39 C. M. R. 682 (ABR), aff'd, *18 U. S. C. M. A. 372, 40 C. M. R. 84.*

For a listing of other representative convictions under Art. 133, see H. Moyer, Justice and the Military 1028-1034 (1972). See also Nelson, Conduct Expected of an Officer and a Gentleman: Ambiguity, 12 AF JAG L. Rev. 124.

[18] *United States v. Sanchez,* 11 U. S. C. M. A. 216, 29 C. M. R. 32.

[19] *United States v. Clark,* 22 C. M. R. 888 (AFBR), petition for review denied, *7 U. S. C. M. A. 790, 22 C. M. R. 331.*

[20] *United States v. Holt,* 7 U. S. C. M. A. 617, 23 C. M. R. 81.

[21] The drafters of the Manual for Courts-Martial have admitted as much, characterizing the discredit clause of Art. 134 as the "catch-all" in military law. Legal and Legislative Basis,

conviction, and the military courts have sometimes overturned convictions when the conduct involved was so marginally related to military discipline as to offend even the loosest interpretations of the general articles. [22] But these circumstances can hardly be thought to validate the otherwise vague statutes. As the Court said in *United States v. Reese, 92 U.S. 214, 221*: "It would certainly be dangerous if the legislature could set a net large enough to catch all possible offenders, and leave it to the courts to step inside and say who could be rightfully detained, and who should be set at large." At best, the general articles are just such a net, and suffer from all the vices that our previous decisions condemn.

II

Perhaps in recognition of the essential vagueness of the general articles, the Court today adopts several rather periphrastic approaches to the problem before us. Whatever the apparent vagueness of these statutes to us civilians, we are told, they are models of clarity to "'practical men in the navy and army.'" *Ante*, at 747, quoting from *Dynes v. Hoover, 20 How. 65, 82*. Moreover, the Court says, the appellee should have been well aware that his conduct fell within the proscriptions of the general articles, since the Manual for Courts-Martial gives specific content to these facially uncertain statutes. I believe that neither of these propositions can withstand analysis.

A

It is true, of course, that a line of prior decisions of this Court, beginning with *Dynes v. Hoover, supra*, in 1858 and concluding with *Carter v. McClaughry, 183 U.S. 365*, in 1902, have upheld against constitutional attack the ancestors of today's

---

Manual for Courts-Martial United States 294 (1951). Admitting that the language of Art. 134 is "vague," the drafters state:

"By judicial interpretation these 'vague words' have since been expanded from the narrow construction placed on them by their author to the point where they have been used as the legal justification to sustain convictions for practically any offense committed by one in the military service which is not either specifically denounced by some other article, or is not a crime or offense not capital or a disorder or neglect to the prejudice of good order and discipline." *Id., at 295.*

[22] See, *e. g., United States v. Ford, 31 C. M. R. 353* (ABR), petition for review denied, *12 U. S. C. M. A. 763, 31 C. M. R. 314* (conviction under Art. 133 for showing an allegedly obscene photograph to a friend in a private home reversed); *United States v. Waluski, 6 U. S. C. M. A. 724, 21 C. M. R. 46* (conviction under Art. 134 of passenger for leaving scene of accident reversed).

general articles.[23] With all respect for the principle of *stare decisis*, however, I believe that these decisions should be given no authoritative force in view of what is manifestly a vastly "altered historic environment." *Mitchell v. W. T. Grant Co., 416 U.S. 600, 634-635* (dissenting opinion). See also *id., at 627-628* (POWELL, J., concurring).

It might well have been true in 1858 or even 1902 that those in the Armed Services knew, through a combination of military custom and instinct, what sorts of acts fell within the purview of the general articles. But times have surely changed. Throughout much of this country's early history, the standing army and navy numbered in the hundreds. The cadre was small, professional, and voluntary. The military was a unique society, isolated from the mainstream of civilian life, and it is at least plausible to suppose that the volunteer in that era understood what conduct was prohibited by the general articles.[24]

It is obvious that the Army into which Dr. Levy entered was far different. It was part of a military establishment whose members numbered in the millions, a large percentage of whom were conscripts or draft-induced volunteers, with no prior military experience and little expectation of remaining beyond their initial period of obligation.[25] Levy was precisely such an individual, a draft-induced volunteer whose military indoctrination was minimal, at best.[26] To presume that he and others like him who served during the Vietnam era were so imbued with the ancient traditions of the military as to comprehend the arcane meaning of the

---

[23] See also *Swaim v. United States, 165 U.S. 553*; *United States v. Fletcher, 148 U.S. 84*; *Smith v. Whitney, 116 U.S. 167*.

[24] See generally Comment, The Discredit Clause of the UCMJ: An Unrestricted Anachronism, 18 U. C. L. A. L. Rev. 821, 833-837. Cf. Warren, The *Bill of Rights* and the Military, 37 N. Y. U. L. Rev. 181, 187-188; Wiener, Courts-Martial and the *Bill of Rights*: The Original Practice II, 72 Harv. L. Rev. 266, 292, 301-302.

[25] See Comment, 18 U. C. L. A. L. Rev., *supra*, at 836. Cf. *Avrech v. Secretary of the Navy, 155 U. S. App. D. C. 352, 357, 477 F.2d 1237, 1242* (Clark, J.), prob. juris. noted, *414 U.S. 816*.

[26] The record indicates that Dr. Levy, unlike many other medical officers entering active duty, did not attend the basic military orientation course at Fort Sam Houston, Texas. Instead, he came to Fort Jackson directly from civilian life. While at Fort Jackson, he received but 16 to 26 hours of military training, only a small portion of which was devoted to military justice.

general articles is to engage in an act of judicial fantasy.[27] In my view, we do a grave disservice to citizen soldiers in subjecting them to the uncertain regime of Arts. 133 and 134 simply because these provisions did not offend the sensibilities of the federal judiciary in a wholly different period of our history. In today's vastly "altered historic environment," the *Dynes* case and its progeny have become constitutional anachronisms, and I would retire them from active service.

B

The Court suggests that the Manual for Courts-Martial provides some notice of what is proscribed by the general articles, through its Appendix containing "Forms for Charges and Specifications."[28] These specimen charges, which consist of "fill-in-the-blank" accusations covering various fact situations, do offer some indication of what conduct the drafters of the Manual perceived to fall within the prohibitions of Arts. 133 and 134. There are several reasons, however, why the form specifications cannot provide the sort of definitive interpretation of the general articles necessary to save these statutes from unconstitutionality.

For one thing, the specifications covering Arts. 133 and 134 are not exclusive; the military courts have repeatedly held conduct not listed in the Manual's Appendix as

---

[27] The Court suggests, *ante*, at 751-752, that some of the problems with the general articles may be ameliorated by the requirement of Art. 137, *10 U. S. C. § 937*, that the provisions of the Code be "carefully explained to each enlisted member at the time of his entrance on active duty, or within six days thereafter," and that they be "explained again after he has completed six months of active duty." Even assuming, *arguendo*, that it is possible to "carefully explain" the general articles, I do not believe that Art. 137 cures the vagueness of the statutes. The record in this case indicates that Dr. Levy received only a very brief amount of instruction on military justice; presumably, only a fraction of that instruction was devoted to the general articles. See n. 26, *supra*. Moreover, Army regulations indicate that only 20 minutes of instruction at the initial military justice lesson for enlisted men is devoted to Arts. 71 through 134 of the UCMJ; 49 minutes of instruction on Arts. 107 through 134 is provided for at the six-month class. Department of the Army, Army Regulation 350-212, Training, Military Justice, 2 June 1972; Army Subject Schedule No. 21-10, Military Justice (Enlisted Personnel Training), 24 June 1969. Obviously, only a portion of this total of 69 minutes can be set aside for instruction pertaining to the general articles. It would be myopic to pretend that such limited instruction on these amorphous criminal statutes provided military personnel with any genuine expertise on the subject, even assuming that *anybody* could *ever* acquire such expertise.

[28] Manual, App. 6*c*.

nonetheless violative of the general articles. [29] Nor can it be said that the specifications contain any common thread or unifying theme that gives generic definition to the articles' vague words; the specimen charges in the Manual list such widely disparate conduct as kicking a public horse in the belly, [30] subornation of perjury, [31] and wrongful cohabitation [32] as violative of Art. 134. [33] Moreover, the list of offenses included in the Appendix is ever-expanding; the 1951 Manual contained 59 Art. 134 offenses, [34] while the list had increased to 63 in 1969. [35] In view of the nonexclusive and transient character of the specification list, a serviceman wishing to conform his conduct to the requirements of the law would simply find definitive guidance from the Manual impossible.

More significantly, the fact that certain conduct is listed in the Manual is no guarantee that it is in violation of the general articles. The Court of Military Appeals has repeatedly emphasized that the sample specifications are only procedural guides and timesavers for military prosecutors beset by poor research facilities, and are not intended to *create* offenses under the general articles. [36] Consequently, the court has

---

[29] See, *e. g.*, *United States v. Sadinsky*, 14 U. S. C. M. A. 563, 34 C. M. R. 343 (jumping from ship to sea); *United States v. Sanchez*, 11 U. S. C. M. A. 216, 29 C. M. R. 32 (sexual acts with a chicken). See also *Avrech v. Secretary of the Navy*, 155 U. S. App. D. C., at 357, 477 F.2d, at 1242; Manual, App. 6*a*.1: Legal and Legislative Basis, Manual for Courts-Martial United States 296 (1951).

[30] Manual, App. 6*c*, Spec. 126.

[31] *Id.*, App. 6*c*, Spec. 170.

[32] *Id.*, App. 6*c*, Spec. 188.

[33] Similarly, the specifications concerning Art. 133 cover such dissimilar offenses as copying an examination paper, being drunk and disorderly, failing to pay a debt, and failure to keep a promise to pay a debt. *Id.*, App. 6*c*, Specs. 122-125. Nowhere under the Art. 133 specifications is there any mention of the conduct with which Levy was charged.

[34] *Id.*, App. 6*c*, Specs. 118-176 (1951 ed.).

[35] *Id.*, App. 6*c*, Specs. 126-188 (1969).

[36] See *United States v. Smith*, 13 U. S. C. M. A. 105, 32 C. M. R. 105; *United States v. McCormick*, 12 U. S. C. M. A. 26, 30 C. M. R. 26. In these and other cases, the Court of Military Appeals has indicated its belief that Congress did not and could not empower the President to promulgate substantive rules of law for the military. See also *United States v. Barnes*, 14 U. S. C. M. A. 567, 34 C. M. R. 347; *United States v. Margelony*, 14 U. S. C. M. A. 55, 33 C. M. R.

on several occasions disapproved Art. 134 convictions, despite the fact that the precise conduct at issue was listed in the form specifications as falling under that article. [37]

Despite all this, the Court indicates that Levy should have been aware that *his* conduct was violative of Art. 134, since one of the specimen charges relates to the making of statements "disloyal to the United States." [38] That specification, and the brief reference to such conduct in the text of the Manual, [39] is itself so vague and overbroad as to have been declared unconstitutional by one federal court. *Stolte v. Laird, 353 F.Supp. 1392* (DC). But even if a consensus as to the meaning of the word "disloyal" were readily attainable, I am less than confident that Dr. Levy's attacks upon our Vietnam policies could be accurately characterized by such an adjective. However foreign to the military atmosphere of Fort Jackson, the words spoken by him represented a viewpoint shared by many American citizens. Whatever the accuracy of these views, I would be loath to impute "disloyalty" to those who honestly held them. In short, I think it is clear that the form specification concerning disloyal statements cannot be said to have given Levy notice of the illegality of his conduct. The specimen charge is no better than the article that spawned it. It merely substitutes one set of subjective and amorphous phraseology for another. [40]

---

267. Cf. *United States v. Acosta-Vargas, 13 U. S. C. M. A. 388, 32 C. M. R. 388.* The question as to whether the Executive has such an inherent power was apparently left open by this Court in *Reid v. Covert, 354 U.S. 1, 38*, and it is not necessary to resolve it in this case. It is enough to note that the Court of Military Appeals has clearly held that inclusion of specific conduct in the Manual does not necessarily mean that it is violative of the general articles. Given that position of the highest military court, I can hardly conclude that a serviceman could ever receive authoritative notice from the form specifications as to the scope of the articles.

[37] See, *e. g., United States v. McCormick, 12 U. S. C. M. A. 26, 30 C. M. R. 26; United States v. Waluski, 6 U. S. C. M. A. 724, 21 C. M. R. 46.*

[38] Manual, App. 6*c*, Spec. 139.

[39] *Id.*, para. 213f (5).

[40] The Court also holds that even if the general articles might be considered vague as to some offenders, the appellee has no standing to raise such a claim, since he should have known that his conduct was forbidden. *Ante*, at 755-757. To the extent that this conclusion rests on the Court's holdings that the general articles are given content through limiting judicial constructions, military custom, or the Manual for Courts-Martial, I have indicated above my disagreement with its underlying premises. And to the extent that this conclusion rests on

III

What has been said above indicates my view that the general articles are unconstitutionally vague under the standards normally and repeatedly applied by this Court. The remaining question is whether, as the Court concludes, *ante*, at 756, the peculiar situation of the military requires application of a standard of judicial review more relaxed than that embodied in our prior decisions.

It is of course common ground that the military is a "specialized community governed by a separate discipline from that of the civilian." *Orloff v. Willoughby, 345 U.S. 83, 94.* A number of serviceman's individual rights must necessarily be subordinated to the overriding military mission, and I have no doubt that the military may constitutionally prohibit conduct that is quite permissible in civilian life, such as questioning the command of a superior. But this only begins the inquiry. The question before us is not whether the military may adopt substantive rules different from those that govern civilian society, but whether the serviceman has the same right as his civilian counterpart to be informed as to precisely what conduct those rules proscribe before he can be criminally punished for violating them. More specifically, the issue is whether the vagueness of the general articles is required to serve a genuine military objective.

The Solicitor General suggests that a certain amount of vagueness in the general articles is necessary in order to maintain high standards of conduct in the military, since it is impossible to predict in advance every offense that might serve to affect morale or discredit the service. It seems to me that this argument was concisely and eloquently rebutted by Judge Aldisert in the Court of *Appeals, 478 F.2d 772, 795* (CA3):

"What high standard of conduct is served by convicting an individual of conduct he did not reasonably perceive to be criminal? Is not the essence of high standards in

---

the language of the general articles, I think that it is simply mistaken. The words of Arts. 133 and 134 are vague beyond repair; I am no more able to discern objective standards of conduct from phrases such as "conduct unbecoming an officer and a gentleman" and "conduct of a nature to bring discredit upon the armed forces" than I am from such words as "bad" or "reprehensible." Given this essential uncertainty, I cannot conclude that the statutory language clearly warned the appellee that his speech was illegal. It may have been, of course, that Dr. Levy had a subjective feeling that his conduct violated *some* military law. But that is not enough, for as we pointed out in *Bouie v. City of Columbia, 378 U.S. 347, 355-356, n. 5,* "the determination whether a criminal statute provides fair warning of its prohibitions must be made on the basis of the statute itself and the other pertinent law, rather than on the basis of an *ad hoc* appraisal of the subjective expectations of particular defendants."

the military, first, knowing one's duty, and secondly, executing it? And, in this regard, would not an even higher standard be served by delineation of the various offenses under Article 134, followed by obedience to these standards?"

It may be that military necessity justifies the promulgation of substantive rules of law that are wholly foreign to civilian life, but I fail to perceive how any legitimate military goal is served by enshrouding these rules in language so vague and uncertain as to be incomprehensible to the servicemen who are to be governed by them. [41] Indeed, I should suppose that vague laws, with their serious capacity for arbitrary and discriminatory enforcement, can in the end only hamper the military's objectives of high morale and esprit de corps.

In short, I think no case has been made for finding that there is any legitimate military necessity for perpetuation of the vague and amorphous general articles. In this regard, I am not alone. No less an authority than Kenneth J. Hodson, former Judge Advocate General of the Army and Chief Judge of the Army Court of Military Review, has recommended the abolition of Art. 134 because "we don't really need it, and we can't defend our use of it in this modern world." Hodson, The Manual for Courts-Martial -- 1984, 57 Military L. Rev. 1, 12. [42] No different conclusion can be reached as to Art. 133. Both are anachronisms, whose legitimate military usefulness, if any, has long since disappeared.

It is perhaps appropriate to add a final word. I do not for one moment denigrate the importance of our inherited tradition that the commissioned officers of our military forces are expected to be men of honor, nor do I doubt the necessity that servicemen generally must be orderly and dutiful. An efficient and effective military organization depends in large part upon the character and quality of its personnel, particularly its leadership. The internal loyalty and mutual reliance indispensable to

---

[41] Cf. J. Heller, *Catch-22*, p. 395 (Dell ed. 1970):

"'We accuse you also of the commission of crimes and infractions we don't even know about yet. Guilty or innocent?'

"'I don't know, sir. How can I say if you don't tell me what they are?'

"'How can we tell you if we don't know?'"

[42] General Hodson suggests that in place of Art. 134, the Department of Defense and various military commanders could promulgate specific sets of orders, outlawing particular conduct. Those disobeying these orders could be prosecuted under Art. 92 of the UCMJ, *10 U. S. C. § 892*, which outlaws the failure to obey any lawful order. See also Note, Taps for the Real *Catch-22*, 81 Yale L. J. 1518, 1537-1541, containing a similar suggestion.

the ultimate effectiveness of any military organization can exist only among people who can be counted on to do their duty. It is, therefore, not only legitimate but essential that in matters of promotion, retention, duty assignment, and internal discipline, evaluations must repeatedly be made of a serviceman's basic character as reflected in his deportment, whether he be an enlisted man or a commissioned officer. But we deal here with criminal statutes. And I cannot believe that such meaningless statutes as these can be used to send men to prison under a Constitution that guarantees due process of law.

Helstoski v. Meanor

Supreme Court of the United States

March 27, 1979, Argued

June 18, 1979, Decided

No. 78-546

442 U.S. 500
99 S. Ct. 2445
61 L. Ed. 2d 30

HELSTOSKI v. MEANOR, UNITED STATES DISTRICT JUDGE, ET AL.

CERTIORARI TO THE UNITED STATES COURT OF APPEALS FOR THE THIRD CIRCUIT.

Morton Stavis argued the cause for petitioner. With him on the briefs was Louise Halper.

Solicitor General McCree argued the cause for respondents. With him on the brief were Assistant Attorney General Heymann, Deputy Solicitor General Frey, and Louis M. Fischer.

Stanley M. Brand argued the cause for Thomas P. O'Neill, Jr., Speaker of the United States House of Representatives, et al. as amici curiae. With Mr. Brand on the brief was Neal P. Rutledge.

BURGER, C. J., delivered the opinion of the Court, in which STEWART, WHITE, MARSHALL, BLACKMUN, REHNQUIST, and STEVENS, JJ., joined. BRENNAN, J., filed a dissenting opinion.
POWELL, J., took no part in the consideration or decision of the case.

CHIEF JUSTICE BURGER delivered the opinion of the Court.

The question in this case is whether mandamus is an appropriate means of challenging the validity of an indictment of a Member of Congress on the ground that it violates the *Speech or Debate Clause of the Constitution*.[1] The Court of Appeals declined to issue the writ. We affirm.

I

Petitioner Helstoski served in the United States Congress from 1965 through 1976 as a Representative from New Jersey. In 1974, the Department of Justice began investigating reported political corruption, including allegations that aliens had paid money for the introduction and processing of private bills which would suspend the application of the immigration laws so as to allow them to remain in this country.

In June 1976, a grand jury returned a 12-count indictment charging Helstoski and others with various criminal acts. Only the first four counts are involved in this case. The first count charged that Helstoski and others had conspired to violate *18 U. S. C. § 201 (c)(1)* by accepting money in return for Helstoski's "being influenced in the performance of official acts, to wit: the introduction of private bills in the United States House of Representatives." The charge recited 16 overt acts, 4 of which referred to the actual introduction of private bills; a 5th referred to an agreement to introduce a private bill. The entire conspiracy was charged as a violation of the general conspiracy statute, *18 U. S. C. § 371*.

Counts II, III, and IV were substantive counts charging violations of *18 U. S. C. §§ 201 (c)(1) and (2)*:

"Whoever, being a public official[,] directly or indirectly, corruptly *asks, demands, exacts, solicits, seeks, accepts, receives, or agrees to receive* anything of value for himself or for any other person or entity, in return for:

---

[1] The *Speech or Debate Clause* provides that "for any Speech or Debate in either House, they [the Senators and Representatives] shall not be questioned in any other Place." Art. I, § 6.

This case was argued together with No. 78-349, *United States* v. *Helstoski, ante*, p. 477, which concerns the restrictions the *Speech or Debate Clause* places on the admissibility of evidence at a trial on charges that a former Member of the House accepted money in return for promising to introduce and introducing private bills.

"(1) being influenced in his performance of any official act; or

"(2) being influenced to commit or aid in committing, or to collude in, or allow, any fraud, or make opportunity for the commission of any fraud on the United States;

. . . .

"Shall be fined . . . or imprisoned." (Emphasis added.)

"Public official" and "official act" are defined in *18 U. S. C. § 201*:

"(a) For the purpose of this section:

"'public official' means Member of Congress . . . ; and

. . . .

"'official act' means any decision or action on any question, matter, cause, suit, proceeding or controversy, which may at any time be pending, or which may by law be brought before any public official, in his official capacity, or in his place of trust or profit."

Each count charged that Helstoski, acting through his legislative aide, had solicited money from aliens in return for "being influenced in the performance of official acts, to wit: the introduction of private bills in the United States House of Representatives on behalf of" the aliens. Essentially, the charges against Helstoski parallel those dealt with in *United States v. Johnson, 383 U.S. 169 (1966)*, and *United States v. Brewster, 408 U.S. 501 (1972)*.

Each count also charged that Helstoski, again acting through his aide, had accepted a bribe "in return for his being influenced in the performance of official acts, to wit: the introduction of private bills in the United States House of Representatives on behalf of" the aliens. Finally, each count charged that a private bill had been introduced on a particular date.

Helstoski neither appeared before nor submitted material to the particular grand jury that returned the indictment. The prosecutor provided that grand jury with transcripts of most, but not all, of the testimony of witnesses, including Helstoski, before eight other grand juries.[2] The United States Attorney explained that to avoid any possible prejudice to Helstoski he had not told the ninth grand jury of

---

[2] The proceedings before the various grand juries are described in *United States* v. *Helstoski, ante*, p. 477.

Helstoski's invocation of his privilege under the *Fifth Amendment*. Moreover, he sought to avoid any challenge resulting from the fact that the District Judge had appeared before one grand jury to rule on Helstoski's claim of that privilege.

Helstoski moved to dismiss the indictment, contending that the grand jury process had been abused and that the indictment violated the *Speech or Debate Clause*. He supported his allegation of abuse of the grand jury by characterizing the eight grand juries as "discovery tools." The effect, he contended, was to permit the prosecutor to select the information presented to the indicting grand jury and to deprive that grand jury of evidence of the demeanor of witnesses, especially that of Helstoski himself.

District Judge Meanor denied the motion after examining a transcript of the evidence presented to the indicting grand jury. He held that there had been no such abuse to justify invalidating the indictment. He found that most of the material not submitted to the indicting grand jury "was either prejudicial to the defendants, or neither inculpating nor exculpating in nature." He also found that the testimony of two grand jury witnesses should have been presented to the indicting grand jury and concluded that *Brady v. Maryland, 373 U.S. 83 (1963)*, required that the Government provide Helstoski with transcripts of their testimony. Judge Meanor also held that the *Speech or Debate Clause* did not require dismissal.

Approximately three months later, in June 1977, Helstoski petitioned the Court of Appeals for a writ of mandamus directing the District Court to dismiss the indictment.

The Court of Appeals declined to issue the writ of mandamus. *576 F.2d 511 (CA3 1978)*. It concluded that the indictment in this case was indistinguishable from that in *United States v. Brewster, supra*, where an indictment was held not to violate the *Speech or Debate Clause* even though it contained references to legislative acts. The Court of Appeals rejected Helstoski's argument that the indictment was invalid because the grand jury had heard evidence of legislative acts, which he argued was in violation of the *Speech or Debate Clause*. The court declined to go behind the indictment, holding that it was valid on its face.

In seeking reversal here of the Court of Appeals holding, Helstoski argues that the extraordinary remedy of mandamus is appropriate in this case to protect the constitutional command of separation of powers. He contends that the *Speech or Debate Clause* assigns exclusive jurisdiction over all legislative acts to Congress. The indictment itself, he urges, is a violation of that Clause because it represents an impermissible assertion of jurisdiction over the legislative function by the grand jury and the federal courts. He challenges the validity of the indictment on two grounds. First, the indictment itself refers to legislative acts. Any attempt at restricting the proof at trial, as approved by the Court of Appeals, will amount to an amendment of the indictment, thereby violating a *Fifth Amendment* right to be tried only on an indictment in precisely the form issued by a grand jury. Second, he contends the *Speech or Debate Clause* was violated when the grand jury was allowed to consider evidence of his legislative acts notwithstanding that such evidence and testimony was presented by him.

II

Almost 100 years ago, this Court explained: "The general principle which governs proceedings by *mandamus* is, that whatever can be done without the employment of that extraordinary writ, *may not be done with it.* It lies only when there is practically *no other remedy.*" *Ex parte Rowland, 104 U.S. 604, 617 (1882)* (emphasis added). More recently we summarized certain considerations for determining whether the writ should issue:

"Among these are that the party seeking issuance of the writ have no other adequate means to attain the relief he desires, and that he satisfy 'the burden of showing that [his] right to issuance of the writ is "clear and indisputable."' Moreover, it is important to remember that issuance of the writ is in large part a matter of discretion with the court to which the petition is addressed." *Kerr v. United States District Court, 426 U.S. 394, 403 (1976)* (citations omitted).

Helstoski contends that his petition for a writ of mandamus should not be governed by the rules which we have developed for assessing mandamus petitions generally. He argues that the writ is especially appropriate for enforcing the commands of the *Speech or Debate Clause.* We agree that the guarantees of that Clause are vitally important to our system of government and therefore are entitled to be treated by the courts with the sensitivity that such important values require. We are unwilling, however, to accept the contention that mandamus is the appropriate vehicle for assuring protection of the Clause in the circumstances shown here. Helstoski could readily have secured review of the ruling complained of and all objectives now sought, by direct appeal to the Court of Appeals from the District Court order denying his motion to dismiss the indictment.

Only recently in *Abney v. United States, 431 U.S. 651 (1977),* we held that "pretrial orders rejecting claims of former jeopardy . . . constitute 'final decisions' and thus satisfy the jurisdictional prerequisites of [28 U. S. C.] § 1291." *Id.,* at 662. The reasoning undergirding that holding applies with particular force here. The language of the *Abney* opinion is particularly apt, even though the context was the Double Jeopardy Clause:

"[There] can be no doubt that such orders constitute a complete, formal and, in the trial court, final rejection of a criminal defendant's double jeopardy claim. There are simply no further steps that can be taken in the District Court to avoid the trial the defendant maintains is barred by the *Fifth Amendment's* guarantee." *Id., at 659.*

This is equally true for a claim that an indictment violates the fundamental guarantees of the *Speech or Debate Clause*. Once a motion to dismiss is denied, there is nothing the Member can do under that Clause in the trial court to prevent the trial; but it is equally clear an appeal of the District Court ruling was available.

Second, we noted:

"[The] very nature of a double jeopardy claim is such that it is collateral to, and separable from, the principal issue at the accused's impending criminal trial, *i. e.*, whether or not the accused is guilty of the offense charged. In arguing that the *Double Jeopardy Clause of the Fifth Amendment* bars his prosecution, the defendant makes no challenge whatsoever to the merits of the charge against him. Nor does he seek suppression of evidence which the Government plans to use in obtaining a conviction. Rather, he is contesting *the very authority of the Government to hale him into court to face trial on the charge against him.*" [3] *Ibid.* (Emphasis added; citations omitted.)

Abney concludes:

"[The] rights conferred on a criminal accused by the *Double Jeopardy Clause* would be significantly undermined if appellate review of double jeopardy claims were postponed until after conviction and sentence. . . . [This] Court has long recognized that the *Double Jeopardy Clause* protects an individual against more than being subjected to double punishments. It is a guarantee against being twice put to *trial* for the same offense." *Id., at 660-661.*

That characterization of the purpose of the *Double Jeopardy Clause* echoed this Court's statement in *Dombrowski v. Eastland, 387 U.S. 82, 85 (1967)*, that the *Speech or Debate Clause* was designed to protect Congressmen "not only from the consequences of litigation's results but also from the burden of defending themselves."

Here, the holding of *Abney* becomes highly relevant; by analogy, if a Member "is to avoid *exposure* to [being questioned for acts done in either House] and thereby enjoy

---

[3] It is true that Helstoski challenges the admissibility of evidence at his trial; that challenge, however, is raised only if the indictment is allowed to stand.

the full protection of the Clause, his . . . challenge to the indictment must be reviewable before . . . exposure [to trial] occurs." *Abney, supra, at 662.*

Helstoski argues that he should not be penalized for failing to predict our decision in *Abney*. But he cannot be viewed as being penalized since the controlling law of the Third Circuit was announced at the time of the District Court order denying dismissal of the indictment, and our holding did no more than affirm the correctness of the law of that Circuit. See *United States v. DiSilvio, 520 F.2d 247, 248 n. 2*a (CA3), cert. denied, *423 U.S. 1015 (1975)*. The relevance of the *Abney-DiSilvio* holdings, read in light of *Dombrowski v. Eastland, supra,* was predictable. We hold that if Helstoski wished to challenge the District Court's denial of his motion to dismiss the indictment, direct appeal to the Court of Appeals was the proper course under *DiSilvio, supra.* [4]

Affirmed.

MR. JUSTICE POWELL took no part in the consideration or decision of this case.

---

[4] If the petition for a writ of mandamus were treated as an appeal it would, of course, have been jurisdictionally out of time. *Fed. Rule App. Proc. 4.*

JUSTICE BRENNAN, dissenting.

In today's decision, the Court professes to "agree that the guarantees of [the Speech or Debate] Clause are vitally important to our system of government and therefore are entitled to be treated by the courts with the sensitivity that such important values require." *Ante*, at 506. Nonetheless, it refuses to hold mandamus an appropriate vehicle for assuring the protections of the Clause because "Helstoski could readily have secured review of the ruling complained of and all objectives now sought, by direct appeal to the Court of Appeals from the District Court order denying his motion to dismiss the indictment." *Ibid.*

Mr. Helstoski may well be excused if he views the Court's holding as if it were a line out of Joseph Heller's "***Catch-22***." He cannot utilize mandamus because he should have sought a direct appeal. But he cannot seek a direct appeal, because that avenue is time barred. *Ante*, at 508 n. 4. Of course, the dilemma could have been short-circuited had Helstoski brought an immediate appeal at the time his motion for dismissal of the indictment was denied. Unfortunately, he could not have known that avenue of relief was available until today -- for we have never before held that the denial of a claim that an indictment violates the *Speech or Debate Clause* is an exception to the longstanding rule forbidding interlocutory appeals.[*] And, as the Court holds, today it is too late. Values as "vitally important" as those guaranteed by the *Speech or Debate Clause* are entitled to more sensitive treatment.

---

[*] The Court makes the surprising assertion that Helstoski should have anticipated today's holding on the basis of a footnote in a 1975 Third Circuit opinion dealing with a different issue. (That opinion, like this Court's decision in *Abney v. United States, 431 U.S. 651 (1977)*, was limited to the double jeopardy issue. *Abney* was announced far too late to have helped the defendant.) Although I agree with the Court's extension of the *Abney* principle from double jeopardy claims to those based upon the *Speech or Debate Clause*, I do not regard the extension as obvious. Nor, apparently, does the Government, as it carefully refrains from endorsing that view. See Brief for United States 92. I certainly would not use it as a basis for penalizing a former Congressman in his assertion of a principle so "vitally important to our system of government." *Ante*, at 506.

Carey v. Brown

Supreme Court of the United States

April 15, 1980, Argued

June 20, 1980, Decided

No. 79-703

447 U.S. 455
100 S. Ct. 2286
65 L. Ed. 2d 263

CAREY, STATE'S ATTORNEY OF COOK COUNTY v. BROWN ET AL.

APPEAL FROM THE UNITED STATES COURT OF APPEALS FOR THE SEVENTH CIRCUIT.

Ellen G. Robinson argued the cause pro hac vice for appellant. With her on the briefs were Bernard Carey, pro se, and Paul P. Biebel, Jr.

Edward Burke Arnolds argued the cause for appellees. With him on the brief was Michael P. Seng.[*]

BRENNAN, J., delivered the opinion of the Court, in which STEWART, WHITE, MARSHALL, POWELL, and STEVENS, JJ., joined.
STEWART, J., filed a concurring opinion.
REHNQUIST, J., filed a dissenting opinion, in which BURGER, C. J., and BLACKMUN, J., joined.

---

[*] Briefs of amici curiae urging reversal were filed by William W. Becker for the New England Legal Foundation; and by Ronald A. Zumbrun, Robert K. Best, and Robin L. Rivett for the Pacific Legal Foundation et al.

Howard Eglit and David Goldberger filed a brief for the Roger Baldwin Foundation of ACLU, Inc., as amicus curiae urging affirmance.

JUSTICE BRENNAN delivered the opinion of the Court.

At issue in this case is the constitutionality under the *First* and *Fourteenth Amendments* of a state statute that generally bars picketing of residences or dwellings, but exempts from its prohibition "the peaceful picketing of a place of employment involved in a labor dispute."

I

On September 6, 1977, several of the appellees, all of whom are members of a civil rights organization entitled the Committee Against Racism, participated in a peaceful demonstration on the public sidewalk in front of the home of Michael Bilandic, then Mayor of Chicago, protesting his alleged failure to support the busing of schoolchildren to achieve racial integration. They were arrested and charged with unlawful residential picketing in violation of Ill. Rev. Stat., ch. 38, § 21.1-2 (1977), which provides:

"It is unlawful to picket before or about the residence or dwelling of any person, except when the residence or dwelling is used as a place of business. However, this Article does not apply to a person peacefully picketing his own residence or dwelling and does not prohibit the peaceful picketing of a place of employment involved in a labor dispute or the place of holding a meeting or assembly on premises commonly used to discuss subjects of general public interest." [1]

Appellees pleaded guilty to the charge and were sentenced to periods of supervision ranging from six months to a year.

---

[1] A violation of § 21.1-2 is a "Class B" misdemeanor punishable by a fine of up to $ 500 and imprisonment for not more than six months. See Ill. Rev. Stat., ch. 38, §§ 21.1-3, 1005-8-3, 1005-9-1 (1977).

At least four other States have enacted antiresidential picketing laws similar in form to this statute. See Ark. Stat. Ann. §§ 41-2966 to 41-2968 (1977); *Conn. Gen. Stat. § 31-120* (1979); *Haw. Rev. Stat. § 379A-1* (1976); *Md. Ann. Code, Art. 27, § 580A* (1976). Connecticut's law has been construed to permit all picketing in a residential area except for labor picketing that is not conducted at the situs of a labor dispute. *State v. Anonymous, 6 Conn. Cir. 372, 274 A. 2d 897 (App. Div. 1970)*; *DeGregory v. Giesing, 427 F.Supp. 910 (Conn. 1977)* (three-judge court). The Maryland statute was declared unconstitutional by the Maryland Court of Appeals in *State v. Schuller, 280 Md. 305, 372 A. 2d 1076 (1977)*. See also *People Acting Through Community Effort v. Doorley, 468 F.2d 1143 (CA1 1972)* (invalidating municipal ordinance virtually identical to the Illinois residential picketing statute); but see *Wauwatosa v. King, 49 Wis. 2d 398, 182 N. W. 2d 530 (1971)* (upholding validity of similar ordinance).

In April 1978, appellees commenced this lawsuit in the United States District Court for the Northern District of Illinois, seeking a declaratory judgment that the Illinois residential picketing statute is unconstitutional on its face and as applied, and an injunction prohibiting defendants -- various state, county, and city officials -- from enforcing the statute. Appellees did not attempt to attack collaterally their earlier state-court convictions, but requested only prospective relief. Alleging that they wished to renew their picketing in residential neighborhoods but were inhibited from doing so by the threat of criminal prosecution under the residential picketing statute, appellees challenged the Act under the *First* and *Fourteenth Amendments* as an overbroad, vague, and, in light of the exception for labor picketing, impermissible content-based restriction on protected expression. The District Court, ruling on cross-motions for summary judgment, denied all relief. *Brown v. Scott, 462 F.Supp. 518 (1978).*

The Court of Appeals for the Seventh Circuit reversed. *Brown v. Scott, 602 F.2d 791 (1979).* Discerning "no principled basis" for distinguishing the Illinois statute from a similar picketing prohibition invalidated in *Police Department of Chicago v. Mosley, 408 U.S. 92 (1972),* the court concluded that the Act's differential treatment of labor and nonlabor picketing could not be justified either by the important state interest in protecting the peace and privacy of the home or by the special character of a residence that is also used as a "place of employment." Accordingly, the court held that the statute, both on its face and as applied to appellees, violated the *Equal Protection Clause of the Fourteenth Amendment.* [2] We noted probable jurisdiction. *444 U.S. 1011 (1980).* We affirm.

II

As the Court of Appeals observed, this is not the first instance in which this Court has had occasion to consider the constitutionality of an enactment selectively proscribing peaceful picketing on the basis of the placard's message. *Police Department of Chicago v. Mosley, supra,* arose out of a challenge to a Chicago ordinance that prohibited picketing in front of any school other than one "involved in a labor

---

[2] Because the Court of Appeals concluded that the labor dispute exception was not severable from the remainder of the statute, it invalidated the enactment in its entirety. Cf. *State v. Schuller, supra, at 318-321, 372 A. 2d, at 1083-1084.* The court therefore found it unnecessary to consider the constitutionality under the *First Amendment* of a statute that prohibited all residential picketing. *Brown v. Scott, 602 F.2d 791, 795, n. 6 (1979).* Because we find the present statute defective on equal protection principles, we likewise do not consider whether a statute barring all residential picketing regardless of its subject matter would violate the *First* and *Fourteenth Amendments.*

dispute."³ We held that the ordinance violated the *Equal Protection Clause* because it impermissibly distinguished between labor picketing and all other peaceful picketing without any showing that the latter was "clearly more disruptive" than the former. *408 U.S., at 100*. Like the Court of Appeals, we find the Illinois residential picketing statute at issue in the present case constitutionally indistinguishable from the ordinance invalidated in *Mosley*.

There can be no doubt that in prohibiting peaceful picketing on the public streets and sidewalks in residential neighborhoods, the Illinois statute regulates expressive conduct that falls within the *First Amendment's* preserve. See, *e. g.*, *Thornhill v. Alabama, 310 U.S. 88 (1940)*; *Gregory v. Chicago, 394 U.S. 111, 112 (1969)*; *Shuttlesworth v. Birmingham, 394 U.S. 147, 152 (1969)*. "Wherever the title of streets and parks may rest, they have immemorially been held in trust for the use of the public and, time out of mind, have been used for purposes of assembly, communicating thoughts between citizens, and discussing public questions." *Hague v. CIO, 307 U.S. 496, 515 (1939)* (opinion of Roberts, J.). "'[Streets], sidewalks, parks, and other similar public places are so historically associated with the exercise of *First Amendment* rights that access to them for the purpose of exercising such rights cannot constitutionally be denied broadly and absolutely.'" *Hudgens v. NLRB, 424 U.S. 507, 515 (1976)* (quoting *Food Employees v. Logan Valley Plaza, 391 U.S. 308, 315 (1968)*).

Nor can it be seriously disputed that in exempting from its general prohibition only the "peaceful picketing of a place of employment involved in a labor dispute," the Illinois statute discriminates between lawful and unlawful conduct based upon the content of the demonstrator's communication.⁴ On its face, the Act accords

---

³ Chicago Municipal Code, ch. 193-1 (i) (1968), provided:

"A person commits disorderly conduct when he knowingly:

. . . .

"(i) Pickets or demonstrates on a public way within 150 feet of any primary or secondary school building while the school is in session and one-half hour before the school is in session and one-half hour after the school session has been concluded, *provided that this subsection does not prohibit the peaceful picketing of any school involved in a labor dispute. . . ."* (Emphasis supplied.)

⁴ The Illinois residential picketing statute apparently has not been construed by the state courts. Throughout this litigation, however, all parties and the courts below have interpreted the statutory exception for "peaceful picketing of a place of employment involved in a labor dispute" as embodying the additional requirement that the subject of the picketing be related

preferential treatment to the expression of views on one particular subject; information about labor disputes may be freely disseminated, but discussion of all other issues is restricted. The permissibility of residential picketing under the Illinois statute is thus dependent solely on the nature of the message being conveyed. [5]

In these critical respects, then, the Illinois statute is identical to the ordinance in *Mosley*, and it suffers from the same constitutional infirmities. When government regulation discriminates among speech-related activities in a public forum, the *Equal Protection Clause* mandates that the legislation be finely tailored to serve substantial state interests, and the justifications offered for any distinctions it draws must be carefully scrutinized. *Police Department of Chicago v. Mosley, 408 U.S., at 98-99, 101;* see *United States v. O'Brien, 391 U.S. 367, 376-377 (1968);Williams v. Rhodes, 393 U.S. 23, 30-31 (1968);Dunn v. Blumstein, 405 U.S. 330, 342-343 (1972);San Antonio Independent School Dist. v. Rodriguez, 411 U.S. 1, 34, n. 75 (1973).*As we explained in *Mosley*: "Chicago may not vindicate its interest in preventing disruption by the

---

to the ongoing labor dispute. *Police Department of Chicago v. Mosley, 408 U.S. 92 (1972),* was premised upon an identical construction. See *id., at 94, n. 2* (statutory exemption for "the peaceful picketing of any school involved in a labor dispute" applies only to *labor* picketing of a school involved in such a dispute).

[5] The District Court read the labor exception in this statute as creating two separate classifications: one between "places of employment" and all other "residences," and a second between "places of employment involved in a labor dispute" and "places of employment *not* involved in a labor dispute." The court held that the first classification was a permissible content-neutral regulation of the location of picketing. And although recognizing that the second distinction may well be based on the subject matter of the demonstration, see n. 4, *supra*, the court held that appellees lacked standing to challenge it because they were not seeking to picket "a place of employment," and thus would not have benefitted from a determination that the second classification was unconstitutional. *Brown v. Scott, 462 F.Supp. 518, 534-535 (1978)*.

The Court of Appeals, in reversing the District Court, refused to adopt the lower court's interpretation of the statute. Rather, it read the "place of employment" exception to divide "residences and dwellings" into but two categories -- those at which picketing is lawful (*i. e.*, all places of employment involved in labor disputes) and those at which it is unlawful (*i. e.*, all other residences and dwellings). *Brown v. Scott, 602 F.2d, at 793-794.* We accept the construction of the Court of Appeals. Appellees sought to picket at a residence and were denied permission to do so. They clearly have standing to attack the statutory classification on which that denial was premised. Indeed, appellant does not challenge the Court of Appeals' interpretation of the statute, Tr. of Oral Arg. 13, and he concedes that this restriction is content-based, *id.,* at 21.

wholesale exclusion of picketing on all but one preferred subject. Given what Chicago tolerates from labor picketing, the excesses of some nonlabor picketing may not be controlled by a broad ordinance prohibiting both peaceful and violent picketing. Such excesses 'can be controlled by narrowly drawn statutes,' *Saia* v. *New York*, 334 U.S., at 562, focusing on the abuses and dealing evenhandedly with picketing regardless of subject matter." *408 U.S., at 101-102.* Yet here, under the guise of preserving residential privacy, Illinois has flatly prohibited all nonlabor picketing even though it permits labor picketing that is equally likely to intrude on the tranquility of the home.

Moreover, it is the content of the speech that determines whether it is within or without the statute's blunt prohibition. [6] What we said in *Mosley* has equal force in the present case:

"The central problem with Chicago's ordinance is that it describes permissible picketing in terms of its subject matter. Peaceful picketing on the subject of a school's labor-management dispute is permitted, but all other peaceful picketing is prohibited. The operative distinction is the message on a picket sign. . . . Any restriction on expressive activity because of its content would completely undercut the 'profound national commitment to the principle that debate on public issues should be uninhibited, robust, and wide-open.' *New York Times Co.* v. *Sullivan*, [*376 U.S. 254*], 270.

"Necessarily, then, under the *Equal Protection Clause*, not to mention the *First Amendment* itself, government may not grant the use of a forum to people whose views it finds acceptable, but deny use to those wishing to express less favored or more controversial views. And it may not select which issues are worth discussing or debating in public facilities. There is an 'equality of status in the field of ideas,' and government must afford all points of view an equal opportunity to be heard. Once a forum is opened up to assembly or speaking by some groups, government may not prohibit others from assembling or speaking on the basis of what they intend to say. Selective exclusions from a public forum may not be based on

---

[6] It is, of course, no answer to assert that the Illinois statute does not discriminate on the basis of the speaker's viewpoint, but only on the basis of the subject matter of his message. "The *First Amendment's* hostility to content-based regulation extends not only to restrictions on particular viewpoints, but also to prohibition of public discussion of an entire topic." *Consolidated Edison Co.* v. *Public Service Comm'n, post,* at 537.

content alone, and may not be justified by reference to content alone." *Id., at 95-96* (citations and footnote omitted). [7]

III

Appellant nonetheless contends that this case is distinguishable from *Mosley*. He argues that the state interests here are especially compelling and particularly well served by a statute that accords differential treatment to labor and nonlabor picketing. We explore in turn each of these interests, and the manner in which they are said to be furthered by this statute.

A

Appellant explains that whereas the Chicago ordinance sought to prevent disruption of the schools, concededly a "substantial" and "legitimate" governmental concern, see *id., at 99, 100*, the Illinois statute was enacted to ensure privacy in the home, a right which appellant views as paramount in our constitutional scheme. [8]

---

[7] *Mosley* was neither the Court's first nor its last pronouncement that the *First* and *Fourteenth Amendments* forbid discrimination in the regulation of expression on the basis of the content of that expression. See *Cox v. Louisiana, 379 U.S. 536, 581 (1965)* (Black, J., concurring):

"Standing, patrolling, or marching back and forth on streets is conduct, not speech, and as conduct can be regulated or prohibited. But by specifically permitting picketing for the publication of labor union views, Louisiana is attempting to pick and choose among the views it is willing to have discussed on its streets. It thus is trying to prescribe by law what matters of public interest people whom it allows to assemble on its streets may and may not discuss. This seems to me to be censorship in a most odious form, unconstitutional under the *First* and *Fourteenth Amendments*. And to deny this appellant and his group use of the streets because of their views against racial discrimination, while allowing other groups to use the streets to voice opinions on other subjects, also amounts, I think, to an invidious discrimination forbidden by the *Equal Protection Clause of the Fourteenth Amendment*."

See also *Erznoznik v. City of Jacksonville, 422 U.S. 205, 209, 215 (1975)*; *Hudgens v. NLRB, 424 U.S. 507, 520 (1976)*; *Madison Joint School District No. 8 v. Wisconsin Employment Relations Comm'n, 429 U.S. 167, 175-176 (1976)*; *First National Bank of Boston v. Bellotti, 435 U.S. 765, 784-785 (1978)*; *Consolidated Edison Co.* v. *Public Service Comm'n, post,* at 536-538.

[8] The importance which the State attaches to the interest in maintaining residential privacy is reflected in the Illinois Legislature's finding accompanying the residential picketing statute:

"The Legislature finds and declares that men in a free society have the right to quiet enjoyment of their homes; that the stability of community and family life cannot be maintained unless the right to privacy and a sense of security and peace in the home are

For this reason, he contends that the same content-based distinctions held invalid in the *Mosley* context may be upheld in the present case.

We find it unnecessary, however, to consider whether the State's interest in residential privacy outranks its interest in quiet schools in the hierarchy of societal values. For even the most legitimate goal may not be advanced in a constitutionally impermissible manner. And though we might agree that certain state interests may be so compelling that where no adequate alternatives exist a content-based distinction -- if narrowly drawn -- would be a permissible way of furthering those objectives, cf. *Schenck v. United States, 249 U.S. 47 (1919)*, this is not such a case.

First, the generalized classification which the statute draws suggests that Illinois itself has determined that residential privacy is not a transcendent objective: While broadly permitting all peaceful labor picketing notwithstanding the disturbances it would undoubtedly engender, the statute makes no attempt to distinguish among various sorts of nonlabor picketing on the basis of the harms they would inflict on the privacy interest. The apparent overinclusiveness and under inclusiveness of the statute's restriction would seem largely to undermine appellant's claim that the prohibition of all nonlabor picketing can be justified by reference to the State's interest in maintaining domestic tranquility. [9]

More fundamentally, the exclusion for labor picketing cannot be upheld as a means of protecting residential privacy for the simple reason that nothing in the content-based labor-nonlabor distinction has any bearing whatsoever on privacy. Appellant can point to nothing inherent in the nature of peaceful labor picketing that would make it any less disruptive of residential privacy than peaceful picketing on issues of broader social concern. Standing alone, then, the State's asserted interest in promoting the privacy of the home is not sufficient to save the statute.

B

---

respected and encouraged; that residential picketing, however just the cause inspiring it, disrupts home, family and communal life; that residential picketing is inappropriate in our society, where the jealously guarded rights of free speech and assembly have always been associated with respect for the rights of others. For these reasons the Legislature finds and declares this Article to be necessary." Ill. Rev. Stat., ch. 38, § 21.1-1 (1977).

[9] Cf. Kalven, The Concept of the Public Forum: Cox v. Louisiana, 1965 Sup. Ct. Rev. 1, 29 (quoted in *Young v. American Mini Theatres, Inc., 427 U.S. 50, 67, n. 27 (1976)* (opinion of STEVENS, J.)): "If some groups are exempted from a prohibition on parades and pickets, the rationale for regulation is fatally impeached." See also *Police Department of Chicago v. Mosley, 408 U.S., at 100; Village of Schaumburg v. Citizens for a Better Environment, 444 U.S. 620, 638-639 (1980)*.

The second important objective advanced by appellant in support of the statute is the State's interest in providing special protection for labor protests. He maintains that federal [10] and state [11] law has long exhibited an unusual concern for such activities, and he contends that this solicitude may be furthered by a narrowly drawn exemption for labor picketing.

The central difficulty with this argument is that it forthrightly presupposes that labor picketing is more deserving of *First Amendment* protection than are public protests over other issues, particularly the important economic, social, and political subjects about which these appellees wish to demonstrate. We reject that proposition. Cf. T. Emerson, The System of Freedom of Expression 444-449 (1970) (suggesting that nonlabor picketing is more akin to pure expression than labor picketing and thus should be subject to fewer restrictions). Public-issue picketing, "an exercise of . . . basic constitutional rights in their most pristine and classic form," *Edwards v. South Carolina, 372 U.S. 229, 235 (1963)*, has always rested on the highest rung of the hierarchy of *First Amendment* values: "The maintenance of the opportunity for free political discussion to the end that government may be responsive to the will of the people and that changes may be obtained by lawful means, an opportunity essential to the security of the Republic, is a fundamental principle of our constitutional system." *Stromberg v. California, 283 U.S. 359, 369 (1931)*. See generally A. Meiklejohn, Free Speech and Its Relation to Self-Government (1948). While the State's motivation in protecting the *First Amendment* rights of employees involved in labor disputes is commendable, that factor, without more, cannot justify the labor picketing exemption.

---

[10] See generally *29 U. S. C. § 141 et seq.; Thornhill v. Alabama, 310 U.S. 88 (1940); AFL v. Swing, 312 U.S. 312 (1941)*. Appellant does not go so far as to suggest that the National Labor Relations Act preempts the State from enacting a law prohibiting the picketing of residences involved in labor disputes. Such an argument has dubious merit. See *Machinists v. Wisconsin Employment Relations Comm'n, 427 U.S. 132, 136, and n. 2 (1976)*.

[11] See Ill. Rev. Stat., ch. 48, § 2a (1977), which provides:

"No restraining order or injunction shall be granted by any court of this State . . . in any case involving or growing out of a dispute concerning terms or conditions of employment, enjoining or restraining any person or persons, either singly or in concert, . . . from peaceably and without threats or intimidation being upon any public street, or thoroughfare or highway for the purpose of obtaining or communicating information, or to peaceably and without threats or intimidation persuade any person or persons to work or to abstain from working, or to employ or to peaceably and without threats or intimidation cease to employ any party to a labor dispute, or to recommend, advise, or persuade others so to do."

C

Appellant's final contention is that the statute can be justified by some combination of the preceding objectives. This argument is fashioned on two different levels. In its elemental formulation, it posits simply that a distinction between labor and nonlabor picketing is uniquely suited to furthering the legislative judgment that residential privacy should be preserved to the greatest extent possible without also compromising the special protection owing to labor picketing. In short, the statute is viewed as a reasonable attempt to accommodate the competing rights of the homeowner to enjoy his privacy and the employee to demonstrate over labor disputes.[12] But this attempt to justify the statute hinges on the validity of both of these goals, and we have already concluded that the latter -- the desire to favor one form of speech over all others -- is illegitimate.

The second and more complex formulation of appellant's position characterizes the statute as a carefully drafted attempt to prohibit that picketing which would impinge on residential privacy while permitting that picketing which would not. In essence, appellant asserts that the exception for labor picketing does not contravene the State's interest in preserving residential tranquility because of the unique character of a residence that is a "place of employment." By "inviting" a worker into his home and converting that dwelling into a place of employment, the argument goes, the resident has diluted his entitlement to total privacy. In other words, he has "waived" his right to be free from picketing with respect to disputes arising out of the employment relationship, thereby justifying the statute's narrow labor exception at those locations.[13]

---

[12] We note that the statute's labor dispute exemption is overbroad in this respect, for it not only protects the rights of the employee to picket the residence of his employer, but it also permits third parties to picket both the employer and his employee, even when there is no dispute between those individuals. As appellant's counsel explained at oral argument: "[The] labor dispute could exist even if the employee wasn't part of the dispute. For example, if you have a condominium that employs non-union janitors and the non-union janitor is perfectly happy to be there, conceivably union janitors could engage in picketing, very much like a traditional labor law case." Tr. of Oral Arg. 14.

[13] An alternative justification for the statute -- one not pressed by appellant -- is that it is intended to protect privacy in the home, but only insofar as that objective can be accomplished without prohibiting those forms of speech that are peculiarly appropriate to residential neighborhoods *and cannot effectively be exercised elsewhere.* Since labor picketing arising out of disputes occurring in residential neighborhoods can only be carried out in those neighborhoods, the argument would continue, it is permitted under the statute while other forms of picketing, for which suitable alternative forums will generally exist, are barred.

The flaw in this argument is that it proves too little. Numerous types of peaceful picketing other than labor picketing would have but a negligible impact on privacy interests, [14] and numerous other actions of a homeowner might constitute "nonresidential" uses of his property and would thus serve to vitiate the right to residential privacy. For example, the resident who prominently decorates his windows and front yard with posters promoting the qualifications of one candidate for political office might be said to "invite" a counter-demonstration from supporters of an opposing candidate. Similarly, a county chairman who uses his home to meet with his district captains and to discuss some controversial issue might well expect that those who are deeply concerned about the decision the chairman will ultimately reach would want to make their views known by demonstrating outside his home during the meeting. And, with particular regard to the facts of the instant case, it borders on the frivolous to suggest that a resident who invites a repairman into his home to fix his television set has "waived" his right to privacy with respect to a dispute between the repairman and the local union, [15] but that the official who has voluntarily chosen to enter the public arena has not likewise "waived" his right to privacy with respect to a challenge to his views on significant issues of social and economic policy. [16]

Even assuming that a content-based distinction might in some cases be permissible on these grounds, but see *Schneider v. State*, 308 U.S. 147, 163 (1939) ("one is not to have the exercise of his liberty of expression in appropriate places abridged on the plea that it may be exercised in some other place"), this is not such a case because the Illinois statute is seriously underinclusive in this respect. It singles out for special protection only one of the many sorts of picketing which must be carried out in residential neighborhoods or not at all. Protests arising out of landlord-tenant relationships, zoning disputes, and historic preservation issues are just some of the many demonstrations that bear a direct relation to residential neighborhoods. See generally Comment, Picketers at the Doorstep, 9 Harv. Civ. Rights -- Civ. Lib. L. Rev. 95, 101-102, 106 (1974). Indeed, appellees themselves assert that they want to engage in residential picketing because it is the only effective means they have of communicating their concern about the issue of busing to the desired neighborhood audience. Yet the Illinois statute bars all of these groups from picketing in residential areas while those wishing to picket at the site of a labor dispute are permitted to do so.

[14] See *supra, at 461-462.*

[15] See n. 12, *supra.*

[16] Cf. *Gertz v. Robert Welch, Inc., 418 U.S. 323 (1974).*

IV

We therefore conclude that appellant has not successfully distinguished *Mosley*. We are not to be understood to imply, however, that residential picketing is beyond the reach of uniform and nondiscriminatory regulation. For the right to communicate is not limitless. *E. g., Cox v. Louisiana, 379 U.S. 536, 554-555 (1965); Cox v. Louisiana, 379 U.S. 559, 563-564 (1965)*.[17] Even peaceful picketing may be prohibited when it interferes with the operation of vital governmental facilities, see, *e. g., ibid.* (picketing or parading prohibited near courthouses); *Adderley v. Florida, 385 U.S. 39 (1966)* (demonstrations prohibited on jailhouse grounds), or when it is directed toward an illegal purpose, see, *e. g., Teamsters v. Vogt, Inc., 354 U.S. 284 (1957)* (prohibition of picketing directed toward achieving "union shop" in violation of state law).

Moreover, we have often declared that "[a] state or municipality may protect individual privacy by enacting reasonable time, place, and manner regulations applicable to all speech *irrespective of content.*" *Erznoznik v. City of Jacksonville, 422 U.S. 205, 209 (1975)* (emphasis supplied). See, *e. g., Cox v. New Hampshire, 312 U.S. 569 (1941);Kovacs v. Cooper, 336 U.S. 77 (1949);Poulos v. New Hampshire, 345 U.S. 395 (1953);Cox v. Louisiana, 379 U.S., at 554;Grayned v. City of Rockford, 408 U.S. 104 (1972)*. In sum, "no mandate in our Constitution leaves States and governmental units powerless to pass laws to protect the public from the kind of boisterous and threatening conduct that disturbs the tranquility of spots selected by the people either for homes, wherein they can escape the hurly-burly of the outside business and political world, or for public and other buildings that require peace and quiet to carry out their functions, such as courts, libraries, schools, and hospitals." *Gregory v. Chicago, 394 U.S. 111, 118 (1969)* (Black, J., concurring).

Preserving the sanctity of the home, the one retreat to which men and women can repair to escape from the tribulations of their daily pursuits, is surely an important value. Our decisions reflect no lack of solicitude for the right of an individual "to be let alone" in the privacy of the home, "sometimes the last citadel of the tired, the weary, and the sick." *Id., at 125* (Black, J., concurring). See generally *Stanley v. Georgia, 394 U.S. 557 (1969); Rowan v. United States Post Office Dept., 397 U.S. 728 (1970); FCC v. Pacifica Foundation, 438 U.S. 726 (1978); Payton v. New York, 445 U.S.*

---

[17] Mr. Justice Goldberg's opinion for the Court in the first *Cox* case stated: "The rights of free speech and assembly, while fundamental in our democratic society, still do not mean that everyone with opinions or beliefs to express may address a group at any public place and at any time. The constitutional guarantee of liberty implies the existence of an organized society maintaining public order, without which liberty itself would be lost in the excesses of anarchy." *379 U.S., at 554.*

573 (1980). The State's interest in protecting the well-being, tranquility, and privacy of the home is certainly of the highest order in a free and civilized society. "'The crucial question, however, is whether [the Illinois' statute] advances that objective in a manner consistent with the command of the *Equal Protection Clause.*' *Reed* v. *Reed*, 404 U.S. 71, 76 [(1971)]." *Police Department of Chicago v. Mosley*, *408 U.S., at 99*. And because the statute discriminates among pickets based on the subject matter of their expression, the answer must be "No."

The judgment of the Court of Appeals is

Affirmed.

JUSTICE STEWART, concurring.

The opinion of the Court in this case, as did the Court's opinion in *Police Department of Chicago v. Mosley, 408 U.S. 92,* invokes the *Equal Protection Clause of the Fourteenth Amendment* as the basis of decision. But what was actually at stake in *Mosley*, and is at stake here, is the basic meaning of the constitutional protection of free speech:

"[While] a municipality may constitutionally impose reasonable time, place, and manner regulations on the use of its streets and sidewalks for *First Amendment* purposes, and may even forbid altogether such use of some of its facilities; what a municipality may *not* do under the *First* and *Fourteenth Amendments* is to discriminate in the regulation of expression on the basis of the content of that expression." *Hudgens v. NLRB, 424 U.S. 507, 520.* (Citations omitted.)

It is upon this understanding that I join the opinion and judgment of the Court.

JUSTICE REHNQUIST, with whom CHIEF JUSTICE and JUSTICE BLACKMUN join, dissenting.

I address the merits of the Court's constitutional decision first, although I also seriously question the appellees' standing to assert the grounds for invalidity on which the Court apparently relies.[1] One who reads the opinion of the Court is probably left with the impression that Illinois has enacted a residential picketing statute which reads: "All residential picketing, except for labor picketing, is prohibited." Such an impression is entirely understandable; indeed, it is created by the Court's own phrasing throughout the opinion. The Court asserts that Illinois, "in exempting from its general prohibition *only* the 'peaceful picketing of a place of employment involved in a labor dispute,' . . . discriminates between lawful and unlawful conduct based upon . . . content. . . ." (Emphasis added.) *Ante*, at 460. It states that "information about labor disputes may be freely disseminated, but discussion of all other issues is restricted." *Ante*, at 461. The Court finds that the permissibility of residential picketing in Illinois is dependent "*solely* on the nature of the message being conveyed." *Ibid*. (Emphasis added.) And again the Court states that "Illinois has flatly prohibited all nonlabor picketing" while the statute is said to "broadly [permit] all peaceful labor picketing." *Ante*, at 462, 465.

Dissenting opinions are more likely than not to quarrel with the Court's exposition of the law, but my initial quarrel is with the accuracy of the Court's paraphrasing and selective quotation from the Illinois statute. The complete language of the statute, set out accurately in the text of the Court's opinion, reveals a legislative

---

[1] The Court premises its finding that the appellees have standing to challenge the statute at least in part on the basis of the appellant's "concessions" at oral argument that the State was not persisting in its challenge to appellees' standing in this Court. See *ante*, at 461, n. 5. But we have said that "[we] are loath to attach conclusive weight to the relatively spontaneous responses of counsel to equally spontaneous questioning from the Court during oral argument." *Moose Lodge No. 107 v. Irvis, 407 U.S. 163, 170 (1972)*. Moreover, while appellant may have chosen not to challenge appellees' standing to argue that they had been denied equal protection under the statute, appellant certainly did not concede that appellees had standing to argue that other individuals desiring to picket under circumstances dissimilar to appellees might be denied equal protection under the statute. In fact, counsel quite explicitly stated that the Court should only consider the constitutionality of prohibiting the appellees' conduct: "I would urge that the . . . *First Amendment* question only be as applied to the plaintiffs, to the conduct that the plaintiffs actually engaged in. . . ." Tr. of Oral Arg. 17. And this is the standing question that is implicated by the Court's opinion. See *infra*, at 486-489.

scheme quite different from that described by the Court in its narrative paraphrasing of the enactment.[2]

The statute provides that residential picketing is prohibited, but goes on to exempt four categories of residences from this general ban. *First*, if the residence is used as a "place of business" *all* peaceful picketing is allowed. *Second*, if the residence is being used to "[hold] a meeting or assembly on premises commonly used to discuss subjects of general public interest" *all* peaceful picketing is allowed. *Third*, if the residence is also used as a "place of employment" which is involved in a labor dispute, labor-related picketing is allowed. *Finally*, the statute provides that a resident is entitled to picket his own home. Thus it is clear that information about labor disputes may *not* be "freely disseminated" since labor picketing is restricted to a narrow category of residences. And Illinois has *not* "flatly prohibited all nonlabor picketing" since it allows nonlabor picketing at residences used as a place of business, residences used as public meeting places, and at an individual's own residence.

Only through this mischaracterization of the Illinois statute may the Court attempt to fit this case into the *Mosley* rule prohibiting regulation on the basis of *"content alone."* (Emphasis added.) *Police Department of Chicago v. Mosley*, 408 U.S. 92, 96 (1972). For in *Mosley*, the sole determinant of an individual's right to picket near a school was the content of the speech. As the Court today aptly observes, such a regulation warrants exacting scrutiny. In contrast, the principal determinant of a person's right to picket a residence in Illinois is not content, as the Court suggests, but rather the character of the residence sought to be picketed. Content is relevant only in one of the categories established by the legislature.

The cases appropriate to the analysis therefore are those establishing the limits on a State's authority to impose time, place, and manner restrictions on speech activities. Under this rubric, even taking into account the limited content distinction made by the statute, Illinois has readily satisfied its constitutional obligation to draft statutes in conformity with *First Amendment* and equal protection principles. In fact, the very

---

[2] The simplistic construction of the statute reflected in the Court's opinion apparently is also justified by supposed "concessions" of appellant's counsel at oral argument. *Ante*, at 461, n. 5. Appellant, however, has never suggested that the statute regulates picketing solely by permitting labor, but not nonlabor, issues to be aired through residential picketing. While admitting the use of some content differentiation, the appellant asserts throughout his argument that the statute is a "place" regulation; it allows picketing at homes used for nonresidential purposes but not at those homes used exclusively for residential purposes. See, *e. g.*, the question presented for review in the Juris. Statement 4.

statute which the Court today cavalierly invalidates has been hailed by commentators as "an excellent model" of legislation achieving a delicate balance among rights to privacy, free expression, and equal protection. See Kamin, Residential Picketing and the *First Amendment*, 61 Nw. U. L. Rev. 177, 207 (1966); Comment, 34 U. Chi. L. Rev. 106, 139 (1966). The state legislators of the Nation will undoubtedly greet today's decision with nothing less than exasperation and befuddlement. Time after time, the States have been assured that they may properly promote residential privacy even though free expression must be reduced. To be sure, our decisions have adopted a virtual laundry list of "Don'ts" that must be adhered to in the process. Heading up that list of course is the rule that legislatures must curtail free expression through the "least restrictive means" consistent with the accomplishment of their purpose, and they must avoid standards which are either vague or capable of discretionary application. But somewhere, the Court says in these cases (with a reassuring pat on the head to the legislatures), there *is* the constitutional pot of gold at the end of the rainbow of litigation.

Here, where Illinois has drafted such a statute, avoiding an outright ban on all residential picketing, avoiding reliance on any vague or discretionary standards, and permitting categories of permissible picketing activity at residences where the State has determined the resident's own actions have substantially reduced his interest in privacy, the Court in response confronts the State with the "***Catch-22***' that the less restrictive categories are constitutionally infirm under principles of equal protection. Under the Court's approach today, the State would fare better by adopting *more* restrictive means, a judicial incentive I had thought this Court would hesitate to afford. Either that, or uniform restrictions will be found invalid under the *First Amendment* and categorical exceptions found invalid under the *Equal Protection Clause*, with the result that speech and only speech will be entitled to protection. This can only mean that the hymns of praise in prior opinions celebrating carefully drawn statutes are no more than sympathetic clucking, and in fact the State is damned if it does and damned if it doesn't.

Equally troublesome is the methodology by which these difficult questions of constitutional law have been reached. The Court today figuratively walked a country mile to find a potential unconstitutional application of this statute, and it is primarily on that potential which the total nullification of this statute rests. Just because it is a statute which is in issue does not relieve this Court of its duty to decide only the concrete controversy presented by the case. As discussed below, I think it quite clear that the statute does not prohibit the appellees in this action from engaging in conduct which must be protected under the *First Amendment*, the state interests would not be satisfied by a statute employing less restrictive means, the statute is not facially overbroad by prohibiting conduct which clearly must be permitted under the *First Amendment*, and the appellees have not themselves been denied equal protection because they do not seek to picket under circumstances which are indistinguishable from the circumstances where picketing is allowed. Only by speculating that there *might* be an individual or group that will be denied equal protection by the statute can the Court invalidate it. This is speculation this Court is not permitted to indulge in when nullifying the acts of a legislative branch.

I

The Illinois statute in issue simply does not contravene the *First Amendment*.

A

Repeatedly, this Court has upheld state authority to restrict the time, place, and manner of speech, if those regulations "protect a substantial governmental interest unrelated to the suppression of free expression" and are narrowly tailored, limiting the restrictions to those reasonably necessary to protect the substantial government interest. *Brown v. Glines, 444 U.S. 348, 354 (1980)*; *Village of Schaumburg v. Citizens for a Better Environment, 444 U.S. 620 (1980)*. This standard of measuring permissible state regulation, often echoed in this Court's opinions, is readily satisfied in this case.

The interest which the State here seeks to protect is residential privacy, as clearly demonstrated by the legislature's statement of purpose. *Ante*, at 464, n. 8. When a residence is used for exclusively residential purposes, the State recognizes no exception to the ban on picketing. As in this case, it has not been asserted that Mayor Bilandic's home fell into any category other than a residence used solely for residential purposes. The appellees nevertheless assert that their interest in publicizing their opinions on the issue of school integration outweigh the State's asserted interest in protecting residential privacy.

Our cases simply do not support such a construction of the *First Amendment*. In *Kovacs v. Cooper, 336 U.S. 77, 81 (1949)*, the state interest in preventing interference with the "social activities in which [city residents] are engaged or the quiet that they would like to enjoy" warranted the prohibition of sound trucks on residential streets. In *Rowan v. United States Post Office Dept., 397 U.S. 728, 736 (1970)*, this Court held that "[the] right of every person 'to be let alone' must be placed in the scales with the right of others to communicate." The Court recognized a "very basic right to be free from sights, sounds, and tangible matter we do not want" in the home. *Ibid.* These interests were sufficient to justify a resident's ability to absolutely preclude delivery of unwanted mail to his address. Similarly, in *FCC v. Pacifica Foundation, 438 U.S. 726, 748 (1978)*, the Court found that an offensive broadcast could be absolutely banned from the airwaves because it "confronts the citizen, not only in public, but also in the privacy of the home, where the individual's right to be left alone plainly outweighs the *First Amendment* rights of an intruder." Under these authorities, the appellees have no fundamental *First Amendment* right to picket in front of a residence.

B

Nor can it be said that the state interest could be fully protected by a less restrictive statute. An absolute ban on picketing at residences used solely for residential purposes permissibly furthers the state interest in protecting residential privacy. The State could certainly conclude that the presence of even a solitary picket in front of a residence is an intolerable intrusion on residential privacy. The Court today suggests that some picketing activities would have but a "negligible impact on privacy interests," intimating that Illinois could satisfy its interests through more limited restrictions on picketing, such as regulating the hours and numbers of pickets. *Ante*, at 469. But I find nothing in the cases of this Court to suggest that a State may not permissibly conclude that even one individual camped in front of the home is unacceptable. It is the State, and not this Court, which legislates to prohibit evils which its citizens find unescapable, subject only to the limitations of the United States Constitution. Unlike sound trucks, it is not just the distraction of the noise which is in issue -- it is the very presence of an unwelcome visitor at the home. As a Wisconsin court described in *Wauwatosa v. King*, 49 Wis. 2d 398, 411-412, 182 N. W. 2d 530, 537 (1971):

"To those inside . . . the home becomes something less than a home when and while the picketing . . . [continues]. . . . [The] tensions and pressures may be psychological, not physical, but they are not, for that reason, less inimical to family privacy and truly domestic tranquility."

Whether noisy or silent, alone or accompanied by others, whether on the streets or on the sidewalk, I think that there are few of us that would feel comfortable knowing that a stranger lurks outside our home. The State's prohibition of this conduct is even easier to justify than regulations previously upheld by this Court limiting mailings and broadcasts into the home. In *Rowan*, as in *Pacifica*, the resident at least could have short-circuited the annoyance by throwing away the mail or turning off the radio. Even that alternative redress, however, was held not sufficient to preclude the legislative authorities from prohibiting the initial intrusion. Where, as here, the resident has no recourse of escape whatsoever, the State may quite justifiably conclude that the protection afforded by a statute such as this seems even more necessary.

C

Thus the appellees cannot secure the invalidation of this statute by urging that they seek to engage in expression which must be protected by the *First Amendment* or by demonstrating that a statute less restrictive of picketing would satisfy the state interest. On occasion this Court has, of course, permitted invalidation of a statute even though the plaintiff's conduct was not protected if the statute clearly "sweeps within its prohibitions what may not be punished under the First . . . [Amendment]." *Grayned v. City of Rockford, 408 U.S. 104, 114-115 (1972).*

But this statute satisfies even the overbreadth challenge. It is arguable that when a resident has voluntarily used his home for nonresidential uses in a way which reduces the resident's privacy interest, and the person seeking to picket the home has no alternative forum for effectively airing the grievance because it relates to this nonresidential use of the home, some form of residential picketing might be protected under the *First Amendment.* The courts which have found general prohibitions on residential picketing to be permissible under the *First Amendment* have considered the question more difficult under such circumstances. For example, in *Walinsky v. Kennedy, 94 Misc. 2d 121, 404 N. Y. S. 2d 491 (1977)*, the New York court enjoined all residential picketing but concluded that

"[a] more difficult question would be raised if the [resident's] office were in his home and there was thus no other suitable forum wherein he could be confronted or the picket's viewpoints could be heard." *Id., at 132, n. 15, 404 N. Y. S. 2d, at 498, n. 15.*

Similarly, in *Hibbs v. Neighborhood Organization to Rejuvenate Tenant Housing, 433 Pa. 578, 580, 252 A. 2d 622, 623-624 (1969)*, the court found that a slumlord could be picketed at his home, but only because he effectively operated his business out of his residence and no other alternative situs was available to air the dispute. This Court has intimated a similar concern in dicta in *Senn v. Tile Layers, 301 U.S. 468 (1937).* There the right of laborers under a state statute to picket the residence of an employer who operated his business in his home was upheld, and the Court went on to say that "[members] of a union might, without special statutory authorization by a state, make known the facts of a labor dispute, for freedom of speech is guaranteed by the Federal Constitution." *Id., at 478.*

I would by no means say without more that the State would have to permit such residential picketing, but such circumstances would, as the courts have found, present the greatest potential for a complaint of overbreadth. The State in the present case has forestalled any such challenge, however, by exempting such groups from the ban on residential picketing. Whether *required* by the Constitution or not, such exemptions are the concern of this Court only if they *violate* the Constitution. This Court in fact upheld enforcement of a statute permitting similar residential picketing in *Senn v. Tile Layers, supra.* Since the State has a legitimate interest in protecting speech activity and in particular, providing a forum where no other is reasonably available, excluding residences used for nonresidential purposes from the general prohibition on residential picketing is an entirely rational legislative policy, even if not mandated by the *First Amendment.* Thus no overbreadth challenge should succeed here.

II

Even though the statute does not prohibit conduct which is protected, the statute must also survive the hurdle of the *Equal Protection Clause of the Fourteenth Amendment.* By choosing a less-restrictive-means approach and excluding pickets at residences used for nonresidential purposes from the general prohibition, the Court concludes the State has violated equal protection. I do not think this result can be sustained because the appellees have not been denied equal protection and that is the only question this Court may properly review.

A

Police Department of Chicago v. Mosley, 408 U.S. 92 (1972), states a standard by which equal protection requirements in the *First Amendment* context must be measured. The Court in that case identified the "crucial question" as "whether there is an appropriate governmental interest suitably furthered by the differential treatment" of the appellees' picketing. *Id., at 95.* The interest asserted by the city was the prevention of disruption in the schools. Thus the statute, to satisfy *Mosley*, should have prohibited all picketing which could reasonably be categorized as disruptive. Yet the ordinance permitted labor picketing while prohibiting picketing relating to race discrimination (and all other nonlabor topics), even though both forms of picketing were equally disruptive.

Thus the question is whether the State has a substantial interest in differentiating between the picketing which appellees seek to conduct and the picketing which is permitted under the statute. For equal protection does not require that "things which are different in fact . . . be treated in law as though they were the same." *Tigner v. Texas, 310 U.S. 141, 147 (1940).* Appellees seek to picket a residence to voice their views on school integration. There has been no showing that the resident has used his home for nonresidential purposes, or that no other forum is available where appellees may publicize their dispute. [3] All pickets who fall within this category, no matter what the content of their expression may be, are prohibited from residential picketing. School integration, public housing, labor disputes, and the recognition of Red China are treated alike in this respect. The State has differentiated only when the residence has been used as a place of business, a place for public meetings, or a place of employment, or is occupied by the picket himself. In each of these categories, the State has determined that the resident has waived some measure of privacy through voluntary use of his home for these purposes.

Our cases clearly support a State's authority to design the permissibility of picketing in relation to the use to which a particular building is put. As stated in *Grayned v. City of Rockford, 408 U.S., at 116*: "The nature of a place, 'the pattern of its normal activities, dictate the kinds of regulations of time, place, and manner that are reasonable.' . . . The crucial question is whether the manner of expression is basically incompatible with the normal activity of a particular place at a particular time." The fact that all areas could be classified as school grounds, however, would not mean that all school grounds had to be subject to the same restrictions. As the Court in *Grayned* noted: "Different considerations, of course, apply in different circumstances. For example, restrictions appropriate to a single-building high school during class hours would be inappropriate in many open areas on a college campus. . . ." *Id., at 120, n. 45*. And just as surely the State may differentiate between residences used exclusively for residential purposes and those which are not. It is far from nonsensical or arbitrary for a legislature to conclude that privacy interests are reduced when the residence is used for these other purposes. In another *First Amendment* case, *Paris Adult Theatre I v. Slaton, 413 U.S. 49, 61 (1973)*, we stated: "From the beginning of civilized societies, legislators and judges have acted on various unprovable assumptions. Such assumptions underlie much lawful state regulation of commercial and business affairs."

Despite the state interest in treating residences which are used for nonresidential purposes differently from residences which are not, the Court finds that the categories are improper because there is an element of content regulation in the statutory scheme. While content is clearly not the principal focus of the statutory categories, since content is only relevant in the one subcategory of "places of

---

[3] If it is the Mayor the appellees seek to reach, they have not shown they cannot do so at city hall. If it is the neighborhoods they seek to reach, they have not shown that they cannot do so in neighborhood parks. I think it is now clear that when speech interests are countered by other substantial governmental interests, the availability of another forum is a highly relevant factor in determining the appropriate balance. See *Pell v. Procunier, 417 U.S. 817, 823-824 (1974)*.

employment," the content restriction is quite clearly related to a legitimate state purpose. When an individual hires an employee to perform services in his home, it would not seem reasonable to conclude that the resident had so greatly compromised his residential status so as to permit picketing on any subject. The State may quite properly decide that the balance is better struck by the rule embodied in this statute which recognizes a more limited waiver of privacy interests by allowing only picketing relating to any labor dispute involving the resident *as employer* which has arisen out of the resident's choice of using his residence as a place of employment.

Content regulation, when closely related to a permissible state purpose, is clearly permitted. Surely the Court would not prohibit a city from preventing an individual from interrupting an orderly city council discussion of public housing to orate on the vices or virtues of nuclear power. Yet this is content regulation. More accurately, it is restriction of topics to those appropriate to the forum. In this case, the forum is a confined one -- residences used as a place of employment -- and clearly labor picketing in that forum is the relevant topic.

This differentiation is supported by *Cox v. Louisiana, 379 U.S. 559 (1965)*. There the Court upheld a state prohibition on picketing in front of a government building which was used as a courthouse if the content of the picketing could be presumed to demonstrate an intent to influence the judiciary. In *Cox* then, because of the nature of the state interest invoked, both the content of the picketing as well as the use of the building were considered determinative. The Court noted that if a mayor had an office in the courthouse and individuals were picketing on a topic relevant to the mayor, rather than the judiciary, then the speech would be permissible. Thus use and content, or as MR. JUSTICE STEVENS stated for the plurality in *Young v. American Mini Theatres, Inc., 427 U.S. 50 (1976)*, "content and context" are important determinants. As in *Cox*, a State need not treat residences which are used for different purposes in the same fashion, and when reasonably related to the state purpose, distinctions in content are permissible. See also *FCC v. Pacifica Foundation, 438 U.S. 726 (1978)*; *Erznoznik v. City of Jacksonville, 422 U.S. 205 (1975)*; *Young v. American Mini Theatres, supra.*

The question, therefore, is not whether there is some differentiation on the basis of content, but whether the appellees' prohibited conduct can be said to share the same characteristics of the conduct which is permitted. The Court devotes less than one page to what purports to be an equal protection analysis of this determinative question. In fact, only one sentence relates to the differences between the litigants in this case and the permitted picketing:

"And, with particular regard to the facts of the instant case, it borders on the frivolous to suggest that a resident who invites a repairman into his home to fix his television set has 'waived' his right to privacy with respect to a dispute between the repairman and the local union, but that the official who has voluntarily chosen to enter the public arena has not likewise 'waived' his right to privacy with respect to a challenge to his views on significant issues of social and economic policy." *Ante*, at 469.

First, it is unclear whether the Illinois statute would be construed to permit the type of labor picketing described in the Court's example where the dispute is not between the employer and the employee. [4] Second, the fact that an official has chosen to enter the public arena has no bearing on the question of how he uses his residence -- the only question of relevance to the Illinois Legislature. Further, just as the State had an interest in *Cox* in preventing picketing which might tend to improperly influence the judicial process, the State certainly has an equal interest in preventing residential picketing of their officials where the result might be influence through the harassment of the official's family. This is not the type of influence that a democratic society has traditionally held high as a part of the *Bill of Rights*. Finally, at least in the case of the repairman, the home in fact is the situs of the publicized dispute, while the Mayor's home is not. The appellees do not seek to picket the situs of the dispute; they do not seek to picket the home of an individual who has used his residence for nonresidential purposes relevant to that dispute; they have not established the unavailability of any alternative forum. These are the characteristics of residential picketing which the State has allowed. The appellees have thereby failed to establish that they seek to picket under circumstances rationally indistinguishable from the circumstances under which the State has permitted picketing. They have therefore not been denied equal protection.

B

The Court makes little effort to establish that the appellees seek to picket under circumstances which are indistinguishable from the picketing permitted under the statute. Instead, it places the fulcrum of its equal protection argument on the fact that there might well be other actions of a homeowner which would constitute a "nonresidential" use of his property, warranting additional statutory exceptions.

---

[4] If given an opportunity, the Illinois courts might determine that many repairmen are not "employees" under the statute. Further, it is also possible that the state courts would limit the disputes covered by the exception to those between the resident and his employee. More importantly, these are questions with which this court should not be concerned until the state courts have had an opportunity to address them. See *infra*, at 488.

While I am not persuaded that the Court has identified an example of another picket who should likewise be permitted to picket under the justification forwarded by the State, [5] the flaws in the analysis are more fundamental. First, the fact that there may be someone other than the appellees who has a right to be treated similarly to those permitted to picket is irrelevant to the question of constitutional validity in this case. The Court apparently believes it has a license to import the more relaxed standing requirements of *First Amendment* overbreadth into equal protection challenges. This, however, is not and should not be the law. Precedent supports no such approach and the rationale underlying the expanded standing principles in the overbreadth context are inapposite in the equal protection realm.

As we stated in *Grayned*, standing to challenge an ordinance which has been constitutionally applied to the plaintiff is permitted because otherwise the statute, if allowed to stand until a later challenge, will "deter privileged activity." *408 U.S., at 114*. In the equal protection context, however, we are not concerned that conduct

---

[5] The Court identifies several examples of picketing which the State would allegedly have to allow in order to avoid a successful equal protection attack. The Court indicates that there is no ground for differentiating between the picketing which is permitted and picketing relating to landlord-tenant disputes, zoning disputes, and historic preservation issues. *Ante*, at 468-469, n. 13. The first of these examples seems particularly inappropriate since picketing in relation to landlord-tenant disputes would most likely be permissible under the statute just as written. The statute exempts picketing by an individual at his residence, so it would certainly appear that a tenant could picket in front of his own dwelling (which also happens to be the situs of the dispute). If the landlord operates his business out of his home, the tenants would also be able to picket there under the statute. Thus there is no reason to believe that the picketing opportunities of tenants have been substantially limited by the statutory classifications, and in fact would appear to be at least as broad as those afforded to employees with labor disputes. Zoning disputes and historic preservation issues are distinguishable in several respects. First, those issues have no relationship to the use of an individual's residence (other than their own, which of course they may picket) and the individual resident would not have waived any privacy interests. Second, alternative forums would theoretically include residential parks as well as the office of the authorities responsible for the relevant decisions.

The Court's citation of lawn decorations as a waiver of residential privacy seems odd since that act does not involve the voluntary admission of strangers into the home for some nonresidential purposes -- a characteristic shared by each of the other exceptions. *Ante*, at 469. The Court's citation of a political party meeting is also distinguishable since this example does not share the commercial attributes of the other exemptions -- where "nonresidential use" seems most readily found. An alternative forum would also not seem difficult to obtain in those circumstances.

which *must* be permitted under the *First Amendment* will be prohibited, but only that conduct which could be and is properly prohibited be permitted if indistinguishable from other permitted conduct. The impact on speech is therefore a minimal one, while the jurisprudential considerations for declining to consider alternative applications loom large.

In *Barrows v. Jackson, 346 U.S. 249, 256 (1953)*, an equal protection case, the Court identified the ordinary rule that, "even though a party will suffer a direct substantial injury from application of a statute, he cannot challenge its constitutionality unless he can show that he is within the class whose constitutional rights are allegedly infringed." The Court justified the rule, stating:

"One reason for this ruling is that the state court, when actually faced with the question, might narrowly construe the statute to obliterate the objectionable feature, or it might declare the unconstitutional provision separable. *New York ex rel. Hatch* v. *Reardon*, [204 U.S.], at 160-161. . . . It would indeed be undesirable for this Court to consider every conceivable situation which might possibly arise in the application of complex and comprehensive legislation. Nor are we so ready to frustrate the expressed will of Congress or that of the state legislatures. Cf. *Southern Pacific Co.* v. *Gallagher, 306 U.S. 167, 172*." *Id., at 256-257*.

More recently in *Craig v. Boren, 429 U.S. 190, 193 (1976)*, we emphasized that standing is "designed to minimize unwarranted intervention into controversies where the applicable constitutional questions are ill-defined and speculative." Sound principles of standing simply do not permit this Court to entertain any claim by the appellees in this action that someone other than themselves *might* be denied equal protection by the operation of the statute. See also *Young v. American Mini Theatres, Inc., 427 U.S., at 58-59, 60*; *Broadrick v. Oklahoma, 413 U.S. 601 (1973)*. This consideration is particularly compelling in this case since the appellees had an opportunity to seek a limiting construction of the statute by the Illinois courts when originally prosecuted for their picketing, but chose to plead guilty instead, thereby denying the one court system that could authoritatively limit the statute the opportunity to do so.

Even if this Court could properly take cognizance of the fact that some identifiable person not clearly encompassed in the statutory categories permitting picketing should also be allowed to picket, under equal protection standards, that fact alone would not justify wholesale invalidation of the entire statutory framework. In *Califano v. Jobst, 434 U.S. 47, 53-55 (1977)*, this Court emphasized that sound equal protection analysis must uphold general rules "even though such rules inevitably produce seemingly arbitrary consequences in some individual cases," and that "the broad legislative classification must be judged by reference to characteristics typical of the affected classes rather than by focusing on selected, atypical examples." Any other standard of review, such as that employed by the Court today, will inevitably lead to invalidation, for this or any other court will always be able to conceive of a hypothetical not properly accounted for by the statutory categories. The state courts, if given an opportunity, have the tools to correct such minor deficiencies. This Court has soundly permitted state legislatures far more room for error in the drafting of its categories than what the Court today allows. As it stated in *Ginsberg v. New York, 390 U.S. 629, 642-643 (1968)*, "[we] do not demand of legislatures 'scientifically certain criteria of legislation,' *Noble State Bank v. Haskell, 219 U.S. 104, 110.*" And more recently, we recognized a compelling need to allow to local government "a reasonable opportunity to experiment with solutions to admittedly serious problems." *Young v. American Mini Theatres, supra, at 71.*

I can conclude this dissent with no more apt words than those of Mr. Justice Frankfurter in his concurring opinion in *Kovacs v. Cooper, 336 U.S., at 97*: "[It] is not for us to supervise the limits the legislature may impose in safeguarding the steadily narrowing opportunities for serenity and reflection."

Aguilar v. Felton

Supreme Court of the United States

December 5, 1984, Argued

July 1, 1985, Decided [*]

No. 84-237

473 U.S. 402
105 S. Ct. 3232
87 L. Ed. 2d 290

AGUILAR ET AL. v. FELTON ET AL.

APPEAL FROM THE UNITED STATES COURT OF APPEALS FOR THE SECOND CIRCUIT.

Solicitor General Lee argued the cause for appellants in all cases. With him on the briefs for appellant in No. 84-238 were Acting Assistant Attorney General Willard, Deputy Solicitor General Bator, Anthony J. Steinmeyer, and Michael Jay Singer. Charles H. Wilson filed a brief for appellant in No. 84-237. Frederick A. O. Schwarz, Jr., Leonard Koerner, and Stephen J. McGrath filed briefs for appellant in No. 84-239.

Stanley Geller argued the cause and filed briefs for appellees in all cases. [+]

---

[*] Together with No. 84-238, Secretary, United States Department of Education v. Felton et al., and No. 84-239, Chancellor of the Board of Education of the City of New York v. Felton et al., also on appeal from the same court.

[+] Briefs of amici curiae urging reversal were filed for the Council for American Private Education et al. by Edward McGlynn Gaffney, Jr.; for the Catholic League for Religious and Civil Rights by Steven Frederick McDowell; for Citizens for Educational Freedom by Charles E. Rice; for the National Jewish Commission on Law and Public Affairs by Nathan Lewin, Dennis Rapps, and Daniel D. Chazin; for Parents Rights, Inc., by John J. Donnelly; and for the United States Catholic Conference by Wilfred R. Caron and Mark E. Chopko.

Briefs of amici curiae urging affirmance were filed for the American Civil Liberties Union et al. by Burt Neuborne, Charles Sims, and Marc D. Stern; for Americans United for Separation of Church and State et al. by Lee Boothby; and for the Anti-Defamation League of B'nai B'rith by Justin J. Finger, Meyer Eisenberg, and Jeffrey P. Sinensky.

BRENNAN, J., delivered the opinion of the Court, in which MARSHALL, BLACKMUN, POWELL, and STEVENS, JJ., joined.
POWELL, J., filed a concurring opinion.
BURGER, C. J., WHITE, J., and REHNQUIST, J., filed dissenting opinions.
O'CONNOR, J., filed a dissenting opinion, in which REHNQUIST, J., joined as to Parts II and III.

JUSTICE BRENNAN delivered the opinion of the Court.

The City of New York uses federal funds to pay the salaries of public employees who teach in parochial schools. In this companion case to *School District of Grand Rapids* v. *Ball, ante,* p. 373, we determine whether this practice violates the Establishment Clause of the First Amendment.

I

A

The program at issue in this case, originally enacted as Title I of the Elementary and Secondary Education Act of 1965,[1] authorizes the Secretary of Education to distribute financial assistance to local educational institutions to meet the needs of educationally deprived children from low-income families. The funds are to be appropriated in accordance with programs proposed by local educational agencies

---

[1] Title I, 92 Stat. 2153, was codified at *20 U. S. C. § 2701 et seq. Section 2701* provided:

"In recognition of the special educational needs of children of low-income families and the impact that concentrations of low-income families have on the ability of local educational agencies to support adequate educational programs, the Congress hereby declares it to be the policy of the United States to provide financial assistance (as set forth in the following parts of this subchapter) to local educational agencies serving areas with concentrations of children from low-income families to expand and improve their educational programs by various means (including preschool programs) which contribute particularly to meeting the special educational needs of educationally deprived children."

Effective October 1, 1982, Title I was superseded by Chapter I of the Education Consolidation and Improvement Act of 1981, 95 Stat. 464, *20 U. S. C. § 3801 et seq.* See *20 U. S. C. § 3801* (current Chapter I analogue of *§ 2701*). The provisions concerning the participation of children in private schools under Chapter I are virtually identical to those in Title I. Compare 20 U. S. C. § 2740 (former Title I provision) with 20 U. S. C. § 3806 (current Chapter I provision). For the sake of convenience, we will adopt the usage of the parties and continue to refer to the program as "Title I."

and approved by state educational agencies. 20 U. S. C. § 3805(a). [2] "To the extent consistent with the number of educationally deprived children in the school district of the local educational agency who are enrolled in private elementary and secondary schools, such agency shall make provisions for including special educational services and arrangements . . . in which such children can participate." § 3806(a). [3] The proposed programs must also meet the following statutory requirements: the children involved in the program must be educationally deprived, § 3804(a), [4] the children must reside in areas comprising a high concentration of low-income families, § 3805(b), [5] and the programs must supplement, not supplant, programs that would exist absent funding under Title I. § 3807(b). [6]

---

[2] The statute provides:

"A local educational agency may receive a grant under this subchapter for any fiscal year if it has on file with the State educational agency an application which describes the programs and projects to be conducted with such assistance for a period of not more than three years, and such application has been approved by the State educational agency."

See also *20 U. S. C. § 2731* (former Title I analogue).

[3] In *Wheeler v. Barrera, 417 U.S. 402, 41 L. Ed. 2d 159, 94 S. Ct. 2274 (1974)*, we addressed the question whether this provision requires the assignment of publicly employed teachers to provide instruction during regular school hours in parochial schools. We held that Title I mandated that private school students receive services comparable to, but not identical to, the Title I services received by public school students. *Id., at 420-421.* Therefore, the statute would permit, but not require, that on-site services be provided in the parochial schools. In reaching this conclusion as a matter of statutory interpretation, we explicitly noted that "we intimate no view as to the *Establishment Clause* effect of any particular program." *Id., at 426.* *Wheeler* thus provides no authority for the constitutionality of the program before us today.

[4] The statute provides:

"Each State and local educational agency shall use the payments under this subchapter for programs and projects (including the acquisition of equipment and, where necessary, the construction of school facilities) which are designed to meet the special educational needs of educationally deprived children."

[5] The statute provides:

"The application described in subsection (a) of this section shall be approved if . . . the programs and projects described --

"(1)(A) are conducted in attendance areas of such agency having the highest concentration of low-income children . . . ."

[6] The statute provides:

Since 1966, the City of New York has provided instructional services funded by Title I to parochial school students on the premises of parochial schools. Of those students eligible to receive funds in 1981-1982, 13.2% were enrolled in private schools. Of that group, 84% were enrolled in schools affiliated with the Roman Catholic Archdiocese of New York and the Diocese of Brooklyn and 8% were enrolled in Hebrew day schools. With respect to the religious atmosphere of these schools, the Court of Appeals concluded that "the picture that emerges is of a system in which religious considerations play a key role in the selection of students and teachers, and which has as its substantial purpose the inculcation of religious values." *739 F.2d 48, 68 (CA2 1984)*.

The programs conducted at these schools include remedial reading, reading skills, remedial mathematics, English as a second language, and guidance services. These programs are carried out by regular employees of the public schools (teachers, guidance counselors, psychologists, psychiatrists, and social workers) who have volunteered to teach in the parochial schools. The amount of time that each professional spends in the parochial school is determined by the number of students in the particular program and the needs of these students.

The City's Bureau of Nonpublic School Reimbursement makes teacher assignments, and the instructors are supervised by field personnel, who attempt to pay at least one unannounced visit per month. The field supervisors, in turn, report to program coordinators, who also pay occasional unannounced supervisory visits to monitor Title I classes in the parochial schools. The professionals involved in the program are directed to avoid involvement with religious activities that are conducted within the private schools and to bar religious materials in their classrooms. All material and equipment used in the programs funded under Title I are supplied by the Government and are used only in those programs. The professional personnel are solely responsible for the selection of the students. Additionally, the professionals are informed that contact with private school personnel should be kept to a minimum. Finally, the administrators of the parochial

---

"A local educational agency may use funds received under this subchapter only so as to supplement and, to the extent practical, increase the level of funds that would, in the absence of such Federal funds, be made available from non-Federal sources for the education of pupils participating in programs and projects assisted under this subchapter, and in no case may such funds be so used as to supplant such funds from such non-Federal sources. In order to demonstrate compliance with this subsection a local education agency shall not be required to provide services under this subchapter outside the regular classroom or school program."

schools are required to clear the classrooms used by the public school personnel of all religious symbols.

B

In 1978, six taxpayers commenced this action in the District Court for the Eastern District of New York, alleging that the Title I program administered by the City of New York violates the *Establishment Clause*. These taxpayers, appellees in today's case, sought to enjoin the further distribution of funds to programs involving instruction on the premises of parochial schools. Initially the case was held for the outcome of *National Coalition for Public Education and Religious Liberty v. Harris, 489 F. Supp. 1248 (SDNY 1980) (PEARL)*, which involved an identical challenge to the Title I program. When the District Court in *PEARL* affirmed the constitutionality of the Title I program, *ibid.*, and this Court dismissed the appeal for want of jurisdiction, *449 U.S. 808 (1980)*, the challenge of the present appellees was renewed. The District Court granted appellants' motion for summary judgment based upon the evidentiary record developed in *PEARL*.

A unanimous panel of the Court of Appeals for the Second Circuit reversed, holding that

"[the] *Establishment Clause*, as it has been interpreted by the Supreme Court in *Public Funds for Public Schools v. Marburger, 358 F. Supp. 29 (D. N. J. 1973), aff'd mem., 417 U.S. 961* . . . (1974); *Meek v. Pittenger, 421 U.S. 349, 44 L. Ed. 2d 217, 95 S. Ct. 1753* . . . (1975) (particularly Part V, pp. 367-72); and *Wolman v. Walter, 433 U.S. 229, 53 L. Ed. 2d 714, 97 S. Ct. 2593* . . . (1977), constitutes an insurmountable barrier to the use of federal funds to send public school teachers and other professionals into religious schools to carry on instruction, remedial or otherwise, or to provide clinical and guidance services of the sort at issue here." *739 F.2d at 49-50*.

We postponed probable jurisdiction. *469 U.S. 878 (1984)*. We conclude that jurisdiction by appeal does not properly lie.[7] Treating the papers as a petition for a

---

[7] The Court of Appeals held that the plan adopted and administered by the City of New York violates the *Establishment Clause*. *739 F.2d 48, 72 (1984)*. Appeals from this ruling were taken pursuant to *28 U. S. C. § 1252*. An appeal under § 1252, however, may be taken only from an interlocutory or final judgment that has held an Act of Congress unconstitutional as applied ("*i. e.*, that the section, by its own terms, infringed constitutional freedoms in the circumstances of that particular case") or as a whole. *United States v. Christian Echoes National Ministry, Inc., 404 U.S. 561, 563-565, 30 L. Ed. 2d 716, 92 S. Ct. 663 (1972)*. Because the ruling appealed from is not such a judgment, the appeals must be dismissed for want of jurisdiction. *Ibid.*

writ of certiorari, see *28 U. S. C. § 2103*, we grant the petition and now affirm the judgment below.

II

In *School District of Grand Rapids* v. *Ball,* ante, p. 373, the Court has today held unconstitutional under the *Establishment Clause* two remedial and enhancement programs operated by the Grand Rapids Public School District, in which classes were provided to private school children at public expense in classrooms located in and leased from the local private schools. The New York City programs challenged in this case are very similar to the programs we examined in *Ball*. In both cases, publicly funded instructors teach classes composed exclusively of private school students in private school buildings. In both cases, an overwhelming number of the participating private schools are religiously affiliated. In both cases, the publicly funded programs provide not only professional personnel, but also all materials and supplies necessary for the operation of the programs. Finally, the instructors in both cases are told that they are public school employees under the sole control of the public school system.

Appellants attempt to distinguish this case on the ground that the City of New York, unlike the Grand Rapids Public School District, has adopted a system for monitoring the religious content of publicly funded Title I classes in the religious schools. At best, the supervision in this case would assist in preventing the Title I program from being used, intentionally or unwittingly, to inculcate the religious beliefs of the surrounding parochial school. But appellants' argument fails in any event, because the supervisory system established by the City of New York inevitably results in the excessive entanglement of church and state, an *Establishment Clause* concern distinct from that addressed by the effects doctrine. Even where state aid to parochial institutions does not have the primary effect of advancing religion, the provision of such aid may nonetheless violate the *Establishment Clause* owing to the nature of the interaction of church and state in the administration of that aid.

The principle that the state should not become too closely entangled with the church in the administration of assistance is rooted in two concerns. When the

---

As we have in comparable cases, we shall continue in this opinion to refer to the parties as appellants and appellees in order to minimize confusion. See, *e. g., Kulko v. California Superior Court, 436 U.S. 84, 90, n. 4, 56 L. Ed. 2d 132, 98 S. Ct. 1690 (1978).*

state becomes enmeshed with a given denomination in matters of religious significance, the freedom of religious belief of those who are not adherents of that denomination suffers, even when the governmental purpose underlying the involvement is largely secular. In addition, the freedom of even the adherents of the denomination is limited by the governmental intrusion into sacred matters. "[The] *First Amendment* rests upon the premise that both religion and government can best work to achieve their lofty aims if each is left free from the other within its respective sphere." *McCollum v. Board of Education, 333 U.S. 203, 212, 92 L. Ed. 649, 68 S. Ct. 461 (1948).*

In *Lemon v. Kurtzman, 403 U.S. 602, 29 L. Ed. 2d 745, 91 S. Ct. 2105 (1971),* the Court held that the supervision necessary to ensure that teachers in parochial schools were not conveying religious messages to their students would constitute the excessive entanglement of church and state:

"A comprehensive, discriminating, and continuing state surveillance will inevitably be required to ensure that these restrictions are obeyed and the *First Amendment* otherwise respected. Unlike a book, a teacher cannot be inspected once so as to determine the extent and intent of his or her personal beliefs and subjective acceptance of the limitations imposed by the *First Amendment*. These prophylactic contacts will involve excessive and enduring entanglement between state and church." *Id., at 619.*

Similarly, in *Meek v. Pittenger, 421 U.S. 349, 44 L. Ed. 2d 217, 95 S. Ct. 1753 (1975),* we invalidated a state program that offered, *inter alia,* guidance, testing, and remedial and therapeutic services performed by public employees on the premises of the parochial schools. *Id., at 352-353.* As in *Lemon,* we observed that though a comprehensive system of supervision might conceivably prevent teachers from having the primary effect of advancing religion, such a system would inevitably lead to an unconstitutional administrative entanglement between church and state.

"The prophylactic contacts required to ensure that teachers play a strictly nonideological role, the Court held [in *Lemon*], necessarily give rise to a constitutionally intolerable degree of entanglement between church and state. *Id., at 619.* The same excessive entanglement would be required for Pennsylvania to be 'certain,' as it must be, that . . . personnel do not advance the religious mission of the church-related schools in which they serve. *Public Funds for Public Schools v. Marburger, 358 F. Supp. 29, 40-41,* aff'd, *417 U.S. 961, 41 L. Ed. 2d 1134, 94 S. Ct. 3163." 421 U.S. at 370.*

In *Roemer v. Maryland Public Works Board*, 426 U.S. 736, 49 L. Ed. 2d 179, 96 S. Ct. 2337 (1976), the Court sustained state programs of aid to religiously affiliated institutions of higher learning. The State allowed the grants to be used for any nonsectarian purpose. The Court upheld the grants on the ground that the institutions were not "'pervasively sectarian,'" *id., at 758-759*, and therefore a system of supervision was unnecessary to ensure that the grants were not being used to effect a religious end. In so holding, the Court identified "what is crucial to a nonentangling aid program: the ability of the State to identify and subsidize separate secular functions carried out at the school, without on-the-site inspections being necessary to prevent diversion of the funds to sectarian purposes." *Id., at 765*. Similarly, in *Tilton v. Richardson*, 403 U.S. 672, 29 L. Ed. 2d 790, 91 S. Ct. 2091 (1971), the Court upheld one-time grants to sectarian institutions because ongoing supervision was not required. See also *Hunt v. McNair*, 413 U.S. 734, 37 L. Ed. 2d 923, 93 S. Ct. 2868 (1973).

As the Court of Appeals recognized, the elementary and secondary schools here are far different from the colleges at issue in *Roemer*, *Hunt*, and *Tilton*. *739 F.2d at 68-70*. Unlike the colleges, which were found not to be "pervasively sectarian," many of the schools involved in this case are the same sectarian schools which had "'as a substantial purpose the inculcation of religious values'" in *Committee for Public Education & Religious Liberty v. Nyquist*, 413 U.S. 756, 768, 37 L. Ed. 2d 948, 93 S. Ct. 2955 (1973), quoting *Committee for Public Education & Religious Liberty v. Nyquist*, 350 F. Supp. 655, 663 (SDNY 1972). Moreover, our holding in *Meek* invalidating instructional services much like those at issue in this case rested on the ground that the publicly funded teachers were "performing important educational services in schools in which education is an integral part of the dominant sectarian mission and in which an atmosphere dedicated to the advancement of religious belief is constantly maintained." *Meek*, *supra, at 371*. The court below found that the schools involved in this case were "well within this characterization." *739 F.2d at 70*. [8]

---

[8] Appellants suggest that the degree of sectarianism differs from school to school. This has little bearing on our analysis. As Judge Friendly, writing for the court below, noted: "It may well be that the degree of sectarianism in Catholic schools in, for example, black neighborhoods, with considerable proportions of non-Catholic pupils and teachers, is relatively low; by the same token, in other schools it may be relatively high. Yet . . . enforcement of the *Establishment Clause* does not rest on means or medians. If any significant number of the Title I schools create the risks described in *Meek*, *Meek* applies. It would be simply incredible, and the affidavits do not aver, that all, or almost all, New York City's parochial schools receiving Title I aid have . . . abandoned 'the religious mission that is the only reason for the schools' existence.'" *739 F.2d at 70* (quoting *Lemon v. Kurtzman*, 403 U.S. 602, 650, 29 L. Ed. 2d 745, 91 S. Ct. 2105 (1971)* (opinion of BRENNAN, J.).

Unlike the schools in *Roemer*, many of the schools here receive funds and report back to their affiliated church, require attendance at church religious exercises, begin the schoolday or class period with prayer, and grant preference in admission to members of the sponsoring denominations. *739 F.2d at 70*. In addition, the Catholic schools at issue here, which constitute the vast majority of the aided schools, are under the general supervision and control of the local parish. *Ibid.*

The critical elements of the entanglement proscribed in *Lemon* and *Meek* are thus present in this case. First, as noted above, the aid is provided in a pervasively sectarian environment. Second, because assistance is provided in the form of teachers, ongoing inspection is required to ensure the absence of a religious message. Compare *Lemon, supra, at 619*, with *Tilton, supra, at 688*, and *Roemer, supra, at 765*. In short, the scope and duration of New York City's Title I program would require a permanent and pervasive state presence in the sectarian schools receiving aid.

This pervasive monitoring by public authorities in the sectarian schools infringes precisely those *Establishment Clause* values at the root of the prohibition of excessive entanglement. Agents of the city must visit and inspect the religious school regularly, alert for the subtle or overt presence of religious matter in Title I classes. Cf. *Lemon v. Kurtzman, 403 U.S. at 619* ("What would appear to some to be essential to good citizenship might well for others border on or constitute instruction in religion"). In addition, the religious school must obey these same agents when they make determinations as to what is and what is not a "religious symbol" and thus off limits in a Title I classroom. In short, the religious school, which has as a primary purpose the advancement and preservation of a particular religion must endure the ongoing presence of state personnel whose primary purpose is to monitor teachers and students in an attempt to guard against the infiltration of religious thought.

The administrative cooperation that is required to maintain the educational program at issue here entangles church and state in still another way that infringes interests at the heart of the *Establishment Clause*. Administrative personnel of the public and parochial school systems must work together in resolving matters related to schedules, classroom assignments, problems that arise in the implementation of the program, requests for additional services, and the dissemination of information regarding the program. Furthermore, the program necessitates "frequent contacts between the regular and the remedial teachers (or other professionals), in which each side reports on individual student needs, problems encountered, and results achieved." *739 F.2d at 65*.

We have long recognized that underlying the *Establishment Clause* is "the objective . . . to prevent, as far as possible, the intrusion of either [church or state] into the precincts of the other." *Lemon v. Kurtzman, supra, at 614*. See also *McCollum v. Board of Education, 333 U.S. at 212*. Although "[separation] in this context cannot mean absence of all contact," *Walz v. Tax Comm'n, 397 U.S. 664, 676, 25 L. Ed. 2d 697, 90 S. Ct. 1409 (1970)*, the detailed monitoring and close administrative contact required to maintain New York City's Title I program can only produce "a kind of continuing day-to-day relationship which the policy of neutrality seeks to minimize." *Id., at 674*. The numerous judgments that must be made by agents of the city concern matters that may be subtle and controversial, yet may be of deep religious significance to the controlling denominations. As government agents must make these judgments, the dangers of political divisiveness along religious lines increase. At the same time, "[the] picture of state inspectors prowling the halls of parochial schools and auditing classroom instruction surely raises more than an imagined specter of governmental 'secularization of a creed.'" *Lemon v. Kurtzman, supra, at 650* (opinion of BRENNAN, J.).

III

Despite the well-intentioned efforts taken by the City of New York, the program remains constitutionally flawed owing to the nature of the aid, to the institution receiving the aid, and to the constitutional principles that they implicate -- that neither the State nor Federal Government shall promote or hinder a particular faith or faith generally through the advancement of benefits or through the excessive entanglement of church and state in the administration of those benefits.

Affirmed.

JUSTICE POWELL, concurring.

I concur in the Court's opinions and judgments today in this case and in *School District of Grand Rapids v. Ball, ante*, p. 373, holding that the aid to parochial schools involved in those cases violates the *Establishment Clause of the First Amendment*. I write to emphasize additional reasons why precedents of this Court require us to invalidate these two educational programs that concededly have "done so much good and little, if any, detectable harm." *739 F.2d 48, 72 (CA2 1984)*. The Court has previously recognized the important role of parochial schools:

"'Parochial schools, quite apart from their sectarian purpose, have provided an educational alternative for millions of young Americans; they often afford wholesome competition with our public schools; and in some States they relieve substantially the tax burden incident to the operation of public schools.'" *Mueller v. Allen, 463 U.S. 388, 401-402, 77 L. Ed. 2d 721, 103 S. Ct. 3062 (1983)* (quoting *Wolman v. Walter, 433 U.S. 229, 262, 53 L. Ed. 2d 714, 97 S. Ct. 2593 (1977)* (POWELL, J., concurring in part, concurring in judgment in part, and dissenting in part)).

"The State has, moreover, a legitimate interest in facilitating education of the highest quality for all children within its boundaries, whatever school their parents have chosen for them." *433 U.S. at 262*. Regrettably, however, the Title I and Grand Rapids programs do not survive the scrutiny required by our *Establishment Clause* cases.

I agree with the Court that in this case the *Establishment Clause* is violated because there is too great a risk of government entanglement in the administration of the religious schools; the same is true in *Ball, ante*, p. 373. As beneficial as the Title I program appears to be in accomplishing its secular goal of supplementing the education of deprived children, its elaborate structure, the participation of public school teachers, and the government surveillance required to ensure that public funds are used for secular purposes inevitably present a serious risk of excessive entanglement. Our cases have noted that "'[the] State must be *certain*, given the Religion Clauses, that subsidized teachers do not inculcate religion.'" *Meek v. Pittenger, 421 U.S. 349, 371, 44 L. Ed. 2d 217, 95 S. Ct. 1753 (1975)* (emphasis added) (quoting *Lemon v. Kurtzman, 403 U.S. 602, 619, 29 L. Ed. 2d 745, 91 S. Ct. 2105 (1971)*). This is true whether the subsidized teachers are religious school teachers, as in *Lemon*, or public school teachers teaching secular subjects to parochial school children at the parochial schools. Judge Friendly, writing for the unanimous Court of Appeals, agreed with this assessment of our cases. He correctly observed that the structure of the Title I program required the active and extensive surveillance that the City has provided, and, "under *Meek*, this very surveillance constitutes excessive entanglement even if it has succeeded in preventing the fostering of religion." *739 F.2d at 66.*

This risk of entanglement is compounded by the additional risk of political divisiveness stemming from the aid to religion at issue here. I do not suggest that at this point in our history the Title I program or similar parochial aid plans could result in the establishment of a state religion. There likewise is small chance that these programs would result in significant religious or denominational control over our democratic processes. See *Wolman v. Walter, supra,* at 263 (POWELL, J., concurring in part, concurring in judgment in part, and dissenting in part). Nonetheless, there remains a considerable risk of continuing political strife over the propriety of direct aid to religious schools and the proper allocation of limited governmental resources. As this Court has repeatedly recognized, there is a likelihood whenever direct governmental aid is extended to some groups that there will be competition and strife among them and others to gain, maintain, or increase the financial support of government. *E. g., Committee for Public Education & Religious Liberty v. Nyquist, 413 U.S. 756, 796-797, 37 L. Ed. 2d 948, 93 S. Ct. 2955 (1973); Lemon v. Kurtzman, supra, at 623.* In States such as New York that have large and varied sectarian populations, one can be assured that politics will enter into any state decision to aid parochial schools. Public schools, as well as private schools, are under increasing financial pressure to meet real and perceived needs. Thus, any proposal to extend direct governmental aid to parochial schools alone is likely to spark political disagreement from taxpayers who support the public schools, as well as from nonrecipient sectarian groups, who may fear that needed funds are being diverted from them. In short, aid to parochial schools of the sort at issue here potentially leads to "that kind and degree of government involvement in religious life that, as history teaches us, is apt to lead to strife and frequently strain a political system to the breaking point." *Walz v. Tax Comm'n, 397 U.S. 664, 694, 25 L. Ed. 2d 697, 90 S. Ct. 1409 (1970)* (opinion of Harlan, J.). Although the Court's opinion does not discuss it at length, see *ante,* at 413, the potential for such divisiveness is a strong additional reason for holding that the Title I and Grand Rapids programs are invalid on entanglement grounds.

The Title I program at issue in this case also would be invalid under the "effects" prong of the test adopted in *Lemon v. Kurtzman, supra.* [*] As has been discussed

---

[*] Nothing that I say here should be construed as suggesting that a court inevitably must determine whether all three prongs of the *Lemon* test have been violated. See, *e. g., Committee*

thoroughly in *Ball, ante*, at 392-397, with respect to the Grand Rapids programs, the type of aid provided in New York by the Title I program amounts to a state subsidy of the parochial schools by relieving those schools of the duty to provide the remedial and supplemental education their children require. This is not the type of "indirect and incidental effect beneficial to [the] religious institutions" that we suggested in *Nyquist* would survive *Establishment Clause* scrutiny. *413 U.S. at 775.* Rather, by directly assuming part of the parochial schools' education function, the effect of the Title I aid is "inevitably . . . to subsidize and advance the religious mission of [the] sectarian schools," *id., at 779-780*, even though the program provides that only secular subjects will be taught. As in *Meek v. Pittenger, 421 U.S. 349, 44 L. Ed. 2d 217, 95 S. Ct. 1753 (1975)*, the secular education these schools provide goes "'hand in hand'" with the religious mission that is the reason for the schools' existence. *421 U.S. at 366* (quoting *Lemon v. Kurtzman, 403 U.S. at 657* (opinion of BRENNAN, J.)). Because of the predominantly religious nature of the schools, the substantial aid provided by the Title I program "inescapably results in the direct and substantial advancement of religious activity." *Meek v. Pittenger, supra, at 366.*

I recognize the difficult dilemma in which governments are placed by the interaction of the "effects" and entanglement prongs of the *Lemon* test. Our decisions require governments extending aid to parochial schools to tread an extremely narrow line between being certain that the "principal or primary effect" of the aid is not to advance religion, *Lemon v. Kurtzman, supra, at 612*, and avoiding excessive entanglement. Nonetheless, the Court has never foreclosed the possibility that some types of aid to parochial schools could be valid under the *Establishment Clause*. *Mueller v. Allen, 463 U.S. at 393*. Our cases have upheld evenhanded secular assistance to both parochial and public school children in some areas. *E. g., ibid.* (tax deductions for educational expenses); *Board of Education v. Allen, 392 U.S. 236, 20 L. Ed. 2d 1060, 88 S. Ct. 1923 (1968)* (provision of secular textbooks); *Everson v. Board of Education, 330 U.S. 1, 91 L. Ed. 711, 67 S. Ct. 504 (1947)* (reimbursements for bus fare to school). I do not read the Court's opinion as precluding these types of indirect aid to parochial schools. In the cases cited, the assistance programs made funds available equally to public and nonpublic schools without entanglement. The constitutional defect in the Title I program, as indicated above, is that it provides a direct financial subsidy to be administered in significant part by public school teachers within parochial schools -- resulting in both the advancement of religion and forbidden entanglement. If, for example, Congress

---

for Public Education & Religious Liberty v. Nyquist, 413 U.S. 756, 794, 37 L. Ed. 2d 948, 93 S. Ct. 2955 (1973). I discuss an additional infirmity of the programs at issue in these cases only to emphasize why even a beneficial program may be invalid because of the way it is structured.

could fashion a program of evenhanded financial assistance to both public and private schools that could be administered, without governmental supervision in the private schools, so as to prevent the diversion of the aid from secular purposes, we would be presented with a different question.

I join the opinions and judgments of the Court.

CHIEF JUSTICE BURGER, dissenting.

Under the guise of protecting Americans from the evils of an Established Church such as those of the 18th century and earlier times, today's decision will deny countless schoolchildren desperately needed remedial teaching services funded under Title I. The program at issue covers remedial reading, reading skills, remedial mathematics, English as a second language, and assistance for children needing special help in the learning process. The "remedial reading" portion of this program, for example, reaches children who suffer from dyslexia, a disease known to be difficult to diagnose and treat. Many of these children now will not receive the special training they need, simply because their parents desire that they attend religiously affiliated schools.

What is disconcerting about the result reached today is that, in the face of the human cost entailed by this decision, the Court does not even attempt to identify any threat to religious liberty posed by the operation of Title I. I share JUSTICE WHITE's concern that the Court's obsession with the criteria identified in *Lemon v. Kurtzman*, *403 U.S. 602, 29 L. Ed. 2d 745, 91 S. Ct. 2105 (1971)*, has led to results that are "contrary to the long-range interests of the country," *ante*, at 400. As I wrote in *Wallace v. Jaffree*, *472 U.S. 38, 89, 86 L. Ed. 2d 29, 105 S. Ct. 2479 (1985)* (dissenting opinion), "our responsibility is not to apply tidy formulas by rote; our duty is to determine whether the statute or practice at issue is a step toward establishing a state religion." Federal programs designed to prevent a generation of children from growing up without being able to read effectively are not remotely steps in that direction. It borders on paranoia to perceive the Archbishop of Canterbury or the Bishop of Rome lurking behind programs that are just as vital to the Nation's schoolchildren as textbooks, see generally *Board of Education v. Allen*, *392 U.S. 236, 20 L. Ed. 2d 1060, 88 S. Ct. 1923 (1968)*, transportation to and from school, see generally *Everson v. Board of Education*, *330 U.S. 1, 91 L. Ed. 711, 67 S. Ct. 504 (1947)*, and school nursing services.

On the merits of this case, I dissent for the reasons stated in my separate opinion in *Meek v. Pittenger*, *421 U.S. 349, 44 L. Ed. 2d 217, 95 S. Ct. 1753 (1975)*. We have frequently recognized that some interaction between church and state is unavoidable, and that an attempt to eliminate all contact between the two would be both futile and undesirable. Justice Douglas, writing for the Court in *Zorach v. Clauson*, *343 U.S. 306, 312, 96 L. Ed. 954, 72 S. Ct. 679 (1952)*, stated:

"The *First Amendment* . . . does not say that in every and all respects there shall be a separation of Church and State. . . . Otherwise the state and religion would be aliens to each other -- hostile, suspicious, and even unfriendly."

The Court today fails to demonstrate how the interaction occasioned by the program at issue presents any threat to the values underlying the *Establishment Clause*.

I cannot join in striking down a program that, in the words of the Court of Appeals, "has done so much good and little, if any, detectable harm." *739 F.2d 48, 72 (CA2 1984)*. The notion that denying these services to students in religious schools is a neutral act to protect us from an Established Church has no support in logic, experience, or history. Rather than showing the neutrality the Court boasts of, it exhibits nothing less than hostility toward religion and the children who attend church-sponsored schools.

JUSTICE REHNQUIST, dissenting.

I dissent for the reasons stated in my dissenting opinion in *Wallace v. Jaffree, 472 U.S. 38, 91, 86 L. Ed. 2d 29, 105 S. Ct. 2479 (1985)*. In this case the Court takes advantage of the "***Catch-22***" paradox of its own creation, see *Wallace, supra, at 109-110* (REHNQUIST, J., dissenting), whereby aid must be supervised to ensure no entanglement but the supervision itself is held to cause an entanglement. The Court today strikes down nondiscriminatory nonsectarian aid to educationally deprived children from low-income families. The *Establishment Clause* does not prohibit such sorely needed assistance; we have indeed traveled far afield from the concerns which prompted the adoption of the *First Amendment* when we rely on gossamer abstractions to invalidate a law which obviously meets an entirely secular need. I would reverse.

JUSTICE O'CONNOR, with whom JUSTICE REHNQUIST joins as to Parts II and III, dissenting.

Today the Court affirms the holding of the Court of Appeals that public school teachers can offer remedial instruction to disadvantaged students who attend religious schools "only if such instruction . . . [is] afforded at a neutral site off the premises of the religious school." *739 F.2d 48, 64 (CA2 1984).* This holding rests on the theory, enunciated in Part V of the Court's opinion in *Meek v. Pittenger, 421 U.S. 349, 367-373, 44 L. Ed. 2d 217, 95 S. Ct. 1753 (1975),* that public school teachers who set foot on parochial school premises are likely to bring religion into their classes, and that the supervision necessary to prevent religious teaching would unduly entangle church and state. Even if this theory were valid in the abstract, it cannot validly be applied to New York City's 19-year-old Title I program. The Court greatly exaggerates the degree of supervision necessary to prevent public school teachers from inculcating religion, and thereby demonstrates the flaws of a test that condemns benign cooperation between church and state. I would uphold Congress' efforts to afford remedial instruction to disadvantaged schoolchildren in both public and parochial schools.

I

As in *Wallace v. Jaffree, 472 U.S. 38, 86 L. Ed. 2d 29, 105 S. Ct. 2479 (1985)*, and *Thornton v. Caldor, Inc., 472 U.S. 703, 86 L. Ed. 2d 557, 105 S. Ct. 2914 (1985)*, the Court in this litigation adheres to the three-part *Establishment Clause* test enunciated in *Lemon v. Kurtzman, 403 U.S. 602, 612-613, 29 L. Ed. 2d 745, 91 S. Ct. 2105 (1971).* To survive the *Lemon* test, a statute must have both a secular legislative purpose and a principal or primary effect that neither advances nor inhibits religion. Under *Lemon* and its progeny, direct state aid to parochial schools that has the purpose or effect of furthering the religious mission of the schools is unconstitutional. I agree with that principle. According to the Court, however, the New York City Title I program is defective not because of any improper purpose or effect, but rather because it fails the third part of the *Lemon* test: the Title I program allegedly fosters excessive government entanglement with religion. I disagree with the Court's analysis of entanglement, and I question the utility of entanglement as a separate *Establishment Clause* standard in most cases. Before discussing entanglement, however, it is worthwhile to explore the purpose and effect of the New York City Title I program in greater depth than does the majority opinion.

The purpose of Title I is to provide special educational assistance to disadvantaged children who would not otherwise receive it. Congress recognized that poor academic performance by disadvantaged children is part of the cycle of poverty. S.

Rep. No. 146, 89th Cong., 1st Sess., 4 (1965). Congress sought to break the cycle by providing classes in remedial reading, mathematics, and English to disadvantaged children in parochial as well as public schools, for public schools enjoy no monopoly on education in low-income areas. *Wheeler v. Barrera, 417 U.S. 402, 405-406, 41 L. Ed. 2d 159, 94 S. Ct. 2274 (1974).* See 20 U. S. C. §§ 2740(a), 3806(a). Congress permitted remedial instruction by public school teachers on parochial school premises only if such instruction is "not normally provided by the nonpublic school" and would "contribute particularly to meeting the special educational needs of educationally deprived children." S. Rep. No. 146, *supra*, at 12. See *34 CFR § 200.73 (1984)* (Department of Education regulations implementing Title I and precluding instruction on parochial school premises except where necessary and where such instruction is not normally provided by the school).

After reviewing the text of the statute and its legislative history, the District Court concluded that Title I serves a secular purpose of aiding needy children regardless of where they attend school. App. to Juris. Statement in No. 84-238, p. 56a, incorporating findings of the District Court in *National Coalition for Public Education and Religious Liberty v. Harris, 489 F. Supp. 1248, 1258 (SDNY 1980) (PEARL).* The Court of Appeals did not dispute this finding, and no party in this Court contends that the purpose of the statute or of the New York City Title I program is to advance or endorse religion. Indeed, the record demonstrates that New York City public school teachers offer Title I classes on the premises of parochial schools solely because alternative means to reach the disadvantaged parochial school students -- such as instruction for parochial school students at the nearest public school, either after or during regular school hours -- were unsuccessful. *PEARL, supra,* at 1255. As the Court of Appeals acknowledged, New York City" could reasonably have regarded [Title I instruction on parochial school premises] as the most effective way to carry out the purposes of the Act." *739 F.2d at 49.* Whether one looks to the face of the statute or to its implementation, the Title I program is undeniably animated by a legitimate secular purpose.

The Court's discussion of the effect of the New York City Title I program is even more perfunctory than its analysis of the program's purpose. The Court's opinion today in *School District of Grand Rapids* v. *Ball, ante,* p. 373, which strikes down a Grand Rapids scheme that the Court asserts is very similar to the New York City program, identifies three ways in which public instruction on parochial school premises may have the impermissible effect of advancing religion. First, "state-paid instructors, influenced by the pervasively sectarian nature of the religious schools in which they work, may subtly or overtly indoctrinate the students in particular religious tenets at public expense." Second, "state-provided instruction in the religious school buildings threatens to convey a message of state support for

113

religion to students and to the general public." Third, "the programs in effect subsidize the religious functions of the parochial schools by taking over a substantial portion of their responsibility for teaching secular subjects." *Ante*, at 397. While addressing the effect of the Grand Rapids program at such length, the Court overlooks the effect of Title I in New York City.

One need not delve too deeply in the record to understand why the Court does not belabor the effect of the Title I program. The abstract theories explaining why on-premises instruction might possibly advance religion dissolve in the face of experience in New York City. As the District Court found in 1980:

"New York City has been providing Title I services in nonpublic schools for fourteen years. The evidence presented in this action includes: extensive background information on Title I; an in-depth description of New York City's program; a detailed review of Title I rules and regulations and the ways in which they are enforced; and the testimony and affidavits of federal officials, state officers, school administrators, Title I teachers and supervisors, and parents of children receiving Title I services. The evidence establishes that the result feared in other cases has not materialized in the City's Title I program. The presumption -- that the 'religious mission' will be advanced by providing educational services on parochial school premises -- is not supported by the facts of this case." *PEARL, supra*, at 1265.

Indeed, in 19 years there has never been a single incident in which a Title I instructor "subtly or overtly" attempted to "indoctrinate the students in particular religious tenets at public expense." *Grand Rapids, ante*, at 397.

Common sense suggests a plausible explanation for this unblemished record. New York City's public Title I instructors are professional educators who can and do follow instructions not to inculcate religion in their classes. They are unlikely to be influenced by the sectarian nature of the parochial schools where they teach, not only because they are carefully supervised by public officials, but also because the vast majority of them visit several different schools each week and are not of the same religion as their parochial students.* In light of the ample record, an objective observer of the implementation of the Title I program in New York City would hardly view it as endorsing the tenets of the participating parochial schools. To the contrary, the actual and perceived effect of the program is precisely the effect intended by Congress: impoverished schoolchildren are being helped to overcome

---

* It is undisputed that 78% of Title I instructors who teach in parochial schools visit more than one school each week. Almost three-quarters of the instructors do not share the religious affiliation of any school they teach in. App. 49.

learning deficits, improving their test scores, and receiving a significant boost in their struggle to obtain both a thorough education and the opportunities that flow from it.

The only type of impermissible effect that arguably could carry over from the *Grand Rapids* decision to this litigation, then, is the effect of subsidizing "the religious functions of the parochial schools by taking over a substantial portion of their responsibility for teaching secular subjects." *Ibid.* That effect is tenuous, however, in light of the statutory directive that Title I funds may be used only to provide services that otherwise would not be available to the participating students. 20 U. S. C. § 3807(b). The Secretary of Education has vigorously enforced the requirement that Title I funds supplement rather than supplant the services of local education agencies. See *Bennett v. Kentucky Dept. of Ed., 470 U.S. 656, 84 L. Ed. 2d 590, 105 S. Ct. 1544 (1985); Bennett v. New Jersey, 470 U.S. 632, 84 L. Ed. 2d 572, 105 S. Ct. 1555 (1985).*

Even if we were to assume that Title I remedial classes in New York City may have duplicated to some extent instruction parochial schools would have offered in the absence of Title I, the Court's delineation of this third type of effect proscribed by the *Establishment Clause* would be seriously flawed. Our *Establishment Clause* decisions have not barred remedial assistance to parochial school children, but rather remedial assistance *on the premises of the parochial school.* Under *Wolman v. Walter, 433 U.S. 229, 244-248, 53 L. Ed. 2d 714, 97 S. Ct. 2593 (1977)*, the New York City classes prohibited by the Court today would have survived *Establishment Clause* scrutiny if they had been offered in a neutral setting off the property of the private school. Yet it is difficult to understand why a remedial reading class offered on parochial school premises is any more likely to supplant the secular course offerings of the parochial school than the same class offered in a portable classroom next door to the school. Unless *Wolman* was wrongly decided, the defect in the Title I program cannot lie in the risk that it will supplant secular course offerings.

II

Recognizing the weakness of any claim of an improper purpose or effect, the Court today relies entirely on the entanglement prong of *Lemon* to invalidate the New York City Title I program. The Court holds that the occasional presence of peripatetic public school teachers on parochial school grounds threatens undue entanglement of church and state because (1) the remedial instruction is afforded in a pervasively sectarian environment; (2) ongoing supervision is required to assure that the public school teachers do not attempt to inculcate religion; (3) the administrative personnel of the parochial and public school systems must work together in resolving administrative and scheduling problems; and (4) the instruction is likely to result in political divisiveness over the propriety of direct aid. *Ante*, at 412-414; *ante*, at 415-416 (concurring opinion of POWELL, J.).

This analysis of entanglement, I acknowledge, finds support in some of this Court's precedents. In *Meek v. Pittenger, 421 U.S. at 369*, the Court asserted that it could not rely "on the good faith and professionalism of the secular teachers and counselors functioning in church-related schools to ensure that a strictly nonideological posture is maintained." Because "a teacher remains a teacher," the Court stated, there remains a risk that teachers will intertwine religious doctrine with secular instruction. The continuing state surveillance necessary to prevent this from occurring would produce undue entanglement of church and state. *Id., at 370-372*. The Court's opinion in *Meek* further asserted that public instruction on parochial school premises creates a serious risk of divisive political conflict over the issue of aid to religion. *Ibid. Meek*'s analysis of entanglement was reaffirmed in *Wolman* two Terms later.

I would accord these decisions the appropriate deference commanded by the doctrine of *stare decisis* if I could discern logical support for their analysis. But experience has demonstrated that the analysis in Part V of the *Meek* opinion is flawed. At the time *Meek* was decided, thoughtful dissents pointed out the absence of any record support for the notion that public school teachers would attempt to inculcate religion simply because they temporarily occupied a parochial school classroom, or that such instruction would produce political divisiveness. *Id., at 385* (opinion of BURGER, C. J.); *id., at 387* (opinion of REHNQUIST, J.). Experience has given greater force to the arguments of the dissenting opinions in *Meek*. It is not intuitively obvious that a dedicated public school teacher will tend to disobey instructions and commence proselytizing students at public expense merely because the classroom is within a parochial school. *Meek* is correct in asserting that a teacher of remedial reading "remains a teacher," but surely it is significant that the teacher involved is a professional, full-time public school employee who is unaccustomed to bringing religion into the classroom. Given that not a single incident of religious indoctrination has been identified as occurring in the thousands of classes offered in Grand Rapids and New York City over the past two decades, it is time to acknowledge that the risk identified in *Meek* was greatly exaggerated.

Just as the risk that public school teachers in parochial classrooms will inculcate religion has been exaggerated, so has the degree of supervision required to manage that risk. In this respect the New York City Title I program is instructive. What supervision has been necessary in New York City to enable public school teachers to help disadvantaged children for 19 years without once proselytizing? Public officials have prepared careful instructions warning public school teachers of their exclusively secular mission, and have required Title I teachers to study and observe them. App. 50-51. Under the rules, Title I teachers are not accountable to parochial or private school officials; they have sole responsibility for selecting the students who participate in their class, must administer their own tests for determining eligibility, cannot engage in team teaching or cooperative activities with parochial school teachers, must make sure that all materials and equipment they use are not otherwise used by the parochial school, and must not participate in religious activities in the schools or introduce any religious matter into their teaching. To ensure compliance with the rules, a field supervisor and a program coordinator, who are full-time public school employees, make unannounced visits to each teacher's classroom at least once a month. *Id., at 53.*

The Court concludes that this degree of supervision of public school employees by other public school employees constitutes excessive entanglement of church and state. I cannot agree. The supervision that occurs in New York City's Title I program does not differ significantly from the supervision any public school teacher receives, regardless of the location of the classroom. JUSTICE POWELL suggests that the required supervision is extensive because the State must be *certain* that public school teachers do not inculcate religion. *Ante,* at 415. That reasoning would require us to close our public schools, for there is always some chance that a public school teacher will bring religion into the classroom, regardless of its location. See *Wallace v. Jaffree, 472 U.S. at 44-45, n. 23.* Even if I remained confident of the usefulness of entanglement as an *Establishment Clause* test, I would conclude that New York City's efforts to prevent religious indoctrination in Title I classes have been adequate and have not caused excessive institutional entanglement of church and state.

The Court's reliance on the potential for political divisiveness as evidence of undue entanglement is also unpersuasive. There is little record support for the proposition that New York City's admirable Title I program has ignited any controversy other than this litigation. In *Mueller v. Allen, 463 U.S. 388, 403-404, n. 11, 77 L. Ed. 2d 721, 103 S. Ct. 3062 (1983),* the Court cautioned that the "elusive inquiry" into political divisiveness should be confined to a narrow category of parochial aid cases. The concurring opinion in *Lynch v. Donnelly, 465 U.S. 668, 687, 79 L. Ed. 2d 604, 104 S. Ct. 1355 (1984),* went further, suggesting that *Establishment Clause* analysis should focus solely on the character of the government activity that might cause political divisiveness, and that "the entanglement prong of the *Lemon* test is properly limited to institutional entanglement."

I adhere to the doubts about the entanglement test that were expressed in *Lynch*. It is curious indeed to base our interpretation of the Constitution on speculation as to the likelihood of a phenomenon which the parties may create merely by prosecuting a lawsuit. My reservations about the entanglement test, however, have come to encompass its institutional aspects as well. As JUSTICE REHNQUIST has pointed out, many of the inconsistencies in our *Establishment Clause* decisions can be ascribed to our insistence that parochial aid programs with a valid purpose and effect may still be invalid by virtue of undue entanglement. *Wallace v. Jaffree, supra, at 109-110*. For example, we permit a State to pay for bus transportation to a parochial school, *Everson v. Board of Education, 330 U.S. 1, 91 L. Ed. 711, 67 S. Ct. 504 (1947)*, but preclude States from providing buses for parochial school field trips, on the theory such trips involve excessive state supervision of the parochial officials who lead them. *Wolman, 433 U.S. at 254*. To a great extent, the anomalous results in our *Establishment Clause* cases are "attributable to [the] 'entanglement' prong." Choper, The Religion Clauses of the *First Amendment*: Reconciling the Conflict, 41 U. Pitt. L. Rev. 673, 681 (1980).

Pervasive institutional involvement of church and state may remain relevant in deciding the *effect* of a statute which is alleged to violate the *Establishment Clause, Walz v. Tax Comm'n, 397 U.S. 664 (1970)*, but state efforts to ensure that public resources are used only for nonsectarian ends should not in themselves serve to invalidate an otherwise valid statute. The State requires sectarian organizations to cooperate on a whole range of matters without thereby advancing religion or giving the impression that the government endorses religion. *Wallace v. Jaffree, supra, at 110* (dissenting opinion of REHNQUIST, J.) (noting that state educational agencies impose myriad curriculum, attendance, certification, fire, and safety regulations on sectarian schools). If a statute lacks a purpose or effect of advancing or endorsing religion, I would not invalidate it merely because it requires some ongoing cooperation between church and state or some state supervision to ensure that state funds do not advance religion.

III

Today's ruling does not spell the end of the Title I program of remedial education for disadvantaged children. Children attending public schools may still obtain the benefits of the program. Impoverished children who attend parochial schools may also continue to benefit from Title I programs offered off the premises of their schools -- possibly in portable classrooms just over the edge of school property. The only disadvantaged children who lose under the Court's holding are those in cities where it is not economically and logistically feasible to provide public facilities for remedial education adjacent to the parochial school. But this subset is significant, for it includes more than 20,000 New York City school-children and uncounted others elsewhere in the country.

For these children, the Court's decision is tragic. The Court deprives them of a program that offers a meaningful chance at success in life, and it does so on the untenable theory that public school teachers (most of whom are of different faiths than their students) are likely to start teaching religion merely because they have walked across the threshold of a parochial school. I reject this theory and the analysis in *Meek* v. *Pittenger* on which it is based. I cannot close my eyes to the fact that, over almost two decades, New York City's public school teachers have helped thousands of impoverished parochial school children to overcome educational disadvantages without once attempting to inculcate religion. Their praiseworthy efforts have not eroded and do not threaten the religious liberty assured by the *Establishment Clause*. The contrary judgment of the Court of Appeals should be reversed.

I respectfully dissent.

Bowen v. Kendrick

Supreme Court of the United States

March 30, 1988, Argued

June 29, 1988, Decided

No. 87-253 [*]

487 U.S. 589
108 S. Ct. 2562
101 L. Ed. 2d 520

BOWEN, SECRETARY OF HEALTH AND HUMAN SERVICES v. KENDRICK ET AL.

APPEAL FROM THE UNITED STATES DISTRICT COURT FOR THE DISTRICT OF COLUMBIA.

Solicitor General Fried argued the cause for appellant in Nos. 87-253 and 87-431, and for the federal appellee in No. 87-462. With him on the briefs were Assistant Attorney General Willard, Acting Assistant Attorney General Spears, Deputy Solicitor General Ayer, Deputy Assistant Attorney General Cynkar, Lawrence S. Robbins, Michael Jay Singer, Jay S. Bybee, and Theodore C. Hirt. Michael W. McConnell argued the cause for appellant in No. 87-775. With him on the briefs were Edward R. Grant, Clarke D. Forsythe, Paul Arneson, and Michael J. Woodruff.

Janet Benshoof argued the cause for appellees in Nos. 87-253, 87-431, and 87-775 and appellants in No. 87-462. With her on the briefs were Lynn M. Paltrow, Nan D. Hunter, Rachael N. Pine, and Bruce J. Ennis, Jr. [+]

---

[*] Together with No. 87-431, Bowen, Secretary of Health and Human Services v. Kendrick et al., No. 87-462, Kendrick et al. v. Bowen, Secretary of Health and Human Services, et al., and No. 87-775, United Families of America v. Kendrick et al., also on appeal from the same court.

[+] Briefs of amici curiae urging reversal were filed for the Attorney General of Arizona et al. by Gary B. Born and James S. Campbell; for the Catholic League for Religious and Civil Rights et al. by Steven Frederick McDowell; for the Institute for Youth Advocacy by Gregory A. Loken; for the National Jewish Commission on Law and Public Affairs by

REHNQUIST, C. J., delivered the opinion of the Court, in which White, O'Connor, Scalia, and Kennedy, JJ., joined.
O'CONNOR, J., filed a concurring opinion.
KENNEDY, J., filed a concurring opinion, in which Scalia, J., joined.
BLACKMUN, J., filed a dissenting opinion, in which Brennan, Marshall, and Stevens, JJ., joined.

CHIEF JUSTICE REHNQUIST delivered the opinion of the Court.

This litigation involves a challenge to a federal grant program that provides funding for services relating to adolescent sexuality and pregnancy. Considering the federal statute both "on its face" and "as applied," the District Court ruled that the statute violated the *Establishment Clause of the First Amendment* insofar as it provided for the involvement of religious organizations in the federally funded programs. We conclude, however, that the statute is not unconstitutional on its face, and that a determination of whether any of the grants made pursuant to the statute violate the *Establishment Clause* requires further proceedings in the District Court.

I

The Adolescent Family Life Act (AFLA or Act), Pub. L. 97-35, 95 Stat. 578, *42 U. S. C. § 300z et seq. (1982 ed. and Supp. IV),* was passed by Congress in 1981 in

---

Nathan Lewin and Dennis Rapps; for the National Right to Life Committee, Inc., by James Bopp, Jr.; for the Rutherford Institute et al. by John W. Whitehead, David E. Morris, Alfred J. Lindh, Ira W. Still III, William B. Hollberg, Randall A. Pentiuk, Thomas W. Strahan, William Bonner, John F. Southworth, Jr., and W. Charles Bundren; and for the United States Catholic Conference by Mark E. Chopko and Philip H. Harris.

Briefs of amici curiae urging affirmance were filed for the American Public Health Association et al. by John H. Hall, Nadine Taub, and Judith Levin; for the Baptist Joint Committee on Public Affairs et al. by Oliver S. Thomas; for the Committee for Public Education and Religious Liberty by Leo Pfeffer; for the Council on Religious Freedom by Lee Boothby, Robert W. Nixon, and Rolland Truman; for the National Coalition for Public Education and Religious Liberty et al. by David B. Isbell, David H. Remes, and Herman Schwartz; and for the NOW Legal Defense and Education Fund et al. by Sarah E. Burns and Marsha Levick.

Briefs of amici curiae were filed for the Anti-Defamation League of B'nai B'rith et al. by Ruti G. Teitel, Justin J. Finger, Jeffrey P. Sinensky, Meyer Eisenberg, and Steven M. Freeman; for Catholic Charities, U. S. A., et al. by Patrick Francis Geary; and for the Unitarian Universalist Association et al. by Patricia Hennessey.

response to the "severe adverse health, social, and economic consequences" that often follow pregnancy and childbirth among unmarried adolescents. *42 U. S. C. § 300z(a)(5) (1982 ed., Supp. IV)*. Like its predecessor, the Adolescent Health Services and Pregnancy Prevention and Care Act of 1978, Pub. L. 95-626, Tit. VI, 92 Stat. 3595-3601 (Title VI), the AFLA is essentially a scheme for providing grants to public or nonprofit private organizations or agencies "for services and research in the area of premarital adolescent sexual relations and pregnancy." S. Rep. No. 97-161, p. 1 (1981) (hereinafter Senate Report). These grants are intended to serve several purposes, including the promotion of "self discipline and other prudent approaches to the problem of adolescent premarital sexual relations," *§ 300z(b)(1)*, the promotion of adoption as an alternative for adolescent parents, *§ 300z(b)(2)*, the establishment of new approaches to the delivery of care services for pregnant adolescents, *§ 300z(b)(3)*, and the support of research and demonstration projects "concerning the societal causes and consequences of adolescent premarital sexual relations, contraceptive use, pregnancy, and child rearing," *§ 300z(b)(4)*.

In pertinent part, grant recipients are to provide two types of services: "care services," for the provision of care to pregnant adolescents and adolescent parents, *§ 300z-1(a)(7)*, and "prevention services," for the prevention of adolescent sexual relations, *§ 300z-1(a)(8)*. [1] While the AFLA leaves it up to the Secretary of Health and Human Services (the Secretary) to define exactly what types of services a grantee must provide, see *§§ 300z-1(a)(7), (8), 300z-1(b)*, the statute contains a listing of "necessary services" that may be funded. These services include pregnancy testing and maternity counseling, adoption counseling and referral services, prenatal and postnatal health care, nutritional information, counseling, child care, mental health services, and perhaps most importantly for present purposes, "educational services relating to family life and problems associated with adolescent premarital sexual relations," *§ 300z-1(a)(4)*. [2]

---

[1] In addition to these services, the AFLA also provides funding for research projects. See *§§ 300z(b)(4)-(6), 300z-7*. This aspect of the statute is not involved in this case.

[2] *Section 300z-1(a)(4)* provides in full:

"(4) 'necessary services' means services which may be provided by grantees which are --

"(A) pregnancy testing and maternity counseling;

"(B) adoption counseling and referral services which present adoption as an option for pregnant adolescents, including referral to licensed adoption agencies in the community if the eligible grant recipient is not a licensed adoption agency;

"(C) primary and preventive health services including prenatal and postnatal care;

In drawing up the AFLA and determining what services to provide under the Act, Congress was well aware that "the problems of adolescent premarital sexual relations, pregnancy, and parenthood are multiple and complex." § 300z(a)(8)(A). Indeed, Congress expressly recognized that legislative or governmental action alone would be insufficient:

> "[S]uch problems are best approached through a variety of integrated and essential services provided to adolescents and their families by other family

"(D) nutrition information and counseling;

"(E) referral for screening and treatment of venereal disease;

"(F) referral to appropriate pediatric care;

"(G) educational services relating to family life and problems associated with adolescent premarital sexual relations, including --

"(i) information about adoption;

"(ii) education on the responsibilities of sexuality and parenting;

"(iii) the development of material to support the role of parents as the provider of sex education; and

"(iv) assistance to parents, schools, youth agencies, and health providers to educate adolescents and preadolescents concerning self-discipline and responsibility in human sexuality;

"(H) appropriate educational and vocational services and referral to such services;

"(I) referral to licensed residential care or maternity home services; and

"(J) mental health services and referral to mental health services and to other appropriate physical health services;

"(K) child care sufficient to enable the adolescent parent to continue education or to enter into employment;

"(L) consumer education and homemaking;

"(M) counseling for the immediate and extended family members of the eligible person;

"(N) transportation;

"(O) outreach services to families of adolescents to discourage sexual relations among unemancipated minors;

"(P) family planning services; and

"(Q) such other services consistent with the purposes of this subchapter as the Secretary may approve in accordance with regulations promulgated by the Secretary."

members, religious and charitable organizations, voluntary associations, and other groups in the private sector as well as services provided by publicly sponsored initiatives." § 300z(a)(8)(B).

Accordingly, the AFLA expressly states that federally provided services in this area should promote the involvement of parents, and should "emphasize the provision of support by other family members, religious and charitable organizations, voluntary associations, and other groups." § 300z(a)(10)(C). The AFLA implements this goal by providing in § 300z-2 that demonstration projects funded by the government

> "shall use such methods as will strengthen the capacity of families to deal with the sexual behavior, pregnancy, or parenthood of adolescents and to make use of support systems such as other family members, friends, religious and charitable organizations, and voluntary associations."

In addition, AFLA requires grant applicants, among other things, to describe how they will, "as appropriate in the provision of services[,] involve families of adolescents[, and] involve religious and charitable organizations, voluntary associations, and other groups in the private sector as well as services provided by publicly sponsored initiatives." § 300z-5(a)(21). This broad-based involvement of groups outside of the government was intended by Congress to "establish better coordination, integration, and linkages" among existing programs in the community, § 300z(b)(3) (1982 ed., Supp. IV), to aid in the development of "strong family values and close family ties," § 300z(a)(10)(A), and to "help adolescents and their families deal with complex issues of adolescent premarital sexual relations and the consequences of such relations." § 300z(a)(10)(C).

In line with its purposes, the AFLA also imposes limitations on the use of funds by grantees. First, the AFLA expressly states that no funds provided for demonstration projects under the statute may be used for family planning services (other than counseling and referral services) unless appropriate family planning services are not otherwise available in the community. § 300z-3(b)(1). Second, the AFLA restricts the awarding of grants to "programs or projectswhich do not provide abortions or abortion counseling or referral," except that the program may provide referral for abortion counseling if the adolescent and her parents request such referral. § 300z-10(a). Finally, the AFLA states that "grants may be made only to projects or programs which do not advocate, promote, or encourage abortion." § 300z-10(a). [3]

---

[3] Section 300z-10(a) reads in full:

Since 1981, when the AFLA was adopted, the Secretary has received 1,088 grant applications and awarded 141 grants. Brief for Federal Appellant 8. Funding has gone to a wide variety of recipients, including state and local health agencies, private hospitals, community health associations, privately operated health care centers, and community and charitable organizations. It is undisputed that a number of grantees or subgrantees were organizations with institutional ties to religious denominations. See App. 748-756 (listing grantees).

In 1983, this lawsuit against the Secretary was filed in the United States District Court for the District of Columbia by appellees, a group of federal taxpayers, clergymen, and the American Jewish Congress. Seeking both declaratory and injunctive relief, appellees challenged the constitutionality of the AFLA on the grounds that on its face and as applied the statute violates the Religion Clauses of the *First Amendment*.[4] Following cross-motions for summary judgment, the District Court held for appellees and declared that the AFLA was invalid both on its face and as applied "insofar as religious organizations are involved in carrying out the programs and purposes of the Act." *657 F. Supp. 1547, 1570 (DC 1987).*

The court first found that under *Flast v. Cohen, 392 U.S. 83 (1968),* appellees had standing to challenge the statute both on its face and as applied. Turning to the merits, the District Court applied the three-part test for *Establishment Clause* cases set forth in *Lemon v. Kurtzman, 403 U.S. 602 (1971).*[5] The court concluded that the

---

"Grants or payments may be made only to programs or projects which do not provide abortions or abortion counseling or referral, or which do not subcontract with or make any payment to any person who provides abortions or abortion counseling or referral, except that any such program or project may provide referral for abortion counseling to a pregnant adolescent if such adolescent and the parents or guardians of such adolescent request such referral; and grants may be made only to projects or programs which do not advocate, promote, or encourage abortion."

[4] On October 2, 1984, the District Court allowed United Families of America (UFA) to intervene and participate as a defendant-intervenor in support of the constitutionality of the AFLA.

[5] The court rejected appellees' claim that a strict-scrutiny standard should apply to the AFLA because the statute's restriction of funding to organizations that oppose abortion explicitly and deliberately discriminates among religious denominations. See *Larson v. Valente, 456 U.S. 228 (1982).* The court found that the AFLA does not precondition the award of a grant on a grantee's having a particular religious belief; it merely restricts the grantees from using federal tax dollars to advocate a certain course of action. See § 300z-10. While the AFLA's restriction on the advocacy of abortion does coincide with certain religious beliefs, that fact by itself did not, in the District Court's opinion, trigger the application of strict scrutiny

125

AFLA has a valid secular purpose: the prevention of social and economic injury caused by teenage pregnancy and premarital sexual relations. In the court's view, however, the AFLA does not survive the second prong of the *Lemon* test because it has the "direct and immediate" effect of advancing religion insofar as it expressly requires grant applicants to describe how they will involve religious organizations in the provision of services. § 300z-5(a)(21)(B). The statute also permits religious organizations to be grantees and "envisions a direct role for those organizations in the education and counseling components of AFLA grants." *657 F. Supp., at 1562.* As written, the AFLA makes it possible for religiously affiliated grantees to teach adolescents on issues that can be considered "fundamental elements of religious doctrine." The AFLA does all this without imposing any restriction whatsoever against the teaching of "religion *qua* religion" or the inculcation of religious beliefs in federally funded programs. As the District Court put it, "[t]o presume that AFLA counselors from religious organizations can put their beliefs aside when counseling an adolescent on matters that are part of religious doctrine is simply unrealistic." *Id., at 1563* (citing *Grand Rapids School District v. Ball,* 473 U.S. 373 (1985)).

The District Court then concluded that the statute as applied also runs afoul of the *Lemon* effects test. [6] The evidence presented by appellees revealed that AFLA grants had gone to various organizations that were affiliated with religious denominations and that had corporate requirements that the organizations abide by religious doctrines. Other AFLA grantees were not explicitly affiliated with organized religions, but were "religiously inspired and dedicated to teaching the dogma that inspired them." *657 F. Supp., at 1564.* In the District Court's view, the record clearly established that the AFLA, as it has been administered by the Secretary, has in fact directly advanced religion, provided funding for institutions that were "pervasively sectarian," or allowed federal funds to be used for education and counseling that "amounts to the teaching of religion." *Ibid.* As to the entanglement prong of *Lemon,* the court ruled that because AFLA funds are used largely for counseling and teaching, it would require overly intrusive monitoring or oversight to ensure that religion is not advanced by religiously affiliated AFLA grantees. Indeed, the court felt that "it is impossible to comprehend entanglement

---

under *Larson*. This aspect of the District Court's opinion has not been challenged on this appeal.

[6] Prior to this, the court reviewed "the motions, the statements of material fact not in dispute, the allegations of disputed facts, the golconda of documents submitted to the Court, and the case law," and concluded that the material facts were not in dispute and that summary judgment would be proper. *657 F. Supp., at 1554.*

more extensive and continuous than that necessitated by the AFLA." *657 F. Supp., at 1568.*[7]

In a separate order, filed August 13, 1987, the District Court ruled that the "constitutionally infirm language of the AFLA, namely its references to 'religious organizations,'" App. to Juris. Statement in No. 431, p. 53a, is severable from the Act pursuant to *Alaska Airlines, Inc. v. Brock,* 480 U.S. 678 (1987). The court also denied the Secretary's *Federal Rule of Civil Procedure 59(e)* motion to clarify what the court meant by "religious organizations" for purposes of determining the scope of its injunction. On the same day that this order was entered, appellants docketed their appeal on the merits directly with this Court pursuant to *28 U. S. C. § 1252.* A separate appeal from the District Court's August 13 order was also docketed, as was a cross-appeal by appellees on the severability issue. On November 9, 1987, we noted probable jurisdiction in all three appeals and consolidated the cases for argument. *484 U.S. 942 (1987).*

II

The District Court in this lawsuit held the AFLA unconstitutional both on its face and as applied. Few of our cases in the *Establishment Clause* area have explicitly distinguished between facial challenges to a statute and attacks on the statute as applied. Several cases have clearly involved challenges to a statute "on its face." For example, in *Edwards v. Aguillard,* 482 U.S. 578 (1987), we considered the validity of the Louisiana "Creationism Act," finding the Act "facially invalid." Indeed, in that case it was clear that only a facial challenge could have been considered, as the Act had not been implemented. *Id., at 581, n. 1.* Other cases, as well, have considered the validity of statutes without the benefit of a record as to how the statute had actually been applied. See *Wolman v. Walter,* 433 U.S. 229 (1977); *Committee for Public Education & Religious Liberty v. Nyquist,* 413 U.S. 756 (1973).

In other cases we have, in the course of determining the constitutionality of a statute, referred not only to the language of the statute but also to the manner in which it had been administered in practice. *Levitt v. Committee for Public Education & Religious Liberty,* 413 U.S. 472, 479 (1973); *Meek v. Pittenger,* 421 U.S. 349 (1975). See also *Grand Rapids School District v. Ball, supra, at 377-379; Aguilar v. Felton,* 473 U.S. 402 (1985). In several cases we have expressly recognized that an otherwise valid statute authorizing grants might be challenged on the grounds that the award of a

---

[7] The court also found that the AFLA's funding of religious organizations is likely to incite political divisiveness. See *id., at 1569* (citing, *e. g., Lynch v. Donnelly,* 465 U.S. 668, 689 (1984) (O'CONNOR, J., concurring)).

grant in a particular case would be impermissible. *Hunt v. McNair, 413 U.S. 734 (1973),* involved a challenge to a South Carolina statute that provided for the issuance of revenue bonds to assist "institutions of higher learning" in constructing new facilities. The plaintiffs in that case did not contest the validity of the statute as a whole, but contended only that a statutory grant to a religiously affiliated college would be invalid. *Id., at 736.* In *Tilton v. Richardson, 403 U.S. 672 (1971),* the Court reviewed a federal statute authorizing construction grants to colleges exclusively for secular educational purposes. We rejected the contention that the statute was invalid "on its face" and "as applied" to the four church-related colleges that were named as defendants in the case. However, we did leave open the possibility that the statute might authorize grants which could be invalid, stating that "[i]ndividual projects can be properly evaluated if and when challenges arise with respect to particular recipients and some evidence is then presented to show that the institution does in fact possess" sectarian characteristics that might make a grant of aid to the institution constitutionally impermissible. *Id., at 682.* See also *Roemer v. Maryland Bd. of Public Works, 426 U.S. 736, 760-761 (1976)* (upholding a similar statute authorizing grants to colleges against a "facial" attack and pretermitting the question whether "particular applications may result in unconstitutional use of funds").

There is, then, precedent in this area of constitutional law for distinguishing between the validity of the statute on its face and its validity in particular applications. Although the Court's opinions have not even adverted to (to say nothing of explicitly delineated) the consequences of this distinction between "on its face" and "as applied" in this context, we think they do justify the District Court's approach in separating the two issues as it did here.

This said, we turn to consider whether the District Court was correct in concluding that the AFLA was unconstitutional on its face. As in previous cases involving facial challenges on *Establishment Clause* grounds, *e. g., Edwards v. Aguillard, supra; Mueller v. Allen, 463 U.S. 388 (1983),* we assess the constitutionality of an enactment by reference to the three factors first articulated in *Lemon v. Kurtzman, 403 U.S. 602 (1971).* Under the *Lemon* standard, which guides "[t]he general nature of our inquiry in this area," *Mueller v. Allen, supra, at 394,* a court may invalidate a statute only if it is motivated wholly by an impermissible purpose, *Lynch v. Donnelly, 465 U.S. 668, 680 (1984); Stone v. Graham, 449 U.S. 39, 41 (1980),* if its primary effect is the advancement of religion, *Estate of Thornton v. Caldor, Inc., 472 U.S. 703, 708 (1985),* or if it requires excessive entanglement between church and state, *Lemon, supra, at 613; Walz v. Tax Comm'n, 397 U.S. 664, 674 (1970).* We consider each of these factors in turn.

As we see it, it is clear from the face of the statute that the AFLA was motivated primarily, if not entirely, by a legitimate secular purpose -- the elimination or reduction of social and economic problems caused by teenage sexuality, pregnancy, and parenthood. See §§ *300z(a), (b)* (1982 ed. and Supp. IV). Appellees cannot, and do not, dispute that, on the whole, religious concerns were not the sole motivation behind the Act, see *Lynch, supra, at 680*, nor can it be said that the AFLA lacks a legitimate secular purpose, see *Edwards v. Aguillard, 482 U.S., at 585*. In the court below, however, appellees argued that the *real* purpose of the AFLA could only be understood in reference to the AFLA's predecessor, Title VI. Appellees contended that Congress had an impermissible purpose in adopting the AFLA because it specifically amended Title VI to increase the role of religious organizations in the programs sponsored by the Act. In particular, they pointed to the fact that the AFLA, unlike Title VI, requires grant applicants to describe how they will involve religious organizations in the programs funded by the AFLA. § 300z-5(a)(21)(B).

The District Court rejected this argument, however, reasoning that even if it is assumed that the AFLA was motivated in part by improper concerns, the parts of the statute to which appellees object were also motivated by other, entirely legitimate secular concerns. We agree with this conclusion. As the District Court correctly pointed out, Congress amended Title VI in a number of ways, most importantly for present purposes by attempting to enlist the aid of not only "religious organizations," but also "family members . . ., charitable organizations, voluntary associations, and other groups in the private sector," in addressing the problems associated with adolescent sexuality. § *300z(a)(8)(B)*; see also §§ 300z-5(a)(21)(A), (B). Cf. Title VI, § 601(a)(5) ("[T]he problems of adolescent [sexuality] . . . are best approached through a variety of integrated and essential services"). Congress' decision to amend the statute in this way reflects the entirely appropriate aim of increasing broadbased community involvement "in helping adolescent boys and girls understand the implications of premarital sexual relations, pregnancy, and parenthood." See Senate Report, at 2, 15-16. In adopting the AFLA, Congress expressly intended to expand the services already authorized by Title VI, to insure the increased participation of parents in education and support services, to increase the flexibility of the programs, and to spark the development of new, innovative services. *Id.*, at 7-9. These are all legitimate secular goals that are furthered by the AFLA's additions to Title VI, including the challenged provisions that refer to religious organizations. There simply is no evidence that Congress' "actual purpose" in passing the AFLA was one of "endorsing religion." See *Edwards v. Aguillard, 482*

129

U.S., at 589-594. Nor are we in a position to doubt that Congress' expressed purposes are "sincere and not a sham." *Id., at 587.* [8]

As usual in *Establishment Clause* cases, see, *e. g., Grand Rapids School District v. Ball,* 473 U.S. 373 (1985); *Mueller, supra,* the more difficult question is whether the primary effect of the challenged statute is impermissible. Before we address this question, however, it is useful to review again just what the AFLA sets out to do. Simply stated, it authorizes grants to institutions that are capable of providing certain care and prevention services to adolescents. Because of the complexity of the problems that Congress sought to remedy, potential grantees are required to describe how they will involve other organizations, including religious organizations, in the programs funded by the federal grants. § 300z-5(a)(21)(B); see also § 300z-2(a). There is no requirement in the Act that grantees be affiliated with any religious denomination, although the Act clearly does not rule out grants to religious organizations.[9] The services to be provided under the AFLA are not religious in character, see n. 2, *supra*, nor has there been any suggestion that religious institutions or organizations with religious ties are uniquely well qualified to carry out those services.[10] Certainly it is true that a substantial part of the services listed as "necessary services" under the Act involve some sort of education or counseling, see, *e. g.,* §§ *300z-1(a)(4)(D), (G), (H), (J), (L), (M), (O),* but there is nothing

---

[8] We also see no reason to conclude that the AFLA serves an impermissible religious purpose simply because some of the goals of the statute coincide with the beliefs of certain religious organizations. See *Harris v. McRae,* 448 U.S. 297, 319-320 (1980); *McGowan v. Maryland,* 366 U.S. 420, 442 (1961).

[9] Indeed, the legislative history shows that Congress was aware that religious organizations had been grantees under Title VI and that it did not disapprove of that practice. The Senate Report, at 16, states:

"It should be noted that under current law [Title VI], the Office of Adolescent Pregnancy Programs has made grants to two religious-affiliated organizations, two Christian organizations and several other groups that are indirectly affiliated with religious bodies. Religious affiliation is not a criterion for selection as a grantee under the adolescent family life program, but any such grants made by the Secretary would be a simple recognition that nonprofit religious organizations have a role to play in the provision of services to adolescents."

[10] One witness before the Senate Committee testified that "projects which target hispanic and other minority populations are more accepted by the population if they include sectarian, as well as non-sectarian, organizations in the delivery of those services." S. Rep. No. 98-496, p. 10 (1984). This indicates not that sectarian grantees are particularly well qualified to perform AFLA services, but that the inclusion of both secular and sectarian grantees can improve the effectiveness of the Act's programs.

inherently religious about these activities and appellees do not contend that, by themselves, the AFLA's "necessary services" somehow have the primary effect of advancing religion. Finally, it is clear that the AFLA takes a particular approach toward dealing with adolescent sexuality and pregnancy -- for example, two of its stated purposes are to "promote self discipline and other prudent approaches to the problem of adolescent premarital sexual relations," § *300z(b)(1)*, and to "promote adoption as an alternative," 300z(b)(2) -- but again, that approach is not inherently religious, although it may coincide with the approach taken by certain religions.

Given this statutory framework, there are two ways in which the statute, considered "on its face," might be said to have the impermissible primary effect of advancing religion. First, it can be argued that the AFLA advances religion by expressly recognizing that "religious organizations have a role to play" in addressing the problems associated with teenage sexuality. Senate Report, at 16. In this view, even if no religious institution receives aid or funding pursuant to the AFLA, the statute is invalid under the *Establishment Clause* because, among other things, it expressly enlists the involvement of religiously affiliated organizations in the federally subsidized programs, it endorses religious solutions to the problems addressed by the Act, or it creates symbolic ties between church and state. Secondly, it can be argued that the AFLA is invalid on its face because it allows religiously affiliated organizations to participate as grantees or subgrantees in AFLA programs. From this standpoint, the Act is invalid because it authorizes direct federal funding of religious organizations which, given the AFLA's educational function and the fact that the AFLA's "viewpoint" may coincide with the grantee's "viewpoint" on sexual matters, will result unavoidably in the impermissible "inculcation" of religious beliefs in the context of a federally funded program.

We consider the former objection first. As noted previously, the AFLA expressly mentions the role of religious organizations in four places. It states (1) that the problems of teenage sexuality are "best approached through a variety of integrated and essential services provided to adolescents and their families by[, among others,] religious organizations," § *300z(a)(8)(B)*, (2) that federally subsidized services "should emphasize the provision of support by[, among others,] religious and charitable organizations," § *300z(a)(10)(C)*, (3) that AFLA programs "shall use such methods as will strengthen the capacity of families . . . to make use of support systems such as . . . religious . . . organizations," § 300z-2(a), and (4) that grant applicants shall describe how they will involve religious organizations, among other groups, in the provision of services under the Act. § 300z-5(a)(21)(B).

Putting aside for the moment the possible role of religious organizations as grantees, these provisions of the statute reflect at most Congress' considered judgment that religious organizations can help solve the problems to which the AFLA is addressed. See Senate Report, at 15-16. Nothing in our previous cases prevents Congress from making such a judgment or from recognizing the important part that religion or religious organizations may play in resolving certain secular problems. Particularly when, as Congress found, "prevention of adolescent sexual activity and adolescent pregnancy depends primarily upon developing strong family values and close family ties," § *300z(a)(10)(A)*, it seems quite sensible for Congress to recognize that religious organizations can influence values and can have some influence on family life, including parents' relations with their adolescent children. To the extent that this congressional recognition has any effect of advancing religion, the effect is at most "incidental and remote." See *Lynch, 465 U.S., at 683*; *Estate of Thornton v. Caldor, Inc., 472 U.S., at 710*; *Nyquist, 413 U.S., at 771*. In addition, although the AFLA does require potential grantees to describe how they will involve religious organizations in the provision of services under the Act, it also requires grantees to describe the involvement of "charitable organizations, voluntary associations, and other groups in the private sector," § 300z-5(a)(21)(B). [11] In our view, this reflects the statute's successful maintenance of "a course of neutrality among religions, and between religion and nonreligion," *Grand Rapids School District v. Ball, 473 U.S., at 382*.

This brings us to the second ground for objecting to the AFLA: the fact that it allows religious institutions to participate as recipients of federal funds. The AFLA defines an "eligible grant recipient" as a "public or nonprofit private organization or agency" which demonstrates the capability of providing the requisite services. § *300z-1(a)(3)*. As this provision would indicate, a fairly wide spectrum of organizations is eligible to apply for and receive funding under the Act, and nothing on the face of the Act suggests it is anything but neutral with respect to the grantee's status as a sectarian or purely secular institution. See Senate Report, at 16 ("Religious affiliation is not a criterion for selection as a grantee . . ."). In this regard, then, the AFLA is similar to other statutes that this Court has upheld

---

[11] This undercuts any argument that religion has been "advanced" simply because AFLA added to Title VI the various references to religious organizations. As we noted previously, the amendments to Title VI were motivated by the secular purpose of increasing community involvement in the problems associated with adolescent sexuality. Although the AFLA amendments may have the effect of increasing the role of religious organizations in services provided under the AFLA, at least relative to services provided under Title VI, this reflects merely the fact that the AFLA program as a whole was expanded, with the role of all community organizations being increased as a result. This expansion of programs available under the AFLA, as opposed to Title VI, has only the "incidental" effect, if that, of advancing religion.

against *Establishment Clause* challenges in the past. In *Roemer v. Maryland Bd. of Public Works,* 426 U.S. 736 (1976), for example, we upheld a Maryland statute that provided annual subsidies directly to qualifying colleges and universities in the State, including religiously affiliated institutions. As the plurality stated, "religious institutions need not be quarantined from public benefits that are neutrally available to all." *Id.,* at 746 (discussing *Everson v. Board of Education,* 330 U.S. 1 (1947) (approving busing services equally available to both public and private school children), and *Board of Education v. Allen,* 392 U.S. 236 (1968) (upholding state provision of secular textbooks for both public and private school students)). Similarly, in *Tilton v. Richardson,* 403 U.S. 672 (1971), we approved the federal Higher Educational Facilities Act, which was intended by Congress to provide construction grants to "all colleges and universities regardless of any affiliation with or sponsorship by a religious body." *Id.,* at 676. And in *Hunt v. McNair,* 413 U.S. 734 (1973), we rejected a challenge to a South Carolina statute that made certain benefits "available to all institutions of higher education in South Carolina, whether or not having a religious affiliation." *Id.,* at 741. In other cases involving indirect grants of state aid to religious institutions, we have found it important that the aid is made available regardless of whether it will ultimately flow to a secular or sectarian institution. See, *e. g., Witters v. Washington Dept. of Services for Blind,* 474 U.S. 481, 487 (1986); *Mueller v. Allen,* 463 U.S., at 398; *Everson v. Board of Education, supra,* at 17-18; *Walz v. Tax Comm'n,* 397 U.S., at 676.

We note in addition that this Court has never held that religious institutions are disabled by the *First Amendment* from participating in publicly sponsored social welfare programs. To the contrary, in *Bradfield v. Roberts,* 175 U.S. 291 (1899), the Court upheld an agreement between the Commissioners of the District of Columbia and a religiously affiliated hospital whereby the Federal Government would pay for the construction of a new building on the grounds of the hospital. In effect, the Court refused to hold that the mere fact that the hospital was "conducted under the auspices of the Roman Catholic Church" was sufficient to alter the purely secular legal character of the corporation, *id., at 298,* particularly in the absence of any allegation that the hospital discriminated on the basis of religion or operated in any way inconsistent with its secular charter. In the Court's view, the giving of federal aid to the hospital was entirely consistent with the *Establishment Clause,* and the fact that the hospital was religiously affiliated was "wholly immaterial." *Ibid.* The propriety of this holding, and the long history of cooperation and interdependency between governments and charitable or religious organizations is reflected in the legislative history of the AFLA. See S. Rep. No. 98-496, p. 10 (1984) ("Charitable organizations with religious affiliations historically have provided social services with the support of their communities and without controversy").

Of course, even when the challenged statute appears to be neutral on its face, we have always been careful to ensure that direct government aid to religiously affiliated institutions does not have the primary effect of advancing religion. One way in which direct government aid might have that effect is if the aid flows to institutions that are "pervasively sectarian." We stated in *Hunt* that

> "[a]id normally may be thought to have a primary effect of advancing religion when it flows to an institution in which religion is so pervasive that a substantial portion of its functions are subsumed in the religious mission . . . ." 413 U.S., at 743.

The reason for this is that there is a risk that direct government funding, even if it is designated for specific secular purposes, may nonetheless advance the pervasively sectarian institution's "religious mission." See *Grand Rapids School District v. Ball*, 473 U.S., at 385 (discussing how aid to religious schools may impermissibly advance religion). Accordingly, a relevant factor in deciding whether a particular statute on its face can be said to have the improper effect of advancing religion is the determination of whether, and to what extent, the statute directs government aid to pervasively sectarian institutions. In *Grand Rapids School District*, for example, the Court began its "effects" inquiry with "a consideration of the nature of the institutions in which the [challenged] programs operate." *Id., at 384.*

In this lawsuit, nothing on the face of the AFLA indicates that a significant proportion of the federal funds will be disbursed to "pervasively sectarian" institutions. Indeed, the contention that there is a substantial risk of such institutions receiving direct aid is undercut by the AFLA's facially neutral grant requirements, the wide spectrum of public and private organizations which are capable of meeting the AFLA's requirements, and the fact that, of the eligible religious institutions, many will not deserve the label of "pervasively sectarian." [12] This is not a case like *Grand Rapids*, where the challenged aid flowed almost entirely to parochial schools. In that case the State's "Shared Time" program was directed specifically at providing certain classes for nonpublic schools, and 40 of 41 of the

---

[12] The validity of this observation is borne out by the statistics for the AFLA program in fiscal year 1986. According to the record of funding for that year, some $ 10.7 million in funding was awarded under the AFLA to a total of 86 organizations. Of this, about $ 3.3 million went to 23 religiously affiliated grantees, with only $ 1.3 million of this figure going to the 13 projects that were cited by the District Court for constitutional violations. App. 748-756. Of these 13 projects, 4 appear to be state or local government organizations, and at least 1 is a hospital. *Id., at 755.* Of the 13 religiously affiliated organizations listed, 2 are universities. *Id., at 756.*

schools that actually participated in the program were found to be "pervasively sectarian." *Id., at 385.* See also *Nyquist, 413 U.S., at 768* ("'all or practically all'" of the schools entitled to receive grants were religiously affiliated); *Meek v. Pittenger, 421 U.S., at 371.* Instead, this litigation more closely resembles *Tilton* and *Roemer,* where it was foreseeable that some proportion of the recipients of government aid would be religiously affiliated, but that only a small portion of these, if any, could be considered "pervasively sectarian." In those cases we upheld the challenged statutes on their face and as applied to the institutions named in the complaints, but left open the consequences which would ensue if they allowed federal aid to go to institutions that were in fact pervasively sectarian. *Tilton, 403 U.S., at 682; Roemer, 426 U.S., at 760.* As in *Tilton* and *Roemer,* we do not think the possibility that AFLA grants may go to religious institutions that can be considered "pervasively sectarian" is sufficient to conclude that no grants whatsoever can be given under the statute to religious organizations. We think that the District Court was wrong in concluding otherwise.

Nor do we agree with the District Court that the AFLA necessarily has the effect of advancing religion because the religiously affiliated AFLA grantees will be providing educational and counseling services to adolescents. Of course, we have said that the *Establishment Clause* does "prohibit government-financed or government-sponsored indoctrination into the beliefs of a particular religious faith," *Grand Rapids, supra, at 385,* and we have accordingly struck down programs that entail an unacceptable risk that government funding would be used to "advance the religious mission" of the religious institution receiving aid. See, *e. g., Meek, supra, at 370.* But nothing in our prior cases warrants the presumption adopted by the District Court that religiously affiliated AFLA grantees are not capable of carrying out their functions under the AFLA in a lawful, secular manner. Only in the context of aid to "pervasively sectarian" institutions have we invalidated an aid program on the grounds that there was a "substantial" risk that aid to these religious institutions would, knowingly or unknowingly, result in religious indoctrination. *E. g., Grand Rapids, supra, at 387-398; Meek, supra, at 371.* In contrast, when the aid is to flow to religiously affiliated institutions that were not pervasively sectarian, as in *Roemer,* we refused to presume that it would be used in a way that would have the primary effect of advancing religion. *Roemer, 426 U.S., at 760* ("We must assume that the colleges . . . will exercise their delegated control over use of the funds in compliance with the statutory, and therefore the constitutional, mandate"). We think that the type of presumption that the District Court applied in this case is simply unwarranted. As we stated in *Roemer*: "It has not been the Court's practice, in considering facial challenges to statutes of this kind, to strike them down in anticipation that particular applications may result in unconstitutional use of funds." *Id., at 761;* see also *Tilton, supra, at 682.*

We also disagree with the District Court's conclusion that the AFLA is invalid because it authorizes "teaching" by religious grant recipients on "matters [that] are fundamental elements of religious doctrine," such as the harm of premarital sex and the reasons for choosing adoption over abortion. *657 F. Supp., at 1562.* On an issue as sensitive and important as teenage sexuality, it is not surprising that the Government's secular concerns would either coincide or conflict with those of religious institutions. But the possibility or even the likelihood that some of the religious institutions who receive AFLA funding will agree with the message that Congress intended to deliver to adolescents through the AFLA is insufficient to warrant a finding that the statute on its face has the primary effect of advancing religion. See *Lynch, 465 U.S., at 682*; *id., at 715-716* (BRENNAN, J., dissenting); *Harris v. McRae, 448 U.S. 297, 319-320 (1980).* Nor does the alignment of the statute and the religious views of the grantees run afoul of our proscription against "fund[ing] a specifically religious activity in an otherwise substantially secular setting." *Hunt, 413 U.S., at 743.* The facially neutral projects authorized by the AFLA -- including pregnancy testing, adoption counseling and referral services, prenatal and postnatal care, educational services, residential care, child care, consumer education, etc. -- are not themselves "specifically religious activities," and they are not converted into such activities by the fact that they are carried out by organizations with religious affiliations.

As yet another reason for invalidating parts of the AFLA, the District Court found that the involvement of religious organizations in the Act has the impermissible effect of creating a "crucial symbolic link" between government and religion. *657 F. Supp., at 1564* (citing, *e. g., Grand Rapids, 473 U.S., at 390*). If we were to adopt the District Court's reasoning, it could be argued that any time a government aid program provides funding to religious organizations in an area in which the organization also has an interest, an impermissible "symbolic link" could be created, no matter whether the aid was to be used solely for secular purposes. This would jeopardize government aid to religiously affiliated hospitals, for example, on the ground that patients would perceive a "symbolic link" between the hospital -- part of whose "religious mission" might be to save lives -- and whatever government entity is subsidizing the purely secular medical services provided to the patient. We decline to adopt the District Court's reasoning and conclude that, in this litigation, whatever "symbolic link" might in fact be created by the AFLA's disbursement of funds to religious institutions is not sufficient to justify striking down the statute on its face.

A final argument that has been advanced for striking down the AFLA on "effects" grounds is the fact that the statute lacks an express provision preventing the use of federal funds for religious purposes. [13] Cf. *Tilton, 403 U.S., at 675*; *Roemer, supra, at 740-741*. Clearly, if there were such a provision in this statute, it would be easier to conclude that the statute on its face could not be said to have the primary effect of advancing religion, see, *e. g., Roemer, supra, at 760*, but we have never stated that a *statutory* restriction is constitutionally required. The closest we came to such a holding was in *Tilton*, where we struck down a provision of the statute that would have eliminated Government sanctions for violating the statute's restrictions on religious uses of funds after 20 years. *403 U.S., at 683*. The reason we did so, however, was because the 20-year limit on sanctions created a risk that the religious institution would, after the 20 years were up, act as if there were no longer any constitutional or statutory limitations on its use of the federally funded building. This aspect of the decision in *Tilton* was thus intended to indicate that the constitutional limitations on use of federal funds, as embodied in the statutory restriction, could not simply "expire" at some point during the economic life of the benefit that the grantee received from the Government. In this litigation, although there is no express statutory limitation on religious use of funds, there is also no intimation in the statute that at some point, or for some grantees, religious uses are permitted. To the contrary, the 1984 Senate Report on the AFLA states that "the use of Adolescent Family Life Act funds to promote religion, or to teach the religious doctrines of a particular sect, is contrary to the intent of this legislation." S. Rep. No. 98-496, p. 10 (1984). We note in addition that the AFLA requires each grantee to undergo evaluations of the services it provides, § 300z-5(b)(1), and also requires grantees to "make such reports concerning its use of Federal funds as the Secretary may require," § 300z-5(c). The application requirements of the Act, as well, require potential grantees to disclose in detail exactly what services they intend to provide and how they will be provided. § 300z-5(a). These provisions, taken together, create a mechanism whereby the Secretary can police the grants that are given out under the Act to ensure that federal funds are not used for impermissible purposes. Unlike some other grant programs, in which aid might be given out in one-time grants without ongoing supervision by the Government, the programs established under the authority of the AFLA can be monitored to determine whether the funds are, in effect, being used by the grantees in such a way as to advance religion. Given this statutory scheme, we do not think that the absence of an express limitation on the use of federal funds for religious purposes means that the statute, on its face, has the primary effect of advancing religion.

---

[13] Section 300z-3 does, however, expressly define the uses to which federal funds may be put, including providing care and prevention services to eligible individuals. Nowhere in this section is it suggested that use of funds for religious purposes would be permissible.

137

This, of course, brings us to the third prong of the *Lemon Establishment Clause* "test" -- the question whether the AFLA leads to "'an excessive government entanglement with religion.'" *Lemon*, 403 U.S., at 613 (quoting *Walz v. Tax Comm'n, 397 U.S., at 674*). There is no doubt that the monitoring of AFLA grants is necessary if the Secretary is to ensure that public money is to be spent in the way that Congress intended and in a way that comports with the *Establishment Clause*. Accordingly, this litigation presents us with yet another "***Catch-22***" argument: the very supervision of the aid to assure that it does not further religion renders the statute invalid. See *Aguilar v. Felton*, 473 U.S., at 421 (REHNQUIST, J., dissenting); *id., at 418* (Powell, J., concurring) (interaction of entanglement and effects tests forces schools "to tread an extremely narrow line"); *Roemer, 426 U.S., at 768-769* (WHITE, J., concurring in judgment). For this and other reasons, the "entanglement" prong of the *Lemon* test has been much criticized over the years. See, *e. g., Aguilar v. Felton, supra, at 429* (O'CONNOR, J., dissenting); *Wallace v. Jaffree, 472 U.S. 38, 109-110 (1985)* (REHNQUIST, J., dissenting); *Lynch v. Donnelly, 465 U.S., at 689* (O'CONNOR, J., concurring); *Lemon, supra, at 666-668* (WHITE, J., concurring and dissenting). Most of the cases in which the Court has divided over the "entanglement" part of the *Lemon* test have involved aid to parochial schools; in *Aguilar* v. *Felton*, for example, the Court's finding of excessive entanglement rested in large part on the undisputed fact that the elementary and secondary schools receiving aid were "pervasively sectarian" and had "'as a substantial purpose the inculcation of religious values.'" *473 U.S., at 411* (quoting *Nyquist, 413 U.S., at 768*); see also *473 U.S., at 411* (expressly distinguishing *Roemer, Hunt*, and *Tilton* as cases involving aid to institutions that were not pervasively sectarian). In *Aguilar*, the Court feared that an adequate level of supervision would require extensive and permanent on-site monitoring, *473 U.S., at 412-413*, and would threaten both the "freedom of religious belief of those who [were] not adherents of that denomination" and the "freedom of . . . the adherents of the denomination." *Id., at 409-410*.

Here, by contrast, there is no reason to assume that the religious organizations which may receive grants are "pervasively sectarian" in the same sense as the Court has held parochial schools to be. There is accordingly no reason to fear that the less intensive monitoring involved here will cause the Government to intrude unduly in the day-to-day operation of the religiously affiliated AFLA grantees. Unquestionably, the Secretary will review the programs set up and run by the AFLA grantees, and undoubtedly this will involve a review of, for example, the educational materials that a grantee proposes to use. The Secretary may also wish to have Government employees visit the clinics or offices where AFLA programs are being carried out to see whether they are in fact being administered in accordance with statutory and constitutional requirements. But in our view, this type of grant monitoring does not amount to "excessive entanglement," at least in the context of a statute authorizing grants to religiously affiliated organizations that are not necessarily "pervasively sectarian." [14]

In sum, in this somewhat lengthy discussion of the validity of the AFLA on its face, we have concluded that the statute has a valid secular purpose, does not have the primary effect of advancing religion, and does not create an excessive entanglement of church and state. We note, as is proper given the traditional presumption in favor of the constitutionality of statutes enacted by Congress, that our conclusion that the statute does not violate the *Establishment Clause* is consistent with the conclusion Congress reached in the course of its deliberations on the AFLA. As the Senate Committee Report states:

> "In the committee's view, provisions for the involvement of religious organizations [in the AFLA] do not violate the constitutional separation between church and state. Recognizing the limitations of Government in dealing with a problem that has complex moral and social dimensions, the committee believes that promoting the involvement of religious organizations in the solution to these problems is neither inappropriate or illegal." Senate Report, at 15-16.

For the foregoing reasons we conclude that the AFLA does not violate the *Establishment Clause* "on its face."

III

We turn now to consider whether the District Court correctly ruled that the AFLA was unconstitutional as applied. Our first task in this regard is to consider whether appellees had standing to raise this claim. In *Flast v. Cohen, 392 U.S. 83 (1968)*, we held that federal taxpayers have standing to raise *Establishment Clause* claims against exercises of congressional power under the taxing and spending power of Article I, § 8, of the Constitution. Although we have considered the problem of standing and Article III limitations on federal jurisdiction many times since then, we have

---

[14] We also disagree with the District Court's conclusion that the AFLA is invalid because it is likely to create political division along religious lines. See *657 F. Supp., at 1569*. It may well be that because of the importance of the issues relating to adolescent sexuality there may be a division of opinion along religious lines as well as other lines. But the same may be said of a great number of other public issues of our day. In addition, as we said in *Mueller v. Allen, 463 U.S. 388, 404, n. 11 (1983)*, the question of "political divisiveness" should be "regarded as confined to cases where direct financial subsidies are paid to parochial schools or to teachers in parochial schools."

consistently adhered to *Flast* and the narrow exception it created to the general rule against taxpayer standing established in *Frothingham v. Mellon, 262 U.S. 447 (1923)*. Accordingly, in this case there is no dispute that appellees have standing to raise their challenge to the AFLA on its face. What is disputed, however, is whether appellees also have standing to challenge the statute as applied. The answer to this question turns on our decision in *Valley Forge Christian College v. Americans United for Separation of Church & State, Inc., 454 U.S. 464 (1982)*. In *Valley Forge*, we ruled that taxpayers did not have standing to challenge a decision by the Secretary of Health, Education, and Welfare (HEW) to dispose of certain property pursuant to the Federal Property and Administrative Services Act of 1949, 63 Stat. 377, as amended, *40 U. S. C. § 471 et seq.* We rejected the taxpayers' claim of standing for two reasons: first, because "the source of their complaint is not a congressional action, but a decision by HEW to transfer a parcel of federal property," *454 U.S., at 479*, and second, because "the property transfer about which [the taxpayers] complain was not an exercise of authority conferred by the Taxing and Spending Clause of Art. I, § 8," *id., at 480*. Appellants now contend that appellees' standing in this case is deficient for the former reason; they argue that a challenge to the AFLA "as applied" is really a challenge to executive action, not to an exercise of congressional authority under the Taxing and Spending Clause. We do not think, however, that appellees' claim that AFLA funds are being used improperly by individual grantees is any less a challenge to congressional taxing and spending power simply because the funding authorized by Congress has flowed through and been administered by the Secretary. Indeed, *Flast* itself was a suit against the Secretary of HEW, who had been given the authority under the challenged statute to administer the spending program that Congress had created. In subsequent cases, most notably *Tilton*, we have not questioned the standing of taxpayer plaintiffs to raise *Establishment Clause* challenges, even when their claims raised questions about the administratively made grants. See *Tilton, 403 U.S., at 676*; see also *Hunt, 413 U.S., at 735-736* (not questioning standing of state taxpayer to file suit against state executive in an "as applied" challenge); *Roemer, 426 U.S., at 744* (same). This is not a case like *Valley Forge*, where the challenge was to an exercise of executive authority pursuant to the *Property Clause* of Article IV, § 3, see *454 U.S., at 480*, or *Schlesinger v. Reservists Committee to Stop the War, 418 U.S. 208, 228 (1974)*, where the plaintiffs challenged the executive decision to allow Members of Congress to maintain their status as officers of the Armed Forces Reserve. See also *United States v. Richardson, 418 U.S. 166, 175 (1974)* (rejecting standing in challenge to statutes regulating the Central Intelligence Agency's accounting and reporting requirements). Nor is this, as we stated in *Flast*, a challenge to "an incidental expenditure of tax funds in the administration of an essentially regulatory statute." *392 U.S., at 102*. The AFLA is at heart a program of disbursement of funds pursuant to Congress' taxing and spending powers, and appellees' claims call into question how the funds authorized by Congress are being disbursed pursuant to the AFLA's statutory mandate. In this litigation there is thus a sufficient nexus between the taxpayer's standing as a taxpayer and the congressional exercise of taxing and spending power, notwithstanding the role the Secretary plays in administering the statute.[15]

On the merits of the "as applied" challenge, it seems to us that the District Court did not follow the proper approach in assessing appellees' claim that the Secretary is making grants under the Act that violate the *Establishment Clause of the First Amendment.* Although the District Court stated several times that AFLA aid had been given to religious organizations that were " pervasively sectarian," see *657 F. Supp., at 1564, 1565, 1567,* it did not identify which grantees it was referring to, nor did it discuss with any particularity the aspects of those organizations which in its view warranted classification as "pervasively sectarian."[16] The District Court did identify certain instances in which it felt AFLA funds were used for constitutionally improper purposes, but in our view the court did not adequately design its remedy to address the specific problems it found in the Secretary's administration of the statute. Accordingly, although there is no dispute that the record contains evidence of specific incidents of impermissible behavior by AFLA grantees, we feel that this lawsuit should be remanded to the District Court for consideration of the evidence presented by appellees insofar as it sheds light on the manner in which the statute is presently being administered. It is the latter inquiry to which the court must direct itself on remand.

In particular, it will be open to appellees on remand to show that AFLA aid is flowing to grantees that can be considered "pervasively sectarian" religious institutions, such as we have held parochial schools to be. See *Hunt, supra, at 743.* As our previous discussion has indicated, and as *Tilton, Hunt,* and *Roemer* make clear, it is not enough to show that the recipient of a challenged grant is affiliated with a religious institution or that it is "religiously inspired."

---

[15] Because we find that the taxpayer appellees have standing, we need not consider the standing of the clergy or the American Jewish Congress.

[16] The closest the court came was to identify "at least ten AFLA grantees or subgrantees [that] were themselves 'religious organizations,' in the sense that they have explicit corporate ties to a particular religious faith and by-laws or policies that prohibit any deviation from religious doctrine." *657 F. Supp., at 1565.* While these factors are relevant to the determination of whether an institution is "pervasively sectarian," they are not conclusive, and we do not find the court's conclusion that these institutions are "religious organizations" to be equivalent to a finding that their secular purposes and religious mission are "inextricably intertwined."

The District Court should also consider on remand whether in particular cases AFLA aid has been used to fund "specifically religious activit[ies] in an otherwise substantially secular setting." *Hunt, supra, at 743.* In *Hunt,* for example, we deemed it important that the conditions on which the aid was granted were sufficient to preclude the possibility that funds would be used for the construction of a building used for religious purposes. Here it would be relevant to determine, for example, whether the Secretary has permitted AFLA grantees to use materials that have an explicitly religious content or are designed to inculcate the views of a particular religious faith. As we have pointed out in our previous discussion, evidence that the views espoused on questions such as premarital sex, abortion, and the like happen to coincide with the religious views of the AFLA grantee would not be sufficient to show that the grant funds are being used in such a way as to have a primary effect of advancing religion.

If the District Court concludes on the evidence presented that grants are being made by the Secretary in violation of the *Establishment Clause*, it should then turn to the question of the appropriate remedy. We deal here with a funding statute with respect to which Congress has expressed the view that the use of funds by grantees to promote religion, or to teach religious doctrines of a particular sect, would be contrary to the intent of the statute. See S. Rep. No. 98-496, p. 10 (1984). The Secretary has promulgated a series of conditions to each grant, including a prohibition against teaching or promoting religion. See App. 757. While these strictures may not be coterminous with the requirements of the *Establishment Clause*, they make it very likely that any particular grant which would violate the *Establishment Clause* would also violate the statute and the grant conditions imposed by the Secretary. Should the court conclude that the Secretary has wrongfully approved certain AFLA grants, an appropriate remedy would require the Secretary to withdraw such approval.

IV

We conclude, first, that the District Court erred in holding that the AFLA is invalid on its face, and second, that the court should consider on remand whether particular AFLA grants have had the primary effect of advancing religion. Should the court conclude that the Secretary's current practice does allow such grants, it should devise a remedy to insure that grants awarded by the Secretary comply with the Constitution and the statute. The judgment of the District Court is accordingly

Reversed.

JUSTICE O'CONNOR, concurring.

This litigation raises somewhat unusual questions involving a facially valid statute that appears to have been administered in a way that led to violations of the *Establishment Clause*. I agree with the Court's resolution of those questions, and I join its opinion. I write separately, however, to explain why I do not believe that the Court's approach reflects any tolerance for the kind of improper administration that seems to have occurred in the Government program at issue here.

The dissent says, and I fully agree, that "[p]ublic funds may not be used to endorse the religious message." *Post*, at 642. As the Court notes, "there is no dispute that the record contains evidence of specific incidents of impermissible behavior by AFLA grantees." *Ante*, at 620. Because the District Court employed an analytical framework that did not require a detailed discussion of the voluminous record, the extent of this impermissible behavior and the degree to which it is attributable to poor administration by the Executive Branch is somewhat less clear. In this circumstance, two points deserve to be emphasized. First, *any* use of public funds to promote religious doctrines violates the *Establishment Clause*. Second, *extensive* violations -- if they can be proved in this case -- will be highly relevant in shaping an appropriate remedy that ends such abuses. For that reason, appellees may yet prevail on remand, and I do not believe that the Court's approach entails a relaxation of "the unwavering vigilance that the Constitution requires against any law 'respecting an establishment of religion.'" See *post*, at 648 (quoting *U.S. Const., Amdt. 1*); cf. *post*, at 630, n. 4.

The need for detailed factual findings by the District Court stems in part from the delicacy of the task given to the Executive Branch by the Adolescent Family Life Act (AFLA). Government has a strong and legitimate secular interest in encouraging sexual restraint among young people. At the same time, as the dissent rightly points out, "[t]here is a very real and important difference between running a soup kitchen or a hospital, and counseling pregnant teenagers on how to make the difficult decisions facing them." *Post*, at 641. Using religious organizations to advance the secular goals of the AFLA, without thereby permitting religious indoctrination, is inevitably more difficult than in other projects, such as ministering to the poor and the sick. I nonetheless agree with the Court that the partnership between governmental and religious institutions contemplated by the AFLA need not result in constitutional violations, despite an undeniably greater risk than is present in cooperative undertakings that involve less sensitive objectives. If the District Court finds on remand that grants are being made in violation of the *Establishment Clause*, an appropriate remedy would take into account the history of the program's administration as well as the extent of any continuing constitutional violations.

JUSTICE KENNEDY, with whom JUSTICE SCALIA joins, concurring.

I join the Court's opinion, and write this separate concurrence to discuss one feature of the proceedings on remand. The Court states that "it will be open to appellees on remand to show that AFLA aid is flowing to grantees that can be considered 'pervasively sectarian' religious institutions, such as we have held parochial schools to be." *Ante*, at 621. In my view, such a showing will not alone be enough, in an asapplied challenge, to make out a violation of the *Establishment Clause*.

Though I am not confident that the term "pervasively sectarian" is a well-founded juridical category, I recognize the thrust of our previous decisions that a statute which provides for exclusive or disproportionate funding to pervasively sectarian institutions may impermissibly advance religion and as such be invalid on its face. We hold today, however, that the neutrality of the grant requirements and the diversity of the organizations described in the statute before us foreclose the argument that it is disproportionately tied to pervasively sectarian groups. *Ante*, at 610-611. Having held that the statute is not facially invalid, the only purpose of further inquiring whether any particular grantee institution is pervasively sectarian is as a preliminary step to demonstrating that the funds are in fact being used to further religion. In sum, where, as in this litigation, a statute provides that the benefits of a program are to be distributed in a neutral fashion to religious and nonreligious applicants alike, and the program withstands a facial challenge, it is not unconstitutional as applied solely by reason of the religious character of a specific recipient. The question in an as-applied challenge is not whether the entity is of a religious character, but how it spends its grant.

JUSTICE BLACKMUN, with whom JUSTICE BRENNAN, JUSTICE MARSHALL, and JUSTICE STEVENS join, dissenting.

In 1981, Congress enacted the Adolescent Family Life Act (AFLA), 95 Stat. 578, *42 U. S. C. § 300z et seq. (1982 ed. and Supp. IV)*, thereby "involv[ing] families[,] . . . religious and charitable organizations, voluntary associations, and other groups," § 300z-5(a)(21), in a broad-scale effort to alleviate some of the problems associated with teenage pregnancy. It is unclear whether Congress ever envisioned that public funds would pay for a program during a session of which parents and teenagers would be instructed:

> "You want to know the church teachings on sexuality. . . . You are the church. You people sitting here are the body of Christ. The teachings of you and the things you value are, in fact, the values of the Catholic Church." App. 226.

Or of curricula that taught:

> "The Church has always taught that the marriage act, or intercourse, seals the union of husband and wife, (and is a representation of their union on all levels.) Christ commits Himself to us when we come to ask for the sacrament of marriage. We ask Him to be active in our life. God is love. We ask Him to share His love in ours, and God procreates with us, He enters into our physical union with Him, and we begin new life." *Id., at 372.*

Or the teaching of a method of family planning described on the grant application as "not only a method of birth regulation but also a philosophy of procreation," *id., at 143*, and promoted as helping "spouses who are striving . . . to transform their married life into testimony[,] . . . to cultivate their matrimonial spirituality[, and] to make themselves better instruments in God's plan," and as "facilitat[ing] the evangelization of homes." *Id., at 385.*

Whatever Congress had in mind, however, it enacted a statute that facilitated and, indeed, encouraged the use of public funds for such instruction, by giving religious groups a central pedagogical and counseling role without imposing any restraints on the sectarian quality of the participation. As the record developed thus far in this litigation makes all too clear, federal tax dollars appropriated for AFLA purposes have been used, with Government approval, to support religious teaching. Today the majority upholds the facial validity of this statute and remands the action to the District Court for further proceedings concerning appellees' challenge to the manner in which the statute has been applied. Because I am firmly convinced that our cases require invalidating this statutory scheme, I dissent.

I

The District Court, troubled by the lack of express guidance from this Court as to the appropriate manner in which to examine *Establishment Clause* challenges to an entire statute as well as to specific instances of its implementation, reluctantly proceeded to analyze the AFLA both "on its face" and "as applied." Thereafter, on cross-motions for summary judgment supported by an extensive record of undisputed facts, the District Court applied the three-pronged analysis of *Lemon v. Kurtzman, 403 U.S. 602 (1971)*, and declared the AFLA unconstitutional both facially and as applied. *657 F. Supp. 1547 (DC 1987)*. The majority acknowledges that this Court in some cases has passed on the facial validity of a legislative enactment and in others limited its analysis to the particular applications at issue; yet, while confirming that the District Court was justified in analyzing the AFLA both ways, the Court fails to elaborate on the consequences that flow from the analytical division.

While the distinction is sometimes useful in constitutional litigation, the majority misuses it here to divide and conquer appellees' challenge. [1] By designating appellees' broad attack on the statute as a "facial" challenge, the majority justifies divorcing its analysis from the extensive record developed in the District Court, and thereby strips the challenge of much of its force and renders the evaluation of

---

[1] A related point on which I do agree with the majority is worth acknowledging explicitly. In his appeal to this Court, the Secretary of Health and Human Services vigorously criticized the District Court's analysis of the AFLA on its face, asserting that it "cannot be squared with this Court's explanation in *United States v. Salerno, [481 U.S. 739, 745 (1987)],*" that in mounting a facial challenge to a legislative Act, 'the challenger must establish that no set of circumstances exists under which the Act would be valid.'" Brief for Federal Appellant 30. The Court, however, rejects the application of such rigid analysis in *Establishment Clause* cases, explaining: "As in previous cases involving facial challenges on *Establishment Clause* grounds, . . . we assess the constitutionality of an enactment by reference to the three factors first articulated in *Lemon v. Kurtzman, 403 U.S. 602 (1971)*." *Ante*, at 602. Indeed, the Secretary's proposed test is wholly incongruous with analysis of an *Establishment Clause* challenge under *Lemon*, which requires our examination of the purpose of the legislative enactment, as well as its primary effect or potential for fostering excessive entanglement. Although I may differ with the majority in the application of the *Lemon* analysis to the AFLA, I join it in rejecting the Secretary's approach which would render review under the *Establishment Clause* a nullity. Even in a statute like the AFLA, with its solicitude for, and specific averment to, the participation of religious organizations, one could hypothesize some "set of circumstances . . . under which the Act would be valid," as, for example, might be the case if no religious organization ever actually applied for or participated under an AFLA grant. The *Establishment Clause* cannot be eviscerated by such artifice.

the *Lemon* "effects" prong particularly sterile and meaningless. By characterizing appellees' objections to the real-world operation of the AFLA an "as-applied" challenge, the Court risks misdirecting the litigants and the lower courts toward piecemeal litigation continuing indefinitely throughout the life of the AFLA. In my view, a more effective way to review *Establishment Clause* challenges is to look to the type of relief prayed for by the plaintiffs, and the force of the arguments and supporting evidence they marshal. Whether we denominate a challenge that focuses on the systematically unconstitutional operation of a statute a "facial" challenge -- because it goes to the statute as a whole -- or an "as-applied" challenge -- because we rely on real-world events -- the Court should not blind itself to the facts revealed by the undisputed record. [2]

As is evident from the parties' arguments, the record compiled below, and the decision of the District Court, this lawsuit has been litigated primarily as a broad challenge to the statutory scheme as a whole, not just to the awarding of grants to a few individual applicants. The thousands of pages of depositions, affidavits, and documentary evidence were not intended to demonstrate merely that particular grantees should not receive further funding. Indeed, because of the 5-year grant cycle, some of the original grantees are no longer AFLA participants. This record was designed to show that the AFLA had been interpreted and implemented by the Government in a manner that was clearly unconstitutional, and appellees sought declaratory and injunctive relief as to the entire statute.

In discussing appellees' as-applied challenge, the District Court recognized that their objections went further than the validity of the particular grants under review:

> "The undisputed record before the Court transforms the inherent conflicts between the AFLA and the Constitution into reality. . . . While the Court will not engage in an exhaustive recitation of the record, references to

---

[2] Of course, the manner in which the challenge is characterized does not limit the relief available. Where justified by the nature of the controversy and the evidence in the record, a federal district court may invoke broad equitable powers to prevent continued unconstitutional activity. See *Hutto v. Finney*, 437 U.S. 678, 687, and n. 9 (1978); *Swann v. Charlotte-Mecklenburg Board of Education*, 402 U.S. 1, 15 (1971) ("[B]readth and flexibility are inherent in equitable remedies"). In *Milliken v. Bradley*, 433 U.S. 267 (1977), the Court reiterated that in exercising its broad equitable powers, a district court should focus on the "nature and scope of the constitutional violation," and ensure that decrees by "remedial in nature." *Id., at 280* (emphasis omitted). On remand, therefore, as instructed by the majority, the District Court must undertake the delicate task of fashioning relief appropriate to the scope of any particular violation it discovers.

representative portions of the record reveal the extent to which the AFLA has in fact 'directly and immediately' advanced religion, funded 'pervasively sectarian' institutions, or permitted the use of federal tax dollars for education and counseling that amounts to the teaching of religion." *657 F. Supp., at 1564* (footnote omitted).

The majority declines to accept the District Court's characterization of the record, yet fails to review it independently, relying instead on its assumptions and casual observations about the character of the grantees and potential grantees.[3] See *ante*, at 610, 611-612, 616-617. In doing so, the Court neglects its responsibilities under the *Establishment Clause* and gives uncharacteristically short shrift to the District Court's understanding of the facts.[4]

---

[3] The majority finds support for its "observation[s]" in the statistics for the AFLA program in fiscal 1986. See *ante*, at 610, n. 12. Because there are some organizations that were funded in 1982, but not in 1986, and vice versa, I find the cumulative funding figures for FY 1982-1986 more helpful. Looking at those figures, and the same group of recipients identified by the majority, I find that of approximately $ 53.5 million in AFLA funding, over $ 10 million went to the 13 organizations specifically cited in the District Court's opinion for constitutional violations. App. 748-756. The District Court, of course, did not "engage in an exhaustive recitation of the record," but made references only to "representative portions." *657 F. Supp. 1547, 1564 (DC 1987)*. Another 13 organizations characterized as "religiously affiliated" in a tabulation prepared by the Department of Health and Human Services in connection with this litigation, received an additional $ 6 million during this period. Looking at the figures from a different perspective, a third of the approximately 100,000 "clients served" by all AFLA grantees during the 1985-1986 period received their services from the "cited" grantees, and nearly 11,000 more from the other "religiously affiliated" institutions. App. 748-756. At a minimum, these figures already demonstrate substantial constitutionally suspect funding through the AFLA, rendering the majority's expectations unrealistic and unwarranted. And, because of the Government's failure to require grantees to report on subgrant and subcontract arrangements, *id., at 745*, we only can speculate as to what additional public funds subsidized the religious missions of groups that the secular grantees brought in to fulfill their statutory obligation to involve religious organizations in the provision of services. See § 300z-5(a)(21)(B).

[4] The Court leaves for the District Court on remand the "consideration of the evidence presented by appellees insofar as it sheds light on the manner in which the statute is presently being administered," *ante*, at 621, conceding, as it must, that the factual record could paint a troubling picture about the true effect of the AFLA as a whole. See *Witters v. Washington Dept. of Services for the Blind, 474 U.S. 481, 488 (1986)* (finding significant that "nothing in the record indicates that, if petitioner succeeds, any significant portion of the aid expended under the . . . program as a whole will end up flowing to religious education");

II

Before proceeding to apply Lemon's three-part analysis to the AFLA, I pause to note a particular flaw in the majority's method. A central premise of the majority opinion seems to be that the primary means of ascertaining whether a statute that appears to be neutral on its face in fact has the effect of advancing religion is to determine whether aid flows to "pervasively sectarian" institutions. See *ante*, at 609-610, 616, 621. This misplaced focus leads the majority to ignore the substantial body of case law the Court has developed in analyzing programs providing direct aid to parochial schools, and to rely almost exclusively on the few cases in which the Court has upheld the supplying of aid to private colleges, including religiously affiliated institutions.

"Pervasively sectarian," a vaguely defined term of art, has its roots in this Court's recognition that government must not engage in detailed supervision of the inner workings of religious institutions, and the Court's sensible distaste for the "picture of state inspectors prowling the halls of parochial schools and auditing classroom instruction," *Lemon v. Kurtzman, 403 U.S.*, at *650* (BRENNAN, J., concurring); see also *Aguilar v. Felton, 473 U.S. 402, 411 (1985)*; *Roemer v. Maryland Public Works Board, 426 U.S. 736, 762 (1976)* (plurality opinion). Under the "effects" prong of the *Lemon* test, the Court has used one variant or another of the pervasively sectarian concept to explain why any but the most indirect forms of government aid to such institutions would necessarily have the effect of advancing religion. For example, in *Meek v. Pittenger, 421 U.S. 349, 365 (1975)*, the Court explained:

> "[I]t would simply ignore reality to attempt to separate secular educational functions from the predominantly religious role performed by many of Pennsylvania's churchrelated elementary and secondary schools and to then characterize Act 195 as channeling aid to the secular without providing direct aid to the sectarian."

See also *Hunt v. McNair, 413 U.S. 734, 743 (1973)*.

Aguilar v. Felton, 473 U.S. 402, 412, n. 8 (1985) ("'If any significant number of the ... schools create the risks described in *Meek*, *Meek* applies'"), quoting *Felton v. Secretary, United States Dept. of Education, 739 F. 2d 48, 70 (CA2 1984)*; *Widmar v. Vincent, 454 U.S. 263, 275 (1981)* (noting absence of empirical evidence that religious groups would dominate university's open forum).

I fully agree with the majority's determination that appellees have standing as taxpayers to challenge the operation of the AFLA, *ante*, at 618-620, and note that appellees may yet prevail on remand.

The majority first skews the *Establishment Clause* analysis by adopting a cramped view of what constitutes a pervasively sectarian institution. Perhaps because most of the Court's decisions in this area have come in the context of aid to parochial schools, which traditionally have been characterized as pervasively sectarian, the majority seems to equate the characterization with the institution.[5] In support of that illusion, the majority relies heavily on three cases in which the Court has upheld direct government funding to liberal arts colleges with some religious affiliation, noting that such colleges were not "pervasively sectarian." But the happenstance that the few cases in which direct-aid statutes have been upheld have concerned religiously affiliated liberal arts colleges no more suggests that only parochial schools should be considered "pervasively sectarian," than it suggests that the only religiously affiliated institutions that may ever receive direct government funding are private liberal arts colleges. In fact, the cases on which the majority relies have stressed that the institutions' "*predominant* higher education mission is to provide their students with a *secular* education." *Tilton v. Richardson, 403 U.S. 672, 687 (1971)* (emphasis added); see *Roemer v. Maryland Public Works Board, 426 U.S., at 755* (noting "high degree of institutional autonomy" and that "the encouragement of spiritual development is only one secondary objective of each college") (internal quotations omitted); *Hunt v. McNair, 413 U.S., at 744* (finding "no basis to conclude that the College's operations are oriented significantly towards sectarian rather than secular education"). In sharp contrast, the District Court here concluded that AFLA grantees and participants included "organizations with institutional ties to religious denominations *and corporate requirements that the organizations abide by and not contradict religious doctrines.* In addition, other recipients of AFLA funds, while not explicitly affiliated with a religious denomination, are religiously inspired *and dedicated to teaching the dogma that inspired them*" (emphasis added). *657 F. Supp., at 1564*. On a continuum of "sectarianism" running from parochial schools at one end to the colleges funded by the statutes upheld in *Tilton, Hunt,* and *Roemer* at the other, the AFLA grantees described by the District Court clearly are much closer to the former than to the latter.

---

[5] In rejecting the claim that the AFLA leads to excessive government entanglement with religion, the Court declines "to assume that the religious organizations which may receive grants are 'pervasively sectarian' in the same sense as the Court has held parochial schools to be." *Ante*, at 616. With respect to the claim that the AFLA is unconstitutional at least as applied, if not on its face, the Court -- apparently unsatisfied with findings the District Court already made to that very effect -- instructs that on remand, appellees may show that "AFLA aid is flowing to grantees that can be considered 'pervasively sectarian' religious institutions, such as we have held parochial schools to be." *Ante*, at 621.

More importantly, the majority also errs in suggesting that the inapplicability of the label is generally dispositive. While a plurality of the Court has framed the inquiry as "whether an institution is so 'pervasively sectarian' that it may receive no direct state aid of any kind," *Roemer v. Maryland Public Works Board, 426 U.S., at 758,* the Court never has treated the absence of such a finding as a license to disregard the potential for impermissible fostering of religion. The characterization of an institution as "pervasively sectarian" allows us to eschew further inquiry into the use that will be made of direct government aid. In that sense, it is a sufficient, but not a necessary, basis for a finding that a challenged program creates an unacceptable *Establishment Clause* risk. The label thus serves in some cases as a proxy for a more detailed analysis of the institution, the nature of the aid, and the manner in which the aid may be used.

The voluminous record compiled by the parties and reviewed by the District Court illustrates the manner in which the AFLA has been interpreted and implemented by the agency responsible for the aid program, and eliminates whatever need there might be to speculate about what kind of institutions *might* receive funds and how they *might* be selected; the record explains the nature of the activities funded with Government money, as well as the content of the educational programs and materials developed and disseminated. There is no basis for ignoring the volumes of depositions, pleadings, and undisputed facts reviewed by the District Court simply because the recipients of the Government funds may not in every sense resemble parochial schools.

III

As is often the case, it is the effect of the statute, rather than its purpose, that creates *Establishment Clause* problems. Because I have no meaningful disagreement with the majority's discussion of the AFLA's essentially secular purpose, and because I find the statute's effect of advancing religion dispositive, I turn to that issue directly.

A

The majority's holding that the AFLA is not unconstitutional on its face marks a sharp departure from our precedents. While aid programs providing nonmonetary, verifiably secular aid have been upheld notwithstanding the indirect effect they might have on the allocation of an institution's own funds for religious activities, see, *e. g., Board of Education v. Allen, 392 U.S. 236 (1968)* (lending secular textbooks to parochial schools); *Everson v. Board of Education, 330 U.S. 1 (1947)* (providing bus services to parochial schools), direct cash subsidies have always required much closer scrutiny into the expected and potential uses of the funds, and much greater guarantees that the funds would not be used inconsistently with the *Establishment Clause*. Parts of the AFLA prescribing various forms of outreach, education, and counseling services [6] specifically authorize the expenditure of funds in ways previously held unconstitutional. For example, the Court has upheld the use of public funds to support a parochial school's purchase of secular textbooks already approved for use in public schools, see *Wolman v. Walter, 433 U.S. 229, 236-238 (1977)*; *Meek v. Pittenger, 421 U.S., at 359-362*, or its grading and administering of state-prepared tests, *Committee for Public Education & Religious Liberty v. Regan, 444 U.S. 646 (1980)*. When the books, teaching materials, or examinations were to be selected or designed by the private schools themselves, however, the Court consistently has held that such government aid risked advancing religion impermissibly. See, *e. g., Wolman v. Walter, 433 U.S., at 248-251*; *Levitt v. Committee for Public Education & Religious Liberty, 413 U.S. 472 (1973)*; *Lemon v. Kurtzman, 403 U.S., at 620-621*. The teaching materials that may be purchased, developed, or disseminated with AFLA funding are in no way restricted to those already selected and approved for use in secular contexts. [7]

Notwithstanding the fact that Government funds are paying for religious organizations to teach and counsel impressionable adolescents on a highly sensitive subject of considerable religious significance, often on the premises of a church or

---

[6] The District Court observed that 9 of 17 "necessary services," see § 300z-1(a)(4), expressly involved some sort of education, counseling, or an intimately related service. *657 F. Supp., at 1562*.

[7] Thus, for example, until discovery began in this lawsuit, St. Ann's, a home for unmarried pregnant teenagers, operated by the Order of the Daughters of Charity and owned by the Archdiocese of Washington, D.C., purchased books containing Catholic doctrine on chastity, masturbation, homosexuality, and abortion, using AFLA funds, and distributed them to participants. See App. 336, 354-359, 362. Catholic Family Services of Amarillo, Tex., used a curriculum outline guide for AFLA-funded parent workshops with explicit theological references, as well as religious "reference" materials, including the film "Everyday Miracle," described as "depicting the miracle of the process of human reproduction as a gift from God." Record 155, Plaintiffs' Appendix, Vol. IV, p. 119. The District Court concluded:

"The record demonstrates that some grantees have included explicitly religious materials, or a curriculum that indicates an intent to teach theological and secular views on sexual conduct, in their HHS-approved grant proposals. . . . One such application, which was funded for one year, included a program designed, *inter alia*, 'to communicate the Catholic diocese, Mormon (Church of Jesus Christ of Latter Day Saints) and Young Buddhist Association's approaches to sex education.'" *657 F. Supp., at 1565-1566*.

parochial school and without any effort to remove religious symbols from the sites, *657 F. Supp., at 1565-1566*, the majority concludes that the AFLA is not facially invalid. The majority acknowledges the constitutional proscription on government-sponsored religious indoctrination but, on the basis of little more than an indefensible assumption that AFLA recipients are not pervasively sectarian and consequently are presumed likely to comply with statutory and constitutional mandates, dismisses as insubstantial the risk that indoctrination will enter counseling. *Ante*, at 611-612. Similarly, the majority rejects the District Court's conclusion that the subject matter renders the risk of indoctrination unacceptable, and does so, it says, because "the likelihood that some of the religious institutions who receive AFLA funding will agree with the message that Congress intended to deliver to adolescents through the AFLA" does not amount to the advancement of religion. *Ante*, at 613. I do not think the statute can be so easily and conveniently saved.

(1)

The District Court concluded that asking religious organizations to teach and counsel youngsters on matters of deep religious significance, yet expect them to refrain from making reference to religion is both foolhardy and unconstitutional. The majority's rejection of this view is illustrative of its doctrinal misstep in relying so heavily on the college-funding cases. The District Court reasoned:

> "To presume that AFLA counselors from religious organizations can put their beliefs aside when counseling an adolescent on matters that are part of religious doctrine is simply unrealistic. . . . Even if it were possible, government would tread impermissibly on religious liberty merely by suggesting that religious organizations instruct *on doctrinal matters* without any conscious or unconscious reference to that doctrine. Moreover, the statutory scheme is fraught with the possibility that religious beliefs might infuse instruction and never be detected by the impressionable and unlearned adolescent to whom the instruction is directed" (emphasis in original). *657 F. Supp., at 1563.*

The majority rejects the District Court's assumptions as unwarranted outside the context of a pervasively sectarian institution. In doing so, the majority places inordinate weight on the nature of the institution receiving the funds, and ignores altogether the targets of the funded message and the nature of its content.

I find it nothing less than remarkable that the majority relies on statements expressing confidence that administrators of religiously affiliated liberal arts colleges would not breach statutory proscriptions and use government funds earmarked "for secular purposes only," to finance theological instruction or religious worship, see *ante*, at 612, citing *Roemer, 426 U.S., at 760-761*, and *Tilton, 403 U.S., at 682*, in order to reject a challenge based on the risk of indoctrination inherent in "educational services relating to family life and problems associated with adolescent premarital sexual relations," or "outreach services to families of adolescents to discourage sexual relations among unemancipated minors." *§§ 300z-1(a)(4)(G), (O)*. The two situations are simply not comparable. [8]

The AFLA, unlike any statute this Court has upheld, pays for teachers and counselors, employed by and subject to the direction of religious authorities, to educate impressionable young minds on issues of religious moment. Time and again we have recognized the difficulties inherent in asking even the best-intentioned individuals in such positions to make "a total separation between secular teaching and religious doctrine." *Lemon v. Kurtzman, 403 U.S., at 619*. Accord, *Levitt v. Committee for Public Education & Religious Liberty, 413 U.S., at 481*; *Meek v. Pittenger, 421 U.S., at 370-371*; *Roemer v. Maryland Public Works Board, 426 U.S., at 749* (plurality opinion); *Wolman v. Walter, 433 U.S., at 254*; *Grand Rapids School District v. Ball, 473 U.S. 373, 388 (1985)*. Where the targeted audience is composed of children, of course, the Court's insistence on adequate safeguards has always been greatest. See, *e. g., Grand Rapids School District v. Ball, 473 U.S., at 383, 390*; *Committee for Public Education & Religious Liberty v. Nyquist, 413 U.S. 756, 796-798 (1973)*, *Lemon v. Kurtzman, 403 U.S., at 622-624*. In those cases in which funding of colleges with religious affiliations has been upheld, the Court has relied on the assumption that "college students are less impressionable and less susceptible to religious indoctrination. . . . The skepticism of the college student is not an

---

[8] In addition to funding activity of a wholly different character, the AFLA differs from the statutes reviewed in those cases in its expressed solicitude for the participation of religious organizations. In *Tilton v. Richardson, 403 U.S. 672, 675 (1971)*, the statute "authorize[d] federal grants and loans to 'institutions of higher education' for the construction of a wide variety of 'academic facilities'"; in *Hunt v. McNair, 413 U.S. 734, 736 (1973)*, South Carolina had established a state agency "the purpose of which [was] 'to assist institutions for higher education in the construction, financing and refinancing of projects' . . . primarily through the issuance of revenue bonds"; in *Roemer v. Maryland Public Works Board, 426 U.S. 736, 740 (1976)* (plurality opinion), the State provided funding to "'any [qualified] private institution of higher learning within the State of Maryland.'" The AFLA, in contrast, expressly requires applicants for grants to describe how they "will, as appropriate in the provision of services . . . (B) involve religious . . . organizations." § 300z-5(a)(21)(B), and the legislative history conclusively shows that Congress intended religious organizations to participate as grantees and as participants under grants awarded to other organizations. See S. Rep. No. 97-161, pp. 15-16 (1981).

inconsiderable barrier to any attempt or tendency to subvert the congressional objectives and limitations" (footnote omitted). *Tilton v. Richardson, 403 U.S., at 686* (plurality opinion). See also *Widmar v. Vincent, 454 U.S. 263, 274, n. 14 (1981)* ("University students are, of course, young adults. They are less impressionable than younger students and should be able to appreciate that the University's policy is one of neutrality toward religion").

(2)

By observing that the alignment of the statute and the religious views of the grantees do not render the AFLA a statute which funds "specifically religious activity," the majority makes light of the religious significance in the counseling provided by some grantees. Yet this is a dimension that Congress specifically sought to capture by enlisting the aid of religious organizations in battling the problems associated with teenage pregnancy. See S. Rep. No. 97-161, pp. 15-16 (1981); S. Rep. No. 98-496, pp. 9-10 (1984). Whereas there may be secular values promoted by the AFLA, including the encouragement of adoption and premarital chastity and the discouragement of abortion, it can hardly be doubted that when promoted in theological terms by religious figures, those values take on a religious nature. Not surprisingly, the record is replete with observations to that effect.[9] It

---

[9] The District Court's conclusion, which I find compelling, is that the AFLA requires teaching and counseling "on matters inseparable from religious dogma." *657 F. Supp., at 1565.* This conclusion is borne out by statements of AFLA administrators and participants. For example, the Lyon County, Kan., Health Department's grant proposal acknowledges that "[s]uch sensitive and intimate material cannot be presented without touching on . . . religious beliefs." Record 155, Plaintiffs' Appendix, Vol. IV, p. 221. Patrick J. Sheeran, the Director of the Division of Program Development and Monitoring in the Office of Adolescent Pregnancy Programs explained:

"Broadly speaking, I find it hard to find any kind of educational or value type of program that doesn't have some kind of basic religious or ethical foundation, and while a sex education class may be completely separate from a religious class, it might relate back to it in terms of principles that are embedded philosophically or theologically or religiously in another discipline." App. 122.

Mr. Sheeran's views were echoed by Dr. Paul Simmons, a Baptist clergyman and professor of Christian Ethics:

"The very purpose of religion is to transmit certain values, and those values associated with sex, marriage, chastity and abortion involve religious values and theological or doctrinal issues. In encouraging premarital chastity, it would be extremely difficult for a religiously

should be undeniable by now that religious dogma may not be employed by government even to accomplish laudable secular purposes such as "the promotion of moral values, the contradiction to the materialistic trends of our times, the perpetuation of our institutions and the teaching of literature." *Abington School District v. Schempp,* 374 U.S. 203, 223 (1963) (holding unconstitutional daily reading of Bible verses and recitation of the Lord's Prayer in public schools); *Stone v. Graham,* 449 U.S. 39 (1980) (holding unconstitutional posting of Ten Commandments despite notation explaining secular application thereof). [10]

It is true, of course, that the Court has recognized that the Constitution does not prohibit the government from supporting secular social-welfare services solely because they are provided by a religiously affiliated organization. See *ante,* at 609. But such recognition has been closely tied to the nature of the subsidized social service: "the State may send a cleric, indeed even a clerical order, to perform *a wholly secular task*" (emphasis added). *Roemer v. Maryland Public Works Board,* 426 U.S., at 746 (plurality opinion). There is a very real and important difference between running a soup kitchen or a hospital, and counseling pregnant teenagers on how to make the difficult decisions facing them. The risk of advancing religion at public

---

affiliated group not to impart its own religious values and doctrinal perspectives when teaching a subject that has always been central to its religious teachings." *Id.,* at 597.

In any event, regardless of the efforts AFLA teachers and counselors may have undertaken in attempting to separate their religious convictions from the advice they actually dispensed to participating teenagers, the District Court found that "the overwhelming number of comments shows that program participants believed that these federally funded programs were also sponsored by the religious denomination." *657 F. Supp.,* at 1566.

[10] Religion plays an important role to many in our society. By enlisting its aid in combating certain social ills, while imposing the restrictions required by the *First Amendment* on the use of public funds to promote religion, we risk secularizing and demeaning the sacred enterprise. Whereas there is undoubtedly a role for churches of all denominations in helping prevent the problems often associated with early sexual activity and unplanned pregnancies, any attempt to confine that role within the strictures of a government-sponsored secular program can only taint the religious mission with a "corrosive secularism." *Grand Rapids School District v. Ball,* 473 U.S. 373, 385 (1985). The *First Amendment* protects not only the State from being captured by the Church, but also protects the Church from being corrupted by the State and adopted for its purposes. A government program that provides funds for religious organizations to carry out secular tasks inevitably risks promoting "the pernicious tendency of a state subsidy to tempt religious schools to compromise their religious mission without wholly abandoning it." *Roemer v. Maryland Public Works Board,* 426 U.S., at 775 (STEVENS, J., dissenting); see also *Lynch v. Donnelly,* 465 U.S. 668, 726-727 (1984) (BLACKMUN, J., dissenting).

expense, and of creating an appearance that the government is endorsing the medium and the message, is much greater when the religious organization is directly engaged in pedagogy, with the express intent of shaping belief and changing behavior, than where it is neutrally dispensing medication, food, or shelter.[11]

There is also, of course, a fundamental difference between government's employing religion *because* of its unique appeal to a higher authority and the transcendental nature of its message, and government's enlisting the aid of religiously committed individuals or organizations without regard to their sectarian motivation. In the latter circumstance, religion plays little or no role; it merely explains why the individual or organization has chosen to get involved in the publicly funded program. In the former, religion is at the core of the subsidized activity, and it affects the manner in which the "service" is dispensed. For some religious organizations, the answer to a teenager's question "Why shouldn't I have an abortion?" or "Why shouldn't I use barrier contraceptives?" will undoubtedly be different from an answer based solely on secular considerations.[12] Public funds may not be used to endorse the religious message.

B

---

[11] In arguing that providing "social welfare services" is categorically different from educating schoolchildren for *Establishment Clause* purposes, appellants relied heavily on *Bradfield v. Roberts, 175 U.S. 291 (1899)*, a case in which the Court upheld the appropriation of money for the construction of two buildings to be part of a religiously affiliated hospital. Unlike the AFLA, however, which seeks "to promote self discipline and other prudent approaches to the problem of adolescent premarital sexual relations," § 300z(b)(1), the Act of Congress by which the hospital at issue in *Bradfield* had been incorporated expressed that "'the specific and limited object of its creation' is the opening and keeping a hospital in the city of Washington for the care of such sick and invalid persons as may place themselves under the treatment and care of the corporation." *175 U.S., at 299-300*.

[12] Employees of some grantees must follow the directives set forth in a booklet entitled "The Ethical and Religious Directives for Catholic Health Facilities," approved by the Committee on Doctrine of the National Conference of Catholic Bishops. App. 526, 540-544. Solely because of religious dictates, some AFLA grantees teach and refer teenagers for only "natural family planning," which "has never been used successfully with teenagers," *id., at 535*, and may not refer couples to programs that offer artificial methods of birth control, because those programs conflict with the teachings of the Roman Catholic Church. *Id.*, at 407, 628. One nurse midwife working at an AFLA program was even reprimanded for contravening the hospital's religious views on sex when she answered "yes" to a teenager who asked, as a medical matter, whether she could have sex during pregnancy. *Id., at 552*.

The problems inherent in a statutory scheme specifically designed to involve religious organizations in a governmentfunded pedagogical program are compounded by the lack of any statutory restrictions on the use of federal tax dollars to promote religion. Conscious of the remarkable omission from the AFLA of any restriction whatsoever on the use of public funds for sectarian purposes, the Court disingenuously argues that we have "never stated that a *statutory* restriction is constitutionally required." *Ante*, at 614. In *Tilton v. Richardson*, this Court upheld a statute providing grants and loans to colleges for the construction of academic facilities because it "expressly prohibit[ed] their use for religious instruction, training, or worship . . . and the record show[ed] that some church-related institutions ha[d] been required to disgorge benefits for failure to obey" the restriction, *403 U.S., at 679-680*, but severed and struck a provision of the statute that permitted the restriction to lapse after 20 years. The *Tilton* Court noted that the statute required applicants to provide assurances only that use of the funded facility would be limited to secular purposes for the initial 20-year period, and that this limitation, "obviously opens the facility to use for any purpose at the end of that period." *Id., at 683*. Because they expired after 20 years, "the statute's enforcement provisions [were] inadequate to ensure that the impact of the federal aid will not advance religion." *Id., at 682*.

The majority interprets *Tilton* "to indicate that the constitutional limitations on use of federal funds, as embodied in the statutory restriction, could not simply 'expire'" after 20 years, but concludes that the absence of a statutory restriction in the AFLA is not troubling, because "there is also no intimation in the statute that at some point, or for some grantees, religious uses are permitted." *Ante*, at 614. Although there is something to the notion that the lifting of a pre-existing restriction may be more likely to be perceived as affirmative authorization than would the absence of any restriction at all, there was in *Tilton* no provision that stated that after 20 years facilities built under the aid program could be converted into chapels. What there was in *Tilton* was an express *statutory* provision, which lapsed, leaving no restrictions; it was that *vacuum* that the Court found constitutionally impermissible. In the AFLA, by way of contrast, there is a vacuum right from the start.[13]

---

[13] This vacuum is particularly noticeable when we consider the pains to which Congress went to specify other restrictions on the use of AFLA funds. For example, the AFLA expressly provides:

"Grants or payments may be made only to programs or projects which do not provide abortions or abortion counseling or referral, or which do not subcontract with or make any payment to any person who provides abortions or abortion counseling or referral, except that any such program or project may provide referral for abortion counseling to a pregnant

If *Tilton* were indeed the only indication that cash-grant programs must include prohibitions on the use of public funds to advance or endorse religion, one might argue more plausibly that ordinary reporting requirements, in conjunction with some presumption that Government agencies administer federal programs in a constitutional fashion, [14] might suffice to protect a statute against facial challenge.

---

adolescent if such adolescent and the parents or guardians of such adolescent request such referral; and grants may be made only to projects or programs which do not advocate, promote, or encourage abortion." § 300z-10. The AFLA also sets certain conditions on funding for family planning services, § 300z-3(b)(1), and requires of applicants some 18 separate "assurances" covering everything from confidentiality of patient records, § 300z-5(a)(11), to a commitment that the applicant will "make every reasonable effort . . . to secure from eligible persons payment for services in accordance with [structured fee] schedules," § 300z-5(a)(16)(B). Yet nowhere in the statute is there a single restriction on the use of federal funds to promote or advance religion. See *ante*, at 614-615.

[14] Appellees have challenged that presumption here, calling into question the manner in which grantees were selected and supervised. Mr. Sheeran, the Director of the Division of Program Development and Monitoring in the Office of Adolescent Pregnancy Programs, testified that he was surprised at the lack of experience, yet high proportion of religious affiliation, among those selected to read and evaluate grant applications. App. 98. Some of the reader's comments strongly suggest *they* considered religious indoctrination indispensable to achieve the AFLA's stated purpose, see, *e. g., id., at 509*; Record 155, Plaintiffs' Appendix Vol. I, pp. 354-355, and that evidence of no involvement by religious organizations was a factor in rejecting applications, see, *e. g.*, Record 155, Plaintiffs' Appendix, Vol. I-A, pp. 505D, 505E, 505G; Record 155, Plaintiffs' Appendix, Vol. I, pp. 340, 346.

Despite the clear religious mission of many applicants, pre-award investigations or admonitions against the use of AFLA funds to promote religion were minimal. Mr. Sheeran was instructed to call Catholic grantees already selected for funding, and obtain assurances that the grant money would not be used for "teaching of morals, dogmas, [or] religious principles." App. 107. The calls lasted two or three minutes, and involved no detailed discussion of the use of church and parochial school facilities, or religious literature. *Id., at 112-113.*

The District Court found that the problems that should have been noted at the application stage remained uncured in implementation:

"Nor do the facts suggest that the programs in operation cured the *First Amendment* problems evident from these approved grant applications. At least one grantee actually included 'spiritual counseling' in its AFLA program. Other AFLA programs used curricula with explicitly religious materials. In addition, a very large number of AFLA programs took place on sites adorned with religious symbols . . . .

That, however, is simply not the case. In *Committee for Public Education & Religious Liberty v. Regan, 444 U.S. 646 (1980)*, for example, the Court upheld a state program whereby private schools were reimbursed for the actual cost of administering state-required tests. The statute specifically required that no payments be made for religious instruction and incorporated an extensive auditing system. The Court warned, however: "Of course, under the relevant cases the outcome would likely be different were there no effective means for insuring that the cash reimbursements would cover only secular services." *Id., at 659*. In this regard, the *Regan* Court merely echoed and reaffirmed what was already well established. In *Committee for Public Education & Religious Liberty* v. *Nyquist*, the Court explained:

> "Nothing in the statute, for instance, bars a qualifying school from paying out of state funds the salaries of employees who maintain the school chapel, or the cost of renovating classrooms in which religion is taught, or the cost of heating and lighting those same facilities. *Absent appropriate restrictions* on expenditures for these and similar purposes, *it simply cannot be denied* that this section has a primary effect that advances religion in that it subsidizes directly the religious activities of sectarian elementary and secondary schools" (emphasis added). *413 U.S., at 774*.

See *id., at 780* ("In the absence of an effective means of guaranteeing that the state aid derived from public funds will be used exclusively for secular, neutral, and nonideological purposes, it is clear from our cases that direct aid in whatever form is invalid"); *Lemon v. Kurtzman, 403 U.S., at 621* ("The history of government grants of a continuing cash subsidy indicates that such programs have almost always been accompanied by varying measures of control and surveillance"). See also *Roemer v. Maryland Public Works Board, 426 U.S., at 760* (upholding grant program containing statutory restriction on using state funds for "sectarian purposes"); *Hunt v. McNair, 413 U.S., at 744* (noting that the statute at issue "specifically states that a project 'shall not include' any buildings or facilities used for religious purposes"). [15]

"Similarly, the record reveals that some grantees attempted to evade restrictions they perceived on AFLA-funded religious teaching by establishing programs in which an AFLA-funded staffer's presentations would be immediately followed, in the same room and in the staffer's presence, by a program presented by a member of a religious order and dedicated to presentation of religious views on the subject covered by the AFLA staffer" (citations omitted). *657 F. Supp., at 1566.*

[15] Indeed, the AFLA stands out among similar grant programs, precisely because of the absence of such restrictions. Cf., *e. g.*, 20 U. S. C. § 27 (support for vocational education); 20 U. S. C. § 241-1(a)(4) (federal disaster relief for local education agencies); 20 U. S. C. §

Despite the glaring omission of a restriction on the use of funds for religious purposes, the Court attempts to resurrect the AFLA by noting a legislative intent not to promote religion, and observing that various reporting provisions of the statute "create a mechanism whereby the Secretary can police the grants." *Ante*, at 615. However effective this "mechanism" might prove to be in enforcing clear statutory directives, it is of no help where, as here, no restrictions are found on the face of the statute, and the Secretary has not promulgated any by regulation. Indeed, the only restriction on the use of AFLA funds for religious purposes is found in the Secretary's "Notice of Grant Award" sent to grantees, which specifies that public funds may not be used to "teach or promote religion," *657 F. Supp., at 1563, n. 13*, and apparently even that clause was not inserted until after this litigation was underway. Furthermore, the "enforcement" of the limitation on sectarian use of AFLA funds, such as it is, lacks any bite. There is no procedure pursuant to which funds used to promote religion must be refunded to the Government, as there was, for example, in *Tilton v. Richardson, 403 U.S., at 682*.

Indeed, nothing in the AFLA precludes the funding of even "pervasively sectarian" organizations, whose work by definition cannot be segregated into religious and secular categories. And, unlike a pre-enforcement challenge, where there is no record to review, or a limited challenge to a specific grant, where the Court is reluctant to invalidate a statute "in anticipation that particular applications may result in unconstitutional use of funds," *Roemer v. Maryland Public Works Board, 426 U.S., at 761*, in this litigation the District Court expressly found that funds have gone to pervasively sectarian institutions and tax dollars have been used for the teaching of religion. *657 F. Supp., at 1564*. Moreover, appellees have specifically called into question the manner in which the grant program was administered and grantees were selected. See n. 14, *supra*. These objections cannot responsibly be answered by reliance on the Secretary's enforcement mechanism. See, *e. g., Levitt v. Committee for Public Education & Religious Liberty, 413 U.S., at 480* ("[T]he State is constitutionally compelled to assure that the state-supported activity is not being used for religious indoctrination"); *Lemon v. Kurtzman, 403 U.S., at 619* ("The State must be certain, given the Religion Clauses, that subsidized teachers do not inculcate religion").

1021(c) (assistance to college and research libraries); *20 U. S. C. § 1070e(c)(1)(B) (1982 ed., Supp. IV)* (assistance to institutions of higher education); *20 U. S. C. § 1134e(g) (1982 ed., Supp. IV)* (fellowships for graduate and professional study); *20 U. S. C. § 1210 (1982 ed. and Supp. IV)* (grants to adult education programs); *42 U. S. C. § 2753(b)(1)(C)* (college work-study grants); *42 U. S. C. § 5001(a)(2)* (grants to retired senior-citizen volunteer service programs).

C

By placing unsupportable weight on the "pervasively sectarian" label, and recharacterizing appellees' objections to the statute, the Court attempts to create an illusion of consistency between our prior cases and its present ruling that the AFLA is not facially invalid. But the Court ignores the unwavering vigilance that the Constitution requires against any law "respecting an establishment of religion," *U.S. Const., Amdt. 1,* which, as we have recognized time and again, calls for fundamentally conservative decisionmaking: our cases do not require a plaintiff to demonstrate that a government action *necessarily* promotes religion, but simply that it creates such a substantial risk. See, *e. g., Grand Rapids School District v. Ball,* 473 U.S., at 387 (observing a "substantial risk that, overtly or subtly, the religious message . . . will infuse the supposedly secular classes"); *Committee for Public Education & Religious Liberty v. Regan,* 444 U.S., at 656 (describing as "minimal" the chance that religious bias would enter process of granding state-drafted tests in secular subjects, given "complete" state safeguards); *Wolman v. Walter,* 433 U.S., at 254 (noting "unacceptable risk of fostering of religion" as "an inevitable byproduct" of teacher-accompanied field trips); *Meek v. Pittenger,* 421 U.S., at 372 (finding "potential for impermissible fostering of religion"); *Levitt v. Committee for Public Education & Religious Liberty,* 413 U.S., at 480 (finding dispositive "the substantial risk that . . . examinations, prepared by teachers under the authority of religious institutions, will be drafted with an eye, unconsciously or otherwise, to inculcate students in the religious precepts of the sponsoring church"); *Lemon v. Kurtzman,* 403 U.S., at 619 (finding "potential for impermissible fostering of religion"). Given the nature of the subsidized activity, the lack of adequate safeguards, and the chronicle of past experience with this statute, there is no room for doubt that the AFLA creates a substantial risk of impermissible fostering of religion.

IV

While it is evident that the AFLA does not pass muster under *Lemon*'s "effects" prong, the unconstitutionality of the statute becomes even more apparent when we consider the unprecedented degree of entanglement between Church and State required to prevent subsidizing the advancement of religion with AFLA funds. The majority's brief discussion of *Lemon*'s "entanglement" prong is limited to (a) criticizing it as a "**Catch-22**," and (b) concluding that because there is "no reason to assume that the religious organizations which may receive grants are 'pervasively sectarian' in the same sense as the Court has held parochial schools to be," there is no need to be concerned about the degree of monitoring which will be necessary to ensure compliance with the AFLA and the *Establishment Clause. Ante,* at 615-616. As to the former, although the majority is certainly correct that the Court's entanglement analysis has been criticized in the separate writings of some Members of the Court, the question whether a government program leads to "'an excessive government entanglement with religion'" nevertheless is and remains a part of the applicable constitutional inquiry. *Lemon v. Kurtzman, 403 U.S., at 613*, quoting *Walz v. Tax Comm'n, 397 U.S. 664, 674 (1970)*. I accept the majority's conclusion that "[t]here is no doubt that the monitoring of AFLA grants is necessary . . . to ensure that public money is to be spent . . . in a way that comports with the *Establishment Clause*," *ante*, at 615, but disagree with its easy characterization of entanglement analysis as a "***Catch-22***." To the extent any metaphor is helpful, I would be more inclined to characterize the Court's excessive entanglement decisions as concluding that to implement the required monitoring, we would have to kill the patient to cure what ailed him. See, *e. g., Lemon v. Kurtzman, 403 U.S., at 614-615; Meek v. Pittenger, 421 U.S., at 370; Aguilar v. Felton, 473 U.S., at 413-414*.

As to the Court's conclusion that our precedents do not indicate that the Secretary's monitoring will have to be exceedingly intensive or entangling, because the grant recipients are not sufficiently like parochial schools, I must disagree. As discussed above, the majority's excessive reliance on the distinction between the Court's parochial-school-aid cases and college-funding cases is unwarranted. *Lemon, Meek*, and *Aguilar* cannot be so conveniently dismissed solely because the majority declines to assume that the "pervasively sectarian" label can be applied here.

To determine whether a statute fosters excessive entanglement, a court must look at three factors: (1) the character and purpose of the institutions benefited; (2) the nature of the aid; and (3) the nature of the relationship between the government and the religious organization. See *Lemon v. Kurtzman, 403 U.S., at 614-615*. Thus, in *Lemon*, it was not solely the fact that teachers performed their duties within the four walls of the parochial school that rendered monitoring difficult and, in the end, unconstitutional. It seems inherent in the pedagogical function that there will be disagreements about what is or is not "religious" and which will require an intolerable degree of government intrusion and censorship.

> "What would appear to some to be essential to good citizenship might well for others border on or constitute instruction in religion. . . .
>
> . . .
>
> ". . . Unlike a book, a teacher cannot be inspected once so as to determine the extent and intent of his or her personal beliefs and subjective acceptance of the limitations imposed by the *First Amendment*." *Id., at 619.*

Accord, *Aguilar v. Felton, 473 U.S., at 413.* See also *New York v. Cathedral Academy, 434 U.S. 125, 133 (1977)* (noting that the State "would have to undertake a search for religious meaning in every classroom examination . . . . The prospect of church and state litigating in court about what does or does not have religious meaning touches the very core of the constitutional guarantee against religious establishment").

In *Roemer, Tilton,* and *Hunt,* the Court relied on "the ability of the State to identify and subsidize separate secular functions carried out at the school, *without on-the-site inspections being necessary to prevent diversion of the funds to sectarian purposes,*" Roemer v. Maryland Public Works Board, 426 U.S., at 765 (emphasis added), and on the fact that onetime grants require "no continuing financial relationships or dependencies, no annual audits, and no government analysis of an institution's expenditures on secular as distinguished from religious activities." *Tilton v. Richardson, 403 U.S., at 688.* AFLA grants, of course, are not simply one-time construction grants. As the majority readily acknowledges, the Secretary will have to "review the programs set up and run by the AFLA grantees[, including] a review of, for example, the educational materials that a grantee proposes to use." *Ante,* at 616-617. And, as the majority intimates, monitoring the use of AFLA funds will undoubtedly require more than the "minimal" inspection "necessary to ascertain that the facilities are devoted to secular education," *Tilton, 403 U.S., at 687.* Since teachers and counselors, unlike buildings, "are not necessarily religiously neutral, greater governmental surveillance would be required to guarantee that state salary aid would not in fact subsidize religious instruction." *Id., at 687-688.*

V

The AFLA, without a doubt, endorses religion. Because of its expressed solicitude for the participation of religious organizations in all AFLA programs in one form or another, the statute creates a symbolic and real partnership between the clergy and the fisc in addressing a problem with substantial religious overtones. Given the delicate subject matter and the impressionable audience, the risk that the AFLA will convey a message of Government endorsement of religion is overwhelming. The statutory language and the extensive record established in the District Court make clear that the problem lies in the statute and its systematically unconstitutional operation, and not merely in isolated instances of misapplication. I therefore would find the statute unconstitutional without remanding to the District Court. I trust, however, that after all its labors thus far, the District Court will not grow weary prematurely and read into the Court's decision a suggestion that the AFLA has been constitutionally implemented by the Government, for the majority deliberately eschews any review of the facts.[16] After such further proceedings as are now to be deemed appropriate, and after the District Court enters findings of fact on the basis of the testimony and documents entered into evidence, it may well decide, as I would today, that the AFLA as a whole indeed has been unconstitutionally applied.[17]

---

[16] JUSTICE KENNEDY, joined by JUSTICE SCALIA, would further constrain the District Court's consideration of the evidence as to how grantees spent their money, regardless of whether the grantee could be labeled "pervasively sectarian," see *ante*, at 624-625, asserting that "[t]he question in an as-applied challenge is not whether the entity is of a religious character." This statement comes without citation to authority and is contrary to the clear import of our cases. As ill-defined as the concept behind the "pervasively sectarian" label may be, this Court consistently has held, and reaffirms today, that "'[a]id normally may be thought to have a primary effect of advancing religion when it flows to an institution in which religion is so pervasive that a substantial portion of its functions are subsumed in the religious mission.'" *Ante*, at 610, quoting *Hunt v. McNair, 413 U.S., at 743.*

See also *Roemer v. Maryland Public Works Board, 426 U.S., at 758* ("[T]he question [is] whether an institution is so 'pervasively sectarian' that it may receive no direct state aid of any kind"). Indeed, to suggest that because a challenge is labeled "as-applied," the character of the institution receiving the aid loses its relevance is to misunderstand the very nature of the concept of a "pervasively sectarian" institution, which is based in part on the conclusion that the secular and sectarian activities of an institution are "inextricably intertwined," see *ante*, at 620, n. 16. Not surprisingly, the Court flatly rejects JUSTICE KENNEDY's suggestion, observing that "it will be open to appellees on remand to show that AFLA aid is flowing to grantees that can be considered 'pervasively sectarian' religious institutions." *Ante*, at 621.

[17] Appellees argued in the District Court, and here as cross-appellants, that the portions of the statute inviting the participation of religious organizations were not severable, and thus that the entire statute must be held unconstitutional. I take no position on this issue.

Price Waterhouse v. Hopkins

Supreme Court of the United States

October 31, 1988, Argued

May 1, 1989, Decided

No. 87-1167

490 U.S. 228
109 S. Ct. 1775
104 L. Ed. 2d 268

PRICE WATERHOUSE v. HOPKINS

CERTIORARI TO THE UNITED STATES COURT OF APPEALS FOR THE DISTRICT OF COLUMBIA CIRCUIT.

Kathryn A. Oberly argued the cause for petitioner. With her on the briefs were Paul M. Bator, Douglas A. Poe, Eldon Olson, and Ulric R. Sullivan.

James H. Heller argued the cause for respondent. With him on the brief was Douglas B. Huron.[*]

---

[*] *Robert E. Williams* and *Douglas S. McDowell* filed a brief for the Equal Employment Advisory Council as *amicus curiae* urging reversal.

Briefs of *amici curiae* urging affirmance were filed for the American Federation of Labor and Congress of Industrial Organizations by *Marsha S. Berzon* and *Laurence Gold;* for the American Psychological Association by *Donald N. Bersoff;* for the Committees on Civil Rights, Labor and Employment Law, and Sex and Law of the Association of the Bar of the City of New York by *Jonathan Lang, Eugene S. Friedman, Arthur Leonard,* and *Colleen McMahon;* and for the NOW Legal Defense and Education Fund et al. by *Sarah E. Burns, Lynn Hecht Schafran, Joan E. Bertin, John A. Powell,* and *Donna R. Lenhoff.*

Solicitor General Fried, Assistant Attorney General Reynolds, Deputy Solicitor General Merrill, Deputy Assistant Attorney General Clegg, Brian J. Martin, and *David K. Flynn* filed a brief for the United States as *amicus curiae.*

BRENNAN, J., announced the judgment of the Court and delivered an opinion, in which Marshall, Blackmun, and Stevens, JJ., joined.
WHITE, J., filed an opinion concurring in the judgment.
O'CONNOR, J., filed an opinion concurring in the judgment.
KENNEDY, J., filed a dissenting opinion, in which Rehnquist, C. J., and Scalia, J., joined.

JUSTICE BRENNAN announced the judgment of the Court and delivered an opinion, in which JUSTICE MARSHALL, JUSTICE BLACKMUN, and JUSTICE STEVENS join.

Ann Hopkins was a senior manager in an office of Price Waterhouse when she was proposed for partnership in 1982. She was neither offered nor denied admission to the partnership; instead, her candidacy was held for reconsideration the following year. When the partners in her office later refused to repropose her for partnership, she sued Price Waterhouse under Title VII of the Civil Rights Act of 1964, 78 Stat. 253, as amended, *42 U. S. C. § 2000e et seq.*, charging that the firm had discriminated against her on the basis of sex in its decisions regarding partnership. Judge Gesell in the Federal District Court for the District of Columbia ruled in her favor on the question of liability, *618 F. Supp. 1109 (1985)*, and the Court of Appeals for the District of Columbia Circuit affirmed. *263 U.S. App. D. C. 321, 825 F. 2d 458 (1987)*. We granted certiorari to resolve a conflict among the Courts of Appeals concerning the respective burdens of proof of a defendant and plaintiff in a suit under Title VII when it has been shown that an employment decision resulted from a mixture of legitimate and illegitimate motives. *485 U.S. 933 (1988)*.

I

At Price Waterhouse, a nationwide professional accounting partnership, a senior manager becomes a candidate for partnership when the partners in her local office submit her name as a candidate. All of the other partners in the firm are then invited to submit written comments on each candidate -- either on a "long" or a "short" form, depending on the partner's degree of exposure to the candidate. Not every partner in the firm submits comments on every candidate. After reviewing the comments and interviewing the partners who submitted them, the firm's Admissions Committee makes a recommendation to the Policy Board. This recommendation will be either that the firm accept the candidate for partnership, put her application on "hold," or deny her the promotion outright. The Policy Board then decides whether to submit the candidate's name to the entire partnership for a vote, to "hold" her candidacy, or to reject her. The recommendation of the Admissions Committee, and the decision of the Policy Board, are not controlled by fixed guidelines: a certain number of positive comments from partners will not guarantee a candidate's admission to the partnership, nor will a specific quantity of negative comments necessarily defeat her application. Price Waterhouse places no limit on the number of persons whom it will admit to the partnership in any given year.

Ann Hopkins had worked at Price Waterhouse's Office of Government Services in Washington, D. C., for five years when the partners in that office proposed her as a candidate for partnership. Of the 662 partners at the firm at that time, 7 were women. Of the 88 persons proposed for partnership that year, only 1 -- Hopkins -- was a woman. Forty-seven of these candidates were admitted to the partnership, 21 were rejected, and 20 -- including Hopkins -- were "held" for reconsideration the following year.[1] Thirteen of the 32 partners who had submitted comments on Hopkins supported her bid for partnership. Three partners recommended that her candidacy be placed on hold, eight stated that they did not have an informed opinion about her, and eight recommended that she be denied partnership.

In a jointly prepared statement supporting her candidacy, the partners in Hopkins' office showcased her successful 2-year effort to secure a $ 25 million contract with the Department of State, labeling it "an outstanding performance" and one that Hopkins carried out "virtually at the partner level." Plaintiff's Exh. 15. Despite Price Waterhouse's attempt at trial to minimize her contribution to this project, Judge Gesell specifically found that Hopkins had "played a key role in Price Waterhouse's successful effort to win a multi-million dollar contract with the Department of State." *618 F. Supp., at 1112.* Indeed, he went on, "[n]one of the other partnership candidates at Price Waterhouse that year had a comparable record in terms of successfully securing major contracts for the partnership." *Ibid.*

---

[1] Before the time for reconsideration came, two of the partners in Hopkins' office withdrew their support for her, and the office informed her that she would not be reconsidered for partnership. Hopkins then resigned. Price Waterhouse does not challenge the Court of Appeals' conclusion that the refusal to repropose her for partnership amounted to a constructive discharge. That court remanded the case to the District Court for further proceedings to determine appropriate relief, and those proceedings have been stayed pending our decision. Brief for Petitioner 15, n. 3. We are concerned today only with Price Waterhouse's decision to place Hopkins' candidacy on hold. Decisions pertaining to advancement to partnership are, of course, subject to challenge under Title VII. *Hishon v. King & Spalding, 467 U.S. 69 (1984).*

The partners in Hopkins' office praised her character as well as her accomplishments, describing her in their joint statement as "an outstanding professional" who had a "deft touch," a "strong character, independence and integrity." Plaintiff's Exh. 15. Clients appear to have agreed with these assessments. At trial, one official from the State Department described her as "extremely competent, intelligent," "strong and forthright, very productive, energetic and creative." Tr. 150. Another high-ranking official praised Hopkins' decisiveness, broadmindedness, and "intellectual clarity"; she was, in his words, "a stimulating conversationalist." *Id., at 156-157*. Evaluations such as these led Judge Gesell to conclude that Hopkins "had no difficulty dealing with clients and her clients appear to have been very pleased with her work" and that she "was generally viewed as a highly competent project leader who worked long hours, pushed vigorously to meet deadlines and demanded much from the multidisciplinary staffs with which she worked." *618 F. Supp., at 1112-1113*.

On too many occasions, however, Hopkins' aggressiveness apparently spilled over into abrasiveness. Staff members seem to have borne the brunt of Hopkins' brusqueness. Long before her bid for partnership, partners evaluating her work had counseled her to improve her relations with staff members. Although later evaluations indicate an improvement, Hopkins' perceived shortcomings in this important area eventually doomed her bid for partnership. Virtually all of the partners' negative remarks about Hopkins -- even those of partners supporting her -- had to do with her "inter-personal skills." Both "[s]upporters and opponents of her candidacy," stressed Judge Gesell, "indicated that she was sometimes overly aggressive, unduly harsh, difficult to work with and impatient with staff." *Id., at 1113*.

There were clear signs, though, that some of the partners reacted negatively to Hopkins' personality because she was a woman. One partner described her as "macho" (Defendant's Exh. 30); another suggested that she "overcompensated for being a woman" (Defendant's Exh. 31); a third advised her to take "a course at charm school" (Defendant's Exh. 27). Several partners criticized her use of profanity; in response, one partner suggested that those partners objected to her swearing only "because it's a lady using foul language." Tr. 321. Another supporter explained that Hopkins "ha[d] matured from a tough-talking somewhat masculine hard-nosed mgr to an authoritative, formidable, but much more appealing lady ptr candidate." Defendant's Exh. 27. But it was the man who, as Judge Gesell found, bore responsibility for explaining to Hopkins the reasons for the Policy Board's decision to place her candidacy on hold who delivered the *coup de grace:* in order to improve her chances for partnership, Thomas Beyer advised, Hopkins should "walk more femininely, talk more femininely, dress more femininely, wear make-up, have her hair styled, and wear jewelry." *618 F. Supp., at 1117.*

Dr. Susan Fiske, a social psychologist and Associate Professor of Psychology at Carnegie-Mellon University, testified at trial that the partnership selection process at Price Waterhouse was likely influenced by sex stereotyping. Her testimony focused not only on the overtly sex-based comments of partners but also on gender-neutral remarks, made by partners who knew Hopkins only slightly, that were intensely critical of her. One partner, for example, baldly stated that Hopkins was "universally disliked" by staff (Defendant's Exh. 27), and another described her as "consistently annoying and irritating" *(ibid.);* yet these were people who had had very little contact with Hopkins. According to Fiske, Hopkins' uniqueness (as the only woman in the pool of candidates) and the subjectivity of the evaluations made it likely that sharply critical remarks such as these were the product of sex stereotyping -- although Fiske admitted that she could not say with certainty whether any particular comment was the result of stereotyping. Fiske based her opinion on a review of the submitted comments, explaining that it was commonly accepted practice for social psychologists to reach this kind of conclusion without having met any of the people involved in the decisionmaking process.

In previous years, other female candidates for partnership also had been evaluated in sex-based terms. As a general matter, Judge Gesell concluded, "[c]andidates were viewed favorably if partners believed they maintained their femin[in]ity while becoming effective professional managers"; in this environment, "[t]o be identified as a 'women's lib[b]er' was regarded as [a] negative comment." *618 F. Supp., at 1117.* In fact, the judge found that in previous years "[o]ne partner repeatedly commented that he could not consider any woman seriously as a partnership candidate and believed that women were not even capable of functioning as senior managers -- yet the firm took no action to discourage his comments and recorded his vote in the overall summary of the evaluations." *Ibid.*

Judge Gesell found that Price Waterhouse legitimately emphasized interpersonal skills in its partnership decisions, and also found that the firm had not fabricated its complaints about Hopkins' interpersonal skills as a pretext for discrimination. Moreover, he concluded, the firm did not give decisive emphasis to such traits only because Hopkins was a woman; although there were male candidates who lacked these skills but who were admitted to partnership, the judge found that these candidates possessed other, positive traits that Hopkins lacked.

The judge went on to decide, however, that some of the partners' remarks about Hopkins stemmed from an impermissibly cabined view of the proper behavior of women, and that Price Waterhouse had done nothing to disavow reliance on such comments. He held that Price Waterhouse had unlawfully discriminated against Hopkins on the basis of sex by consciously giving credence and effect to partners' comments that resulted from sex stereotyping. Noting that Price Waterhouse could avoid equitable relief by proving by clear and convincing evidence that it would have placed Hopkins' candidacy on hold even absent this discrimination, the judge decided that the firm had not carried this heavy burden.

The Court of Appeals affirmed the District Court's ultimate conclusion, but departed from its analysis in one particular: it held that even if a plaintiff proves that discrimination played a role in an employment decision, the defendant will not be found liable if it proves, by clear and convincing evidence, that it would have made the same decision in the absence of discrimination. *263 U.S. App. D. C., at 333-334, 825 F. 2d, at 470-471.* Under this approach, an employer is not deemed to have violated Title VII if it proves that it would have made the same decision in the absence of an impermissible motive, whereas under the District Court's approach, the employer's proof in that respect only avoids equitable relief. We decide today that the Court of Appeals had the better approach, but that both courts erred in requiring the employer to make its proof by clear and convincing evidence.

II

The specification of the standard of causation under Title VII is a decision about the kind of conduct that violates that statute. According to Price Waterhouse, an employer violates Title VII only if it gives decisive consideration to an employee's gender, race, national origin, or religion in making a decision that affects that employee. On Price Waterhouse's theory, even if a plaintiff shows that her gender played a part in an employment decision, it is still her burden to show that the decision would have been different if the employer had not discriminated. In Hopkins' view, on the other hand, an employer violates the statute whenever it allows one of these attributes to play any part in an employment decision. Once a plaintiff shows that this occurred, according to Hopkins, the employer's proof that it would have made the same decision in the absence of discrimination can serve to limit equitable relief but not to avoid a finding of liability. [2] We conclude that, as often happens, the truth lies somewhere in between.

---

[2] This question has, to say the least, left the Circuits in disarray. The Third, Fourth, Fifth, and Seventh Circuits require a plaintiff challenging an adverse employment decision to show that, but for her gender (or race or religion or national origin), the decision would have been in her favor. See, *e. g., Bellissimo v. Westinghouse Electric Corp.,* 764 F. 2d 175, 179 (CA3 1985), cert. denied, 475 U.S. 1035 (1986); *Ross v. Communications Satellite Corp.,* 759 F. 2d 355, 365-366 (CA4 1985); *Peters v. Shreveport,* 818 F. 2d 1148, 1161 (CA5 1987); *McQuillen v. Wisconsin*

A

In passing Title VII, Congress made the simple but momentous announcement that sex, race, religion, and national origin are not relevant to the selection, evaluation, or compensation of employees.[3] Yet, the statute does not purport to limit the other qualities and characteristics that employers *may* take into account in making employment decisions. The converse, therefore, of "for cause" legislation, [4]

Education Assn. Council, 830 F. 2d 659, 664-665 (CA7 1987). The First, Second, Sixth, and Eleventh Circuits, on the other hand, hold that once the plaintiff has shown that a discriminatory motive was a "substantial" or "motivating" factor in an employment decision, the employer may avoid a finding of liability only by proving that it would have made the same decision even in the absence of discrimination. These courts have either specified that the employer must prove its case by a preponderance of the evidence or have not mentioned the proper standard of proof. See, *e. g., Fields v. Clark University*, 817 F. 2d 931, 936-937 (CA1 1987) ("motivating factor"); *Berl v. Westchester County*, 849 F. 2d 712, 714-715 (CA2 1988) ("substantial part"); *Terbovitz v. Fiscal Court of Adair County, Ky.*, 825 F. 2d 111, 115 (CA6 1987) ("motivating factor"); *Bell v. Birmingham Linen Service*, 715 F. 2d 1552, 1557 (CA11 1983). The Court of Appeals for the District of Columbia Circuit, as shown in this case, follows the same rule except that it requires that the employer's proof be clear and convincing rather than merely preponderant. *263 U.S. App. D. C. 321, 333-334, 825 F. 2d 458, 470-471 (1987)*; see also *Toney v. Block*, 227 U.S. App. D. C. 273, 275, 705 F. 2d 1364, 1366 (1983) (Scalia, J.) (it would be "destructive of the purposes of [Title VII] to require the plaintiff to establish . . . the difficult hypothetical proposition that, had there been no discrimination, the employment decision would have been made in his favor"). The Court of Appeals for the Ninth Circuit also requires clear and convincing proof, but it goes further by holding that a Title VII violation is made out as soon as the plaintiff shows that an impermissible motivation played a part in an employment decision -- at which point the employer may avoid reinstatement and an award of backpay by proving that it would have made the same decision in the absence of the unlawful motive. See, *e. g. Fadhl v. City and County of San Francisco*, 741 F. 2d 1163, 1165-1166 (1984) (Kennedy, J.) ("significant factor"). Last, the Court of Appeals for the Eighth Circuit draws the same distinction as the Ninth between the liability and remedial phases of Title VII litigation, but requires only a preponderance of the evidence from the employer. See, *e. g., Bibbs v. Block*, 778 F. 2d 1318, 1320-1324 (1985) (en banc) ("discernible factor").

[3] We disregard, for purposes of this discussion, the special context of affirmative action.

[4] Congress specifically declined to require that an employment decision have been "for cause" in order to escape an affirmative penalty (such as reinstatement or backpay) from a court. As introduced in the House, the bill that became Title VII forbade such affirmative relief if an "individual was . . . refused employment or advancement, or was suspended or discharged *for cause.*" H. R. Rep. No. 7152, 88th Cong., 1st Sess., 77 (1963) (emphasis added). The phrase "for cause" eventually was deleted in favor of the phrase "for any reason other

Title VII eliminates certain bases for distinguishing among employees while otherwise preserving employers' freedom of choice. This balance between employee rights and employer prerogatives turns out to be decisive in the case before us.

Congress' intent to forbid employers to take gender into account in making employment decisions appears on the face of the statute. In now-familiar language, the statute forbids an employer to "fail or refuse to hire or to discharge any individual, or otherwise to discriminate with respect to his compensation, terms, conditions, or privileges of employment," or to "limit, segregate, or classify his employees or applicants for employment in any way which would deprive or tend to deprive any individual of employment opportunities or otherwise adversely affect his status as an employee, *because of* such individual's . . . sex." *42 U. S. C. §§ 2000e-2(a)(1), (2)* (emphasis added). [5] We take these words to mean that gender must be irrelevant to employment decisions. To construe the words "because of" as colloquial shorthand for "but-for causation," as does Price Waterhouse, is to misunderstand them. [6]

But-for causation is a hypothetical construct. In determining whether a particular factor was a but-for cause of a given event, we begin by assuming that that factor was present at the time of the event, and then ask whether, even if that factor had been absent, the event nevertheless would have transpired in the same way. The present, active tense of the operative verbs of § 703(a)(1) ("to fail or refuse"), in

---

than" one of the enumerated characteristics. See 110 Cong. Rec. 2567-2571 (1964). Representative Celler explained that this substitution "specif[ied] cause"; in his view, a court "cannot find any violation of the act which is based on facts other . . . than discrimination on the grounds of race, color, religion, or national origin." *Id.*, at 2567.

[5] In this Court, Hopkins for the first time argues that Price Waterhouse violated § 703(a)(2) when it subjected her to a biased decisionmaking process that "tended to deprive" a woman of partnership on the basis of her sex. Since Hopkins did not make this argument below, we do not address it.

[6] We made passing reference to a similar question in *McDonald v. Santa Fe Trail Transportation Co., 427 U.S. 273, 282, n. 10 (1976)*, where we stated that when a Title VII plaintiff seeks to show that an employer's explanation for a challenged employment decision is pretextual, "no more is required to be shown than that race was a 'but for' cause." This passage, however, does not suggest that the plaintiff *must* show but-for cause; it indicates only that if she does so, she prevails. More important, *McDonald* dealt with the question whether the employer's stated reason for its decision was *the* reason for its action; unlike the case before us today, therefore, *McDonald* did not involve mixed motives. This difference is decisive in distinguishing this case from those involving "pretext." See *infra*, at 247, n. 12.

contrast, turns our attention to the actual moment of the event in question, the adverse employment decision. The critical inquiry, the one commanded by the words of § 703(a)(1), is whether gender was a factor in the employment decision *at the moment it was made*. Moreover, since we know that the words "because of" do not mean "*solely* because of," [7] we also know that Title VII meant to condemn even those decisions based on a mixture of legitimate and illegitimate considerations. When, therefore, an employer considers both gender and legitimate factors at the time of making a decision, that decision was "because of" sex and the other, legitimate considerations -- even if we may say later, in the context of litigation, that the decision would have been the same if gender had not been taken into account.

To attribute this meaning to the words "because of" does not, as the dissent asserts, *post*, at 282, divest them of causal significance. A simple example illustrates the point. Suppose two physical forces act upon and move an object, and suppose that either force acting alone would have moved the object. As the dissent would have it, *neither* physical force was a "cause" of the motion unless we can show that but for one or both of them, the object would not have moved; apparently both forces were simply "in the air" unless we can identify at least one of them as a but-for cause of the object's movement. *Ibid.* Events that are causally overdetermined, in other words, may not have any "cause" at all. This cannot be so.

We need not leave our common sense at the doorstep when we interpret a statute. It is difficult for us to imagine that, in the simple words "because of," Congress meant to obligate a plaintiff to identify the precise causal role played by legitimate and illegitimate motivations in the employment decision she challenges. We conclude, instead, that Congress meant to obligate her to prove that the employer relied upon sex-based considerations in coming to its decision.

Our interpretation of the words "because of" also is supported by the fact that Title VII does identify one circumstance in which an employer may take gender into account in making an employment decision, namely, when gender is a "bona fide occupational qualification [(BFOQ)] reasonably necessary to the normal operation of th[e] particular business or enterprise." *42 U. S. C. § 2000e-2(e)*. The only plausible inference to draw from this provision is that, in all other circumstances, a person's gender may not be considered in making decisions that affect her. Indeed, Title VII even forbids employers to make gender an indirect stumbling block to employment opportunities. An employer may not, we have held, condition employment opportunities on the satisfaction of facially neutral tests or

---

[7] Congress specifically rejected an amendment that would have placed the word "solely" in front of the words "because of." 110 Cong. Rec. 2728, 13837 (1964).

qualifications that have a disproportionate, adverse impact on members of protected groups when those tests or qualifications are not required for performance of the job. See *Watson v. Fort Worth Bank & Trust, 487 U.S. 977 (1988)*; *Griggs v. Duke Power Co., 401 U.S. 424 (1971).*

To say that an employer may not take gender into account is not, however, the end of the matter, for that describes only one aspect of Title VII. The other important aspect of the statute is its preservation of an employer's remaining freedom of choice. We conclude that the preservation of this freedom means that an employer shall not be liable if it can prove that, even if it had not taken gender into account, it would have come to the same decision regarding a particular person. The statute's maintenance of employer prerogatives is evident from the statute itself and from its history, both in Congress and in this Court.

To begin with, the existence of the BFOQ exception shows Congress' unwillingness to require employers to change the very nature of their operations in response to the statute. And our emphasis on "business necessity" in disparate-impact cases, see *Watson* and *Griggs*, and on "legitimate, nondiscriminatory reason[s]" in disparate-treatment cases, see *McDonnell Douglas Corp. v. Green, 411 U.S. 792, 802 (1973)*; *Texas Dept. of Community Affairs v. Burdine, 450 U.S. 248 (1981)*, results from our awareness of Title VII's balance between employee rights and employer prerogatives. In *McDonnell Douglas*, we described as follows Title VII's goal to eradicate discrimination while preserving workplace efficiency: "The broad, overriding interest, shared by employer, employee, and consumer, is efficient and trustworthy workmanship assured through fair and racially neutral employment and personnel decisions. In the implementation of such decisions, it is abundantly clear that Title VII tolerates no racial discrimination, subtle or otherwise." *411 U.S., at 801.*

When an employer ignored the attributes enumerated in the statute, Congress hoped, it naturally would focus on the qualifications of the applicant or employee. The intent to drive employers to focus on qualifications rather than on race, religion, sex, or national origin is the theme of a good deal of the statute's legislative history. An interpretive memorandum entered into the Congressional Record by Senators Case and Clark, comanagers of the bill in the Senate, is representative of this general theme. [8] According to their memorandum, Title VII "'expressly protects the employer's right to insist that any prospective applicant, Negro or

---

[8] We have in the past acknowledged the authoritativeness of this inter-pretive memorandum, written by the two bipartisan "captains" of Title VII. See, *e. g., Firefighters v. Stotts, 467 U.S. 561, 581, n. 14 (1984).*

white, must meet the applicable job qualifications. Indeed, the very purpose of title VII is to promote hiring on the basis of job qualifications, rather than on the basis of race or color.'" [9] 110 Cong. Rec. 7247 (1964), quoted in *Griggs v. Duke Power Co., supra, at 434*. The memorandum went on: "To discriminate is to make a distinction, to make a difference in treatment or favor, and those distinctions or differences in treatment or favor which are prohibited by section 704 are those which are based on any five of the forbidden criteria: race, color, religion, sex, and national origin. Any other criterion or qualification for employment is not affected by this title." 110 Cong. Rec. 7213 (1964).

Many other legislators made statements to a similar effect; we see no need to set out each remark in full here. The central point is this: while an employer may not take gender into account in making an employment decision (except in those very narrow circumstances in which gender is a BFOQ), it is free to decide against a woman for other reasons. We think these principles require that, once a plaintiff in a Title VII case shows that gender played a motivating part in an employment decision, the defendant may avoid a finding of liability [10] only by proving that it

---

[9] Many of the legislators' statements, such as the memorandum quoted in text, focused specifically on race rather than on gender or religion or national origin. We do not, however, limit their statements to the context of race, but instead we take them as general statements on the meaning of Title VII. The somewhat bizarre path by which "sex" came to be included as a forbidden criterion for employment -- it was included in an attempt to *defeat* the bill, see C. & B. Whalen, The Longest Debate: A Legislative History of the 1964 Civil Rights Act 115-117 (1985) -- does not persuade us that the legislators' statements pertaining to race are irrelevant to cases alleging gender discrimination. The amendment that added "sex" as one of the forbidden criteria for employment was passed, of course, and the statute on its face treats each of the enumerated categories exactly the same.

By the same token, our specific references to gender throughout this opinion, and the principles we announce, apply with equal force to discrimination based on race, religion, or national origin.

[10] Hopkins argues that once she made this showing, she was entitled to a finding that Price Waterhouse had discriminated against her on the basis of sex; as a consequence, she says, the partnership's proof could only limit the relief she received. She relies on Title VII's § 706(g), which permits a court to award affirmative relief when it finds that an employer "has intentionally engaged in or is intentionally engaging in an unlawful employment practice," and yet forbids a court to order reinstatement of, or backpay to, "an individual . . . if such individual was refused . . . employment or advancement or was suspended or discharged *for any reason other than* discrimination on account of race, color, religion, sex, or national origin." 42 U. S. C. § 2000e-5(g) (emphasis added). We do not take this provision to mean that a court inevitably can find a violation of the statute without having considered whether the

would have made the same decision even if it had not allowed gender to play such a role. This balance of burdens is the direct result of Title VII's balance of rights.

Our holding casts no shadow on *Burdine*, in which we decided that, even after a plaintiff has made out a prima facie case of discrimination under Title VII, the burden of persuasion does not shift to the employer to show that its stated legitimate reason for the employment decision was the true reason. *450 U.S., at 256-258*. We stress, first, that neither court below shifted the burden of persuasion to Price Waterhouse on this question, and in fact, the District Court found that Hopkins had not shown that the firm's stated reason for its decision was pretextual. *618 F. Supp., at 1114-1115*. Moreover, since we hold that the plaintiff retains the burden of persuasion on the issue whether gender played a part in the employment decision, the situation before us is not the one of "shifting burdens" that we addressed in *Burdine*. Instead, the employer's burden is most appropriately deemed an affirmative defense: the plaintiff must persuade the fact finder on one point, and

---

employment decision would have been the same absent the impermissible motive. That would be to interpret § 706(g) -- a provision defining *remedies* -- to influence the substantive commands of the statute. We think that this provision merely limits courts' authority to award affirmative relief in those circumstances in which a violation of the statute is not dependent upon the effect of the employer's discriminatory practices on a particular employee, as in pattern-or-practice suits and class actions. "The crucial difference between an individual's claim of discrimination and a class action alleging a general pattern or practice of discrimination is manifest. The inquiry regarding an individual's claim is the reason for a particular employment decision, while 'at the liability stage of a pattern-or-practice trial the focus often will not be on individual hiring decisions, but on a pattern of discriminatory decisionmaking.'" *Cooper v. Federal Reserve Bank of Richmond, 467 U.S. 867, 876 (1984)*, quoting *Teamsters v. United States, 431 U.S. 324, 360, n. 46 (1977)*.

Without explicitly mentioning this portion of § 706(g), we have in the past held that Title VII does not authorize affirmative relief for individuals as to whom, the employer shows, the existence of systemic discrimination had no effect. See *Franks v. Bowman Transportation Co., 424 U.S. 747, 772 (1976)*; *Teamsters v. United States, supra, at 367-371*; *East Texas Motor Freight System, Inc. v. Rodriguez, 431 U.S. 395, 404, n. 9 (1977)*. These decisions suggest that the proper focus of § 706(g) is on claims of systemic discrimination, not on charges of individual discrimination. Cf. *NLRB v. Transportation Management Corp., 462 U.S. 393 (1983)* (upholding the National Labor Relations Board's identical interpretation of § 10(c) of the National Labor Relations Act, *29 U. S. C. § 160(c)*, which contains language almost identical to § 706(g)).

then the employer, if it wishes to prevail, must persuade it on another. See *NLRB v. Transportation Management Corp., 462 U.S. 393, 400 (1983).*[11]

Price Waterhouse's claim that the employer does not bear any burden of proof (if it bears one at all) until the plaintiff has shown "substantial evidence that Price Waterhouse's explanation for failing to promote Hopkins was not the 'true reason' for its action" (Brief for Petitioner 20) merely restates its argument that the plaintiff in a mixed-motives case must squeeze her proof into *Burdine*'s framework. Where a decision was the product of a mixture of legitimate and illegitimate motives, however, it simply makes no sense to ask whether the legitimate reason was "*the* 'true reason'" (Brief for Petitioner 20 (emphasis added)) for the decision -- which is the question asked by *Burdine*. See *Transportation Management, supra*, at 400, n. 5.[12]

---

[11] Given that both the plaintiff and defendant bear a burden of proof in cases such as this one, it is surprising that the dissent insists that our approach requires the employer to bear "the ultimate burden of proof." *Post*, at 288. It is, moreover, perfectly consistent to say *both* that gender was a factor in a particular decision when it was made *and* that, when the situation is viewed hypothetically and after the fact, the same decision would have been made even in the absence of discrimination. Thus, we do not see the "internal inconsistency" in our opinion that the dissent perceives. See *post*, at 285-286. Finally, where liability is imposed because an employer is unable to prove that it would have made the same decision even if it had not discriminated, this is not an imposition of liability "where sex made no difference to the outcome." *Post*, at 285. In our adversary system, where a party has the burden of proving a particular assertion and where that party is unable to meet its burden, we assume that that assertion is inaccurate. Thus, where an employer is unable to prove its claim that it would have made the same decision in the absence of discrimination, we are entitled to conclude that gender *did* make a difference to the outcome.

[12] Nothing in this opinion should be taken to suggest that a case must be correctly labeled as either a "pretext" case or a "mixed-motives" case from the beginning in the District Court; indeed, we expect that plaintiffs often will allege, in the alternative, that their cases are both. Discovery often will be necessary before the plaintiff can know whether both legitimate and illegitimate considerations played a part in the decision against her. At some point in the proceedings, of course, the District Court must decide whether a particular case involves mixed motives. If the plaintiff fails to satisfy the factfinder that it is more likely than not that a forbidden characteristic played a part in the employment decision, then she may prevail only if she proves, following *Burdine*, that the employer's stated reason for its decision is pretextual. The dissent need not worry that this evidentiary scheme, if used during a jury trial, will be so impossibly confused and complex as it imagines. See, *e. g., post*, at 292. Juries long have decided cases in which defendants raised affirmative defenses. The dissent fails, moreover, to explain why the evidentiary scheme that we endorsed over 10 years ago in *Mt. Healthy City Bd. of Ed. v. Doyle, 429 U.S. 274 (1977)*, has not proved unworkable in that

Oblivious to this last point, the dissent would insist that *Burdine*'s framework perform work that it was never intended to perform. It would require a plaintiff who challenges an adverse employment decision in which both legitimate and illegitimate considerations played a part to pretend that the decision, in fact, stemmed from a single source -- for the premise of *Burdine* is that *either* a legitimate *or* an illegitimate set of considerations led to the challenged decision. To say that *Burdine*'s evidentiary scheme will not help us decide a case admittedly involving *both* kinds of considerations is not to cast aspersions on the utility of that scheme in the circumstances for which it was designed.

B

In deciding as we do today, we do not traverse new ground. We have in the past confronted Title VII cases in which an employer has used an illegitimate criterion to distinguish among employees, and have held that it is the employer's burden to justify decisions resulting from that practice. When an employer has asserted that gender is a BFOQ within the meaning of § 703(e), for example, we have assumed that it is the employer who must show why it must use gender as a criterion in employment. See *Dothard v. Rawlinson, 433 U.S. 321, 332-337 (1977)*. In a related context, although the Equal Pay Act expressly permits employers to pay different wages to women where disparate pay is the result of a "factor other than sex," see *29 U. S. C. § 206(d)(1)*, we have decided that it is the employer, not the employee, who must prove that the actual disparity is not sex linked. See *Corning Glass Works v. Brennan, 417 U.S. 188, 196 (1974)*. Finally, some courts have held that, under Title VII as amended by the Pregnancy Discrimination Act, it is the employer who has the burden of showing that its limitations on the work that it allows a pregnant woman to perform are necessary in light of her pregnancy. See, *e. g., Hayes v. Shelby Memorial Hospital, 726 F. 2d 1543, 1548 (CA11 1984)*; *Wright v. Olin Corp., 697 F. 2d 1172, 1187 (CA4 1982)*. As these examples demonstrate, our assumption always has been that if an employer allows gender to affect its decision-making process, then it must carry the burden of justifying its ultimate decision. We have not in the past required women whose gender has proved relevant to an employment decision to establish the negative proposition that they would not have been subject to that decision had they been men, and we do not do so today.

We have reached a similar conclusion in other contexts where the law announces that a certain characteristic is irrelevant to the allocation of burdens and benefits. In *Mt. Healthy City Bd. of Ed. v. Doyle, 429 U.S. 274 (1977)*, the plaintiff claimed that he

---

context but would be hopelessly complicated in a case brought under federal antidiscrimination statutes.

had been discharged as a public school teacher for exercising his free-speech rights under the *First Amendment*. Because we did not wish to "place an employee in a better position as a result of the exercise of constitutionally protected conduct than he would have occupied had he done nothing," *id., at 285*, we concluded that such an employee "ought not to be able, by engaging in such conduct, to prevent his employer from assessing his performance record and reaching a decision not to rehire on the basis of that record." *Id., at 286*. We therefore held that once the plaintiff had shown that his constitutionally protected speech was a "substantial" or "motivating factor" in the adverse treatment of him by his employer, the employer was obligated to prove "by a preponderance of the evidence that it would have reached the same decision as to [the plaintiff] even in the absence of the protected conduct." *Id., at 287*. A court that finds for a plaintiff under this standard has effectively concluded that an illegitimate motive was a "but-for" cause of the employment decision. See *Givhan v. Western Line Consolidated School Dist., 439 U.S. 410, 417 (1979)*. See also *Arlington Heights v. Metropolitan Housing Development Corp., 429 U.S. 252, 270-271, n. 21 (1977)* (applying *Mt. Healthy* standard where plaintiff alleged that unconstitutional motive had contributed to enactment of legislation); *Hunter v. Underwood, 471 U.S. 222, 228 (1985)* (same).

In *Transportation Management*, we upheld the NLRB's interpretation of § 10(c) of the National Labor Relations Act, which forbids a court to order affirmative relief for discriminatory conduct against a union member "if such individual was suspended or discharged for cause." *29 U. S. C. § 160(c)*. The Board had decided that this provision meant that once an employee had shown that his suspension or discharge was based in part on hostility to unions, it was up to the employer to prove by a preponderance of the evidence that it would have made the same decision in the absence of this impermissible motive. In such a situation, we emphasized, "[t]he employer is a wrongdoer; he has acted out of a motive that is declared illegitimate by the statute. It is fair that he bear the risk that the influence of legal and illegal motives cannot be separated, because he knowingly created the risk and because the risk was created not by innocent activity but by his own wrongdoing." *462 U.S., at 403*.

We have, in short, been here before. Each time, we have concluded that the plaintiff who shows that an impermissible motive played a motivating part in an adverse employment decision has thereby placed upon the defendant the burden to show that it would have made the same decision in the absence of the unlawful motive. Our decision today treads this well-worn path.

C

In saying that gender played a motivating part in an employment decision, we mean that, if we asked the employer at the moment of the decision what its reasons were and if we received a truthful response, one of those reasons would be that the applicant or employee was a woman. [13] In the specific context of sex stereotyping, an employer who acts on the basis of a belief that a woman cannot be aggressive, or that she must not be, has acted on the basis of gender.

Although the parties do not overtly dispute this last proposition, the placement by Price Waterhouse of "sex stereotyping" in quotation marks throughout its brief seems to us an insinuation either that such stereotyping was not present in this case or that it lacks legal relevance. We reject both possibilities. As to the existence of sex stereotyping in this case, we are not inclined to quarrel with the District Court's conclusion that a number of the partners' comments showed sex stereotyping at work. See *infra*, at 255-256. As for the legal relevance of sex stereotyping, we are beyond the day when an employer could evaluate employees by assuming or insisting that they matched the stereotype associated with their group, for "'[i]n forbidding employers to discriminate against individuals because of their sex, Congress intended to strike at the entire spectrum of disparate treatment of men and women resulting from sex stereotypes.'" *Los Angeles Dept. of Water and Power v. Manhart*, 435 U.S. 702, 707, n. 13 (1978), quoting *Sprogis v. United Air Lines, Inc.*, 444 F. 2d 1194, 1198 (CA7 1971). An employer who objects to aggressiveness in women but whose positions require this trait places women in an intolerable and impermissible **catch 22**: out of a job if they behave aggressively and out of a job if they do not. Title VII lifts women out of this bind.

Remarks at work that are based on sex stereotypes do not inevitably prove that gender played a part in a particular employment decision. The plaintiff must show that the employer actually relied on her gender in making its decision. In making this showing, stereotyped remarks can certainly be *evidence* that gender played a part.

---

[13] After comparing this description of the plaintiff's proof to that offered by Justice O'Connor's opinion concurring in the judgment, *post*, at 276-277, we do not understand why the concurrence suggests that they are meaningfully different from each other, see *post*, at 275, 277-279. Nor do we see how the inquiry that we have described is "hypothetical," see *post*, at 283, n. 1. It seeks to determine the content of the entire set of reasons for a decision, rather than shaving off one reason in an attempt to determine what the decision would have been in the absence of that consideration. The inquiry that we describe thus strikes us as a distinctly nonhypothetical one.

In any event, the stereotyping in this case did not simply consist of stray remarks. On the contrary, Hopkins proved that Price Waterhouse invited partners to submit comments; that some of the comments stemmed from sex stereotypes; that an important part of the Policy Board's decision on Hopkins was an assessment of the submitted comments; and that Price Waterhouse in no way disclaimed reliance on the sex-linked evaluations. This is not, as Price Waterhouse suggests, "discrimination in the air"; rather, it is, as Hopkins puts it, "discrimination brought to ground and visited upon" an employee. Brief for Respondent 30. By focusing on Hopkins' specific proof, however, we do not suggest a limitation on the possible ways of proving that stereotyping played a motivating role in an employment decision, and we refrain from deciding here which specific facts, "standing alone," would or would not establish a plaintiff's case, since such a decision is unnecessary in this case. But see *post*, at 277 (O'Connor, J., concurring in judgment).

As to the employer's proof, in most cases, the employer should be able to present some objective evidence as to its probable decision in the absence of an impermissible motive. [14] Moreover, proving "'that the same decision would have been justified . . . is not the same as proving that the same decision would have been made.'" *Givhan, 439 U.S., at 416*, quoting *Ayers v. Western Line Consolidated School District, 555 F. 2d 1309, 1315 (CA5 1977)*. An employer may not, in other words, prevail in a mixed-motives case by offering a legitimate and sufficient reason for its decision if that reason did not motivate it at the time of the decision. Finally, an employer may not meet its burden in such a case by merely showing that at the time of the decision it was motivated only in part by a legitimate reason. The very premise of a mixed-motives case is that a legitimate reason was present, and indeed, in this case, Price Waterhouse already has made this showing by convincing Judge Gesell that Hopkins' interpersonal problems were a legitimate concern. The employer instead must show that its legitimate reason, standing alone, would have induced it to make the same decision.

III

The courts below held that an employer who has allowed a discriminatory impulse to play a motivating part in an employment decision must prove by clear and convincing evidence that it would have made the same decision in the absence of

---

[14] Justice White's suggestion, *post*, at 261, that the employer's own testimony as to the probable decision in the absence of discrimination is due special credence where the court has, contrary to the employer's testimony, found that an illegitimate factor played a part in the decision, is baffling.

discrimination. We are persuaded that the better rule is that the employer must make this showing by a preponderance of the evidence.

Conventional rules of civil litigation generally apply in Title VII cases, see, *e. g., United States Postal Service Bd. of Governors v. Aikens, 460 U.S. 711, 716 (1983)* (discrimination not to be "treat[ed] . . . differently from other ultimate questions of fact"), and one of these rules is that parties to civil litigation need only prove their case by a preponderance of the evidence. See, *e. g., Herman & MacLean v. Huddleston, 459 U.S. 375, 390 (1983)*. Exceptions to this standard are uncommon, and in fact are ordinarily recognized only when the government seeks to take unusual coercive action -- action more dramatic than entering an award of money damages or other conventional relief -- against an individual. See *Santosky v. Kramer, 455 U.S. 745, 756 (1982)* (termination of parental rights); *Addington v. Texas, 441 U.S. 418, 427 (1979)* (involuntary commitment); *Woodby v. INS, 385 U.S. 276 (1966)* (deportation); *Schneiderman v. United States, 320 U.S. 118, 122, 125 (1943)* (denaturalization). Only rarely have we required clear and convincing proof where the action defended against seeks only conventional relief, see, *e. g., Gertz v. Robert Welch, Inc., 418 U.S. 323, 342 (1974)* (defamation), and we find it significant that in such cases it was the defendant rather than the plaintiff who sought the elevated standard of proof -- suggesting that this standard ordinarily serves as a shield rather than, as Hopkins seeks to use it, as a sword.

It is true, as Hopkins emphasizes, that we have noted the "clear distinction between the measure of proof necessary to establish the fact that petitioner had sustained some damage and the measure of proof necessary to enable the jury to fix the amount." *Story Parchment Co. v. Paterson Parchment Paper Co., 282 U.S. 555, 562 (1931)*. Likewise, an Equal Employment Opportunity Commission (EEOC) regulation does require federal agencies proved to have violated Title VII to show by clear and convincing evidence that an individual employee is not entitled to relief. See 29 CFR § 1613.271(c)(2) (1988). And finally, it is true that we have emphasized the importance of make-whole relief for victims of discrimination. See *Albemarle Paper Co. v. Moody, 422 U.S. 405 (1975)*. Yet each of these sources deals with the proper determination of relief rather than with the initial finding of liability. This is seen most easily in the EEOC's regulation, which operates only after an agency or the EEOC has found that "an employee of the agency was discriminated against." See 29 CFR § 1613.271(c) (1988). Because we have held that, by proving that it would have made the same decision in the absence of discrimination, the employer may avoid a finding of liability altogether and not simply avoid certain equitable relief, these authorities do not help Hopkins to show why we should elevate the standard of proof for an employer in this position.

Significantly, the cases from this Court that most resemble this one, *Mt. Healthy* and *Transportation Management*, did not require clear and convincing proof. *Mt. Healthy, 429 U.S., at 287*; *Transportation Management, 462 U.S., at 400, 403*. We are not inclined to say that the public policy against firing employees because they spoke out on issues of public concern or because they affiliated with a union is less important than the policy against discharging employees on the basis of their gender. Each of these policies is vitally important, and each is adequately served by requiring proof by a preponderance of the evidence.

Although Price Waterhouse does not concretely tell us how its proof was preponderant even if it was not clear and convincing, this general claim is implicit in its request for the less stringent standard. Since the lower courts required Price Waterhouse to make its proof by clear and convincing evidence, they did not determine whether Price Waterhouse had proved by *a preponderance of the evidence* that it would have placed Hopkins' candidacy on hold even if it had not permitted sex-linked evaluations to play a part in the decision-making process. Thus, we shall remand this case so that that determination can be made.

IV

The District Court found that sex stereotyping "was permitted to play a part" in the evaluation of Hopkins as a candidate for partnership. *618 F. Supp., at 1120*. Price Waterhouse disputes both that stereotyping occurred and that it played any part in the decision to place Hopkins' candidacy on hold. In the firm's view, in other words, the District Court's factual conclusions are clearly erroneous. We do not agree.

In finding that some of the partners' comments reflected sex stereotyping, the District Court relied in part on Dr. Fiske's expert testimony. Without directly impugning Dr. Fiske's credentials or qualifications, Price Waterhouse insinuates that a social psychologist is unable to identify sex stereotyping in evaluations without investigating whether those evaluations have a basis in reality. This argument comes too late. At trial, counsel for Price Waterhouse twice assured the court that he did not question Dr. Fiske's expertise (App. 25) and failed to challenge the legitimacy of her discipline. Without contradiction from Price Waterhouse, Fiske testified that she discerned sex stereotyping in the partners' evaluations of Hopkins, and she further explained that it was part of her business to identify stereotyping in written documents. *Id.*, at 64. We are not inclined to accept petitioner's belated and unsubstantiated characterization of Dr. Fiske's testimony as "gossamer evidence" (Brief for Petitioner 20) based only on "intuitive hunches" (*id.*, at 44) and of her detection of sex stereotyping as "intuitively divined" (*id.*, at 43). Nor are we disposed to adopt the dissent's dismissive attitude toward

Dr. Fiske's field of study and toward her own professional integrity, see *post*, at 293-294, n. 5.

Indeed, we are tempted to say that Dr. Fiske's expert testimony was merely icing on Hopkins' cake. It takes no special training to discern sex stereotyping in a description of an aggressive female employee as requiring "a course at charm school." Nor, turning to Thomas Beyer's memorable advice to Hopkins, does it require expertise in psychology to know that, if an employee's flawed "interpersonal skills" can be corrected by a soft-hued suit or a new shade of lipstick, perhaps it is the employee's sex and not her interpersonal skills that has drawn the criticism. [15]

Price Waterhouse also charges that Hopkins produced no evidence that sex stereotyping played a role in the decision to place her candidacy on hold. As we have stressed, however, Hopkins showed that the partnership solicited evaluations from all of the firm's partners; that it generally relied very heavily on such evaluations in making its decision; that some of the partners' comments were the product of stereotyping; and that the firm in no way disclaimed reliance on those particular comments, either in Hopkins' case or in the past. Certainly a plausible -- and, one might say, inevitable -- conclusion to draw from this set of circumstances is that the Policy Board in making its decision did in fact take into account all of the partners' comments, including the comments that were motivated by stereotypical notions about women's proper deportment. [16]

Price Waterhouse concedes that the proof in *Transportation Management* adequately showed that the employer there had relied on an impermissible motivation in firing the plaintiff. Brief for Petitioner 45. But the only evidence in that case that a discriminatory motive contributed to the plaintiff's discharge was that the employer harbored a grudge toward the plaintiff on account of his union activity; there was,

---

[15] We reject the claim, advanced by Price Waterhouse here and by the dissenting judge below, that the District Court clearly erred in finding that Beyer was "responsible for telling [Hopkins] what problems the Policy Board had identified with her candidacy." *618 F. Supp., at 1117*. This conclusion was reasonable in light of the testimony at trial of a member of both the Policy Board and the Admissions Committee, who stated that he had "no doubt" that Beyer would discuss with Hopkins the reasons for placing her candidacy on hold and that Beyer "knew exactly where the problems were" regarding Hopkins. Tr. 316.

[16] We do not understand the dissenters' dissatisfaction with the District Judge's statements regarding the failure of Price Waterhouse to "sensitize" partners to the dangers of sexism. *Post*, at 294. Made in the context of determining that Price Waterhouse had not disclaimed reliance on sex-based evaluations, and following the judge's description of the firm's history of condoning such evaluations, the judge's remarks seem to us justified.

contrary to Price Waterhouse's suggestion, no direct evidence that that grudge had played a role in the decision, and, in fact, the employer had given other reasons in explaining the plaintiff's discharge. See *462 U.S., at 396*. If the partnership considers that proof sufficient, we do not know why it takes such vehement issue with Hopkins' proof.

Nor is the finding that sex stereotyping played a part in the Policy Board's decision undermined by the fact that many of the suspect comments were made by supporters rather than detractors of Hopkins. A negative comment, even when made in the context of a generally favorable review, nevertheless may influence the decisionmaker to think less highly of the candidate; the Policy Board, in fact, did not simply tally the "yesses" and "noes" regarding a candidate, but carefully reviewed the content of the submitted comments. The additional suggestion that the comments were made by "persons outside the decisionmaking chain" (Brief for Petitioner 48) -- and therefore could not have harmed Hopkins -- simply ignores the critical role that partners' comments played in the Policy Board's partnership decisions.

Price Waterhouse appears to think that we cannot affirm the factual findings of the trial court without deciding that, instead of being overbearing and aggressive and curt, Hopkins is, in fact, kind and considerate and patient. If this is indeed its impression, petitioner misunderstands the theory on which Hopkins prevailed. The District Judge acknowledged that Hopkins' conduct justified complaints about her behavior as a senior manager. But he also concluded that the reactions of at least some of the partners were reactions to her as a *woman* manager. Where an evaluation is based on a subjective assessment of a person's strengths and weaknesses, it is simply not true that each evaluator will focus on, or even mention, the same weaknesses. Thus, even if we knew that Hopkins had "personality problems," this would not tell us that the partners who cast their evaluations of Hopkins in sex-based terms would have criticized her as sharply (or criticized her at all) if she had been a man. It is not our job to review the evidence and decide that the negative reactions to Hopkins were based on reality; our perception of Hopkins' character is irrelevant. We sit not to determine whether Ms. Hopkins is nice, but to decide whether the partners reacted negatively to her personality because she is a woman.

V

We hold that when a plaintiff in a Title VII case proves that her gender played a motivating part in an employment decision, the defendant may avoid a finding of liability only by proving by a preponderance of the evidence that it would have made the same decision even if it had not taken the plaintiff's gender into account.

Because the courts below erred by deciding that the defendant must make this proof by clear and convincing evidence, we reverse the Court of Appeals' judgment against Price Waterhouse on liability and remand the case to that court for further proceedings.

It is so ordered.

JUSTICE WHITE, concurring in the judgment.

In my view, to determine the proper approach to causation in this case, we need look only to the Court's opinion in *Mt. Healthy City Bd. of Ed. v. Doyle*, 429 U.S. 274 (1977). In *Mt. Healthy*, a public employee was not rehired, in part because of his exercise of *First Amendment* rights and in part because of permissible considerations. The Court rejected a rule of causation that focused "solely on whether protected conduct played a part, 'substantial' or otherwise, in a decision not to rehire," on the grounds that such a rule could make the employee better off by exercising his constitutional rights than by doing nothing at all. *Id., at 285.* Instead, the Court outlined the following approach:

> "Initially, in this case, the burden was properly placed upon respondent to show that his conduct was constitutionally protected, and that his conduct was a 'substantial factor' -- or, to put it in other words, that it was a 'motivating factor' in the Board's decision not to rehire him. Respondent having carried that burden, however, the District Court should have gone on to determine whether the Board had shown by a preponderance of the evidence that it would have reached the same decision as to respondent's reemployment even in the absence of the protected conduct." *Id., at 287* (footnote omitted).

It is not necessary to get into semantic discussions on whether the *Mt. Healthy* approach is "but-for" causation in another guise or creates an affirmative defense on the part of the employer to see its clear application to the issues before us in this case. As in *Mt. Healthy*, the District Court found that the employer was motivated by both legitimate and illegitimate factors. And here, as in *Mt. Healthy*, and as the Court now holds, Hopkins was not required to prove that the illegitimate factor was the only, principal, or true reason for petitioner's action. Rather, as Justice O'Connor states, her burden was to show that the unlawful motive was a *substantial* factor in the adverse employment action. The District Court, as its opinion was construed by the Court of Appeals, so found, 263 U.S. App. D. C. 321, 333, 334, 825 F. 2d 458, 470, 471 (1987), and I agree that the finding was supported by the record. The burden of persuasion then should have shifted to Price Waterhouse to prove "by a preponderance of the evidence that it would have reached the same decision . . . in the absence of" the unlawful motive. *Mt. Healthy, supra, at 287.*

I agree with Justice Brennan that applying this approach to causation in Title VII cases is not a departure from, and does not require modification of, the Court's holdings in *Texas Dept. of Community Affairs v. Burdine*, 450 U.S. 248 (1981), and

McDonnell Douglas Corp. v. Green, 411 U.S. 792 (1973). The Court has made clear that "mixed-motives" cases, such as the present one, are different from pretext cases such as *McDonnell Douglas* and *Burdine*. In pretext cases, "the issue is whether either illegal or legal motives, but not both, were the 'true' motives behind the decision." *NLRB v. Transportation Management Corp., 462 U.S. 393, 400, n. 5 (1983)*. In mixed-motives cases, however, there is no one "true" motive behind the decision. Instead, the decision is a result of multiple factors, at least one of which is legitimate. It can hardly be said that our decision in this case is a departure from cases that are "inapposite." *Ibid*. I also disagree with the dissent's assertion that this approach to causation is inconsistent with our statement in *Burdine* that "[t]he ultimate burden of persuading the trier of fact that the defendant intentionally discriminated against the plaintiff remains at all times with the plaintiff." *450 U.S., at 253*. As we indicated in *Transportation Management Corp.*, the showing required by *Mt. Healthy* does not improperly shift from the plaintiff the ultimate burden of persuasion on whether the defendant intentionally discriminated against him or her. See *462 U.S., at 400, n. 5*.

Because the Court of Appeals required Price Waterhouse to prove by clear and convincing evidence that it would have reached the same employment decision in the absence of the improper motive, rather than merely requiring proof by a preponderance of the evidence as in *Mt. Healthy*, I concur in the judgment reversing this case in part and remanding. With respect to the employer's burden, however, the plurality seems to require, at least in most cases, that the employer submit objective evidence that the same result would have occurred absent the unlawful motivation. *Ante*, at 252. In my view, however, there is no special requirement that the employer carry its burden by objective evidence. In a mixed-motives case, where the legitimate motive found would have been ample grounds for the action taken, and the employer credibly testifies that the action would have been taken for the legitimate reasons alone, this should be ample proof. This would even more plainly be the case where the employer denies any illegitimate motive in the first place but the court finds that illegitimate, as well as legitimate, factors motivated the adverse action.[*]

---

[*] I agree with the plurality that if the employer carries this burden, there has been no violation of Title VII.

JUSTICE O'CONNOR, concurring in the judgment.

I agree with the plurality that, on the facts presented in this case, the burden of persuasion should shift to the employer to demonstrate by a preponderance of the evidence that it would have reached the same decision concerning Ann Hopkins' candidacy absent consideration of her gender. I further agree that this burden shift is properly part of the liability phase of the litigation. I thus concur in the judgment of the Court. My disagreement stems from the plurality's conclusions concerning the substantive requirement of causation under the statute and its broad statements regarding the applicability of the allocation of the burden of proof applied in this case. The evidentiary rule the Court adopts today should be viewed as a supplement to the careful framework established by our unanimous decisions in *McDonnell Douglas Corp. v. Green, 411 U.S. 792 (1973)*, and *Texas Dept. of Community Affairs v. Burdine, 450 U.S. 248 (1981)*, for use in cases such as this one where the employer has created uncertainty as to causation by knowingly giving substantial weight to an impermissible criterion. I write separately to explain why I believe such a departure from the *McDonnell Douglas* standard is justified in the circumstances presented by this and like cases, and to express my views as to when and how the strong medicine of requiring the employer to bear the burden of persuasion on the issue of causation should be administered.

I

Title VII provides in pertinent part: "It shall be an unlawful employment practice for an employer . . . to fail or refuse to hire or to discharge any individual, or otherwise to discriminate against any individual with respect to his compensation, terms, conditions, or privileges of employment, *because of* such individual's race, color, religion, sex, or national origin." 42 U. S. C. § 2000e-2(a) (emphasis added). The legislative history of Title VII bears out what its plain language suggests: a substantive violation of the statute only occurs when consideration of an illegitimate criterion is the "but-for" cause of an adverse employment action. The legislative history makes it clear that Congress was attempting to eradicate discriminatory actions in the employment setting, not mere discriminatory thoughts. Critics of the bill that became Title VII labeled it a "thought control bill," and argued that it created a "punishable crime that does not require an illegal external act as a basis for judgment." 100 Cong. Rec. 7254 (1964) (remarks of Sen. Ervin). Senator Case, whose views the plurality finds so persuasive elsewhere, responded:

"The man must do or fail to do something in regard to employment. There must be some specific external act, more than a mental act. Only if he does the act because of the grounds stated in the bill would there be any legal consequences." *Ibid.*

Thus, I disagree with the plurality's dictum that the words "because of" do not mean "but-for" causation; manifestly they do. See *Sheet Metal Workers v. EEOC, 478 U.S. 421, 499 (1986)* (White, J., dissenting) ("[T]he general policy under Title VII is to limit relief for racial discrimination in employment practices to actual victims of the discrimination"). We should not, and need not, deviate from that policy today. The question for decision in this case is what allocation of the burden of persuasion on the issue of causation best conforms with the intent of Congress and the purposes behind Title VII.

The evidence of congressional intent as to which party should bear the burden of proof on the issue of causation is considerably less clear. No doubt, as a general matter, Congress assumed that the plaintiff in a Title VII action would bear the burden of proof on the elements critical to his or her case. As the dissent points out, *post*, at 287, n. 3, the interpretative memorandum submitted by sponsors of Title VII indicates that "the plaintiff, *as in any civil case*, would have the burden of proving that discrimination had occurred." 110 Cong. Rec. 7214 (1964) (emphasis added). But in the area of tort liability, from whence the dissent's "but-for" standard of causation is derived, see *post*, at 282, the law has long recognized that in certain "civil cases" leaving the burden of persuasion on the plaintiff to prove "but-for" causation would be both unfair and destructive of the deterrent purposes embodied in the concept of duty of care. Thus, in multiple causation cases, where a breach of duty has been established, the common law of torts has long shifted the burden of proof to multiple defendants to prove that their negligent actions were not the "but-for" cause of the plaintiff's injury. See *e. g., Summers v. Tice, 33 Cal. 2d 80, 84-87, 199 P. 2d 1, 3-4 (1948).* The same rule has been applied where the effect of a defendant's tortious conduct combines with a force of unknown or innocent origin to produce the harm to the plaintiff. See *Kingston v. Chicago & N. W. R. Co., 191 Wis. 610, 616, 211 N. W. 913, 915 (1927)* ("Granting that the union of that fire [caused by defendant's negligence] with another of natural origin, or with another of much greater proportions, is available as a defense, the burden is on the defendant to show that . . . the fire set by him was not the proximate cause of the damage"). See also 2 J. Wigmore, Select Cases on the Law of Torts § 153, p. 865 (1912) ("When two or more persons by their acts are possibly the sole cause of a harm, or when two or more acts of the same person are possibly the sole cause, and the plaintiff has introduced evidence that one of the two persons, or one of the same person's two acts, is culpable, then the defendant has the burden of proving that the other person, or his other act, was the sole cause of the harm").

While requiring that the plaintiff in a tort suit or a Title VII action prove that the defendant's "breach of duty" was the "but-for" cause of an injury does not generally hamper effective enforcement of the policies behind those causes of action,

> "at other times the [but-for] test demands the impossible. It challenges the imagination of the trier to probe into a purely fanciful and unknowable state of affairs. He is invited to make an estimate concerning facts that concededly never existed. The very uncertainty as to what *might* have happened opens the door wide for conjecture. But when conjecture is demanded it can be given a direction that is consistent with the policy considerations that underlie the controversy." Malone, Ruminations on Cause-In-Fact, 9 Stan. L. Rev. 60, 67 (1956).

Like the common law of torts, the statutory employment "tort" created by Title VII has two basic purposes. The first is to deter conduct which has been identified as contrary to public policy and harmful to society as a whole. As we have noted in the past, the award of backpay to a Title VII plaintiff provides "the spur or catalyst which causes employers and unions to self-examine and to self-evaluate their employment practices and to endeavor to eliminate, so far as possible, the last vestiges" of discrimination in employment. *Albemarle Paper Co. v. Moody*, 422 U.S. 405, 417-418 (1975) (citation omitted). The second goal of Title VII is "to make persons whole for injuries suffered on account of unlawful employment discrimination." *Id., at 418.*

Both these goals are reflected in the elements of a disparate treatment action. There is no doubt that Congress considered reliance on gender or race in making employment decisions an evil in itself. As Senator Clark put it, "[t]he bill simply eliminates consideration of color [or other forbidden criteria] from the decision to hire or promote." 110 Cong. Rec. 7218 (1964). See also *id.*, at 13088 (remarks of Sen. Humphrey) ("What the bill does . . . is simply to make it an illegal practice to use race as a factor in denying employment"). Reliance on such factors is exactly what the threat of Title VII liability was meant to deter. While the main concern of the statute was with employment opportunity, Congress was certainly not blind to the stigmatic harm which comes from being evaluated by a process which treats one as an inferior by reason of one's race or sex. This Court's decisions under the *Equal Protection Clause* have long recognized that whatever the final outcome of a decisional process, the inclusion of race or sex as a consideration within it harms both society and the individual. See *Richmond v. J. A. Croson Co.*, 488 U.S. 469 *(1989).* At the same time, Congress clearly conditioned legal liability on a determination that the consideration of an illegitimate factor *caused* a tangible employment injury of some kind.

Where an individual disparate treatment plaintiff has shown by a preponderance of the evidence that an illegitimate criterion was a *substantial* factor in an adverse employment decision, the deterrent purpose of the statute has clearly been triggered. More importantly, as an evidentiary matter, a reasonable factfinder could conclude that absent further explanation, the employer's discriminatory motivation "caused" the employment decision. The employer has not yet been shown to be a violator, but neither is it entitled to the same presumption of good faith concerning its employment decisions which is accorded employers facing only circumstantial evidence of discrimination. Both the policies behind the statute, and the evidentiary principles developed in the analogous area of causation in the law of torts, suggest that at this point the employer may be required to convince the factfinder that, despite the smoke, there is no fire.

We have given recognition to these principles in our cases which have discussed the "remedial phase" of class action disparate treatment cases. Once the class has established that discrimination against a protected group was essentially the employer's "standard practice," there has been harm to the group and injunctive relief is appropriate. But as to the individual members of the class, the liability phase of the litigation is not complete. See *Dillon v. Coles, 746 F. 2d 998, 1004 (CA3 1984)* ("It is misleading to speak of the additional proof required by an individual class member for relief as being a part of the damage phase, that evidence is actually an element of the liability portion of the case") (footnote omitted). Because the class has already demonstrated that, as a rule, illegitimate factors were considered in the employer's decisions, the burden shifts to the employer "to demonstrate that the individual applicant was denied an employment opportunity for legitimate reasons." *Teamsters v. United States, 431 U.S. 324, 362 (1977).* See also *Franks v. Bowman Transportation Co., 424 U.S. 747, 772 (1976).*

The individual members of a class action disparate treatment case stand in much the same position as Ann Hopkins here. There has been a strong showing that the employer has done exactly what Title VII forbids, but the connection between the employer's illegitimate motivation and any injury to the individual plaintiff is unclear. At this point calling upon the employer to show that despite consideration of illegitimate factors the individual plaintiff would not have been hired or promoted in any event hardly seems "unfair" or contrary to the substantive command of the statute. In fact, an individual plaintiff who has shown that an illegitimate factor played a substantial role in the decision in his or her case has proved *more* than the class member in a *Teamsters* type action. The latter receives the

193

benefit of a burden shift to the defendant based on the *likelihood* that an illegitimate criterion was a factor in the individual employment decision.

There is a tension between the *Franks* and *Teamsters* line of decisions and the individual disparate treatment cases cited by the dissent. See *post*, at 286-289. Logically, under the dissent's view, each member of a disparate treatment class action would have to show "but-for" causation as to his or her individual employment decision, since it is not an element of the pattern or practice proof of the entire class and it is statutorily mandated that the plaintiff bear the burden of proof on this issue throughout the litigation. While the Court has properly drawn a distinction between the elements of a class action claim and an individual disparate treatment claim, see *Cooper v. Federal Reserve Bank of Richmond, 467 U.S. 867, 873-878 (1984)*, and I do not suggest the wholesale transposition of rules from one setting to the other, our decisions in *Teamsters* and *Franks* do indicate a recognition that presumptions shifting the burden of persuasion based on evidentiary probabilities and the policies behind the statute are not alien to our Title VII jurisprudence.

Moreover, placing the burden on the defendant in this case to prove that the same decision would have been justified by legitimate reasons is consistent with our interpretation of the constitutional guarantee of equal protection. Like a disparate treatment plaintiff, one who asserts that governmental action violates the *Equal Protection Clause* must show that he or she is "the victim of intentional discrimination." *Burdine, 450 U.S., at 256*. Compare *post*, at 286, 289 (Kennedy, J., dissenting), with *Washington v. Davis, 426 U.S. 229, 240 (1976)*. In *Alexander v. Louisiana, 405 U.S. 625 (1972)*, we dealt with a criminal defendant's allegation that members of his race had been invidiously excluded from the grand jury which indicted him in violation of the *Equal Protection Clause*. In addition to the statistical evidence presented by petitioner in that case, we noted that the State's "selection procedures themselves were not racially neutral." *Id., at 630*. Once the consideration of race in the decisional process had been established, we held that "the burden of proof shifts to the State to rebut the presumption of unconstitutional action by showing that permissible racially neutral selection criteria and procedures have produced the monochromatic result." *Id., at 632*.

We adhered to similar principles in *Arlington Heights v. Metropolitan Housing Development Corp., 429 U.S. 252 (1977)*, a case which, like this one, presented the problems of motivation and causation in the context of a multimember decisionmaking body authorized to consider a wide range of factors in arriving at its decisions. In *Arlington Heights* a group of minority plaintiffs claimed that a municipal governing body's refusal to rezone a plot of land to allow for the construction of low-income integrated housing was racially motivated. On the issue of causation, we indicated that the plaintiff was not required

> "to prove that the challenged action rested solely on racially discriminatory purposes. Rarely can it be said that a legislature or administrative body operating under a broad mandate made a decision motivated solely by a single concern, or even that a particular purpose was the 'dominant' or 'primary' one. In fact, it is because legislators and administrators are properly concerned with balancing numerous competing considerations that courts refrain from reviewing the merits of their decisions, absent a showing of arbitrariness or irrationality. But racial discrimination is not just another competing consideration. When there is a proof that a discriminatory purpose has been a motivating factor in the decision, this judicial deference is no longer justified." *Id., at 265-266* (citation omitted).

If the strong presumption of regularity and rationality of legislative decisionmaking must give way in the face of evidence that race has played a significant part in a legislative decision, I simply cannot believe that Congress intended Title VII to accord *more* deference to a private employer in the face of evidence that its decisional process has been substantially infected by discrimination. Indeed, where a public employee brings a "disparate treatment" claim under *42 U. S. C. § 1983* and the *Equal Protection Clause* the employee is entitled to the favorable evidentiary framework of *Arlington Heights*. See, *e. g., Hervey v. Little Rock, 787 F. 2d 1223, 1233-1234 (CA8 1986)* (applying *Arlington Heights* to public employee's claim of sex discrimination in promotion decision); *Lee v. Russell County Bd. of Education, 684 F. 2d 769, 773-774 (CA11 1982)* (applying *Arlington Heights* to public employees' claims of race discrimination in discharge case). Under the dissent's reading of Title VII, Congress' extension of the coverage of the statute to public employers in 1972 has placed these employees under a less favorable evidentiary regime. In my view, nothing in the language, history, or purpose of Title VII prohibits adoption of an evidentiary rule which places the burden of persuasion on the defendant to demonstrate that legitimate concerns would have justified an adverse employment action where the plaintiff has convinced the factfinder that a forbidden factor played a substantial role in the employment decision. Even the dissenting judge below "[had] no quarrel with [the] principle" that "a party with one permissible motive and one unlawful one may prevail only by affirmatively proving that it would have acted as it did even if the forbidden motive were absent." *263 U.S. App. D. C. 321, 341, 825 F. 2d 458, 478 (1987)* (Williams, J. dissenting).

II

The dissent's summary of our individual disparate treatment cases to date is fair and accurate, and amply demonstrates that the rule we adopt today is at least a change in direction from some of our prior precedents. See *post*, at 286-289. We have indeed emphasized in the past that in an individual disparate treatment action the plaintiff bears the burden of persuasion throughout the litigation. Nor have we confined the word "pretext" to the narrow definition which the plurality attempts to pin on it today. See *ante*, at 244-247. *McDonnell Douglas* and *Burdine* clearly contemplated that a disparate treatment plaintiff could show that the employer's proffered explanation for an event was not "the true reason" either because it *never* motivated the employer in its employment decisions or because it did not do so in a particular case. *McDonnell Douglas* and *Burdine* assumed that the plaintiff would bear the burden of persuasion as to both these attacks, and we clearly depart from that framework today. Such a departure requires justification, and its outlines should be carefully drawn.

First, *McDonnell Douglas* itself dealt with a situation where the plaintiff presented no direct evidence that the employer had relied on a forbidden factor under Title VII in making an employment decision. The prima facie case established there was not difficult to prove, and was based only on the statistical probability that when a number of potential causes for an employment decision are eliminated an inference arises that an illegitimate factor was in fact the motivation behind the decision. See *Teamsters*, 431 U.S., at 358, n. 44 ("[T]he *McDonnell Douglas* formula does not require direct proof of discrimination"). In the face of this inferential proof, the employer's burden was deemed to be only one of production; the employer must articulate a legitimate reason for the adverse employment action. See *Furnco Construction Corp. v. Waters*, 438 U.S. 567, 577 (1978). The plaintiff must then be given an "opportunity to demonstrate by competent evidence that the presumptively valid reasons for his rejection were in fact a coverup for a racially discriminatory decision." *McDonnell Douglas*, 411 U.S., at 805. Our decision in *Texas Dept. of Community Affairs v. Burdine*, 450 U.S. 248 (1981), also involved the "narrow question" whether, after a plaintiff had carried the "not onerous" burden of establishing the prima facie case under *McDonnell Douglas*, the burden of persuasion should be shifted to the employer to prove that a legitimate reason for the adverse employment action existed. *450 U.S., at 250*. As the discussion of *Teamsters* and *Arlington Heights* indicates, I do not think that the employer is entitled to the same presumption of good faith where there is direct evidence that it has placed substantial reliance on factors whose consideration is forbidden by Title VII.

The only individual disparate treatment case cited by the dissent which involved the kind of direct evidence of discriminatory animus with which we are confronted here is *United States Postal Service Bd. of Governors v. Aikens, 460 U.S. 711, 713-714, n. 2 (1983)*. The question presented to the Court in that case involved only a challenge to the elements of the prima facie case under *McDonnell Douglas* and *Burdine*, see Pet. for Cert. in *United States Postal Service Bd. of Governors* v. *Aikens*, O. T. 1981, No. 81-1044, and the question we confront today was neither briefed nor argued to the Court. As should be apparent, the entire purpose of the *McDonnell Douglas* prima facie case is to compensate for the fact that direct evidence of intentional discrimination is hard to come by. That the employer's burden in rebutting such an inferential case of discrimination is only one of production does not mean that the scales should be weighted in the same manner where there *is* direct evidence of intentional discrimination. Indeed, in one Age Discrimination in Employment Act case, the Court seemed to indicate that "the *McDonnell Douglas* test is inapplicable where the plaintiff presents direct evidence of discrimination." *Trans World Airlines, Inc. v. Thurston, 469 U.S. 111, 121 (1985)*. See also *East Texas Motor Freight System, Inc. v. Rodriguez, 431 U.S. 395, 403-404, n. 9 (1977)*.

Second, the facts of this case, and a growing number like it decided by the Courts of Appeals, convince me that the evidentiary standard I propose is necessary to make real the promise of *McDonnell Douglas* that "[i]n the implementation of [employment] decisions, it is abundantly clear that Title VII tolerates no . . . discrimination, subtle or otherwise." *411 U.S., at 801*. In this case, the District Court found that a number of the evaluations of Ann Hopkins submitted by partners in the firm overtly referred to her failure to conform to certain gender stereotypes as a factor militating against her election to the partnership. *618 F. Supp. 1109, 1116-1117 (DC 1985)*. The District Court further found that these evaluations were given "great weight" by the decisionmakers at Price Waterhouse. *Id., at 1118*. In addition, the District Court found that the partner responsible for informing Hopkins of the factors which caused her candidacy to be placed on hold, indicated that her "professional" problems would be solved if she would "walk more femininely, talk more femininely, wear make-up, have her hair styled, and wear jewelry." *Id., at 1117* (footnote omitted). As the Court of Appeals characterized it, Ann Hopkins proved that Price Waterhouse "permitt[ed] stereotypical attitudes towards women to play a significant, though unquantifiable, role in its decision not to invite her to become a partner." *263 U.S. App. D. C., at 324, 825 F. 2d, at 461*.

At this point Ann Hopkins had taken her proof as far as it could go. She had proved discriminatory input into the decisional process, and had proved that participants in the process considered her failure to conform to the stereotypes credited by a number of the decisionmakers had been a substantial factor in the decision. It is as if Ann Hopkins were sitting in the hall outside the room where partnership decisions were being made. As the partners filed in to consider her candidacy, she heard several of them make sexist remarks in discussing her suitability for partnership. As the decisionmakers exited the room, she was *told* by one of those privy to the decisionmaking process that her gender was a major reason for the rejection of her partnership bid. If, as we noted in *Teamsters*, "[p]resumptions shifting the burden of proof are often created to reflect judicial evaluations of probabilities and to conform with a party's superior access to the proof," *431 U.S., at 359, n. 45*, one would be hard pressed to think of a situation where it would be more appropriate to require the defendant to show that its decision would have been justified by wholly legitimate concerns.

Moreover, there is mounting evidence in the decisions of the lower courts that respondent here is not alone in her inability to pinpoint discrimination as the precise cause of her injury, despite having shown that it played a significant role in the decisional process. Many of these courts, which deal with the evidentiary issues in Title VII cases on a regular basis, have concluded that placing the risk of nonpersuasion on the defendant in a situation where uncertainty as to causation has been created by its consideration of an illegitimate criterion makes sense as a rule of evidence and furthers the substantive command of Title VII. See, *e. g., Bell v. Birmingham Linen Service*, 715 F. 2d 1552, 1556 (CA11 1983) (Tjoflat, J.) ("It would be illogical, indeed ironic, to hold a Title VII plaintiff presenting direct evidence of a defendant's intent to discriminate to a more stringent burden of proof, or to allow a defendant to meet that direct proof by merely articulating, but not proving, legitimate, nondiscriminatory reasons for its action"). Particularly in the context of the professional world, where decisions are often made by collegial bodies on the basis of largely subjective criteria, requiring the plaintiff to prove that *any* one factor was the definitive cause of the decisionmakers' action may be tantamount to declaring Title VII inapplicable to such decisions. See, *e. g., Fields v. Clark University*, 817 F. 2d 931, 935-937 (CA1 1987) (where plaintiff produced "strong evidence" that sexist attitudes infected faculty tenure decision, burden properly shifted to defendant to show that it would have reached the same decision absent discrimination); *Thompkins v. Morris Brown College*, 752 F. 2d 558, 563 (CA11 1985) (direct evidence of discriminatory animus in decision to discharge college professor shifted burden of persuasion to defendant).

Finally, I am convinced that a rule shifting the burden to the defendant where the plaintiff has shown that an illegitimate criterion was a "substantial factor" in the employment decision will not conflict with other congressional policies embodied in Title VII. Title VII expressly provides that an employer need not give preferential treatment to employees or applicants of any race, color, religion, sex, or national origin in order to maintain a work force in balance with the general population. See *42 U. S. C. § 2000e-2(j)*. The interpretive memorandum, whose authoritative force is noted by the plurality, see *ante*, at 243, n. 8, specifically provides: "There is no requirement in title VII that an employer maintain a racial balance in his work force. On the contrary, any deliberate attempt to maintain a racial balance, whatever such a balance may be, would involve a violation of title VII because maintaining such a balance would require an employer to hire or refuse to hire on the basis of race." 110 Cong. Rec. 7213 (1964).

Last Term, in *Watson v. Fort Worth Bank & Trust, 487 U.S. 977 (1988)*, the Court unanimously concluded that the disparate impact analysis first enunciated in *Griggs v. Duke Power Co., 401 U.S. 424 (1971)*, should be extended to subjective or discretionary selection processes. At the same time a plurality of the Court indicated concern that the focus on bare statistics in the disparate impact setting could force employers to adopt "inappropriate prophylactic measures" in violation of § 2000e-2(j). The plurality went on to emphasize that in a disparate impact case, the plaintiff may not simply point to a statistical disparity in the employer's work force. Instead, the plaintiff must identify a particular employment practice and "must offer statistical evidence of a kind and degree sufficient to show that the practice in question has caused the exclusion of applicants for jobs or promotions because of their membership in a protected group." *487 U.S., at 994*. The plurality indicated that "the ultimate burden of proving that discrimination against a protected group has been caused by a specific employment practice remains with the plaintiff at all times." *Id., at 997*.

I believe there are significant differences between shifting the burden of persuasion to the employer in a case resting purely on statistical proof as in the disparate impact setting and shifting the burden of persuasion in a case like this one, where an employee has demonstrated by direct evidence that an illegitimate factor played a substantial role in a particular employment decision. First, the explicit consideration of race, color, religion, sex, or national origin in making employment decisions "was the most obvious evil Congress had in mind when it enacted Title VII." *Teamsters, 431 U.S., at 335, n. 15*. While the prima facie case under *McDonnell Douglas* and the statistical showing of imbalance involved in a disparate impact case may both be indicators of discrimination or its "functional equivalent," they are not, in and of themselves, the evils Congress sought to eradicate from the employment setting. Second, shifting the burden of persuasion to the employer in a situation like this one creates no incentive to preferential treatment in violation of § 2000e-(2)(j). To avoid bearing the burden of justifying its decision, the employer need not seek racial or sexual balance in its work force; rather, all it need do is avoid substantial reliance on forbidden criteria in making its employment decisions.

While the danger of forcing employers to engage in unwarranted preferential treatment is thus less dramatic in this setting than in the situation the Court faced in *Watson*, it is far from wholly illusory. Based on its misreading of the words "because of" in the statute, see *ante*, at 240-242, the plurality appears to conclude that if a decisional process is "tainted" by awareness of sex or race in any way, the employer has violated the statute, and Title VII thus *commands* that the burden shift to the employer to justify its decision. *Ante*, at 250-252. The plurality thus effectively reads the causation requirement out of the statute, and then replaces it with an "affirmative defense." *Ante*, at 244-247.

In my view, in order to justify shifting the burden on the issue of causation to the defendant, a disparate treatment plaintiff must show by direct evidence that an illegitimate criterion was a substantial factor in the decision. As the Court of Appeals noted below: "While most circuits have not confronted the question squarely, the consensus among those that have is that once a Title VII plaintiff has demonstrated by direct evidence that discriminatory animus played a significant or substantial role in the employment decision, the burden shifts to the employer to show that the decision would have been the same absent discrimination." *263 U.S. App. D. C., at 333-344, 825 F. 2d, at 470-471*. Requiring that the plaintiff demonstrate that an illegitimate factor played a substantial role in the employment decision identifies those employment situations where the deterrent purpose of Title VII is most clearly implicated. As an evidentiary matter, where a plaintiff has made this type of strong showing of illicit motivation, the factfinder is entitled to presume that the employer's discriminatory animus made a difference to the outcome, absent proof to the contrary from the employer. Where a disparate treatment plaintiff has made such a showing, the burden then rests with the employer to convince the trier of fact that it is more likely than not that the decision would have been the same absent consideration of the illegitimate factor. The employer need not isolate the sole cause for the decision; rather it must demonstrate that with the illegitimate factor removed from the calculus, sufficient business reasons would have induced it to take the same employment action. This evidentiary scheme essentially requires the employer to place the employee in the same position he or she would have occupied absent discrimination. Cf. *Mt. Healthy City Bd. of Ed. v. Doyle, 429 U.S. 274, 286 (1977)*. If the employer fails to carry this burden, the factfinder is justified in concluding that the decision was made "because of" consideration of the illegitimate factor and the substantive standard for liability under the statute is satisfied.

Thus, stray remarks in the workplace, while perhaps probative of sexual harassment, see *Meritor Savings Bank v. Vinson, 477 U.S. 57, 63-69 (1986)*, cannot justify requiring the employer to prove that its hiring or promotion decisions were based on legitimate criteria. Nor can statements by nondecisionmakers, or statements by decisionmakers unrelated to the decisional process itself, suffice to satisfy the plaintiff's burden in this regard. In addition, in my view testimony such as Dr. Fiske's in this case, standing alone, would not justify shifting the burden of persuasion to the employer. Race and gender always "play a role" in an employment decision in the benign sense that these are human characteristics of which decisionmakers are aware and about which they may comment in a perfectly neutral and nondiscriminatory fashion. For example, in the context of this case, a mere reference to "a lady candidate" might show that gender "played a role" in the decision, but by no means could support a rational factfinder's inference that the decision was made "because of" sex. What is required is what Ann Hopkins showed here: direct evidence that decisionmakers placed substantial negative reliance on an illegitimate criterion in reaching their decision.

It should be obvious that the threshold standard I would adopt for shifting the burden of persuasion to the defendant differs substantially from that proposed by the plurality, the plurality's suggestion to the contrary notwithstanding. See *ante*, at 250, n. 13. The plurality proceeds from the premise that the words "because of" in the statute do not embody any causal requirement at all. Under my approach, the plaintiff must produce evidence sufficient to show that an illegitimate criterion was a substantial factor in the particular employment decision such that a reasonable factfinder could draw an inference that the decision was made "because of" the plaintiff's protected status. Only then would the burden of proof shift to the defendant to prove that the decision would have been justified by other, wholly legitimate considerations. See also *ante*, at 259-260 (White, J., concurring in judgment).

In sum, because of the concerns outlined above, and because I believe that the deterrent purpose of Title VII is disserved by a rule which places the burden of proof on plaintiffs on the issue of causation in all circumstances, I would retain but supplement the framework we established in *McDonnell Douglas* and subsequent cases. The structure of the presentation of evidence in an individual disparate treatment case should conform to the general outlines we established in *McDonnell Douglas* and *Burdine*. First, the plaintiff must establish the *McDonnell Douglas* prima facie case by showing membership in a protected group, qualification for the job, rejection for the position, and that after rejection the employer continued to seek applicants of complainant's general qualifications. *McDonnell Douglas, 411 U.S., at 802.* The plaintiff should also present any direct evidence of discriminatory animus in the decisional process. The defendant should then present its case, including its evidence as to legitimate, nondiscriminatory reasons for the employment decision. As the dissent notes, under this framework, the employer "has every incentive to convince the trier of fact that the decision was lawful." *Post*, at 292, citing *Burdine*, *450 U.S., at 258*. Once all the evidence has been received, the court should determine whether the *McDonnell Douglas* or *Price Waterhouse* framework properly applies to the evidence before it. If the plaintiff has failed to satisfy the *Price Waterhouse* threshold, the case should be decided under the principles enunciated in *McDonnell Douglas* and *Burdine*, with the plaintiff bearing the burden of persuasion on the ultimate issue whether the employment action was taken because of discrimination. In my view, such a system is both fair and workable, and it calibrates the evidentiary requirements demanded of the parties to the goals behind the statute itself.

I agree with the dissent, see *post*, at 293, n. 4, that the evidentiary framework I propose should be available to all disparate treatment plaintiffs where an illegitimate consideration played a substantial role in an adverse employment decision. The Court's allocation of the burden of proof in *Johnson v. Transportation Agency, Santa Clara County, 480 U.S. 616, 626-627 (1987)*, rested squarely on "the analytical framework set forth in *McDonnell Douglas*," *id., at 626*, which we alter today. It would be odd to say the least if the evidentiary rules applicable to Title VII actions were themselves dependent on the gender or the skin color of the litigants. But see *ante*, at 239, n. 3.

In this case, I agree with the plurality that petitioner should be called upon to show that the outcome would have been the same if respondent's professional merit had been its only concern. On remand, the District Court should determine whether Price Waterhouse has shown by a preponderance of the evidence that if gender had not been part of the process, its employment decision concerning Ann Hopkins would nonetheless have been the same.

JUSTICE KENNEDY, with whom THE CHIEF JUSTICE and JUSTICE SCALIA join, dissenting.

Today the Court manipulates existing and complex rules for employment discrimination cases in a way certain to result in confusion. Continued adherence to the evidentiary scheme established in *McDonnell Douglas Corp. v. Green, 411 U.S. 792 (1973)*, and *Texas Dept. of Community Affairs v. Burdine, 450 U.S. 248 (1981)*, is a wiser course than creation of more disarray in an area of the law already difficult for the bench and bar, and so I must dissent.

Before turning to my reasons for disagreement with the Court's disposition of the case, it is important to review the actual holding of today's decision. I read the opinions as establishing that in a limited number of cases Title VII plaintiffs, by presenting direct and substantial evidence of discriminatory animus, may shift the burden of persuasion to the defendant to show that an adverse employment decision would have been supported by legitimate reasons. The shift in the burden of persuasion occurs only where a plaintiff proves by direct evidence that an unlawful motive was a substantial factor actually relied upon in making the decision. *Ante*, at 276-277 (opinion of O'Connor, J.); *ante*, at 259-260 (opinion of White, J.). As the opinions make plain, the evidentiary scheme created today is not for every case in which a plaintiff produces evidence of stray remarks in the workplace. *Ante*, at 251 (opinion of Brennan, J.); *ante, at 277* (opinion of O'Connor, J.).

Where the plaintiff makes the requisite showing, the burden that shifts to the employer is to show that legitimate employment considerations would have justified the decision without reference to any impermissible motive. *Ante*, at 260-261 (opinion of White, J.); *ante*, at 278 (opinion of O'Connor, J.). The employer's proof on the point is to be presented and reviewed just as with any other evidentiary question: the Court does not accept the plurality's suggestion that an employer's evidence need be "objective" or otherwise out of the ordinary. *Ante*, at 261 (opinion of White, J.).

In sum, the Court alters the evidentiary framework of *McDonnell Douglas* and *Burdine* for a closely defined set of cases. Although Justice O'Connor advances some thoughtful arguments for this change, I remain convinced that it is unnecessary and unwise. More troubling is the plurality's rationale for today's decision, which includes a number of unfortunate pronouncements on both causation and methods of proof in employment discrimination cases. To demonstrate the defects in the plurality's reasoning, it is necessary to discuss, first, the standard of causation in Title VII cases, and, second, the burden of proof.

I

The plurality describes this as a case about the standard of *causation* under Title VII, *ante*, at 237, but I respectfully suggest that the description is misleading. Much of the plurality's rhetoric is spent denouncing a "but-for" standard of causation. The theory of Title VII liability the plurality adopts, however, essentially incorporates the but-for standard. The importance of today's decision is not the standard of causation it employs, but its shift to the defendant of the burden of proof. The plurality's causation analysis is misdirected, for it is clear that, whoever bears the burden of proof on the issue, Title VII liability requires a finding of but-for causation. See also *ante*, at 261, and n. (opinion of White, J.); *ante*, at 262-263 (opinion of O'Connor, J.).

The words of Title VII are not obscure. The part of the statute relevant to this case provides:

"It shall be an unlawful employment practice for an employer --

"(1) to fail or refuse to hire or to discharge any individual, or otherwise to discriminate against any individual with respect to his compensation, terms, conditions, or privileges of employment, *because of* such individual's race, color, religion, sex, or national origin." *42 U. S. C. § 2000e-2 (a)(1)* (emphasis added).

By any normal understanding, the phrase "because of" conveys the idea that the motive in question made a difference to the outcome. We use the words this way in everyday speech. And assuming, as the plurality does, that we ought to consider the interpretive memorandum prepared by the statute's drafters, we find that this is what the words meant to them as well. "To discriminate is to make a distinction, to make a difference in treatment or favor." 110 Cong. Rec. 7213 (1964). Congress could not have chosen a clearer way to indicate that proof of liability under Title VII requires a showing that race, color, religion, sex, or national origin caused the decision at issue.

Our decisions confirm that Title VII is not concerned with the mere presence of impermissible motives; it is directed to employment decisions that result from those motives. The verbal formulae we have used in our precedents are synonymous with but-for causation. Thus we have said that providing different insurance coverage to male and female employees violates the statute by treating the employee "'in a manner which but-for that person's sex would be different.'" *Newport News Shipbuilding & Dry Dock Co. v. EEOC, 462 U.S. 669, 683 (1983)*, quoting *Los Angeles Dept. of Water and Power v. Manhart, 435 U.S. 702, 711 (1978)*. We have described the relevant question as whether the employment decision was "based on" a discriminatory criterion, *Teamsters v. United States, 431 U.S. 324, 358 (1977)*, or whether the particular employment decision at issue was "made on the basis of" an impermissible factor, *Cooper v. Federal Reserve Bank of Richmond, 467 U.S. 867, 875 (1984)*.

What we term "but-for" cause is the least rigorous standard that is consistent with the approach to causation our precedents describe. If a motive is not a but-for cause of an event, then by definition it did not make a difference to the outcome. The event would have occurred just the same without it. Common-law approaches to causation often require proof of but-for cause as a starting point toward proof of legal cause. The law may require more than but-for cause, for instance proximate cause, before imposing liability. Any standard less than but-for, however, simply represents a decision to impose liability without causation. As Dean Prosser puts it, "[a]n act or omission is not regarded as a cause of an event if the particular event would have occurred without it." W. Keeton, D. Dobbs, R. Keeton, & D. Owen, Prosser and Keeton on Law of Torts 265 (5th ed. 1984).

One of the principal reasons the plurality decision may sow confusion is that it claims Title VII liability is unrelated to but-for causation, yet it adopts a but-for standard once it has placed the burden of proof as to causation upon the employer. This approach conflates the question whether causation must be shown with the question of how it is to be shown. Because the plurality's theory of Title VII causation is ultimately consistent with a but-for standard, it might be said that my disagreement with the plurality's comments on but-for cause is simply academic. See *ante*, at 259 (opinion of White, J.). But since those comments seem to influence the decision, I turn now to that part of the plurality's analysis.

The plurality begins by noting the quite unremarkable fact that Title VII is written in the present tense. *Ante*, at 240-241. It is unlawful "to fail" or "to refuse" to provide employment benefits on the basis of sex, not "to have failed" or "to have refused" to have done so. The plurality claims that the present tense excludes a but-for inquiry as the relevant standard because but-for causation is necessarily concerned with a hypothetical inquiry into how a past event would have occurred absent the contested motivation. This observation, however, tells us nothing of particular relevance to Title VII or the cause of action it creates. I am unaware of any federal prohibitory statute that is written in the past tense. Every liability determination, including the novel one constructed by the plurality, necessarily is concerned with the examination of a past event.[1] The plurality's analysis of verb

---

[1] The plurality's description of its own standard is both hypothetical and retrospective. The inquiry seeks to determine whether "if we asked the employer at the moment of decision

tense serves only to divert attention from the causation requirement that is made part of the statute by the "because of" phrase. That phrase, I respectfully submit, embodies a rather simple concept that the plurality labors to ignore. [2]

We are told next that but-for cause is not required, since the words "because of" do not mean "*solely* because of." *Ante,* at 241. No one contends, however, that sex must be the sole cause of a decision before there is a Title VII violation. This is a separate question from whether consideration of sex must be *a* cause of the decision. Under the accepted approach to causation that I have discussed, sex is a cause for the employment decision whenever, either by itself or in combination with other factors, it made a difference to the decision. Discrimination need not be the sole cause in order for liability to arise, but merely a necessary element of the set of factors that caused the decision, *i. e.,* a but-for cause. See *McDonald v. Santa Fe Trail Transportation Co., 427 U.S. 273, 282, n. 10 (1976).* The plurality seems to say that since we know the words "because of" do not mean "solely because of," they must not mean "because of" at all. This does not follow, as a matter of either semantics or logic.

The plurality's reliance on the "bona fide occupational qualification" (BFOQ) provisions of Title VII, *42 U. S. C. § 2000e-2(e),* is particularly inapt. The BFOQ provisions allow an employer, in certain cases, to make an employment decision of which it is conceded that sex is the cause. That sex may be the legitimate cause of an employment decision where gender is a BFOQ is consistent with the opposite command that a decision caused by sex in any other case justifies the imposition of Title VII liability. This principle does not support, however, the novel assertion that a violation has occurred where sex made no difference to the outcome.

The most confusing aspect of the plurality's analysis of causation and liability is its internal inconsistency. The plurality begins by saying: "When . . . an employer

---

what its reasons were and if we received a truthful response, one of those reasons would be that the applicant or employee was a woman." *Ante,* at 250.

[2] The plurality's discussion of overdetermined causes only highlights the error of its insistence that but-for is not the substantive standard of causation under Title VII. The opinion discusses the situation where two physical forces move an object, and either force acting alone would have moved the object. *Ante,* at 241. Translated to the context of Title VII, this situation would arise where an employer took an adverse action in reliance both on sex and on legitimate reasons, and *either* the illegitimate or the legitimate reason standing alone would have produced the action. If this state of affairs is proved to the factfinder, there will be no liability under the plurality's own test, for the same decision would have been made had the illegitimate reason never been considered.

considers both gender and legitimate factors at the time of making a decision, that decision was 'because of' sex and the other, legitimate considerations -- even if we may say later, in the context of litigation, that the decision would have been the same if gender had not been taken into account." *Ante*, at 241. Yet it goes on to state that "an employer shall not be liable if it can prove that, even if it had not taken gender into account, it would have come to the same decision." *Ante*, at 242.

Given the language of the statute, these statements cannot both be true. Title VII unambiguously states that an employer who makes decisions "because of" sex has violated the statute. The plurality's first statement therefore appears to indicate that an employer who considers illegitimate reasons when making a decision is a violator. But the opinion then tells us that the employer who shows that the same decision would have been made absent consideration of sex is *not* a violator. If the second statement is to be reconciled with the language of Title VII, it must be that a decision that would have been the same absent consideration of sex was not made "because of" sex. In other words, there is no violation of the statute absent but-for causation. The plurality's description of the "same decision" test it adopts supports this view. The opinion states that "[a] court that finds for a plaintiff under this standard has effectively concluded that an illegitimate motive was a 'but-for' cause of the employment decision," *ante*, at 249, and that this "is not an imposition of liability 'where sex made no difference to the outcome,'" *ante*, at 246, n. 11.

The plurality attempts to reconcile its internal inconsistency on the causation issue by describing the employer's showing as an "affirmative defense." This is nothing more than a label, and one not found in the language or legislative history of Title VII. Section 703(a)(1) is the statutory basis of the cause of action, and the Court is obligated to explain how its disparate-treatment decisions are consistent with the terms of § 703(a)(1), not with general themes of legislative history or with other parts of the statute that are plainly inapposite. While the test ultimately adopted by the plurality may not be inconsistent with the terms of § 703(a)(1), see *infra*, at 292, the same cannot be said of the plurality's reasoning with respect to causation. As Justice O'Connor describes it, the plurality "reads the causation requirement out of the statute, and then replaces it with an 'affirmative defense.'" *Ante*, at 276. Labels aside, the import of today's decision is not that Title VII liability can arise without but-for causation, but that in certain cases it is not the plaintiff who must prove the presence of causation, but the defendant who must prove its absence.

II

We established the order of proof for individual Title VII disparate-treatment cases in *McDonnell Douglas Corp. v. Green, 411 U.S. 792 (1973)*, and reaffirmed this allocation in *Texas Dept. of Community Affairs v. Burdine, 450 U.S. 248 (1981)*. Under

Burdine, once the plaintiff presents a prima facie case, an inference of discrimination arises. The employer must rebut the inference by articulating a legitimate nondiscriminatory reason for its action. The final burden of persuasion, however, belongs to the plaintiff. *Burdine* makes clear that the "ultimate burden of persuading the trier of fact that the defendant intentionally discriminated against the plaintiff remains at all times with the plaintiff." *Id., at 253.* See also *Board of Trustees of Keene State College v. Sweeney, 439 U.S. 24, 29 (1978)* (Stevens, J., dissenting).³ I would adhere to this established evidentiary framework, which provides the appropriate standard for this and other individual disparate-treatment cases. Today's creation of a new set of rules for "mixed-motives" cases is not mandated by the statute itself. The Court's attempt at refinement provides limited practical benefits at the cost of confusion and complexity, with the attendant risk that the trier of fact will misapprehend the controlling legal principles and reach an incorrect decision.

In view of the plurality's treatment of *Burdine* and our other disparate-treatment cases, it is important first to state why those cases are dispositive here. The plurality tries to reconcile its approach with *Burdine* by announcing that it applies only to a "pretext" case, which it defines as a case in which the plaintiff attempts to prove that the employer's proffered explanation is itself false. *Ante*, at 245-247, and n. 11. This ignores the language of *Burdine*, which states that a plaintiff may succeed in meeting her ultimate burden of persuasion "*either* directly by persuading the court that a discriminatory reason more likely motivated the employer or indirectly by showing that the employer's proffered explanation is unworthy of credence." *450 U.S., at 256* (emphasis added). Under the first of these two alternative methods, a plaintiff meets her burden if she can "persuade the court that the employment decision more likely than not was motivated by a discriminatory reason." *United States Postal Service Bd. of Governors v. Aikens, 460 U.S. 711, 717-718 (1983)* (Blackmun, J., concurring). The plurality makes no attempt to address this aspect of our cases.

Our opinions make plain that *Burdine* applies to all individual disparate-treatment cases, whether the plaintiff offers direct proof that discrimination motivated the employer's actions or chooses the indirect method of showing that the employer's proffered justification is false, that is to say, a pretext. See *Aikens, supra, at 714,* n. 3

---

³ The interpretive memorandum on which the plurality relies makes plain that "the plaintiff, as in any civil case, would have the burden of proving that discrimination had occurred." 110 Cong. Rec. 7214 (1964). Coupled with its earlier definition of discrimination, the memorandum tells us that the plaintiff bears the burden of showing that an impermissible motive "made a difference" in the treatment of the plaintiff. This is none other than the traditional requirement that the plaintiff show but-for cause.

("As in any lawsuit, the plaintiff may prove his case by direct or circumstantial evidence"). The plurality is mistaken in suggesting that the plaintiff in a so-called "mixed-motives" case will be disadvantaged by having to "squeeze her proof into *Burdine*'s framework." *Ante*, at 247. As we acknowledged in *McDonnell Douglas*, "[t]he facts necessarily will vary in Title VII cases," and the specification of the prima facie case set forth there "is not necessarily applicable in every respect to differing factual situations." *411 U.S., at 802, n. 13*. The framework was "never intended to be rigid, mechanized, or ritualistic." *Aikens, supra, at 715*. *Burdine* compels the employer to come forward with its explanation of the decision and permits the plaintiff to offer evidence under either of the logical methods for proof of discrimination. This is hardly a framework that confines the plaintiff; still less is it a justification for saying that the ultimate burden of proof must be on the employer in a mixed-motives case. *Burdine* provides an orderly and adequate way to place both inferential and direct proof before the factfinder for a determination whether intentional discrimination has caused the employment decision. Regardless of the character of the evidence presented, we have consistently held that the ultimate burden "remains at all times with the plaintiff." *Burdine, supra, at 253*.

Aikens illustrates the point. There, the evidence showed that the plaintiff, a black man, was far more qualified than any of the white applicants promoted ahead of him. More important, the testimony showed that "the person responsible for the promotion decisions at issue had made numerous derogatory comments about blacks in general and Aikens in particular." *460 U.S., at 713-714, n. 2*. Yet the Court in *Aikens* reiterated that the case was to be tried under the proof scheme of *Burdine*. Justice Brennan and Justice Blackmun concurred to stress that the plaintiff could prevail under the *Burdine* scheme in either of two ways, one of which was directly to persuade the court that the employment decision was motivated by discrimination. *460 U.S., at 718*. *Aikens* leaves no doubt that the so-called "pretext" framework of *Burdine* has been considered to provide a flexible means of addressing all individual disparate-treatment claims.

Downplaying the novelty of its opinion, the plurality claims to have followed a "well-worn path" from our prior cases. The path may be well worn, but it is in the wrong forest. The plurality again relies on Title VII's BFOQ provisions, under which an employer bears the burden of justifying the use of a sex-based employment qualification. See *Dothard v. Rawlinson, 433 U.S. 321, 332-337 (1977)*. In the BFOQ context this is a sensible, indeed necessary, allocation of the burden, for there by definition sex is the but-for cause of the employment decision and the only question remaining is how the employer can justify it. The same is true of the plurality's citations to Pregnancy Discrimination Act cases, *ante*, at 248. In such cases there is no question that pregnancy was the cause of the disputed action. The

Pregnancy Discrimination Act and BFOQ cases tell us nothing about the case where the employer claims not that a sex-based decision was justified, but that the decision was not sex-based at all.

Closer analogies to the plurality's new approach are found in *Mt. Healthy City Bd. of Ed. v. Doyle, 429 U.S. 274 (1977)*, and *NRLB v. Transportation Management Corp., 462 U.S. 393 (1983)*, but these cases were decided in different contexts. *Mt. Healthy* was a *First Amendment* case involving the firing of a teacher, and *Transportation Management* involved review of the NLRB's interpretation of the National Labor Relations Act. The *Transportation Management* decision was based on the deference that the Court traditionally accords NLRB interpretations of the statutes it administers. See *462 U.S., at 402-403*. Neither case therefore tells us why the established *Burdine* framework should not continue to govern the order of proof under Title VII.

In contrast to the plurality, Justice O'Connor acknowledges that the approach adopted today is a "departure from the *McDonnell Douglas* standard." *Ante*, at 262. Although her reasons for supporting this departure are not without force, they are not dispositive. As Justice O'Connor states, the most that can be said with respect to the Title VII itself is that "nothing in the language, history, or purpose of Title VII *prohibits* adoption" of the new approach. *Ante*, at 269 (emphasis added). Justice O'Connor also relies on analogies from the common law of torts, other types of Title VII litigation, and our equal protection cases. These analogies demonstrate that shifts in the burden of proof are not unprecedented in the law of torts or employment discrimination. Nonetheless, I believe continued adherence to the *Burdine* framework is more consistent with the statutory mandate. Congress' manifest concern with preventing imposition of liability in cases where discriminatory animus did not actually cause an adverse action, see *ante*, at 262 (opinion of O'Connor, J.), suggests to me that an affirmative showing of causation should be required. And the most relevant portion of the legislative history supports just this view. See n. 3, *supra*. The limited benefits that are likely to be produced by today's innovation come at the sacrifice of clarity and practical application.

The potential benefits of the new approach, in my view, are overstated. First, the Court makes clear that the *Price Waterhouse* scheme is applicable only in those cases where the plaintiff has produced direct and substantial proof that an impermissible motive was relied upon in making the decision at issue. The burden shift properly will be found to apply in only a limited number of employment discrimination cases. The application of the new scheme, furthermore, will make a difference only in a smaller subset of cases. The practical importance of the burden of proof is the "risk of nonpersuasion," and the new system will make a difference only where the evidence is so evenly balanced that the factfinder cannot say that either side's explanation of the case is "more likely" true. This category will not include cases in which the allocation of the burden of proof will be dispositive because of a complete lack of evidence on the causation issue. Cf. *Summers v. Tice, 33 Cal. 2d 80, 199 P. 2d 1 (1948)* (allocation of burden dispositive because no evidence of which of two negligently fired shots hit plaintiff). Rather, *Price Waterhouse* will apply only to cases in which there is substantial evidence of reliance on an impermissible motive, as well as evidence from the employer that legitimate reasons supported its action.

Although the *Price Waterhouse* system is not for every case, almost every plaintiff is certain to ask for a *Price Waterhouse* instruction, perhaps on the basis of "stray remarks" or other evidence of discriminatory animus. Trial and appellate courts will therefore be saddled with the task of developing standards for determining when to apply the burden shift. One of their new tasks will be the generation of a jurisprudence of the meaning of "substantial factor." Courts will also be required to make the often subtle and difficult distinction between "direct" and "indirect" or "circumstantial" evidence. Lower courts long have had difficulty applying *McDonnell Douglas* and *Burdine*. Addition of a second burden-shifting mechanism, the application of which itself depends on assessment of credibility and a determination whether evidence is sufficiently direct and substantial, is not likely to lend clarity to the process. The presence of an existing burden-shifting mechanism distinguishes the individual disparate-treatment case from the tort, class-action discrimination, and equal protection cases on which Justice O'Connor relies. The distinction makes Justice White's assertions that one "need look only to" *Mt. Healthy* and *Transportation Management* to resolve this case, and that our Title VII cases in this area are "inapposite," *ante*, at 258-260, at best hard to understand.

Confusion in the application of dual burden-shifting mechanisms will be most acute in cases brought under *42 U. S. C. § 1981* or the Age Discrimination in Employment Act (ADEA), where courts borrow the Title VII order of proof for the conduct of jury trials. See, *e. g.*, Note, The Age Discrimination in Employment Act of 1967 and Trial by Jury: Proposals for Change, *73 Va. L. Rev. 601 (1987)* (noting high reversal rate caused by use of Title VII burden shifting in a jury setting). Perhaps such cases in the future will require a bifurcated trial, with the jury retiring first to make the credibility findings necessary to determine whether the plaintiff has proved that an impermissible factor played a substantial part in the decision, and later hearing evidence on the "same decision" or "pretext" issues. Alternatively, perhaps the trial judge will have the unenviable task of formulating a single instruction for the jury on all of the various burdens potentially involved in the case.

I do not believe the minor refinement in Title VII procedures accomplished by today's holding can justify the difficulties that will accompany it. Rather, I "remain confident that the *McDonnell Douglas* framework permits the plaintiff meriting relief to demonstrate intentional discrimination." *Burdine, 450 U.S., at 258.* Although the employer does not bear the burden of persuasion under *Burdine*, it must offer clear and reasonably specific reasons for the contested decision, and has every incentive to persuade the trier of fact that the decision was lawful. *Ibid.* Further, the suggestion that the employer should bear the burden of persuasion due to superior access to evidence has little force in the Title VII context, where the liberal discovery rules available to all litigants are supplemented by EEOC investigatory files. *Ibid.* In sum, the *Burdine* framework provides a "sensible, orderly way to evaluate the evidence in light of common experience as it bears on the critical question of discrimination," *Aikens, 460 U.S., at 715*, and it should continue to govern the order of proof in Title VII disparate-treatment cases.[4]

III

The ultimate question in every individual disparate-treatment case is whether discrimination caused the particular decision at issue. Some of the plurality's comments with respect to the District Court's findings in this case, however, are potentially misleading. As the plurality notes, the District Court based its liability determination on expert evidence that some evaluations of respondent Hopkins were based on unconscious sex stereotypes,[5] and on the fact that Price Waterhouse

---

[4] The plurality states that it disregards the special context of affirmative action. *Ante*, at 239, n. 3. It is not clear that this is possible. Some courts have held that in a suit challenging an affirmative-action plan, the question of the plan's validity need not be reached unless the plaintiff shows that the plan was a but-for cause of the adverse decision. See *McQuillen v. Wisconsin Education Association Council, 830 F. 2d 659, 665 (CA7 1987)*, cert. denied, *485 U.S. 914 (1988).* Presumably it will be easier for a plaintiff to show that consideration of race or sex pursuant to an affirmative-action plan was a substantial factor in a decision, and the court will need to move on to the question of a plan's validity. Moreover, if the structure of the burdens of proof in Title VII suits is to be consistent, as might be expected given the identical statutory language involved, today's decision suggests that plaintiffs should no longer bear the burden of showing that affirmative-action plans are illegal. See *Johnson v. Transportation Agency, Santa Clara County, 480 U.S. 616, 626-627 (1987).*

[5] The plaintiff who engages the services of Dr. Susan Fiske should have no trouble showing that sex discrimination played a part in any decision. Price Waterhouse chose not to object to Fiske's testimony, and at this late stage we are constrained to accept it, but I think the plurality's enthusiasm for Fiske's conclusions unwarranted. Fiske purported to discern stereotyping in comments that were gender neutral -- *e. g.*, "overbearing and abrasive" --

failed to disclaim reliance on these comments when it conducted the partnership review. The District Court also based liability on Price Waterhouse's failure to "make partners sensitive to the dangers [of stereotyping], to discourage comments tainted by sexism, or to investigate comments to determine whether they were influenced by stereotypes." *618 F. Supp. 1109, 1119 (DC 1985).*

Although the District Court's version of Title VII liability is improper under any of today's opinions, I think it important to stress that Title VII creates no independent cause of action for sex stereotyping. Evidence of use by decision-makers of sex stereotypes is, of course, quite relevant to the question of discriminatory intent. The ultimate question, however, is whether discrimination caused the plaintiff's harm. Our cases do not support the suggestion that failure to "disclaim reliance" on stereotypical comments itself violates Title VII. Neither do they support creation of a "duty to sensitize." As the dissenting judge in the Court of Appeals observed, acceptance of such theories would turn Title VII "from a prohibition of discriminatory conduct into an engine for rooting out sexist thoughts." *263 U.S. App. D. C. 321, 340, 825 F. 2d 458, 477 (1987)* (Williams, J., dissenting).

Employment discrimination claims require factfinders to make difficult and sensitive decisions. Sometimes this may mean that no finding of discrimination is justified even though a qualified employee is passed over by a less than admirable employer. In other cases, Title VII's protections properly extend to plaintiffs who are by no means model employees. As Justice Brennan notes, *ante*, at 258, courts do not sit to determine whether litigants are nice. In this case, Hopkins plainly presented a strong case both of her own professional qualifications and of the presence of discrimination in Price Waterhouse's partnership process. Had the District Court found on this record that sex discrimination caused the adverse decision, I doubt it would have been reversible error. Cf. *Aikens, supra,* at 714, n. 2. That decision was for the finder of fact, however, and the District Court made plain that sex discrimination was not a but-for cause of the decision to place Hopkins' partnership candidacy on hold. Attempts to evade tough decisions by erecting novel theories of liability or multitiered systems of shifting burdens are misguided.

---

without any knowledge of the comments' basis in reality and without having met the speaker or subject. "To an expert of Dr. Fiske's qualifications, it seems plain that no woman could *be* overbearing, arrogant, or abrasive: any observations to that effect would necessarily be discounted as the product of stereotyping. If analysis like this is to prevail in federal courts, no employer can base any adverse action as to a woman on such attributes." *263 U.S. App. D. C. 321, 340, 825 F. 2d 458, 477 (1987)* (Williams, J., dissenting). Today's opinions cannot be read as requiring factfinders to credit testimony based on this type of analysis. See also *ante*, at 277 (opinion of O'Connor, J.).

IV

The language of Title VII and our well-considered precedents require this plaintiff to establish that the decision to place her candidacy on hold was made "because of" sex. Here the District Court found that the "comments of the individual partners and the expert evidence of Dr. Fiske do not prove an intentional discriminatory motive or purpose," *618 F. Supp., at 1118*, and that "[b]ecause plaintiff has considerable problems dealing with staff and peers, the Court cannot say that she would have been elected to partnership if the Policy Board's decision had not been tainted by sexually based evaluations," *id., at 1120*. Hopkins thus failed to meet the requisite standard of proof after a full trial. I would remand the case for entry of judgment in favor of Price Waterhouse.

Boumediene v. Bush

Supreme Court of the United States

December 5, 2007, argued

June 12, 2008, decided

No. 06-1195, No. 06-1196 *

553 U.S. 723
128 S. Ct. 2229
171 L. Ed. 2d 41

LAKHDAR BOUMEDIENE, et al., Petitioners v. GEORGE W. BUSH, PRESIDENT of the UNITED STATES, et al. KHALED A. F. AL ODAH, next friend of FAWZI KHALID ABDULLAH FAHAD AL ODAH, et al. v. UNITED STATES et al.

ON WRITS OF CERTIORARI TO THE UNITED STATES COURT OF APPEALS FOR THE DISTRICT OF COLUMBIA CIRCUIT.

Boumediene v. Bush, 476 F.3d 981, 375 U.S. App. D.C. 48, 2007 U.S. App. LEXIS 3682 (2007)

Seth P. Waxman argued the cause for petitioners.

Paul D. Clement argued the cause for respondents.

KENNEDY, J., delivered the opinion of the Court, in which Stevens, Souter, Ginsburg, and Breyer, JJ., joined.
SOUTER, J., filed a concurring opinion, in which Ginsburg and Breyer, JJ., joined.
ROBERTS, C. J., filed a dissenting opinion, in which Scalia, Thomas, and Alito, JJ., joined.
SCALIA, J., filed a dissenting opinion, in which Roberts, C. J., and Thomas and Alito, JJ., joined.

---

* Together with No. 06-1196, Al Odah, Next Friend of Al Odah et al. v. United States et al., also on certiorari to the same court.

JUSTICE KENNEDY delivered the opinion of the Court.

Petitioners are aliens designated as enemy combatants and detained at the United States Naval Station at Guantanamo Bay, Cuba. There are others detained there, also aliens, who are not parties to this suit.

Petitioners present a question not resolved by our earlier cases relating to the detention of aliens at Guantanamo: whether they have the constitutional privilege of habeas corpus, a privilege not to be withdrawn except in conformance with the Suspension Clause, Art. I, § 9, cl. 2. We hold these petitioners do have the habeas corpus privilege. Congress has enacted a statute, the Detainee Treatment Act of 2005 (DTA), 119 Stat. 2739, that provides certain procedures for review of the detainees' status. We hold that those procedures are not an adequate and effective substitute for habeas corpus. Therefore § 7 of the Military Commissions Act of 2006 (MCA), 28 U.S.C. § 2241(e), operates as an unconstitutional suspension of the writ. We do not address whether the President has authority to detain these petitioners nor do we hold that the writ must issue. These and other questions regarding the legality of the detention are to be resolved in the first instance by the District Court.

I

Under the Authorization for Use of Military Force (AUMF), § 2(a), 115 Stat. 224, note following 50 U.S.C. § 1541, the President is authorized "to use all necessary and appropriate force against those nations, organizations, or persons he determines planned, authorized, committed, or aided the terrorist attacks that occurred on September 11, 2001, or harbored such organizations or persons, in order to prevent any future acts of international terrorism against the United States by such nations, organizations or persons."

In *Hamdi v. Rumsfeld*, 542 U.S. 507, 124 S. Ct. 2633, 159 L. Ed. 2d 578 (2004), five Members of the Court recognized that detention of individuals who fought against the United States in Afghanistan "for the duration of the particular conflict in which they were captured, is so fundamental and accepted an incident to war as to be an exercise of the 'necessary and appropriate force' Congress has authorized the President to use." *Id.*, at 518, 124 S. Ct. 2633, 159 L. Ed. 2d 578 (plurality opinion of O'Connor, J.); *id.*, at 588-589, 124 S. Ct. 2633, 159 L. Ed. 2d 578 (Thomas, J., dissenting). After *Hamdi*, the Deputy Secretary of Defense established Combatant Status Review Tribunals (CSRTs) to determine whether individuals detained at Guantanamo were "enemy combatants," as the Department defines that term. See App. to Pet. for Cert. in No. 06-1195, p 81a. A later memorandum established procedures to implement the PCSRTs. See App. to Pet. for Cert. in No. 06-1196, p 147. The Government maintains these procedures were designed to comply with the due process requirements identified by the plurality in *Hamdi*. See Brief for Federal Respondents 10.

Interpreting the AUMF, the Department of Defense ordered the detention of these petitioners, and they were transferred to Guantanamo. Some of these individuals were apprehended on the battlefield in Afghanistan, others in places as far away from there as Bosnia and Gambia. All are foreign nationals, but none is a citizen of a nation now at war with the United States. Each denies he is a member of the al Qaeda terrorist network that carried out the September 11 attacks or of the Taliban regime that provided sanctuary for al Qaeda. Each petitioner appeared before a separate CSRT; was determined to be an enemy combatant; and has sought a writ of habeas corpus in the United States District Court for the District of Columbia.

The first actions commenced in February 2002. The District Court ordered the cases dismissed for lack of jurisdiction because the naval station is outside the sovereign territory of the United States. See *Rasul v. Bush*, 215 F. Supp. 2d 55 (2002). The Court of Appeals for the District of Columbia Circuit affirmed. See *Al Odah v. United States*, 355 U.S. App. D.C. 189, 321 F.3d 1134, 1145 (2003). We granted certiorari and reversed, holding that 28 U.S.C. § 2241 extended statutory habeas corpus jurisdiction to Guantanamo. See *Rasul v. Bush*, 542 U.S. 466, 473, 124 S. Ct. 2686, 159 L. Ed. 2d 548 (2004). The constitutional issue presented in the instant cases was not reached in *Rasul*. Id., at 476, 124 S. Ct. 2686, 159 L. Ed. 2d 548.

After *Rasul*, petitioners' cases were consolidated and entertained in two separate proceedings. In the first set of cases, Judge Richard J. Leon granted the Government's motion to dismiss, holding that the detainees had no rights that could be vindicated in a habeas corpus action. In the second set of cases Judge Joyce Hens Green reached the opposite conclusion, holding the detainees had rights under the *Due Process Clause of the Fifth Amendment*. See *Khalid v. Bush*, 355 F. Supp. 2d 311, 314 (DC 2005); *In re Guantanamo Detainee Cases*, 355 F. Supp. 2d 443, 464 (DC 2005).

While appeals were pending from the District Court decisions, Congress passed the DTA. Subsection (e) of § 1005 of the DTA amended 28 U.S.C. § 2241 to provide that "no court, justice, or judge shall have jurisdiction to hear or consider . . . an application for a writ of habeas corpus filed by or on behalf of an alien detained by the Department of Defense at Guantanamo Bay, Cuba." 119 Stat. 2742. Section 1005 further provides that the Court of Appeals for the District of Columbia Circuit shall have "exclusive" jurisdiction to review decisions of the CSRTs. *Ibid.*

In *Hamdan v. Rumsfeld*, 548 U.S. 557, 576-577, 126 S. Ct. 2749, 165 L. Ed. 2d 723 (2006), the Court held this provision did not apply to cases (like petitioners') pending when the DTA was enacted. Congress responded by passing the MCA, *10 U.S.C. § 948a et seq.*, which again amended *§ 2241*. The text of the statutory amendment is discussed below. See Part II, *infra*. (Four Members of the *Hamdan* majority noted that "[n]othing prevent[ed] the President from returning to Congress to seek the authority he believes necessary." *548 U.S., at 636, 126 S. Ct. 2749, 165 L. Ed. 2d 723* (Breyer, J., concurring). The authority to which the concurring opinion referred was the authority to "create military commissions of the kind at issue" in the case. *Ibid.* Nothing in that opinion can be construed as an invitation for Congress to suspend the writ.)

Petitioners' cases were consolidated on appeal, and the parties filed supplemental briefs in light of our decision in *Hamdan*. The Court of Appeals' ruling *375 U.S. App. D.C. 48, 476 F.3d 981 (CADC 2007)*, is the subject of our present review and today's decision.

The Court of Appeals concluded that MCA § 7 must be read to strip from it, and all federal courts, jurisdiction to consider petitioners' habeas corpus applications, *id., at 987*; that petitioners are not entitled to the privilege of the writ or the protections of the Suspension Clause, *id., at 990-991*; and, as a result, that it was unnecessary to consider whether Congress provided an adequate and effective substitute for habeas corpus in the DTA.

We granted certiorari. *551 U.S. 1160, 127 S. Ct. 3078, 168 L. Ed. 2d 755 (2007)*.

II

As a threshold matter, we must decide whether MCA § 7 denies the federal courts jurisdiction to hear habeas corpus actions pending at the time of its enactment. We hold the statute does deny that jurisdiction, so that, if the statute is valid, petitioners' cases must be dismissed.

As amended by the terms of the MCA, *28 U.S.C. § 2241(e)* now provides:

"(1) No court, justice, or judge shall have jurisdiction to hear or consider an application for a writ of habeas corpus filed by or on behalf of an alien detained by the United States who has been determined by the United States to have been properly detained as an enemy combatant or is awaiting such determination.

"(2) Except as provided in [§§ 1005(e)(2) and (e)(3) of the DTA] no court, justice, or judge shall have jurisdiction to hear or consider any other action against the United States or its agents relating to any aspect of the detention, transfer, treatment, trial, or conditions of confinement of an alien who is or was detained by the United States and has been determined by the United States to have been properly detained as an enemy combatant or is awaiting such determination."

Section 7(b) of the MCA provides the effective date for the amendment of § 2241(e). It states:

"The amendment made by [MCA § 7(a)] shall take effect on the date of the enactment of this Act, and shall apply to all cases, without exception, pending on or after the date of the enactment of this Act which relate to any aspect of the detention, transfer, treatment, trial, or conditions of detention of an alien detained by the United States since September 11, 2001." 120 Stat. 2636.

There is little doubt that the effective date provision applies to habeas corpus actions. Those actions, by definition, are cases "which relate to . . . detention." See Black's Law Dictionary 728 (8th ed. 2004) (defining habeas corpus as "[a] writ employed to bring a person before a court, most frequently to ensure that the party's imprisonment or detention is not illegal"). Petitioners argue, nevertheless, that MCA § 7(b) is not a sufficiently clear statement of congressional intent to strip the federal courts of jurisdiction in pending cases. See *Ex parte Yerger, 75 U.S. 85, 8 Wall. 85, 102-103, 19 L. Ed. 332 (1869)*. We disagree.

Their argument is as follows: *Section 2241(e)(1)* refers to "a writ of habeas corpus." The next paragraph, *§ 2241(e)(2)*, refers to "any other action . . . relating to any aspect of the detention, transfer, treatment, trial, or conditions of confinement of an alien who . . . [has] been properly detained as an enemy combatant or is awaiting such determination." There are two separate paragraphs, the argument continues, so there must be two distinct classes of cases. And the effective date subsection, MCA § 7(b), it is said, refers only to the second class of cases, for it largely repeats the language of *§ 2241(e)(2)* by referring to "cases . . . which relate to any aspect of the detention, transfer, treatment, trial, or conditions of detention of an alien detained by the United States."

Petitioners' textual argument would have more force were it not for the phrase "other action" in *§ 2241(e)(2)*. The phrase cannot be understood without referring back to the paragraph that precedes it, *§ 2241(e)(1)*, which explicitly mentions the term "writ of habeas corpus." The structure of the two paragraphs implies that habeas actions are a type of action "relating to any aspect of the detention, transfer,

219

treatment, trial, or conditions of confinement of an alien who is or was detained . . . as an enemy combatant." Pending habeas actions, then, are in the category of cases subject to the statute's jurisdictional bar.

We acknowledge, moreover, the litigation history that prompted Congress to enact the MCA. In *Hamdan* the Court found it unnecessary to address the petitioner's Suspension Clause arguments but noted the relevance of the clear statement rule in deciding whether Congress intended to reach pending habeas corpus cases. See *548 U.S., at 575, 126 S. Ct. 2749, 165 L. Ed. 2d 723* (Congress should "not be presumed to have effected such denial [of habeas relief] absent an unmistakably clear statement to the contrary"). This interpretive rule facilitates a dialogue between Congress and the Court. Cf. *Hilton v. South Carolina Public Railways Comm'n, 502 U.S. 197, 206, 112 S. Ct. 560, 116 L. Ed. 2d 560 (1991)*; H. Hart & A. Sacks, The Legal Process: Basic Problems in the Making and Application of Law 1209-1210 (W. Eskridge & P. Frickey eds. 1994). If the Court invokes a clear statement rule to advise that certain statutory interpretations are favored in order to avoid constitutional difficulties, Congress can make an informed legislative choice either to amend the statute or to retain its existing text. If Congress amends, its intent must be respected even if a difficult constitutional question is presented. The usual presumption is that Members of Congress, in accord with their oath of office, considered the constitutional issue and determined the amended statute to be a lawful one; and the Judiciary, in light of that determination, proceeds to its own independent judgment on the constitutional question when required to do so in a proper case.

If this ongoing dialogue between and among the branches of Government is to be respected, we cannot ignore that the MCA was a direct response to *Hamdan*'s holding that the DTA's jurisdiction-stripping provision had no application to pending cases. The Court of Appeals was correct to take note of the legislative history when construing the statute, see *476 F.3d at 986, n. 2* (citing relevant floor statements); and we agree with its conclusion that the MCA deprives the federal courts of jurisdiction to entertain the habeas corpus actions now before us.

III

In deciding the constitutional questions now presented we must determine whether petitioners are barred from seeking the writ or invoking the protections of the Suspension Clause either because of their status, *i.e.*, petitioners' designation by the Executive Branch as enemy combatants, or their physical location, *i.e.*, their presence at Guantanamo Bay. The Government contends that noncitizens designated as enemy combatants and detained in territory located outside our Nation's borders have no constitutional rights and no privilege of habeas corpus.

Petitioners contend they do have cognizable constitutional rights and that Congress, in seeking to eliminate recourse to habeas corpus as a means to assert those rights, acted in violation of the Suspension Clause.

We begin with a brief account of the history and origins of the writ. Our account proceeds from two propositions. First, protection for the privilege of habeas corpus was one of the few safeguards of liberty specified in a Constitution that, at the outset, had no *Bill of Rights*. In the system conceived by the Framers the writ had a centrality that must inform proper interpretation of the Suspension Clause. Second, to the extent there were settled precedents or legal commentaries in 1789 regarding the extraterritorial scope of the writ or its application to enemy aliens, those authorities can be instructive for the present cases.

A

The Framers viewed freedom from unlawful restraint as a fundamental precept of liberty, and they understood the writ of habeas corpus as a vital instrument to secure that freedom. Experience taught, however, that the common-law writ all too often had been insufficient to guard against the abuse of monarchial power. That history counseled the necessity for specific language in the Constitution to secure the writ and ensure its place in our legal system.

Magna Carta decreed that no man would be imprisoned contrary to the law of the land. Art. 39, in Sources of Our Liberties 17 (R. Perry & J. Cooper eds. 1959) ("No free man shall be taken or imprisoned or dispossessed, or outlawed, or banished, or in any way destroyed, nor will we go upon him, nor send upon him, except by the legal judgment of his peers or by the law of the land"). Important as the principle was, the Barons at Runnymede prescribed no specific legal process to enforce it. Holdsworth tells us, however, that gradually the writ of habeas corpus became the means by which the promise of Magna Carta was fulfilled. 9 W. Holdsworth, A History of English Law 112 (1926) (hereinafter Holdsworth).

The development was painstaking, even by the centuries-long measures of English constitutional history. The writ was known and used in some form at least as early as the reign of Edward I. *Id.*, at 108-125. Yet at the outset it was used to protect not the rights of citizens but those of the King and his courts. The early courts were considered agents of the Crown, designed to assist the King in the exercise of his power. See J. Baker, An Introduction to English Legal History 38-39 (4th ed. 2002). Thus the writ, while it would become part of the foundation of liberty for the King's subjects, was in its earliest use a mechanism for securing compliance with the King's laws. See Halliday & White, The Suspension Clause: English Text, Imperial Contexts, and American Implications, *94 Va. L. Rev 575, 585 (2008)* (hereinafter Halliday & White) (manuscript, at 11, online at http://papers.ssrn.com/sol3/papers.cfm?abstract_id=1008252 (all Internet materials as visited June 9, 2008, and available in Clerk of Court's case file) (noting that "conceptually the writ arose from a theory of power rather than a theory of liberty")). Over time it became clear that by issuing the writ of habeas corpus common-law courts sought to enforce the King's prerogative to inquire into the authority of a jailer to hold a prisoner. See M. Hale, Prerogatives of the King 229 (D. Yale ed. 1976); 2 J. Story, Commentaries on the Constitution of the United States § 1341, p 237 (3d ed. 1858) (noting that the writ ran "into all parts of the king's dominions; for it is said, that the king is entitled, at all times, to have an account, why the liberty of any of his subjects is restrained").

Even so, from an early date it was understood that the King, too, was subject to the law. As the writers said of Magna Carta, "it means this, that the king is and shall be below the law." 1 F. Pollock & F. Maitland, History of English Law 173 (2d ed. 1909); see also 2 Bracton On the Laws and Customs of England 33 (S. Thorne transl. 1968) ("The king must not be under man but under God and under the law, because law makes the king"). And, by the 1600's, the writ was deemed less an instrument of the King's power and more a restraint upon it. See Collings, Habeas Corpus for Convicts--Constitutional Right or Legislative Grace, 40 Cali. L. Rev. 335, 336 (1952) (noting that by this point the writ was "the appropriate process for checking illegal imprisonment by public officials").

Still, the writ proved to be an imperfect check. Even when the importance of the writ was well understood in England, habeas relief often was denied by the courts or suspended by Parliament. Denial or suspension occurred in times of political unrest, to the anguish of the imprisoned and the outrage of those in sympathy with them.

A notable example from this period was *Darnel's Case*, 3 How. St. Tr. 1 (K. B. 1627). The events giving rise to the case began when, in a display of the Stuart penchant for authoritarian excess, Charles I demanded that Darnel and at least four others lend him money. Upon their refusal, they were imprisoned. The prisoners sought a writ of habeas corpus; and the King filed a return in the form of a warrant signed by the Attorney General. *Ibid.* The court held this was a sufficient answer and justified the subjects' continued imprisonment. *Id.*, at 59.

There was an immediate outcry of protest. The House of Commons promptly passed the Petition of Right, 3 Car. 1, ch. 1 (1627), 5 Statutes of the Realm 23, 24 (reprint 1963), which condemned executive "imprison[ment] without any cause" shown, and declared that "no freeman in any such manner as is before mencioned [shall] be imprisoned or deteined." Yet a full legislative response was long delayed.

The King soon began to abuse his authority again, and Parliament was dissolved. See W. Hall & R. Albion, A History of England and the British Empire 328 (3d ed. 1953) (hereinafter Hall & Albion). When Parliament reconvened in 1640, it sought to secure access to the writ by statute. The Act of 1640, 16 Car. 1, ch. 10, 5 Statutes of the Realm, at 110, expressly authorized use of the writ to test the legality of commitment by command or warrant of the King or the Privy Council. Civil strife and the Interregnum soon followed, and not until 1679 did Parliament try once more to secure the writ, this time through the Habeas Corpus Act of 1679, 31 Car. 2, ch. 2, *id.,* at 935. The Act, which later would be described by Blackstone as the "stable bulwark of our liberties," 1 W. Blackstone, Commentaries *137 (hereinafter Blackstone), established procedures for issuing the writ; and it was the model upon which the habeas statutes of the 13 American Colonies were based, see Collings, *supra,* at 338-339.

This history was known to the Framers. It no doubt confirmed their view that pendular swings to and away from individual liberty were endemic to undivided, uncontrolled power. The Framers' inherent distrust of governmental power was the driving force behind the constitutional plan that allocated powers among three independent branches. This design serves not only to make Government accountable but also to secure individual liberty. See *Loving v. United States, 517 U.S. 748, 756, 116 S. Ct. 1737, 135 L. Ed. 2d 36 (1996)* (noting that "[e]ven before the birth of this country, separation of powers was known to be a defense against tyranny"); cf. *Youngstown Sheet & Tube Co. v. Sawyer, 343 U.S. 579, 635, 72 S. Ct. 863, 96 L. Ed. 1153, 62 Ohio Law Abs. 417 (1952)* (Jackson, J., concurring) ("[T]he Constitution diffuses power the better to secure liberty"); *Clinton v. City of New York, 524 U.S. 417, 450, 118 S. Ct. 2091, 141 L. Ed. 2d 393 (1998)* (Kennedy, J., concurring) ("Liberty is always at stake when one or more of the branches seek to transgress the separation of powers"). Because the Constitution's separation-of-powers structure, like the substantive guarantees of the *Fifth* and *Fourteenth Amendments,* see *Yick Wo v. Hopkins, 118 U.S. 356, 374, 6 S. Ct. 1064, 30 L. Ed. 220 (1886),* protects persons as well as citizens, foreign nationals who have the privilege of litigating in our courts can seek to enforce separation-of-powers principles, see, *e.g., INS v. Chadha, 462 U.S. 919, 958-959, 103 S. Ct. 2764, 77 L. Ed. 2d 317 (1983).*

That the Framers considered the writ a vital instrument for the protection of individual liberty is evident from the care taken to specify the limited grounds for its suspension: "The Privilege of the Writ of Habeas Corpus shall not be suspended, unless when in Cases of Rebellion or Invasion the public Safety may require it." Art. I, § 9, cl. 2; see Amar, Of Sovereignty and Federalism, *96 Yale L. J. 1425, 1509, n. 329 (1987)* ("[T]he non-suspension clause is the original Constitution's most explicit reference to remedies"). The word "privilege" was used, perhaps, to avoid mentioning some rights to the exclusion of others. (Indeed, the only mention of the term "right" in the Constitution, as ratified, is in its clause giving Congress the power to protect the rights of authors and inventors. See Art. I, § 8, cl. 8.)

Surviving accounts of the ratification debates provide additional evidence that the Framers deemed the writ to be an essential mechanism in the separation-of-powers scheme. In a critical exchange with Patrick Henry at the Virginia ratifying convention Edmund Randolph referred to the Suspension Clause as an "exception" to the "power given to Congress to regulate courts." See 3 Debates in the Several State Conventions on the Adoption of the Federal Constitution 460-464 (J. Elliot 2d ed. 1876). A resolution passed by the New York ratifying convention made clear its understanding that the Clause not only protects against arbitrary suspensions of the writ but also guarantees an affirmative right to judicial inquiry into the causes of detention. See Resolution of the New York Ratifying Convention (July 26, 1788), in 1 *id.*, at 328 (noting the convention's understanding "[t]hat every person restrained of his liberty is entitled to an inquiry into the lawfulness of such restraint, and to a removal thereof if unlawful; and that such inquiry or removal ought not to be denied or delayed, except when, on account of public danger, the Congress shall suspend the privilege of the writ of *habeas corpus*"). Alexander Hamilton likewise explained that by providing the detainee a judicial forum to challenge detention, the writ preserves limited government. As he explained in The Federalist No. 84:

> "[T]he practice of arbitrary imprisonments, have been, in all ages, the favorite and most formidable instruments of tyranny. The observations of the judicious Blackstone . . . are well worthy of recital: 'To bereave a man of life . . . or by violence to confiscate his estate, without accusation or trial, would be so gross and notorious an act of despotism as must at once convey the alarm of tyranny throughout the whole nation; but confinement of the person, by secretly hurrying him to jail, where his sufferings are unknown or forgotten, is a less public, a less striking, and therefore a *more dangerous engine* of arbitrary government.' And as a remedy for this fatal evil he is everywhere peculiarly emphatical in his encomiums on the *habeas corpus* act, which in one place he calls 'the bulwark of the British Constitution.'" C. Rossiter ed., p 512 (1961) (quoting 1 Blackstone *136, 4 *id.*, at *438).

Post-1789 habeas developments in England, though not bearing upon the Framers' intent, do verify their foresight. Those later events would underscore the need for structural barriers against arbitrary suspensions of the writ. Just as the writ had been vulnerable to executive and parliamentary encroachment on both sides of the Atlantic before the American Revolution, despite the Habeas Corpus Act of 1679, the writ was suspended with frequency in England during times of political unrest after 1789. Parliament suspended the writ for much of the period from 1792 to 1801, resulting in rampant arbitrary imprisonment. See Hall & Albion 550. Even as late as World War I, at least one prominent English jurist complained that the Defence of the Realm Act, 1914, 4 & 5 Geo. 5, ch. 29(1)(a), effectively had suspended the privilege of habeas corpus for any person suspected of "communicating with the enemy." See *King* v. *Halliday*, [1917] A. C. 260, 299 (Lord Shaw, dissenting); see generally A. Simpson, In the Highest Degree Odious: Detention Without Trial in Wartime Britain 6-7, 24-25 (1992).

In our own system the Suspension Clause is designed to protect against these cyclical abuses. The Clause protects the rights of the detained by a means consistent with the essential design of the Constitution. It ensures that, except during periods of formal suspension, the Judiciary will have a time-tested device, the writ, to maintain the "delicate balance of governance" that is itself the surest safeguard of liberty. See *Hamdi, 542 U.S., at 536, 124 S. Ct. 2633, 159 L. Ed. 2d 578* (plurality opinion). The Clause protects the rights of the detained by affirming the duty and authority of the Judiciary to call the jailer to account. See *Preiser v. Rodriguez, 411 U.S. 475, 484, 93 S. Ct. 1827, 36 L. Ed. 2d 439 (1973)* ("[T]he essence of habeas corpus is an attack by a person in custody upon the legality of that custody"); cf. *In re Jackson, 15 Mich. 417, 439-440 (1867)* (Cooley, J., concurring) ("The important fact to be observed in regard to the mode of procedure upon this [habeas] writ is, that it is directed to, and served upon, not the person confined, but his jailer"). The separation-of-powers doctrine, and the history that influenced its design, therefore must inform the reach and purpose of the Suspension Clause.

B

The broad historical narrative of the writ and its function is central to our analysis, but we seek guidance as well from founding-era authorities addressing the specific question before us: whether foreign nationals, apprehended and detained in distant countries during a time of serious threats to our Nation's security, may assert the privilege of the writ and seek its protection. The Court has been careful not to foreclose the possibility that the protections of the Suspension Clause have expanded along with post-1789 developments that define the present scope of the writ. See *INS v. St. Cyr, 533 U.S. 289, 300-301, 121 S. Ct. 2271, 150 L. Ed. 2d 347 (2001)*. But the analysis may begin with precedents as of 1789, for the Court has said that "at the absolute minimum" the Clause protects the writ as it existed when the Constitution was drafted and ratified. *Id., at 301, 121 S. Ct. 2271, 150 L. Ed. 2d 347*.

To support their arguments, the parties in these cases have examined historical sources to construct a view of the common-law writ as it existed in 1789--as have *amici* whose expertise in legal history the Court has relied upon in the past. See Brief for Legal Historians as *Amici Curiae;* see also *St. Cyr, supra,* at 302, n. 16, 121 S. Ct. 2271, 150 L. Ed. 2d 347. The Government argues the common-law writ ran only to those territories over which the Crown was sovereign. See Brief for Federal Respondents 27. Petitioners argue that jurisdiction followed the King's officers. See Brief for Petitioner Boumediene et al. 11. Diligent search by all parties reveals no certain conclusions. In none of the cases cited do we find that a common-law court would or would not have granted, or refused to hear for lack of jurisdiction, a petition for a writ of habeas corpus brought by a prisoner deemed an enemy combatant, under a standard like the one the Department of Defense has used in these cases, and when held in a territory, like Guantanamo, over which the Government has total military and civil control.

We know that at common law a petitioner's status as an alien was not a categorical bar to habeas corpus relief. See, *e.g., Sommersett's Case,* 20 How. St. Tr. 1, 80-82 (1772) (ordering an African slave freed upon finding the custodian's return insufficient); see generally *Khera* v. *Secretary of State for the Home Dept.,* [1984] A. C. 74, 111 ("Habeas corpus protection is often expressed as limited to 'British subjects.' Is it really limited to British nationals? Suffice it to say that the case law has given an emphatic 'no' to the question"). We know as well that common-law courts entertained habeas petitions brought by enemy aliens detained in England--"entertained" at least in the sense that the courts held hearings to determine the threshold question of entitlement to the writ. See *Case of Three Spanish Sailors,* 2 Black. W. 1324, 96 Eng. Rep. 775 (C. P. 1779); *King* v. *Schiever,* 2 Burr. 765, 97 Eng. Rep. 551 (K. B. 1759); *Du Castro's Case,* Fort. 195, 92 Eng. Rep. 816 (K. B. 1697).

In *Schiever* and the *Spanish Sailors*' case, the courts denied relief to the petitioners. Whether the holdings in these cases were jurisdictional or based upon the courts' ruling that the petitioners were detained lawfully as prisoners of war is unclear. See *Spanish Sailors, supra,* at 1324, 96 Eng. Rep., at 776; *Schiever, supra,* at 766, 97 Eng. Rep., at 552. In *Du Castro's Case,* the court granted relief, but that case is not analogous to petitioners' because the prisoner there appears to have been detained in England. See Halliday & White 27, n 72. To the extent these authorities suggest the common-law courts abstained altogether from matters involving prisoners of war, there was greater justification for doing so in the context of declared wars with other nation states. Judicial intervention might have complicated the military's ability to negotiate exchange of prisoners with the enemy, a wartime practice well known to the Framers. See Resolution of Mar. 30, 1778, 10 Journals of the Continental Congress 1774-1789, p 295 (W. Ford ed. 1908) (directing General Washington not to exchange prisoners with the British unless the enemy agreed to exempt citizens from capture).

We find the evidence as to the geographic scope of the writ at common law informative, but, again, not dispositive. Petitioners argue the site of their detention is analogous to two territories outside of England to which the writ did run: the so-called "exempt jurisdictions," like the Channel Islands; and (in former times) India. There are critical differences between these places and Guantanamo, however.

As the Court noted in *Rasul*, *542 U.S., at 481-482, 124 S. Ct. 2686, 159 L. Ed. 2d 548*, common-law courts granted habeas corpus relief to prisoners detained in the exempt jurisdictions. But these areas, while not in theory part of the realm of England, were nonetheless under the Crown's control. See 2 H. Hallam, Constitutional History of England: From the Accession of Henry VII to the Death of George II, pp 232-233 (reprint 1989). And there is some indication that these jurisdictions were considered sovereign territory. *King* v. *Cowle*, 2 Burr. 834, 854, 855, 856, 97 Eng. Rep. 587, 599 (K. B. 1759) (describing one of the exempt jurisdictions, Berwick-upon-Tweed, as under the "sovereign jurisdiction" and "subjection of the Crown of England"). Because the United States does not maintain formal sovereignty over Guantanamo Bay, see Part IV, *infra*, the naval station there and the exempt jurisdictions discussed in the English authorities are not similarly situated.

Petitioners and their *amici* further rely on cases in which British courts in India granted writs of habeas corpus to noncitizens detained in territory over which the Moghul Emperor retained formal sovereignty and control. See Brief for Petitioner Boumediene et al. Brief for Legal Historians as *Amici Curiae* 12-13. The analogy to the present cases breaks down, however, because of the geographic location of the courts in the Indian example. The Supreme Court of Judicature (the British Court) sat in Calcutta; but no federal court sits at Guantanamo. The Supreme Court of Judicature was, moreover, a special court set up by Parliament to monitor certain conduct during the British Raj. See Regulating Act of 1773, 13 Geo. 3, ch. 63, §§ 13-14. That it had the power to issue the writ in nonsovereign territory does not prove that common-law courts sitting in England had the same power. If petitioners were to have the better of the argument on this point, we would need some demonstration of a consistent practice of common-law courts sitting in England and entertaining petitions brought by alien prisoners detained abroad. We find little support for this conclusion.

The Government argues, in turn, that Guantanamo is more closely analogous to Scotland and Hanover, territories that were not part of England but nonetheless controlled by the English monarch (in his separate capacities as King of Scotland and Elector of Hanover). See *Cowle*, 2 Burr., at 856, 97 Eng. Rep., at 600. Lord Mansfield can be cited for the proposition that, at the time of the founding, English courts lacked the "power" to issue the writ to Scotland and Hanover, territories

Lord Mansfield referred to as "foreign." *Ibid.* But what matters for our purposes is why common-law courts lacked this power. Given the English Crown's delicate and complicated relationships with Scotland and Hanover in the 1700's, we cannot disregard the possibility that the common-law courts' refusal to issue the writ to these places was motivated not by formal legal constructs but by what we would think of as prudential concerns. This appears to have been the case with regard to other British territories where the writ did not run. See 2 R. Chambers, A Course of Lectures on English Law 1767-1773, p 8 (T. Curley ed. 1986) (discussing the view of Lord Mansfield in *Cowle* that "[n]otwithstanding the *power* which the judges have, yet where they cannot judge of the cause, or give relief upon it, they would not think *proper* to interpose; and therefore in the case of imprisonments in *Guernsey, Jersey, Minorca,* or the *plantations,* the most usual way is to complain to the *king in Council*" (internal quotation marks omitted)). And after the Act of Union in 1707, through which the kingdoms of England and Scotland were merged politically, Queen Anne and her successors, in their new capacity as sovereign of Great Britain, ruled the entire island as one kingdom. Accordingly, by the time Lord Mansfield penned his opinion in *Cowle* in 1759, Scotland was no longer a "foreign" country vis-a-vis England--at least not in the sense in which Cuba is a foreign country vis-a-vis the United States.

Scotland remained "foreign" in Lord Mansfield's day in at least one important respect, however. Even after the Act of Union, Scotland (like Hanover) continued to maintain its own laws and court system. See 1 Blackstone *98, *106. Under these circumstances prudential considerations would have weighed heavily when courts sitting in England received habeas petitions from Scotland or the Electorate. Common-law decisions withholding the writ from prisoners detained in these places easily could be explained as efforts to avoid either or both of two embarrassments: conflict with the judgments of another court of competent jurisdiction; or the practical inability, by reason of distance, of the English courts to enforce their judgments outside their territorial jurisdiction. Cf. *Munaf v. Geren, ante,* at _ 128 S. Ct. 2207, 171 L. Ed. 2d 1 (opinion of the Court) (recognizing that "'prudential concerns' . . . such as comity and the orderly administration of criminal justice" affect the appropriate exercise of habeas jurisdiction).

By the mid-19th century, British courts could issue the writ to Canada, notwithstanding the fact that Canadian courts also had the power to do so. See 9 Holdsworth 124 (citing *Ex parte Anderson*, 3 El. and El. 487 (1861)). This might be seen as evidence that the existence of a separate court system was no barrier to the running of the common-law writ. The Canada of the 1800's, however, was in many respects more analogous to the exempt jurisdictions or to Ireland, where the writ ran, than to Scotland or Hanover in the 1700's, where it did not. Unlike

Scotland and Hanover, Canada followed English law. See B. Laskin, The British Tradition in Canadian Law 50-51 (1969).

In the end a categorical or formal conception of sovereignty does not provide a comprehensive or altogether satisfactory explanation for the general understanding that prevailed when Lord Mansfield considered issuance of the writ outside England. In 1759 the writ did not run to Scotland but did run to Ireland, even though, at that point, Scotland and England had merged under the rule of a single sovereign, whereas the Crowns of Great Britain and Ireland remained separate (at least in theory). See *Cowle, supra*, at 856-857, 97 Eng. Rep., at 600; 1 Blackstone *100-*101. But there was at least one major difference between Scotland's and Ireland's relationship with England during this period that might explain why the writ ran to Ireland but not to Scotland. English law did not generally apply in Scotland (even after the Act of Union), but it did apply in Ireland. Blackstone put it as follows: "[A]s Scotland and England are now one and the same kingdom, and yet differ in their municipal laws; so England and Ireland are, on the other hand, distinct kingdoms, and yet in general agree in their laws." *Id.*, at *100 (footnote omitted). This distinction, and not formal notions of sovereignty, may well explain why the writ did not run to Scotland (and Hanover) but would run to Ireland.

The prudential barriers that may have prevented the English courts from issuing the writ to Scotland and Hanover are not relevant here. We have no reason to believe an order from a federal court would be disobeyed at Guantanamo. No Cuban court has jurisdiction to hear these petitioners' claims, and no law other than the laws of the United States applies at the naval station. The modern-day relations between the United States and Guantanamo thus differ in important respects from the 18th-century relations between England and the kingdoms of Scotland and Hanover. This is reason enough for us to discount the relevance of the Government's analogy.

Each side in the present matter argues that the very lack of a precedent on point supports its position. The Government points out there is no evidence that a court sitting in England granted habeas relief to an enemy alien detained abroad; petitioners respond there is no evidence that a court refused to do so for lack of jurisdiction.

Both arguments are premised, however, upon the assumption that the historical record is complete and that the common law, if properly understood, yields a definite answer to the questions before us. There are reasons to doubt both assumptions. Recent scholarship points to the inherent shortcomings in the historical record. See Halliday & White 14-15 (noting that most reports of 18th-century habeas proceedings were not printed). And given the unique status of

Guantanamo Bay and the particular dangers of terrorism in the modern age, the common-law courts simply may not have confronted cases with close parallels to this one. We decline, therefore, to infer too much, one way or the other, from the lack of historical evidence on point. Cf. *Brown v. Board of Education,* 347 U.S. 483, 489, 74 S. Ct. 686, 98 L. Ed. 873 (1954) (noting evidence concerning the circumstances surrounding the adoption of the *Fourteenth Amendment,* discussed in the parties' briefs and uncovered through the Court's own investigation, "convince us that, although these sources cast some light, it is not enough to resolve the problem with which we are faced. At best, they are inconclusive"); *Reid v. Covert,* 354 U.S. 1, 64, 77 S. Ct. 1222, 1 L. Ed. 2d 1148 (1957) (Frankfurter, J., concurring in result) (arguing constitutional adjudication should not be based upon evidence that is "too episodic, too meager, to form a solid basis in history, preceding and contemporaneous with the framing of the Constitution").

IV

Drawing from its position that at common law the writ ran only to territories over which the Crown was sovereign, the Government says the Suspension Clause affords petitioners no rights because the United States does not claim sovereignty over the place of detention.

Guantanamo Bay is not formally part of the United States. See DTA § 1005(g), 119 Stat. 2743. And under the terms of the lease between the United States and Cuba, Cuba retains "ultimate sovereignty" over the territory while the United States exercises "complete jurisdiction and control." See Lease of Lands for Coaling and Naval Stations, Feb. 23, 1903, U. S.-Cuba, Art. III, T. S. No. 418 (hereinafter 1903 Lease Agreement); *Rasul,* 542 U.S., at 471, 124 S. Ct. 2686, 159 L. Ed. 2d 548. Under the terms of the 1934 treaty, however, Cuba effectively has no rights as a sovereign until the parties agree to modification of the 1903 Lease Agreement or the United States abandons the base. See Treaty Defining Relations with Cuba, May 29, 1934, U. S.-Cuba, Art. III, 48 Stat. 1683, T. S. No. 866.

The United States contends, nevertheless, that Guantanamo is not within its sovereign control. This was the Government's position well before the events of September 11, 2001. See, *e.g.,* Brief for Petitioners in *Sale* v. *Haitian Centers Council, Inc.,* O. T. 1992, No. 92-344, p 31 (arguing that Guantanamo is territory "*outside* the United States"). And in other contexts the Court has held that questions of sovereignty are for the political branches to decide. See *Vermilya-Brown Co. v. Connell,* 335 U.S. 377, 380, 69 S. Ct. 140, 93 L. Ed. 76 (1948) ("[D]etermination of sovereignty over an area is for the legislative and executive departments"); see also *Jones v. United States,* 137 U.S. 202, 11 S. Ct. 80, 34 L. Ed. 691 (1890); *Williams v. Suffolk Ins. Co.,* 38 U.S. 415, 13 Pet. 415, 420, 10 L. Ed. 226 (1839). Even if this were a treaty interpretation case that did not involve a political question, the President's construction of the lease agreement would be entitled to great respect. See *Sumitomo Shoji America, Inc. v. Avagliano*, 457 U.S. 176, 184-185, 102 S. Ct. 2374, 72 L. Ed. 2d 765 (1982).

We therefore do not question the Government's position that Cuba, not the United States, maintains sovereignty, in the legal and technical sense of the term, over Guantanamo Bay. But this does not end the analysis. Our cases do not hold it is improper for us to inquire into the objective degree of control the Nation asserts over foreign territory. As commentators have noted, "'[s]overeignty' is a term used in many senses and is much abused." See *1 Restatement (Third) of Foreign Relations Law of the United States* § 206, Comment b, p. 94 (1986). When we have stated that sovereignty is a political question, we have referred not to sovereignty in the general, colloquial sense, meaning the exercise of dominion or power, see Webster's New International Dictionary 2406 (2d ed. 1934) ("sovereignty," definition 3), but sovereignty in the narrow, legal sense of the term, meaning a claim of right, see *1 Restatement (Third) of Foreign Relations, supra*, § 206, Comment b, at 94 (noting that sovereignty "implies a state's lawful control over its territory generally to the exclusion of other states, authority to govern in that territory, and authority to apply law there"). Indeed, it is not altogether uncommon for a territory to be under the *de jure* sovereignty of one nation, while under the plenary control, or practical sovereignty, of another. This condition can occur when the territory is seized during war, as Guantanamo was during the Spanish-American War. See, *e.g., Fleming v. Page*, 50 U.S. 603, 9 How. 603, 614, 13 L. Ed. 276 (1850) (noting that the port of Tampico, conquered by the United States during the war with Mexico, was "undoubtedly . . . subject to the sovereignty and dominion of the United States," but that it "does not follow that it was a part of the United States, or that it ceased to be a foreign country"); *King v. Earl of Crewe ex parte Sekgome*, [1910] 2 K. B. 576, 603-604 (C. A.) (opinion of Williams, L. J.) (arguing that the Bechuanaland Protectorate in South Africa was "under His Majesty's dominion in the sense of power and jurisdiction, but is not under his dominion in the sense of territorial dominion"). Accordingly, for purposes of our analysis, we accept the Government's position that Cuba, and not the United States, retains *de jure* sovereignty over Guantanamo Bay. As we did in *Rasul*, however, we take notice of the obvious and uncontested fact that the United States, by virtue of its complete jurisdiction and control over the base, maintains *de facto* sovereignty over this territory. See *542 U.S., at 480, 124 S. Ct. 2686, 159 L. Ed. 2d 548*; *id., at 487, 124 S. Ct. 2686, 159 L. Ed. 2d 548* (Kennedy, J., concurring in judgment).

Were we to hold that the present cases turn on the political question doctrine, we would be required first to accept the Government's premise that *de jure* sovereignty is the touchstone of habeas corpus jurisdiction. This premise, however, is unfounded. For the reasons indicated above, the history of common-law habeas corpus provides scant support for this proposition; and, for the reasons indicated below, that position would be inconsistent with our precedents and contrary to fundamental separation-of-powers principles.

A

The Court has discussed the issue of the Constitution's extraterritorial application on many occasions. These decisions undermine the Government's argument that, at least as applied to noncitizens, the Constitution necessarily stops where *de jure* sovereignty ends.

The Framers foresaw that the United States would expand and acquire new territories. See *American Ins. Co. v. 356 Bales of Cotton, 26 U.S. 511, 1 Pet. 511, 542, 7 L. Ed. 242, 1 F. Cas. 658 (1828)*. Article IV, § 3, cl. 1, grants Congress the power to admit new States. Clause 2 of the same section grants Congress the "Power to dispose of and make all needful Rules and Regulations respecting the Territory or other Property belonging to the United States." Save for a few notable (and notorious) exceptions, *e.g., Dred Scott v. Sandford, 60 U.S. 393, 19 How. 393, 15 L. Ed. 691 (1857)*, throughout most of our history there was little need to explore the outer boundaries of the Constitution's geographic reach. When Congress exercised its power to create new territories, it guaranteed constitutional protections to the inhabitants by statute. See, *e.g.*, An Act: to establish a Territorial Government for Utah, *9 Stat. 458* ("[T]he Constitution and laws of the United States are hereby extended over and declared to be in force in said Territory of Utah"); Rev. Stat. § 1891 ("The Constitution and all laws of the United States which are not locally inapplicable shall have the same force and effect within all the organized Territories, and in every Territory hereafter organized as elsewhere within the United States"); see generally Burnett, United States: American Expansion and Territorial Deannexation, *72 U. Chi. L. Rev. 797, 825-827 (2005)*. In particular, there was no need to test the limits of the Suspension Clause because, as early as 1789, Congress extended the writ to the Territories. See Act of Aug. 7, 1789, *1 Stat. 52* (reaffirming Art. II of Northwest Ordinance of 1787, which provided that "[t]he inhabitants of the said territory, shall always be entitled to the benefits of the writ of habeas corpus").

Fundamental questions regarding the Constitution's geographic scope first arose at the dawn of the 20th century when the Nation acquired noncontiguous Territories: Puerto Rico, Guam, and the Philippines--ceded to the United States by Spain at the conclusion of the Spanish-American War--and Hawaii--annexed by the United States in 1898. At this point Congress chose to discontinue its previous practice of extending constitutional rights to the Territories by statute. See, *e.g.*, An Act Temporarily to provide for the administration of the affairs of civil government in the Philippine Islands, and for other purposes, 32 Stat. 692 (noting that Rev. Stat. § 1891 did not apply to the Philippines).

In a series of opinions later known as the Insular Cases, the Court addressed whether the Constitution, by its own force, applies in any territory that is not a State. See *De Lima v. Bidwell, 182 U.S. 1, 21 S. Ct. 743, 45 L. Ed. 1041 (1901)*; *Dooley v. United States, 182 U.S. 222, 21 S. Ct. 762, 45 L. Ed. 1074 (1901)*; *Armstrong v. United States, 182 U.S. 243, 21 S. Ct. 827, 45 L. Ed. 1086 (1901)*; *Downes v. Bidwell, 182 U.S. 244, 21 S. Ct. 770, 45 L. Ed. 1088 (1901)*; *Hawaii v. Mankichi, 190 U.S. 197, 23 S. Ct. 787, 47 L. Ed. 1016 (1903)*; *Dorr v. United States, 195 U.S. 138, 24 S. Ct. 808, 49 L. Ed. 128 (1904)*. The Court held that the Constitution has independent force in these Territories, a force not contingent upon acts of legislative grace. Yet it took note of the difficulties inherent in that position.

Prior to their cession to the United States, the former Spanish colonies operated under a civil-law system, without experience in the various aspects of the Anglo-American legal tradition, for instance the use of grand and petit juries. At least with regard to the Philippines, a complete transformation of the prevailing legal culture would have been not only disruptive but also unnecessary, as the United States intended to grant independence to that Territory. See An Act To declare the purpose of the people of the United States as to the future political status of the people of the Philippine Islands, and to provide a more autonomous government for those islands (Jones Act), *39 Stat. 545* (noting that "it was never the intention of the people of the United States in the incipiency of the War with Spain to make it a war of conquest or for territorial aggrandizement" and that "it is, as it has always been, the purpose of the people of the United States to withdraw their sovereignty over the Philippine Islands and to recognize their independence as soon as a stable government can be established therein"). The Court thus was reluctant to risk the uncertainty and instability that could result from a rule that displaced altogether the existing legal systems in these newly acquired Territories. See *Downes, supra, at 282, 21 S. Ct. 770, 45 L. Ed. 1088* ("It is obvious that in the annexation of outlying and distant possessions grave questions will arise from differences of race, habits, laws and customs of the people, and from differences of soil, climate and production . . .").

These considerations resulted in the doctrine of territorial incorporation, under which the Constitution applies in full in incorporated Territories surely destined for statehood but only in part in unincorporated Territories. See *Dorr, supra, at 143, 24 S. Ct. 808, 49 L. Ed. 128* ("Until Congress shall see fit to incorporate territory

233

ceded by treaty into the United States, . . . the territory is to be governed under the power existing in Congress to make laws for such territories and subject to such constitutional restrictions upon the powers of that body as are applicable to the situation"); *Downes, supra*, at 293, *21 S. Ct. 770, 45 L. Ed. 1088* (White, J., concurring) ("[T]he determination of what particular provision of the Constitution is applicable, generally speaking, in all cases, involves an inquiry into the situation of the territory and its relations to the United States"). As the Court later made clear, "the real issue in the *Insular Cases* was not whether the Constitution extended to the Philippines or Porto Rico when we went there, but which of its provisions were applicable by way of limitation upon the exercise of executive and legislative power in dealing with new conditions and requirements." *Balzac v. Porto Rico, 258 U.S. 298,* 312, *42 S. Ct. 343, 66 L. Ed. 627 (1922)*. It may well be that over time the ties between the United States and any of its unincorporated Territories strengthen in ways that are of constitutional significance. Cf. *Torres v. Puerto Rico, 442 U.S. 465,* 475-476, *99 S. Ct. 2425, 61 L. Ed. 2d 1 (1979)* (Brennan, J., concurring in judgment) ("Whatever the validity of the [Insular Cases] in the particular historical context in which they were decided, those cases are clearly not authority for questioning the application of the *Fourth Amendment*--or any other provision of the *Bill of Rights*--to the Commonwealth of Puerto Rico in the 1970's"). But, as early as *Balzac* in 1922, the Court took for granted that even in unincorporated Territories the Government of the United States was bound to provide to noncitizen inhabitants "guaranties of certain fundamental personal rights declared in the Constitution." *258 U.S., at 312, 312, 42 S. Ct. 343, 66 L. Ed. 627*; see also *Late Corp. of Church of Jesus Christ of Latter-day Saints v. United States, 136 U.S. 1,* 44, *10 S. Ct. 792, 34 L. Ed. 478 (1890)* ("Doubtless Congress, in legislating for the Territories would be subject to those fundamental limitations in favor of personal rights which are formulated in the Constitution and its amendments"). Yet noting the inherent practical difficulties of enforcing all constitutional provisions "always and everywhere," *Balzac, supra, at 312, 312, 42 S. Ct. 343, 66 L. Ed. 627*, the Court devised in the Insular Cases a doctrine that allowed it to use its power sparingly and where it would be most needed. This century-old doctrine informs our analysis in the present matter.

Practical considerations likewise influenced the Court's analysis a half century later in *Reid, 354 U.S. 1, 77 S. Ct. 1222, 1 L. Ed. 2d 1148*. The petitioners there, spouses of American servicemen, lived on American military bases in England and Japan. They were charged with crimes committed in those countries and tried before military courts, consistent with executive agreements the United States had entered into with the British and Japanese Governments. *Id., at 15-16, 77 S. Ct. 1222, 1 L. Ed. 2d 1148* (plurality opinion). Because the petitioners were not themselves military personnel, they argued they were entitled to trial by jury.

Justice Black, writing for the plurality, contrasted the cases before him with the Insular Cases, which involved territories "with wholly dissimilar traditions and institutions" that Congress intended to govern only "temporarily." *Id., at 14, 77 S. Ct. 1222, 1 L. Ed. 2d 1148*. Justice Frankfurter argued that the "specific circumstances of each particular case" are relevant in determining the geographic scope of the Constitution. *Id., at 54, 77 S. Ct. 1222, 1 L. Ed. 2d 1148* (opinion concurring in result). And Justice Harlan, who had joined an opinion reaching the opposite result in the case in the previous Term, *Reid v. Covert*, 351 U.S. 487, 76 S. Ct. 880, 100 L. Ed. 1352 (1956), was most explicit in rejecting a "rigid and abstract rule" for determining where constitutional guarantees extend. *Reid, 354 U.S., at 74, 77 S. Ct. 1222, 1 L. Ed. 2d 1148* (opinion concurring in result). He read the Insular Cases to teach that whether a constitutional provision has extraterritorial effect depends upon the "particular circumstances, the practical necessities, and the possible alternatives which Congress had before it" and, in particular, whether judicial enforcement of the provision would be "impracticable and anomalous." *Id., at 74-75, 77 S. Ct. 1222, 1 L. Ed. 2d 1148*; see also *United States v. Verdugo-Urquidez*, 494 U.S. 259, 277-278, 110 S. Ct. 1056, 108 L. Ed. 2d 222 (1990) (Kennedy, J., concurring) (applying the "impracticable and anomalous" extraterritoriality test in the *Fourth Amendment* context).

That the petitioners in *Reid* were American citizens was a key factor in the case and was central to the plurality's conclusion that the *Fifth* and *Sixth Amendments* apply to American civilians tried outside the United States. But practical considerations, related not to the petitioners' citizenship but to the place of their confinement and trial, were relevant to each Member of the *Reid* majority. And to Justices Harlan and Frankfurter (whose votes were necessary to the Court's disposition) these considerations were the decisive factors in the case.

Indeed the majority splintered on this very point. The key disagreement between the plurality and the concurring Justices in *Reid* was over the continued precedential value of the Court's previous opinion in *In re Ross*, 140 U.S. 453, 11 S. Ct. 897, 35 L. Ed. 581 (1891), which the *Reid* Court understood as holding that under some circumstances Americans abroad have no right to indictment and trial by jury. The petitioner in *Ross* was a sailor serving on an American merchant vessel in Japanese waters who was tried before an American consular tribunal for the murder of a fellow crewman. *140 U.S., at 459, 479, 11 S. Ct. 897, 35 L. Ed. 581*. The *Ross* Court held that the petitioner, who was a British subject, had no rights under the *Fifth* and *Sixth Amendments. Id., at 464, 11 S. Ct. 897, 35 L. Ed. 581*. The petitioner's citizenship played no role in the disposition of the case, however. The Court assumed (consistent with the maritime custom of the time) that Ross had all the rights of a similarly situated American citizen. *Id., at 479, 11 S. Ct. 897, 35 L. Ed.*

581 (noting that Ross was "under the protection and subject to the laws of the United States equally with the seaman who was native born"). The Justices in *Reid* therefore properly understood *Ross* as standing for the proposition that, at least in some circumstances, the jury provisions of the *Fifth* and *Sixth Amendments* have no application to American citizens tried by American authorities abroad. See *354 U.S., at 11-12, 77 S. Ct. 1222, 1 L. Ed. 2d 1148* (plurality opinion) (describing *Ross* as holding that "constitutional protections applied 'only to citizens and others within the United States . . . and not to residents or temporary sojourners abroad'" (quoting *Ross, supra, at 464, 11 S. Ct. 897, 35 L. Ed. 581*)); *354 U.S., at 64, 77 S. Ct. 1222, 1 L. Ed. 2d 1148* (Frankfurter, J., concurring in result) (noting that the consular tribunals upheld in *Ross* "w[ere] based on long-established custom and they were justified as the best possible means for securing justice for the few Americans present in [foreign] countries"); *354 U.S., at 75, 77 S. Ct. 1222, 1 L. Ed. 2d 1148* (Harlan, J., concurring in result) ("What *Ross* and the *Insular Cases* hold is that the particular local setting, the practical necessities, and the possible alternatives are relevant to a question of judgment, namely, whether jury trial *should* be deemed a necessary condition of the exercise of Congress' power to provide for the trial of Americans overseas").

The *Reid* plurality doubted that *Ross* was rightly decided, precisely because it believed the opinion was insufficiently protective of the rights of American citizens. See *354 U.S., at 10-12, 77 S. Ct. 1222, 1 L. Ed. 2d 1148*; see also *id., at 78, 77 S. Ct. 1222, 1 L. Ed. 2d 1148* (Clark, J., dissenting) (noting that "four of my brothers would specifically overrule and two would impair the long-recognized vitality of an old and respected precedent in our law, the case of In re Ross, 140 U.S. 453, 11 S. Ct. 897, 35 L. Ed. 581 (1891)"). But Justices Harlan and Frankfurter, while willing to hold that the American citizen petitioners in the cases before them were entitled to the protections of *Fifth* and *Sixth Amendments*, were unwilling to overturn *Ross*. *354 U.S., at 64, 77 S. Ct. 1222, 1 L. Ed. 2d 1148* (Frankfurter, J., concurring in result); *id., at 75, 77 S. Ct. 1222, 1 L. Ed. 2d 1148* (Harlan, J., concurring in result). Instead, the two concurring Justices distinguished *Ross* from the cases before them, not on the basis of the citizenship of the petitioners, but on practical considerations that made jury trial a more feasible option for them than it was for the petitioner in *Ross*. If citizenship had been the only relevant factor in the case, it would have been necessary for the Court to overturn *Ross*, something Justices Harlan and Frankfurter were unwilling to do. See *Verdugo-Urquidez, supra, at 277, 110 S. Ct. 1056, 108 L. Ed. 2d 222* (Kennedy, J., concurring) (noting that *Ross* had not been overruled).

Practical considerations weighed heavily as well in *Johnson v. Eisentrager, 339 U.S. 763, 70 S. Ct. 936, 94 L. Ed. 1255 (1950)*, where the Court addressed whether habeas corpus jurisdiction extended to enemy aliens who had been convicted of violating the laws of war. The prisoners were detained at Landsberg Prison in Germany during the Allied Powers' post-war occupation. The Court stressed the difficulties of ordering the Government to produce the prisoners in a habeas corpus proceeding. It "would require allocation of shipping space, guarding personnel, billeting and rations" and would damage the prestige of military commanders at a sensitive time. *Id.*, at 779, 70 S. Ct. 936, 94 L. Ed. 1255. In considering these factors the Court sought to balance the constraints of military occupation with constitutional necessities. *Id.*, at 769-779, 70 S. Ct. 936, 94 L. Ed. 1255; see *Rasul*, 542 U.S., at 475-476, 124 S. Ct. 2686, 159 L. Ed. 2d 548 (discussing the factors relevant to *Eisentrager*'s constitutional holding); 542 U.S., at 486, 124 S. Ct. 2686, 159 L. Ed. 2d 548 (Kennedy, J., concurring in judgment) (same).

True, the Court in *Eisentrager* denied access to the writ, and it noted the prisoners "at no relevant time were within any territory over which the United States is sovereign, and [that] the scenes of their offense, their capture, their trial and their punishment were all beyond the territorial jurisdiction of any court of the United States." 339 U.S., at 778, 70 S. Ct. 936, 94 L. Ed. 1255. The Government seizes upon this language as proof positive that the *Eisentrager* Court adopted a formalistic, sovereignty-based test for determining the reach of the Suspension Clause. See Brief for Federal Respondents 18-20. We reject this reading for three reasons.

First, we do not accept the idea that the above-quoted passage from *Eisentrager* is the only authoritative language in the opinion and that all the rest is dicta. The Court's further determinations, based on practical considerations, were integral to Part II of its opinion and came before the decision announced its holding. See *339 U.S., at 781, 70 S. Ct. 936, 94 L. Ed. 1255.*

Second, because the United States lacked both *de jure* sovereignty and plenary control over Landsberg Prison, see *infra*, at 768, 171 L. Ed. 2d, at 76-77, it is far from clear that the *Eisentrager* Court used the term sovereignty only in the narrow technical sense and not to connote the degree of control the military asserted over the facility. See *supra*, at 751-752, 171 L. Ed. 2d, at 68. The Justices who decided *Eisentrager* would have understood sovereignty as a multifaceted concept. See Black's Law Dictionary 1568 (4th ed. 1951) (defining "sovereignty" as "[t]he supreme, absolute, and uncontrollable power by which any independent state is governed"; "the international independence of a state, combined with the right and power of regulating its internal affairs without foreign dictation"; and "[t]he power to do everything in a state without accountability"); Ballentine's Law Dictionary With Pronunciations 1216 (2d ed. 1948) (defining "sovereignty" as "[t]hat public authority which commands in civil society, and orders and directs what each citizen is to perform to obtain the end of its institution"). In its principal brief in *Eisentrager*, the Government advocated a bright-line test for determining the scope of the writ, similar to the one it advocates in these cases. See Brief for Petitioners in *Johnson* v. *Eisentrager*, O. T. 1949, No. 306, pp 74-75. Yet the Court mentioned the concept of territorial sovereignty only twice in its opinion. See *Eisentrager, supra, at 778, 780, 70 S. Ct. 936, 94 L. Ed. 1255*. That the Court devoted a significant portion of Part II to a discussion of practical barriers to the running of the writ suggests that the Court was not concerned exclusively with the formal legal status of Landsberg Prison but also with the objective degree of control the United States asserted over it. Even if we assume the *Eisentrager* Court considered the United States' lack of formal legal sovereignty over Landsberg Prison as the decisive factor in that case, its holding is not inconsistent with a functional approach to questions of extraterritoriality. The formal legal status of a given territory affects, at least to some extent, the political branches' control over that territory. *De jure* sovereignty is a factor that bears upon which constitutional guarantees apply there.

Third, if the Government's reading of *Eisentrager* were correct, the opinion would have marked not only a change in, but a complete repudiation of, the Insular Cases' (and later *Reid*'s) functional approach to questions of extraterritoriality. We cannot accept the Government's view. Nothing in *Eisentrager* says that *de jure* sovereignty is or has ever been the only relevant consideration in determining the geographic reach of the Constitution or of habeas corpus. Were that the case, there would be considerable tension between *Eisentrager*, on the one hand, and the Insular Cases and *Reid*, on the other. Our cases need not be read to conflict in this manner. A constricted reading of *Eisentrager* overlooks what we see as a common thread uniting the Insular Cases, *Eisentrager*, and *Reid:* the idea that questions of extraterritoriality turn on objective factors and practical concerns, not formalism.

B

The Government's formal sovereignty-based test raises troubling separation-of-powers concerns as well. The political history of Guantanamo illustrates the deficiencies of this approach. The United States has maintained complete and uninterrupted control of the bay for over 100 years. At the close of the Spanish-American War, Spain ceded control over the entire island of Cuba to the United States and specifically "relinquishe[d] all claim[s] of sovereignty . . . and title." See Treaty of Paris, Dec. 10, 1898, U. S.-Spain, Art. I, 30 Stat. 1755, T. S. No. 343. From the date the treaty with Spain was signed until the Cuban Republic was established on May 20, 1902, the United States governed the territory "in trust" for the benefit of the Cuban people. *Neely v. Henkel, 180 U.S. 109, 120, 21 S. Ct. 302, 45 L. Ed. 448 (1901)*; H. Thomas, Cuba or The Pursuit of Freedom 436, 460 (1998). And although it recognized, by entering into the 1903 Lease Agreement, that Cuba retained "ultimate sovereignty" over Guantanamo, the United States continued to maintain the same plenary control it had enjoyed since 1898. Yet the Government's view is that the Constitution had no effect there, at least as to noncitizens, because the United States disclaimed sovereignty in the formal sense of the term. The necessary implication of the argument is that by surrendering formal sovereignty over any unincorporated territory to a third party, while at the same time entering into a lease that grants total control over the territory back to the United States, it would be possible for the political branches to govern without legal constraint.

Our basic charter cannot be contracted away like this. The Constitution grants Congress and the President the power to acquire, dispose of, and govern territory, not the power to decide when and where its terms apply. Even when the United States acts outside its borders, its powers are not "absolute and unlimited" but are subject "to such restrictions as are expressed in the Constitution." *Murphy v. Ramsey, 114 U.S. 15, 44, 5 S. Ct. 747, 29 L. Ed. 47 (1885)*. Abstaining from questions involving formal sovereignty and territorial governance is one thing. To hold the political branches have the power to switch the Constitution on or off at will is quite another. The former position reflects this Court's recognition that certain matters requiring political judgments are best left to the political branches. The latter would permit a striking anomaly in our tripartite system of government, leading to a regime in which Congress and the President, not this Court, say "what the law is." *Marbury v. Madison, 5 U.S. 137, 1 Cranch 137, 177, 2 L. Ed. 60 (1803)*.

These concerns have particular bearing upon the Suspension Clause question in the cases now before us, for the writ of habeas corpus is itself an indispensable mechanism for monitoring the separation of powers. The test for determining the scope of this provision must not be subject to manipulation by those whose power it is designed to restrain.

C

As we recognized in *Rasul, 542 U.S., at 476, 124 S. Ct. 2686, 159 L. Ed. 2d 548; id., at 487, 124 S. Ct. 2686, 159 L. Ed. 2d 548* (Kennedy, J., concurring in judgment), the outlines of a framework for determining the reach of the Suspension Clause are suggested by the factors the Court relied upon in *Eisentrager*. In addition to the practical concerns discussed above, the *Eisentrager* Court found relevant that each petitioner:

> "(a) is an enemy alien; (b) has never been or resided in the United States; (c) was captured outside of our territory and there held in military custody as a prisoner of war; (d) was tried and convicted by a Military Commission sitting outside the United States; (e) for offenses against laws of war committed

outside the United States; (f) and is at all times imprisoned outside the United States." *339 U.S., at 777, 70 S. Ct. 936, 94 L. Ed. 1255.*

Based on this language from *Eisentrager*, and the reasoning in our other extraterritoriality opinions, we conclude that at least three factors are relevant in determining the reach of the Suspension Clause: (1) the citizenship and status of the detainee and the adequacy of the process through which that status determination was made; (2) the nature of the sites where apprehension and then detention took place; and (3) the practical obstacles inherent in resolving the prisoner's entitlement to the writ.

Applying this framework, we note at the onset that the status of these detainees is a matter of dispute. Petitioners, like those in *Eisentrager*, are not American citizens. But the petitioners in *Eisentrager* did not contest, it seems, the Court's assertion that they were "enemy alien[s]." *Ibid.* In the instant cases, by contrast, the detainees deny they are enemy combatants. They have been afforded some process in CSRT proceedings to determine their status; but, unlike in *Eisentrager, supra, at 766, 70 S. Ct. 936, 94 L. Ed. 1255*, there has been no trial by military commission for violations of the laws of war. The difference is not trivial. The records from the *Eisentrager* trials suggest that, well before the petitioners brought their case to this Court, there had been a rigorous adversarial process to test the legality of their detention. The *Eisentrager* petitioners were charged by a bill of particulars that made detailed factual allegations against them. See 14 United Nations War Crimes Commission, Law Reports of Trials of War Criminals 8-10 (1949) (reprint 1997). To rebut the accusations, they were entitled to representation by counsel, allowed to introduce evidence on their own behalf, and permitted to cross-examine the prosecution's witnesses. See Memorandum by Command of Lt. Gen. Wedemeyer, Jan. 21, 1946 (establishing "Regulations Governing the Trial of War Criminals" in the China Theater), in Tr. of Record in *Johnson v. Eisentrager*, O. T. 1949, No. 306, pp 34-40.

In comparison the procedural protections afforded to the detainees in the CSRT hearings are far more limited, and, we conclude, fall well short of the procedures and adversarial mechanisms that would eliminate the need for habeas corpus review. Although the detainee is assigned a "Personal Representative" to assist him during CSRT proceedings, the Secretary of the Navy's memorandum makes clear that person is not the detainee's lawyer or even his "advocate." See App. to Pet. for Cert. in No. 06-1196, at 155, ¶ F(1),172. The Government's evidence is accorded a presumption of validity. *Id.*, at 159. The detainee is allowed to present "reasonably available" evidence, *id.*, at 155, ¶(F)1, but his ability to rebut the Government's evidence against him is limited by the circumstances of his confinement and his lack of counsel at this stage. And although the detainee can seek review of his status determination in the Court of Appeals, that review process cannot cure all defects in the earlier proceedings. See Part V, *infra*.

As to the second factor relevant to this analysis, the detainees here are similarly situated to the *Eisentrager* petitioners in that the sites of their apprehension and detention are technically outside the sovereign territory of the United States. As noted earlier, this is a factor that weighs against finding they have rights under the Suspension Clause. But there are critical differences between Landsberg Prison, circa 1950, and the United States Naval Station at Guantanamo Bay in 2008. Unlike its present control over the naval station, the United States' control over the prison in Germany was neither absolute nor indefinite. Like all parts of occupied Germany, the prison was under the jurisdiction of the combined Allied Forces. See Declaration Regarding the Defeat of Germany and the Assumption of Supreme Authority with Respect to Germany, June 5, 1945, U. S.-U. S. S. R.-U. K.-Fr., *60 Stat. 1649*, T. I. A. S. No. 1520. The United States was therefore answerable to its Allies for all activities occurring there. Cf. *Hirota v. MacArthur, 338 U.S. 197, 198, 69 S. Ct. 197, 93 L. Ed. 1902 (1948) (per curiam)* (military tribunal set up by Gen. Douglas MacArthur, acting as "the agent of the Allied Powers," was not a "tribunal of the United States"). The Allies had not planned a long-term occupation of Germany, nor did they intend to displace all German institutions even during the period of occupation. See Agreements Respecting Basic Principles for Merger of the Three Western German Zones of Occupation, and Other Matters, Apr. 8, 1949, U. S.-U. K.-Fr., Art. 1, 63 Stat. 2819, T. I. A. S. No. 2066 (establishing a governing framework "[d]uring the period in which it is necessary that the occupation continue" and expressing the desire "that the German people shall enjoy self-government to the maximum possible degree consistent with such occupation"). The Court's holding in *Eisentrager* was thus consistent with the Insular Cases, where it had held there was no need to extend full constitutional protections to territories the United States did not intend to govern indefinitely. Guantanamo Bay, on the other hand, is no transient possession. In every practical sense Guantanamo is not abroad; it is within the constant jurisdiction of the United States. See *Rasul, 542 U.S., at 480, 124 S. Ct. 2686, 159 L. Ed. 2d 548*; *id., at 487, 124 S. Ct. 2686, 159 L. Ed. 2d 548* (Kennedy, J., concurring in judgment).

As to the third factor, we recognize, as the Court did in *Eisentrager*, that there are costs to holding the Suspension Clause applicable in a case of military detention abroad. Habeas corpus proceedings may require expenditure of funds by the Government and may divert the attention of military personnel from other pressing tasks. While we are sensitive to these concerns, we do not find them dispositive. Compliance with any judicial process requires some incremental expenditure of resources. Yet civilian courts and the Armed Forces have functioned alongside each other at various points in our history. See, *e.g., Duncan v. Kahanamoku, 327 U.S. 304, 66 S. Ct. 606, 90 L. Ed. 688 (1946); Ex parte Milligan, 71 U.S. 2, 4 Wall. 2, 18 L. Ed. 281 (1866).* The Government presents no credible arguments that the military mission at Guantanamo would be compromised if habeas corpus courts had jurisdiction to hear the detainees' claims. And in light of the plenary control the United States asserts over the base, none are apparent to us.

The situation in *Eisentrager* was far different, given the historical context and nature of the military's mission in post-War Germany. When hostilities in the European Theater came to an end, the United States became responsible for an occupation zone encompassing over 57,000 square miles with a population of 18 million. See Letter from President Truman to Secretary of State Byrnes (Nov. 28, 1945), in 8 Documents on American Foreign Relations 257 (R. Dennett & R. Turner eds. 1948); Pollock, A Territorial Pattern for the Military Occupation of Germany, 38 Am. Pol. Sci. Rev. 970, 975 (1944). In addition to supervising massive reconstruction and aid efforts the American forces stationed in Germany faced potential security threats from a defeated enemy. In retrospect the post-War occupation may seem uneventful. But at the time *Eisentrager* was decided, the Court was right to be concerned about judicial interference with the military's efforts to contain "enemy elements, guerilla fighters, and 'werewolves.'" *339 U.S., at 784, 70 S. Ct. 936, 94 L. Ed. 1255.*

Similar threats are not apparent here; nor does the Government argue that they are. The United States Naval Station at Guantanamo Bay consists of 45 square miles of land and water. The base has been used, at various points, to house migrants and refugees temporarily. At present, however, other than the detainees themselves, the only long-term residents are American military personnel, their families, and a small number of workers. See History of Guantanamo Bay, online at https://www.cnic.navy.mil/Guantanamo/AboutGTMO/gtmohistgeneral/ gtmohistgeneral. The detainees have been deemed enemies of the United States. At present, dangerous as they may be if released, they are contained in a secure prison facility located on an isolated and heavily fortified military base.

There is no indication, furthermore, that adjudicating a habeas corpus petition would cause friction with the host government. No Cuban court has jurisdiction over American military personnel at Guantanamo or the enemy combatants detained there. While obligated to abide by the terms of the lease, the United States is, for all practical purposes, answerable to no other sovereign for its acts on the base. Were that not the case, or if the detention facility were located in an active theater of war, arguments that issuing the writ would be "impracticable or anomalous" would have more weight. See *Reid, 354 U.S., at 74, 77 S. Ct. 1222, 1 L.*

Ed. 2d 1148 (Harlan, J., concurring in result). Under the facts presented here, however, there are few practical barriers to the running of the writ. To the extent barriers arise, habeas corpus procedures likely can be modified to address them. See Part VI-B, *infra*.

It is true that before today the Court has never held that noncitizens detained by our Government in territory over which another country maintains *de jure* sovereignty have any rights under our Constitution. But the cases before us lack any precise historical parallel. They involve individuals detained by executive order for the duration of a conflict that, if measured from September 11, 2001, to the present, is already among the longest wars in American history. See Oxford Companion to American Military History 849 (1999). The detainees, moreover, are held in a territory that, while technically not part of the United States, is under the complete and total control of our Government. Under these circumstances the lack of a precedent on point is no barrier to our holding.

We hold that *Art. I, § 9, cl. 2, of the Constitution* has full effect at Guantanamo Bay. If the privilege of habeas corpus is to be denied to the detainees now before us, Congress must act in accordance with the requirements of the Suspension Clause. Cf. *Hamdi, 542 U.S., at 564, 124 S. Ct. 2633, 159 L. Ed. 2d 578* (Scalia, J., dissenting) ("[I]ndefinite imprisonment on reasonable suspicion is not an available option of treatment for those accused of aiding the enemy, absent a suspension of the writ"). This Court may not impose a *de facto* suspension by abstaining from these controversies. See *Hamdan, 548 U.S., at 585, n. 16, 126 S. Ct. 2749, 165 L. Ed. 2d 723* ("[A]bstention is not appropriate in cases . . . in which the legal challenge 'turn[s] on the status of the persons as to whom the military asserted its power'" (quoting *Schlesinger v. Councilman, 420 U.S. 738, 759, 95 S. Ct. 1300, 43 L. Ed. 2d 591 (1975)))*. The MCA does not purport to be a formal suspension of the writ; and the Government, in its submissions to us, has not argued that it is. Petitioners, therefore, are entitled to the privilege of habeas corpus to challenge the legality of their detention.

V

In light of this holding the question becomes whether the statute stripping jurisdiction to issue the writ avoids the Suspension Clause mandate because Congress has provided adequate substitute procedures for habeas corpus. The Government submits there has been compliance with the Suspension Clause because the DTA review process in the Court of Appeals, see DTA § 1005(e), provides an adequate substitute. Congress has granted that court jurisdiction to consider "(i) whether the status determination of the [CSRT] . . . was consistent with the standards and procedures specified by the Secretary of Defense . . . and (ii) to the extent the Constitution and laws of the United States are applicable, whether the use of such standards and procedures to make the determination is consistent with the Constitution and laws of the United States." § 1005(e)(2)(C), 119 Stat. 2742.

The Court of Appeals, having decided that the writ does not run to the detainees in any event, found it unnecessary to consider whether an adequate substitute has been provided. In the ordinary course we would remand to the Court of Appeals to consider this question in the first instance. See *Youakim v. Miller, 425 U.S. 231, 234, 96 S. Ct. 1399, 47 L. Ed. 2d 701 (1976) (per curiam)*. It is well settled, however, that the Court's practice of declining to address issues left unresolved in earlier proceedings is not an inflexible rule. *Ibid.* Departure from the rule is appropriate in "exceptional" circumstances. See *Cooper Industries, Inc. v. Aviall Services, Inc., 543 U.S. 157, 169, 125 S. Ct. 577, 160 L. Ed. 2d 548 (2004); Duignan v. United States, 274 U.S. 195, 200, 47 S. Ct. 566, 71 L. Ed. 996 (1927)*.

The gravity of the separation-of-powers issues raised by these cases and the fact that these detainees have been denied meaningful access to a judicial forum for a period of years render these cases exceptional. The parties before us have addressed the adequacy issue. While we would have found it informative to consider the reasoning of the Court of Appeals on this point, we must weigh that against the harms petitioners may endure from additional delay. And, given there are few precedents addressing what features an adequate substitute for habeas corpus must contain, in all likelihood a remand simply would delay ultimate resolution of the issue by this Court.

We do have the benefit of the Court of Appeals' construction of key provisions of the DTA. When we granted certiorari in these cases, we noted "it would be of material assistance to consult any decision" in the parallel DTA review proceedings pending in the Court of Appeals, specifically any rulings in the matter of *Bismullah v. Gates. 551 U.S. 1160, 127 S. Ct. 3078, 168 L. Ed. 2d 755 (2007)*. Although the Court of Appeals has yet to complete a DTA review proceeding, the three-judge panel in *Bismullah* has issued an interim order giving guidance as to what evidence can be made part of the record on review and what access the detainees can have to counsel and to classified information. See *378 U.S. App. D.C. 179, 501 F.3d 178 (CADC) (Bismullah I)*, reh'g denied*378 U.S. App. D.C. 238, 503 F.3d 137 (CADC 2007) (Bismullah II)*. In that matter the full court denied the Government's motion for rehearing en banc, see *Bismullah v. Gates, 379 U.S. App. D.C. 382, 514 F.3d 1291 (CADC 2008) (Bismullah III)*. The order denying rehearing was accompanied by five separate statements from members of the court, which offer differing views as to the scope of the judicial review Congress intended these detainees to have. *Ibid.*

Under the circumstances we believe the costs of further delay substantially outweigh any benefits of remanding to the Court of Appeals to consider the issue it did not address in these cases.

A

Our case law does not contain extensive discussion of standards defining suspension of the writ or of circumstances under which suspension has occurred. This simply confirms the care Congress has taken throughout our Nation's history to preserve the writ and its function. Indeed, most of the major legislative enactments pertaining to habeas corpus have acted not to contract the writ's protection but to expand it or to hasten resolution of prisoners' claims. See, *e.g.,* Habeas Corpus Act of 1867, ch. 28, § 1, 14 Stat. 385 (current version codified at *28 U.S.C. § 2241 (2000 ed. and Supp. V)* (extending the federal writ to state prisoners)); Cf. *Harris v. Nelson, 394 U.S. 286, 299-300, 89 S. Ct. 1082, 22 L. Ed. 2d 281 (1969)* (interpreting the All Writs Act, 28 U.S.C. § 1651, to allow discovery in habeas corpus proceedings); *Peyton v. Rowe, 391 U.S. 54, 64-65, 88 S. Ct. 1549, 20 L. Ed. 2d 426 (1968)* (interpreting the then-existing version of § 2241 to allow petitioner to proceed with his habeas corpus action, even though he had not yet begun to serve his sentence).

There are exceptions, of course. Title I of the Antiterrorism and Effective Death Penalty Act of 1996 (AEDPA), § 106, 110 Stat. 1220, contains certain gatekeeping provisions that restrict a prisoner's ability to bring new and repetitive claims in "second or successive" habeas corpus actions. We upheld these provisions against a Suspension Clause challenge in *Felker v. Turpin, 518 U.S. 651, 662-664, 116 S. Ct. 2333, 135 L. Ed. 2d 827 (1996).* The provisions at issue in *Felker,* however, did not constitute a substantial departure from common-law habeas procedures. The provisions, for the most part, codified the longstanding abuse-of-the-writ doctrine. *Id., at 664, 116 S. Ct. 2333, 135 L. Ed. 2d 827*; see also *McCleskey v. Zant, 499 U.S. 467, 489, 111 S. Ct. 1454, 113 L. Ed. 2d 517 (1991).* AEDPA applies, moreover, to federal, postconviction review after criminal proceedings in state court have taken place. As of this point, cases discussing the implementation of that statute give little helpful instruction (save perhaps by contrast) for the instant cases, where no trial has been held.

The two leading cases addressing habeas substitutes, *Swain v. Pressley, 430 U.S. 372, 97 S. Ct. 1224, 51 L. Ed. 2d 411 (1977),* and *United States v. Hayman, 342 U.S. 205,*

72 S. Ct. 263, 96 L. Ed. 232 (1952), likewise provide little guidance here. The statutes at issue were attempts to streamline habeas corpus relief, not to cut it back.

The statute discussed in *Hayman* was *28 U.S.C. § 2255.* It replaced traditional habeas corpus for federal prisoners (at least in the first instance) with a process that allowed the prisoner to file a motion with the sentencing court on the ground that his sentence was, *inter alia,* "'imposed in violation of the Constitution or laws of the United States.'" *342 U.S., at 207, n. 1, 72 S. Ct. 263, 96 L. Ed. 232.* The purpose and effect of the statute was not to restrict access to the writ but to make postconviction proceedings more efficient. It directed claims not to the court that had territorial jurisdiction over the place of the petitioner's confinement but to the sentencing court, a court already familiar with the facts of the case. As the *Hayman* Court explained:

> "*Section 2255* . . . was passed at the instance of the Judicial Conference to meet practical difficulties that had arisen in administering the habeas corpus jurisdiction of the federal courts. Nowhere in the history of *Section 2255* do we find any purpose to impinge upon prisoners' rights of collateral attack upon their convictions. On the contrary, the sole purpose was to minimize the difficulties encountered in habeas corpus hearings by affording the same rights in another and more convenient forum." *Id., at 219, 72 S. Ct. 263, 96 L. Ed. 232.*

See also *Hill v. United States, 368 U.S. 424, 427, 428, 82 S. Ct. 468, 7 L. Ed. 2d 417* (1962) (noting that *§ 2255* provides a remedy in the sentencing court that is "exactly commensurate" with the pre-existing federal habeas corpus remedy).

The statute in *Swain, D. C. Code Ann. § 23-110(g)* (1973), applied to prisoners in custody under sentence of the Superior Court of the District of Columbia. Before enactment of the District of Columbia Court Reform and Criminal Procedure Act of 1970 (D. C. Court Reform Act), *84 Stat. 473,* those prisoners could file habeas petitions in the United States District Court for the District of Columbia. The Act, which was patterned on *§ 2255,* substituted a new collateral process in the Superior Court for the pre-existing habeas corpus procedure in the District Court. See *Swain, 430 U.S., at 374-378, 97 S. Ct. 1224, 51 L. Ed. 2d 411.* But, again, the purpose and effect of the statute was to expedite consideration of the prisoner's claims, not to delay or frustrate it. See *id., at 375, n. 4, 97 S. Ct. 1224, 51 L. Ed. 2d 411* (noting that the purpose of the D. C. Court Reform Act was to "alleviate" administrative burdens on the District Court).

That the statutes in *Hayman* and *Swain* were designed to strengthen, rather than dilute, the writ's protections was evident, furthermore, from this significant fact:

Neither statute eliminated traditional habeas corpus relief. In both cases the statute at issue had a saving clause, providing that a writ of habeas corpus would be available if the alternative process proved inadequate or ineffective. *Swain, supra, at 381, 97 S. Ct. 1224, 51 L. Ed. 2d 411*; *Hayman, supra, at 223, 72 S. Ct. 263, 96 L. Ed. 232*. The Court placed explicit reliance upon these provisions in upholding the statutes against constitutional challenges. See *Swain, supra, at 381, 97 S. Ct. 1224, 51 L. Ed. 2d 411* (noting that the provision "avoid[ed] any serious question about the constitutionality of the statute"); *Hayman, supra, at 223, 72 S. Ct. 263, 96 L. Ed. 232* (noting that, because habeas remained available as a last resort, it was unnecessary to "reach constitutional questions").

Unlike in *Hayman* and *Swain*, here we confront statutes, the DTA and the MCA, that were intended to circumscribe habeas review. Congress' purpose is evident not only from the unequivocal nature of MCA § 7's jurisdiction-stripping language, *28 U.S.C. § 2241(e)(1)* ("No court, justice, or judge shall have jurisdiction to hear or consider an application for a writ of habeas corpus . . ."), but also from a comparison of the DTA to the statutes at issue in *Hayman* and *Swain*. When interpreting a statute, we examine related provisions in other parts of the U. S. Code. See, *e.g., West Virginia Univ. Hospitals, Inc. v. Casey, 499 U.S. 83, 88-97, 111 S. Ct. 1138, 113 L. Ed. 2d 68 (1991)*; *Babbitt v. Sweet Home Chapter, Communities for Great Ore., 515 U.S. 687, 717-718, 115 S. Ct. 2407, 132 L. Ed. 2d 597 (1995)* (Scalia, J., dissenting); see generally W. Eskridge, P. Frickey, & E. Garrett, Cases and Materials on Legislation: Statutes and the Creation of Public Policy 1039 (3d ed. 2001). When Congress has intended to replace traditional habeas corpus with habeas-like substitutes, as was the case in *Hayman* and *Swain*, it has granted to the courts broad remedial powers to secure the historic office of the writ. In the § 2255 context, for example, Congress has granted to the reviewing court power to "determine the issues and make findings of fact and conclusions of law" with respect to whether "the judgment [of conviction] was rendered without jurisdiction, or . . . the sentence imposed was not authorized by law or otherwise open to collateral attack." *28 U.S.C. § 2255(b)*. The D. C. Court Reform Act, the statute upheld in *Swain*, contained a similar provision. *§ 23-110(g), 84 Stat. 609*.

In contrast the DTA's jurisdictional grant is quite limited. The Court of Appeals has jurisdiction not to inquire into the legality of the detention generally but only to assess whether the CSRT complied with the "standards and procedures specified by the Secretary of Defense" and whether those standards and procedures are lawful. DTA § 1005(e)(2)(C), 119 Stat. 2742. If Congress had envisioned DTA review as coextensive with traditional habeas corpus, it would not have drafted the statute in this manner. Instead, it would have used language similar to what it used in the statutes at issue in *Hayman* and *Swain*. Cf. *Russello v. United States, 464 U.S. 16, 23,*

104 S. Ct. 296, 78 L. Ed. 2d 17 (1983) ("'[W]here Congress includes particular language in one section of a statute but omits it in another section of the same Act, it is generally presumed that Congress acts intentionally and purposely in the disparate inclusion or exclusion'" (quoting *United States v. Wong Kim Bo, 472 F.2d 720, 722 (CA5 1972)*. *(per curiam)*))) Unlike in *Hayman* and *Swain*, moreover, there has been no effort to preserve habeas corpus review as an avenue of last resort. No saving clause exists in either the MCA or the DTA. And MCA § 7 eliminates habeas review for these petitioners.

The differences between the DTA and the habeas statute that would govern in MCA § 7's absence, *28 U.S.C. § 2241 (2000 ed. and Supp. V)*, are likewise telling. In § 2241 (2000 ed.) Congress confirmed the authority of "any justice" or "circuit judge" to issue the writ. Cf. *Felker, 518 U.S., at 660-661, 116 S. Ct. 2333, 135 L. Ed. 2d 827* (interpreting Title I of AEDPA to not strip from this Court the power to entertain original habeas corpus petitions). That statute accommodates the necessity for factfinding that will arise in some cases by allowing the appellate judge or Justice to transfer the case to a district court of competent jurisdiction, whose institutional capacity for factfinding is superior to his or her own. See *28 U.S.C. § 2241(b)*. By granting the Court of Appeals "exclusive" jurisdiction over petitioners' cases, see DTA § 1005(e)(2)(A), 119 Stat. 2742, Congress has foreclosed that option. This choice indicates Congress intended the Court of Appeals to have a more limited role in enemy combatant status determinations than a district court has in habeas corpus proceedings. The DTA should be interpreted to accord some latitude to the Court of Appeals to fashion procedures necessary to make its review function a meaningful one, but, if congressional intent is to be respected, the procedures adopted cannot be as extensive or as protective of the rights of the detainees as they would be in a § 2241 proceeding. Otherwise there would have been no, or very little, purpose for enacting the DTA.

To the extent any doubt remains about Congress' intent, the legislative history confirms what the plain text strongly suggests: In passing the DTA Congress did not intend to create a process that differs from traditional habeas corpus process in name only. It intended to create a more limited procedure. See, *e.g.*, 151 Cong. Rec. S14263 (Dec. 21, 2005) (statement of Sen. Graham) (noting that the DTA "extinguish[es] these habeas and other actions in order to effect a transfer of jurisdiction over these cases to the DC Circuit Court"); *ibid.* (statement of Sen. Kyl) (agreeing that the bill "create[s] in their place a very limited judicial review of certain military administrative decisions"); *id.*, at S14268 ("It is important to note that the limited judicial review authorized by paragraphs 2 and 3 of subsection (e) [of DTA § 1005] are not habeas-corpus review. It is a limited judicial review of its own nature").

It is against this background that we must interpret the DTA and assess its adequacy as a substitute for habeas corpus. The present cases thus test the limits of the Suspension Clause in ways that *Hayman* and *Swain* did not.

B

We do not endeavor to offer a comprehensive summary of the requisites for an adequate substitute for habeas corpus. We do consider it uncontroversial, however, that the privilege of habeas corpus entitles the prisoner to a meaningful opportunity to demonstrate that he is being held pursuant to "the erroneous application or interpretation" of relevant law. *St. Cyr*, 533 U.S., at 302, 121 S. Ct. 2271, 150 L. Ed. 2d 347. And the habeas court must have the power to order the conditional release of an individual unlawfully detained --though release need not be the exclusive remedy and is not the appropriate one in every case in which the writ is granted. See *Ex parte Bollman*, 8 U.S. 75, 4 Cranch 75, 136, 2 L. Ed. 554 (1807) (where imprisonment is unlawful, the court "can only direct [the prisoner] to be discharged"); R. Hurd, Treatise on the Right of Personal Liberty, and On the Writ of Habeas Corpus and the Practice Connected With It: With a View of the Law of Extradition of Fugitives 222 (2d ed. 1876) ("It cannot be denied where 'a probable ground is shown that the party is imprisoned without just cause, and therefore, hath a right to be delivered,' for the writ then becomes a 'writ of right, which may not be denied but ought to be granted to every man that is committed or detained in prison or otherwise restrained of his liberty'"). But see *Chessman v. Teets*, 354 U.S. 156, 165-166, 77 S. Ct. 1127, 1 L. Ed. 2d 1253 (1957) (remanding in a habeas case for retrial within a "reasonable time"). These are the easily identified attributes of any constitutionally adequate habeas corpus proceeding. But, depending on the circumstances, more may be required.

Indeed, common-law habeas corpus was, above all, an adaptable remedy. Its precise application and scope changed depending upon the circumstances. See 3 Blackstone *131 (describing habeas as "the great and efficacious writ, in all manner of illegal confinement"); see also *Schlup v. Delo*, 513 U.S. 298, 319, 115 S. Ct. 851, 130 L. Ed. 2d 808 (1995) (Habeas "is, at its core, an equitable remedy"); *Jones v. Cunningham*, 371 U.S. 236, 243, 83 S. Ct. 373, 9 L. Ed. 2d 285 (1963) (Habeas is not "a static, narrow, formalistic remedy; its scope has grown to achieve its grand purpose"). It appears the common-law habeas court's role was most extensive in cases of pretrial and noncriminal detention, where there had been little or no previous judicial review of the cause for detention. Notably, the black-letter rule that prisoners could not controvert facts in the jailer's return was not followed (or at least not with consistency) in such cases. Hurd, *supra*, at 271 (noting that the general rule was "subject to exceptions" including cases of bail and impressment);

Oaks, Legal History in the High Court--Habeas Corpus, 64 Mich. L. Rev. 451, 457 (1966) ("[W]hen a prisoner applied for habeas corpus before indictment or trial, some courts examined the written depositions on which he had been arrested or committed, and others even heard oral testimony to determine whether the evidence was sufficient to justify holding him for trial" (footnotes omitted)); Fallon & Meltzer, Habeas Corpus Jurisdiction, Substantive Rights, and the War on Terror, *120 Harv. L. Rev. 2029, 2102 (2007)* ("[T]he early practice was not consistent: courts occasionally permitted factual inquiries when no other opportunity for judicial review existed").

There is evidence from 19th-century American sources indicating that, even in States that accorded strong res judicata effect to prior adjudications, habeas courts in this country routinely allowed prisoners to introduce exculpatory evidence that was either unknown or previously unavailable to the prisoner. See, *e.g., Ex parte Pattison, 56 Miss. 161, 164 (1878)* (noting that "[w]hile the former adjudication must be considered as conclusive on the testimony then adduced" "newly developed exculpatory evidence . . . may authorize the admission to bail"); *Ex parte Foster, 5 Tex. Ct. App. 625, 644 (1879)* (construing the State's habeas statute to allow for the introduction of new evidence "where important testimony has been obtained, which, though not newly discovered, or which, though known to [the petitioner], it was not in his power to produce at the former hearing; [and] where the evidence was newly discovered"); *People v. Martin, 7 N. Y. Leg. Obs. 49, 56 (1848)* ("If in custody on criminal process before indictment, the prisoner has an absolute right to demand that the original depositions be looked into to see whether any crime is in fact imputed to him, and the inquiry will by no means be confined to the return. Facts out of the return may be gone into to ascertain whether the committing magistrate may not have arrived at an illogical conclusion upon the evidence given before him . . ."); see generally W. Church, Treatise on the Writ of Habeas Corpus § 182, p 235 1886) (hereinafter Church) (noting that habeas courts would "hear evidence anew if justice require it"). Justice McLean, on Circuit in 1855, expressed his view that a habeas court should consider a prior judgment conclusive "where there was clearly jurisdiction and a full and fair hearing; but that it might not be so considered when any of these requisites were wanting." *Ex parte Robinson, 20 F. Cas. 969, 971, F. Cas. No. 11935, (No. 11,935)* (CC Ohio). To illustrate the circumstances in which the prior adjudication did not bind the habeas court, he gave the example of a case in which "[s]everal unimpeached witnesses" provided new evidence to exculpate the prisoner. *Ibid.*

The idea that the necessary scope of habeas review in part depends upon the rigor of any earlier proceedings accords with our test for procedural adequacy in the due process context. See *Mathews v. Eldridge, 424 U.S. 319, 335, 96 S. Ct. 893, 47 L. Ed.*

2d 18 (1976) (noting that the *Due Process Clause* requires an assessment of, *inter alia*, "the risk of an erroneous deprivation of [a liberty interest;] and the probable value, if any, of additional or substitute procedural safeguards"). This principle has an established foundation in habeas corpus jurisprudence as well, as Chief Justice Marshall's opinion in *Ex parte Watkins, 28 U.S. 193, 3 Pet. 193, 7 L. Ed. 650 (1830)*, demonstrates. Like the petitioner in *Swain*, Watkins sought a writ of habeas corpus after being imprisoned pursuant to a judgment of a District of Columbia court. In holding that the judgment stood on "high ground," 28 U.S. 193, 3 Pet., at 209, 7 L. Ed. 650, the Chief Justice emphasized the character of the court that rendered the original judgment, noting it was a "court of record, having general jurisdiction over criminal cases." *Id.*, at 203, 3 Pet. 193, 7 L. Ed. 650. In contrast to "inferior" tribunals of limited jurisdiction, *ibid.*, courts of record had broad remedial powers, which gave the habeas court greater confidence in the judgment's validity. See generally Neuman, Habeas Corpus, Executive Detention, and the Removal of Aliens, *98 Colum. L. Rev. 961*, 982-983 *(1998)*.

Accordingly, where relief is sought from a sentence that resulted from the judgment of a court of record, as was the case in *Watkins* and indeed in most federal habeas cases, considerable deference is owed to the court that ordered confinement. See *Brown v. Allen, 344 U.S. 443, 506, 73 S. Ct. 397, 97 L. Ed. 469 (1953)* (opinion of Frankfurter, J.) (noting that a federal habeas court should accept a state court's factual findings unless "a vital flaw be found in the process of ascertaining such facts in the State court"). Likewise in those cases the prisoner should exhaust adequate alternative remedies before filing for the writ in federal court. See *Ex parte Royall, 117 U.S. 241, 251-252, 6 S. Ct. 734, 29 L. Ed. 868 (1886)* (requiring exhaustion of state collateral processes). Both aspects of federal habeas corpus review are justified because it can be assumed that, in the usual course, a court of record provides defendants with a fair, adversary proceeding. In cases involving state convictions this framework also respects federalism; and in federal cases it has added justification because the prisoner already has had a chance to seek review of his conviction in a federal forum through a direct appeal. The present cases fall outside these categories, however; for here the detention is by executive order.

Where a person is detained by executive order, rather than, say, after being tried and convicted in a court, the need for collateral review is most pressing. A criminal conviction in the usual course occurs after a judicial hearing before a tribunal disinterested in the outcome and committed to procedures designed to ensure its own independence. These dynamics are not inherent in executive detention orders or executive review procedures. In this context the need for habeas corpus is more urgent. The intended duration of the detention and the reasons for it bear upon the precise scope of the inquiry. Habeas corpus proceedings need not resemble a criminal trial, even when the detention is by executive order. But the writ must be effective. The habeas court must have sufficient authority to conduct a meaningful review of both the cause for detention and the Executive's power to detain.

To determine the necessary scope of habeas corpus review, therefore, we must assess the CSRT process, the mechanism through which petitioners' designation as enemy combatants became final. Whether one characterizes the CSRT process as direct review of the Executive's battlefield determination that the detainee is an enemy combatant--as the parties have and as we do--or as the first step in the collateral review of a battlefield determination makes no difference in a proper analysis of whether the procedures Congress put in place are an adequate substitute for habeas corpus. What matters is the sum total of procedural protections afforded to the detainee at all stages, direct and collateral.

Petitioners identify what they see as myriad deficiencies in the CSRTs. The most relevant for our purposes are the constraints upon the detainee's ability to rebut the factual basis for the Government's assertion that he is an enemy combatant. As already noted, see Part IV-C, *supra*, at the CSRT stage the detainee has limited means to find or present evidence to challenge the Government's case against him. He does not have the assistance of counsel and may not be aware of the most critical allegations that the Government relied upon to order his detention. See App. to Pet. for Cert. in No. 06-1196, at 156, P F(8) (noting that the detainee can access only the "unclassified portion of the Government Information"). The detainee can confront witnesses that testify during the CSRT proceedings. *Id.*, at 144, P g(8). But given that there are in effect no limits on the admission of hearsay evidence--the only requirement is that the tribunal deem the evidence "relevant and helpful," *ibid.*, P g(9)--the detainee's opportunity to question witnesses is likely to be more theoretical than real.

The Government defends the CSRT process, arguing that it was designed to conform to the procedures suggested by the plurality in *Hamdi*. See *542 U.S., at 538, 124 S. Ct. 2633, 159 L. Ed. 2d 578*. Setting aside the fact that the relevant language in *Hamdi* did not garner a majority of the Court, it does not control the matter at hand. None of the parties in *Hamdi* argued there had been a suspension of the writ. Nor could they. The § 2241 habeas corpus process remained in place, *id., at 525, 124 S. Ct. 2633, 159 L. Ed. 2d 578*. Accordingly, the plurality concentrated on whether the Executive had the authority to detain and, if so, what rights the detainee had under the *Due Process Clause*. True, there are places in the *Hamdi* plurality opinion where it is difficult to tell where its extrapolation of § 2241 ends and its analysis of the petitioner's due process rights begins. But the Court had no occasion to define the necessary scope of habeas review, for Suspension Clause purposes, in the context of enemy combatant detentions. The closest the plurality came to doing so was in discussing whether, in] light of separation-of-powers concerns, § 2241 should be construed to prohibit the District Court from inquiring beyond the affidavit Hamdi's custodian provided in answer to the detainee's habeas petition. The plurality answered this question with an emphatic "no." *Id.*, *at 527, 124 S. Ct. 2633, 159 L. Ed. 2d 578* (labeling this argument as "extreme"); *id., at 535-536, 124 S. Ct. 2633, 159 L. Ed. 2d 578*.

Even if we were to assume that the CSRTs satisfy due process standards, it would not end our inquiry. Habeas corpus is a collateral process that exists, in Justice Holmes' words, to "cu[t] through all forms and g[o] to the very tissue of the structure. It comes in from the outside, not in subordination to the proceedings, and although every form may have been preserved opens the inquiry whether they have been more than an empty shell." *Frank v. Mangum, 237 U.S. 309, 346, 35 S. Ct. 582, 59 L. Ed. 969 (1915)* (dissenting opinion). Even when the procedures authorizing detention are structurally sound, the Suspension Clause remains applicable and the writ relevant. See 2 Chambers, Course of Lectures on English Law 1767-1773, at 6 ("Liberty may be violated either by arbitrary *imprisonment* without law or the appearance of law, or by a lawful magistrate for an unlawful reason"). This is so, as *Hayman* and *Swain* make clear, even where the prisoner is detained after a criminal trial conducted in full accordance with the protections of the *Bill of Rights*. Were this not the case, there would have been no reason for the Court to inquire into the adequacy of substitute habeas procedures in *Hayman* and *Swain*. That the prisoners were detained pursuant to the most rigorous proceedings imaginable, a full criminal trial, would have been enough to render any habeas substitute acceptable *per se*.

Although we make no judgment whether the CSRTs, as currently constituted, satisfy due process standards, we agree with petitioners that, even when all the parties involved in this process act with diligence and in good faith, there is considerable risk of error in the tribunal's findings of fact. This is a risk inherent in any process that, in the words of the former Chief Judge of the Court of Appeals, is "closed and accusatorial." See *Bismullah III, 514 F.3d at 1296* (Ginsburg, C. J., concurring in denial of rehearing en banc). And given that the consequence of error may be detention of persons for the duration of hostilities that may last a generation or more, this is a risk too significant to ignore.

For the writ of habeas corpus, or its substitute, to function as an effective and proper remedy in this context, the court that conducts the habeas proceeding must have the means to correct errors that occurred during the CSRT proceedings.

This includes some authority to assess the sufficiency of the Government's evidence against the detainee. It also must have the authority to admit and consider relevant exculpatory evidence that was not introduced during the earlier proceeding. Federal habeas petitioners long have had the means to supplement the record on review, even in the postconviction habeas setting. See *Townsend v. Sain*, *372 U.S. 293, 313, 83 S. Ct. 745, 9 L. Ed. 2d 770 (1963)*, overruled in part by *Keeney v. Tamayo-Reyes*, *504 U.S. 1, 5, 112 S. Ct. 1715, 118 L. Ed. 2d 318 (1992)*. Here that opportunity is constitutionally required.

Consistent with the historic function and province of the writ, habeas corpus review may be more circumscribed if the underlying detention proceedings are more thorough than they were here. In two habeas cases involving enemy aliens tried for war crimes, *In re Yamashita, 327 U.S. 1, 66 S. Ct. 340, 90 L. Ed. 499 (1946)*, and *Ex parte Quirin, 317 U.S. 1, 63 S. Ct. 2, 87 L. Ed. 3 (1942)*, for example, this Court limited its review to determining whether the Executive had legal authority to try the petitioners by military commission. See *Yamashita, supra, at 8, 66 S. Ct. 340, 90 L. Ed. 499* ("[O]n application for habeas corpus we are not concerned with the guilt or innocence of the petitioners. We consider here only the lawful power of the commission to try the petitioner for the offense charged"); *Quirin, supra, at 25, 63 S. Ct. 2, 87 L. Ed. 3* ("We are not here concerned with any question of the guilt or innocence of petitioners"). Military courts are not courts of record. See *Watkins*, 3 Pet., at 209; Church 513. And the procedures used to try General Yamashita have been sharply criticized by Members of this Court. See *Hamdan, 548 U.S., at 617, 126 S. Ct. 2749, 165 L. Ed. 2d 723*; *Yamashita, supra, at 41-81, 66 S. Ct. 340, 90 L. Ed. 499* (Rutledge, J., dissenting). We need not revisit these cases, however. For on their own terms, the proceedings in *Yamashita* and *Quirin*, like those in *Eisentrager*, had an adversarial structure that is lacking here. See *Yamashita, supra, at 5, 66 S. Ct. 340, 90 L. Ed. 499* (noting that General Yamashita was represented by six military lawyers and that "[t]hroughout the proceedings . . . defense counsel . . . demonstrated their professional skill and resourcefulness and their proper zeal for the defense with which they were charged"); *Quirin, supra, at 23-24, 63 S. Ct. 2, 87 L. Ed. 3*; Exec. Order No. 9185, 7 Fed. Reg. 5103 (1942) (appointing counsel to represent the German saboteurs).

The extent of the showing required of the Government in these cases is a matter to be determined. We need not explore it further at this stage. We do hold that when the judicial power to issue habeas corpus properly is invoked the judicial officer must have adequate authority to make a determination in light of the relevant law and facts and to formulate and issue appropriate orders for relief, including, if necessary, an order directing the prisoner's release.

C

We now consider whether the DTA allows the Court of Appeals to conduct a proceeding meeting these standards. "[W]e are obligated to construe the statute to avoid [constitutional] problems" if it is "'fairly possible'" to do so. *St. Cyr, 533 U.S., at 299-300, 121 S. Ct. 2271, 150 L. Ed. 2d 347* (quoting *Crowell v. Benson, 285 U.S. 22, 62, 52 S. Ct. 285, 76 L. Ed. 598 (1932)*). There are limits to this principle, however. The canon of constitutional avoidance does not supplant traditional modes of statutory interpretation. See *Clark v. Martinez, 543 U.S. 371, 385, 125 S. Ct. 716, 160 L. Ed. 2d 734 (2005)* ("The canon of constitutional avoidance comes into play only when, after the application of ordinary textual analysis, the statute is found to be susceptible of more than one construction; and the canon functions as *a means of choosing between them*"). We cannot ignore the text and purpose of a statute in order to save it.

The DTA does not explicitly empower the Court of Appeals to order the applicant in a DTA review proceeding released should the court find that the standards and procedures used at his CSRT hearing were insufficient to justify detention. This is troubling. Yet, for present purposes, we can assume congressional silence permits a constitutionally required remedy. In that case it would be possible to hold that a remedy of release is impliedly provided for. The DTA might be read, furthermore, to allow petitioners to assert most, if not all, of the legal claims they seek to advance, including their most basic claim: that the President has no authority under the AUMF to detain them indefinitely. (Whether the President has such authority turns on whether the AUMF authorizes--and the Constitution permits--the indefinite detention of "enemy combatants" as the Department of Defense defines that term. Thus a challenge to the President's authority to detain is, in essence, a challenge to the Department's definition of enemy combatant, a "standard" used by the CSRTs in petitioners' cases.) At oral argument, the Solicitor General urged us to adopt both these constructions, if doing so would allow MCA § 7 to remain intact. See Tr. of Oral Arg. 37, 53.

The absence of a release remedy and specific language allowing AUMF challenges are not the only constitutional infirmities from which the statute potentially suffers, however. The more difficult question is whether the DTA permits the Court of Appeals to make requisite findings of fact. The DTA enables petitioners to request "review" of their CSRT determination in the Court of Appeals, DTA § 1005(e)(2)(B)(i), 119 Stat. 2742; but the "Scope of Review" provision confines the Court of Appeals' role to reviewing whether the CSRT followed the "standards and procedures" issued by the Department of Defense and assessing whether those "standards and procedures" are lawful, § 1005(e)(2)(C), *ibid.* Among these standards is "the requirement that the conclusion of the Tribunal be supported by a preponderance of the evidence . . . allowing a rebuttable presumption in favor of the Government's evidence." § 1005(e)(2)(C)(i), *ibid.*

Assuming the DTA can be construed to allow the Court of Appeals to review or correct the CSRT's factual determinations, as opposed to merely certifying that the tribunal applied the correct standard of proof, we see no way to construe the statute to allow what is also constitutionally required in this context: an opportunity for the detainee to present relevant exculpatory evidence that was not made part of the record in the earlier proceedings.

On its face the statute allows the Court of Appeals to consider no evidence outside the CSRT record. In the parallel litigation, however, the Court of Appeals determined that the DTA allows it to order the production of all "'reasonably available information in the possession of the U. S. Government bearing on the issue whether the detainee meets the criteria to be designated as an enemy combatant,'" regardless of whether this evidence was put before the CSRT. *Bismullah I, 501 F.3d at 180.* The Government, see Pet. for Cert. pending in *Gates* v. *Bismullah*, No. 07-1054 (hereinafter *Bismullah* Pet.), with support from five members of the Court of Appeals, see *Bismullah III, 514 F.3d at 1299* (Henderson, J., dissenting from denial of rehearing en banc); *id., at 1302* (opinion of Randolph, J.) (same); *id., at 1306* (opinion of Brown, J.) (same), disagrees with this interpretation. For present purposes, however, we can assume that the Court of Appeals was correct that the DTA allows introduction and consideration of relevant exculpatory evidence that was "reasonably available" to the Government at the time of the CSRT but not made part of the record. Even so, the DTA review proceeding falls short of being a constitutionally adequate substitute, for the detainee still would have no opportunity to present evidence discovered after the CSRT proceedings concluded.

Under the DTA the Court of Appeals has the power to review CSRT determinations by assessing the legality of standards and procedures. This implies the power to inquire into what happened at the CSRT hearing and, perhaps, to remedy certain deficiencies in that proceeding. But should the Court of Appeals determine that the CSRT followed appropriate and lawful standards and procedures, it will have reached the limits of its jurisdiction. There is no language in the DTA that can be construed to allow the Court of Appeals to admit and consider newly discovered evidence that could not have been made part of the CSRT record because it was unavailable to either the Government or the detainee when the CSRT made its findings. This evidence, however, may be critical to the detainee's argument that he is not an enemy combatant and there is no cause to detain him.

This is not a remote hypothetical. One of the petitioners, Mohamed Nechla, requested at his CSRT hearing that the Government contact his employer. Petitioner claimed the employer would corroborate Nechla's contention he had no affiliation with al Qaeda. Although the CSRT determined this testimony would be relevant, it also found the witness was not reasonably available to testify at the time of the hearing. Petitioner's counsel, however, now represents the witness is available to be heard. See Brief for Boumediene Petitioners 5. If a detainee can present reasonably available evidence demonstrating there is no basis for his continued detention, he must have the opportunity to present this evidence to a habeas corpus court. Even under the Court of Appeals' generous construction of the DTA, however, the evidence identified by Nechla would be inadmissible in a DTA review proceeding. The role of an Article III court in the exercise of its habeas corpus function cannot be circumscribed in this manner.

By foreclosing consideration of evidence not presented or reasonably available to the detainee at the CSRT proceedings, the DTA disadvantages the detainee by limiting the scope of collateral review to a record that may not be accurate or complete. In other contexts, *e.g.*, in post-trial habeas cases where the prisoner already has had a full and fair opportunity to develop the factual predicate of his claims, similar limitations on the scope of habeas review may be appropriate. See *Williams v. Taylor, 529 U.S. 420, 436-437, 120 S. Ct. 1479, 146 L. Ed. 2d 435 (2000)* (noting that § 2254 "does not equate prisoners who exercise diligence in pursuing their claims with those who do not"). In this context, however, where the underlying detention proceedings lack the necessary adversarial character, the detainee cannot be held responsible for all deficiencies in the record.

The Government does not make the alternative argument that the DTA allows for the introduction of previously unavailable exculpatory evidence on appeal. It does point out, however, that if a detainee obtains such evidence, he can request that the Deputy Secretary of Defense convene a new CSRT. See Supp. Brief for Federal Respondents 4. Whatever the merits of this procedure, it is an insufficient replacement for the factual review these detainees are entitled to receive through habeas corpus. The Deputy Secretary's determination whether to initiate new proceedings is wholly a discretionary one. See Dept. of Defense, Office for the Administrative Review of the Detention of Enemy Combatants, Instruction 5421.1, Procedure for Review of "New Evidence" Relating to Enemy Combatant (EC) Status P 5(d) (May 7, 2007) (Instruction 5421.1) ("The decision to convene a CSRT to reconsider the basis of the detainee's [enemy combatant] status in light of 'new evidence' is a matter vested in the unreviewable discretion of the [Deputy Secretary of Defense]"). And we see no way to construe the DTA to allow a detainee to challenge the Deputy Secretary's decision not to open a new CSRT pursuant to

Instruction 5421.1. Congress directed the Secretary of Defense to devise procedures for considering new evidence, see DTA § 1005(a)(3), 119 Stat. 2741; but the detainee has no mechanism for ensuring that those procedures are followed. DTA § 1005(e)(2)(C), *id.* at 2742, makes clear that the Court of Appeals' jurisdiction is "limited to consideration of . . . whether the status determination of the [CSRT] with regard to such alien was consistent with the standards and procedures specified by the Secretary of Defense . . . and . . . whether the use of such standards and procedures to make the determination is consistent with the Constitution and laws of the United States." DTA § 1005(e)(2)(A), *ibid.*, further narrows the Court of Appeals' jurisdiction to reviewing "any final decision of a [CSRT] that an alien is properly detained as an enemy combatant." The Deputy Secretary's determination whether to convene a new CSRT is not a "status determination of the [CSRT]," much less a "final decision" of that body.

We do not imply DTA review would be a constitutionally sufficient replacement for habeas corpus but for these limitations on the detainee's ability to present exculpatory evidence. For even if it were possible, as a textual matter, to read into the statute each of the necessary procedures we have identified, we could not overlook the cumulative effect of our doing so. To hold that the detainees at Guantanamo may, under the DTA, challenge the President's legal authority to detain them, contest the CSRT's findings of fact, supplement the record on review with exculpatory evidence, and request an order of release would come close to reinstating the *§ 2241* habeas corpus process Congress sought to deny them. The language of the statute, read in light of Congress' reasons for enacting it, cannot bear this interpretation. Petitioners have met their burden of establishing that the DTA review process is, on its face, an inadequate substitute for habeas corpus.

Although we do not hold that an adequate substitute must duplicate *§ 2241* in all respects, it suffices that the Government has not established that the detainees' access to the statutory review provisions at issue is an adequate substitute for the writ of habeas corpus. MCA § 7 thus effects an unconstitutional suspension of the writ. In view of our holding we need not discuss the reach of the writ with respect to claims of unlawful conditions of treatment or confinement.

VI

A

In light of our conclusion that there is no jurisdictional bar to the District Court's entertaining petitioners' claims the question remains whether there are prudential barriers to habeas corpus review under these circumstances.

The Government argues petitioners must seek review of their CSRT determinations in the Court of Appeals before they can proceed with their habeas corpus actions in the District Court. As noted earlier, in other contexts and for prudential reasons this Court has required exhaustion of alternative remedies before a prisoner can seek federal habeas relief. Most of these cases were brought by prisoners in state custody, *e.g., Ex parte Royall,* 117 U.S. 241, 6 S. Ct. 734, 29 L. Ed. 868, and thus involved federalism concerns that are not relevant here. But we have extended this rule to require defendants in courts-martial to exhaust their military appeals before proceeding with a federal habeas corpus action. See *Schlesinger,* 420 U.S., at 758, 95 S. Ct. 1300, 43 L. Ed. 2d 591.

The real risks, the real threats, of terrorist attacks are constant and not likely soon to abate. The ways to disrupt our life and laws are so many and unforeseen that the Court should not attempt even some general catalogue of crises that might occur. Certain principles are apparent, however. Practical considerations and exigent circumstances inform the definition and reach of the law's writs, including habeas corpus. The cases and our tradition reflect this precept.

In cases involving foreign citizens detained abroad by the Executive, it likely would be both an impractical and unprecedented extension of judicial power to assume that habeas corpus would be available at the moment the prisoner is taken into custody. If and when habeas corpus jurisdiction applies, as it does in these cases, then proper deference can be accorded to reasonable procedures for screening and initial detention under lawful and proper conditions of confinement and treatment for a reasonable period of time. Domestic exigencies, furthermore, might also impose such onerous burdens on the Government that here, too, the Judicial Branch would be required to devise sensible rules for staying habeas corpus proceedings until the Government can comply with its requirements in a responsible way. Cf. *Ex parte Milligan,* 4 Wall., at 127, 18 L. Ed. 281 ("If, in foreign invasion or civil war, the courts are actually closed, and it is impossible to administer criminal justice according to law, *then*, on the theatre of active military operations, where war really prevails, there is a necessity to furnish a substitute for the civil authority, thus overthrown, to preserve the safety of the army and society; and as no power is left but the military, it is allowed to govern by martial rule until the laws can have their free course"). Here, as is true with detainees apprehended abroad, a relevant consideration in determining the courts' role is whether there are suitable alternative processes in place to protect against the arbitrary exercise of governmental power.

The cases before us, however, do not involve detainees who have been held for a short period of time while awaiting their CSRT determinations. Were that the case, or were it probable that the Court of Appeals could complete a prompt review of their applications, the case for requiring temporary abstention or exhaustion of alternative remedies would be much stronger. These qualifications no longer pertain here. In some of these cases six years have elapsed without the judicial oversight that habeas corpus or an adequate substitute demands. And there has been no showing that the Executive faces such onerous burdens that it cannot respond to habeas corpus actions. To require these detainees to complete DTA review before proceeding with their habeas corpus actions would be to require additional months, if not years, of delay. The first DTA review applications were filed over two years ago, but no decisions on the merits have been issued. While some delay in fashioning new procedures is unavoidable, the costs of delay can no longer be borne by those who are held in custody. The detainees in these cases are entitled to a prompt habeas corpus hearing.

Our decision today holds only that petitioners before us are entitled to seek the writ; that the DTA review procedures are an inadequate substitute for habeas corpus; and that petitioners in these cases need not exhaust the review procedures in the Court of Appeals before proceeding with their habeas actions in the District Court. The only law we identify as unconstitutional is MCA § 7, *28 U.S.C. § 2241(e)*. Accordingly, both the DTA and the CSRT process remain intact. Our holding with regard to exhaustion should not be read to imply that a habeas court should intervene the moment an enemy combatant steps foot in a territory where the writ runs. The Executive is entitled to a reasonable period of time to determine a detainee's status before a court entertains that detainee's habeas corpus petition. The CSRT process is the mechanism Congress and the President set up to deal with these issues. Except in cases of undue delay, federal courts should refrain from entertaining an enemy combatant's habeas corpus petition at least until after the Department, acting via the CSRT, has had a chance to review his status.

B

Although we hold that the DTA is not an adequate and effective substitute for habeas corpus, it does not follow that a habeas corpus court may disregard the dangers the detention in these cases was intended to prevent. *Felker, Swain,* and *Hayman* stand for the proposition that the Suspension Clause does not resist innovation in the field of habeas corpus. Certain accommodations can be made to reduce the burden habeas corpus proceedings will place on the military without impermissibly diluting the protections of the writ.

In the DTA Congress sought to consolidate review of petitioners' claims in the Court of Appeals. Channeling future cases to one district court would no doubt reduce administrative burdens on the Government. This is a legitimate objective that might be advanced even without an amendment to *§ 2241*. If, in a future case, a detainee files a habeas petition in another judicial district in which a proper respondent can be served, see *Rumsfeld v. Padilla, 542 U.S. 426, 435-436, 124 S. Ct. 2711, 159 L. Ed. 2d 513 (2004)*, the Government can move for change of venue to the court that will hear these petitioners' cases, the United States District Court for the District of Columbia. See *28 U.S.C. § 1404(a)*; *Braden v. 30th Judicial Circuit Court of Ky., 410 U.S. 484, 499, n. 15, 93 S. Ct. 1123, 35 L. Ed. 2d 443 (1973)*.

Another of Congress' reasons for vesting exclusive jurisdiction in the Court of Appeals, perhaps, was to avoid the widespread dissemination of classified information. The Government has raised similar concerns here and elsewhere. See Brief for Federal Respondents 55-56; *Bismullah* Pet. 30. We make no attempt to anticipate all of the evidentiary and access-to-counsel issues that will arise during the course of the detainees' habeas corpus proceedings. We recognize, however, that the Government has a legitimate interest in protecting sources and methods of intelligence gathering; and we expect that the District Court will use its discretion to accommodate this interest to the greatest extent possible. Cf. *United States v. Reynolds, 345 U.S. 1, 10, 73 S. Ct. 528, 97 L. Ed. 727 (1953)* (recognizing an evidentiary privilege in a civil damages case where "there is a reasonable danger that compulsion of the evidence will expose military matters which, in the interest of national security, should not be divulged").

These and the other remaining questions are within the expertise and competence of the District Court to address in the first instance.

In considering both the procedural and substantive standards used to impose detention to prevent acts of terrorism, proper deference must be accorded to the political branches. See *United States v. Curtiss-Wright Export Corp., 299 U.S. 304, 320, 57 S. Ct. 216, 81 L. Ed. 255 (1936)*. Unlike the President and some designated Members of Congress, neither the Members of this Court nor most federal judges begin the day with briefings that may describe new and serious threats to our Nation and its people. The law must accord the Executive substantial authority to apprehend and detain those who pose a real danger to our security.

Officials charged with daily operational responsibility for our security may consider a judicial discourse on the history of the Habeas Corpus Act of 1679 and like matters to be far removed from the Nation's present, urgent concerns. Established legal doctrine, however, must be consulted for its teaching. Remote in time it may be; irrelevant to the present it is not. Security depends upon a sophisticated intelligence apparatus and the ability of our Armed Forces to act and to interdict. There are further considerations, however. Security subsists, too, in fidelity to freedom's first principles. Chief among these are freedom from arbitrary and unlawful restraint and the personal liberty that is secured by adherence to the separation of powers. It is from these principles that the judicial authority to consider petitions for habeas corpus relief derives.

Our opinion does not undermine the Executive's powers as Commander in Chief. On the contrary, the exercise of those powers is vindicated, not eroded, when confirmed by the Judicial Branch. Within the Constitution's separation-of-powers structure, few exercises of judicial power are as legitimate or as necessary as the responsibility to hear challenges to the authority of the Executive to imprison a person. Some of these petitioners have been in custody for six years with no definitive judicial determination as to the legality of their detention. Their access to the writ is a necessity to determine the lawfulness of their status, even if, in the end, they do not obtain the relief they seek.

Because our Nation's past military conflicts have been of limited duration, it has been possible to leave the outer boundaries of war powers undefined. If, as some fear, terrorism continues to pose dangerous threats to us for years to come, the Court might not have this luxury. This result is not inevitable, however. The political branches, consistent with their independent obligations to interpret and uphold the Constitution, can engage in a genuine debate about how best to preserve constitutional values while protecting the Nation from terrorism. Cf. *Hamdan*, 548 U.S., at 636, 126 S. Ct. 2749, 165 L. Ed. 2d 723 (Breyer, J., concurring) ("[J]udicial insistence upon that consultation does not weaken our Nation's ability to deal with danger. To the contrary, that insistence strengthens the Nation's ability to determine--through democratic means--how best to do so").

It bears repeating that our opinion does not address the content of the law that governs petitioners' detention. That is a matter yet to be determined. We hold that petitioners may invoke the fundamental procedural protections of habeas corpus. The laws and Constitution are designed to survive, and remain in force, in extraordinary times. Liberty and security can be reconciled; and in our system they are reconciled within the framework of the law. The Framers decided that habeas corpus, a right of first importance, must be a part of that framework, a part of that law.

The determination by the Court of Appeals that the Suspension Clause and its protections are inapplicable to petitioners was in error. The judgment of the Court of Appeals is reversed. The cases are remanded to the Court of Appeals with instructions that it remand the cases to the District Court for proceedings consistent with this opinion.

It is so ordered.

JUSTICE SOUTER, with whom JUSTICE GINSBURG and JUSTICE BREYER join, concurring.

I join the Court's opinion in its entirety and add this afterword only to emphasize two things one might overlook after reading the dissents.

Four years ago, this Court in *Rasul v. Bush*, 542 U.S. 466, 124 S. Ct. 2686, 159 L. Ed. 2d 548 (2004), held that statutory habeas jurisdiction extended to claims of foreign nationals imprisoned by the United States at Guantanamo Bay, "to determine the legality of the Executive's potentially indefinite detention" of them, *id.*, at 485, 124 S. Ct. 2686, 159 L. Ed. 2d 548. Subsequent legislation eliminated the statutory habeas jurisdiction over these claims, so that now there must be constitutionally based jurisdiction or none at all. Justice Scalia is thus correct that here, for the first time, this Court holds there is (he says "confers") constitutional habeas jurisdiction over aliens imprisoned by the military outside an area of *de jure* national sovereignty, see *post*, at 826, 171 L. Ed. 2d, at 115 (dissenting opinion). But no one who reads the Court's opinion in *Rasul* could seriously doubt that the jurisdictional question must be answered the same way in purely constitutional cases, given the Court's reliance on the historical background of habeas generally in answering the statutory question. See, *e.g.*, 542 U.S., at 473, 481-483, and nn 11-14, 124 S. Ct. 2686, 159 L. Ed. 2d 548. Indeed, the Court in *Rasul* directly answered the very historical question that Justice Scalia says is dispositive, see *post*, at 843, 171 L. Ed. 2d, at 125; it wrote that "[a]pplication of the habeas statute to persons detained at [Guantanamo] is consistent with the historical reach of the writ of habeas corpus," 542 U.S., at 481, 124 S. Ct. 2686, 159 L. Ed. 2d 548. Justice Scalia dismisses the statement as dictum, see *post*, at 846, 171 L. Ed. 2d, at 127, but if dictum it was, it was dictum well considered, and it stated the view of five Members of this Court on the historical scope of the writ. Of course, it takes more than a quotation from *Rasul*, however much on point, to resolve the constitutional issue before us here, which the majority opinion has explored afresh in the detail it deserves. But whether one agrees or disagrees with today's decision, it is no bolt out of the blue.

A second fact insufficiently appreciated by the dissents is the length of the disputed imprisonments, some of the prisoners represented here today having been locked up for six years, *ante*, at 794, 171 L. Ed. 2d, at 95 (opinion of the Court). Hence the hollow ring when the dissenters suggest that the Court is somehow precipitating the Judiciary into reviewing claims that the military (subject to appeal to the Court of Appeals for the District of Columbia Circuit) could handle within some reasonable period of time. See, *e.g.*, *post*, at 803, 171 L. Ed. 2d, at 100 (opinion of Roberts, C. J.) ("[T]he Court should have declined to intervene until the D. C. Circuit had assessed the nature and validity of the congressionally mandated proceedings in a given detainee's case"); *post, at 805, 171 L. Ed. 2d, at 102* ("[I]t is not necessary to consider the availability of the writ until the statutory remedies have been shown to be inadequate"); *post, at 807, 171 L. Ed. 2d, at 103* ("[The Court] rushes to decide the fundamental question of the reach of habeas corpus when the functioning of the DTA may make that decision entirely unnecessary"). These suggestions of judicial haste are all the more out of place given the Court's realistic acknowledgment that in periods of exigency the tempo of any habeas review must reflect the immediate peril facing the country. See *ante, at 793-794, 171 L. Ed. 2d, at 94-95*.

It is in fact the very lapse of four years from the time *Rasul* put everyone on notice that habeas process was available to Guantanamo prisoners, and the lapse of six years since some of these prisoners were captured and incarcerated, that stand at odds with the repeated suggestions of the dissenters that these cases should be seen as a judicial victory in a contest for power between the Court and the political branches. See *post, at 801, 802, 826, 171 L. Ed. 2d, at 99-100, 100, 115* (opinion of Roberts, C. J.); *post, at 830-831, 842-843, 849-850, 171 L. Ed. 2d, at 117, 118, 124-125, 125, 129* (opinion of Scalia, J.). The several answers to the charge of triumphalism might start with a basic fact of Anglo-American constitutional history: that the power, first of the Crown and now of the Executive Branch of the United States, is necessarily limited by habeas corpus jurisdiction to enquire into the legality of executive detention. And one could explain that in this Court's exercise of responsibility to preserve habeas corpus something much more significant is involved than pulling and hauling between the judicial and political branches. Instead, though, it is enough to repeat that some of these petitioners have spent six years behind bars. After six years of sustained executive detentions in Guantanamo, subject to habeas jurisdiction but without any actual habeas scrutiny, today's decision is no judicial victory, but an act of perseverance in trying to make habeas review, and the obligation of the courts to provide it, mean something of value both to prisoners and to the Nation. See *ante, at 797, 171 L. Ed. 2d, at 97*.

CHIEF JUSTICE ROBERTS, with whom JUSTICE SCALIA, JUSTICE THOMAS, and JUSTICE ALITO join, dissenting.

Today the Court strikes down as inadequate the most generous set of procedural protections ever afforded aliens detained by this country as enemy combatants. The political branches crafted these procedures amidst an ongoing military conflict, after much careful investigation and thorough debate. The Court rejects them today out of hand, without bothering to say what due process rights the detainees possess, without explaining how the statute fails to vindicate those rights, and before a single petitioner has exhausted the procedures under the law. And to what effect? The majority merely replaces a review system designed by the people's representatives with a set of shapeless procedures to be defined by federal courts at some future date. One cannot help but think, after surveying the modest practical results of the majority's ambitious opinion, that this decision is not really about the detainees at all, but about control of federal policy regarding enemy combatants.

The majority is adamant that the Guantanamo detainees are entitled to the protections of habeas corpus--its opinion begins by deciding that question. I regard the issue as a difficult one, primarily because of the unique and unusual jurisdictional status of Guantanamo Bay. I nonetheless agree with Justice Scalia's analysis of our precedents and the pertinent history of the writ, and accordingly join his dissent. The important point for me, however, is that the Court should have resolved these cases on other grounds. Habeas is most fundamentally a procedural right, a mechanism for contesting the legality of executive detention. The critical threshold question in these cases, prior to any inquiry about the writ's scope, is whether the system the political branches designed protects whatever rights the detainees may possess. If so, there is no need for any additional process, whether called "habeas" or something else.

Congress entrusted that threshold question in the first instance to the Court of Appeals for the District of Columbia Circuit, as the Constitution surely allows Congress to do. See Detainee Treatment Act of 2005 (DTA), § 1005(e)(2)(A), 119 Stat. 2742. But before the D. C. Circuit has addressed the issue, the Court cashiers the statute, and without answering this critical threshold question itself. The Court does eventually get around to asking whether review under the DTA is, as the Court frames it, an "adequate substitute" for habeas, *ante, at 772, 171 L. Ed. 2d, at 81*, but even then its opinion fails to determine what rights the detainees possess and whether the DTA system satisfies them. The majority instead compares the undefined DTA process to an equally undefined habeas right--one that is to be given shape only in the future by district courts on a case-by-case basis. This whole approach is misguided.

It is also fruitless. How the detainees' claims will be decided now that the DTA is gone is anybody's guess. But the habeas process the Court mandates will most likely end up looking a lot like the DTA system it replaces, as the district court judges shaping it will have to reconcile review of the prisoners' detention with the undoubted need to protect the American people from the terrorist threat--precisely the challenge Congress undertook in drafting the DTA. All that today's opinion has done is shift responsibility for those sensitive foreign policy and national security decisions from the elected branches to the Federal Judiciary.

I believe the system the political branches constructed adequately protects any constitutional rights aliens captured abroad and detained as enemy combatants may enjoy. I therefore would dismiss these cases on that ground. With all respect for the contrary views of the majority, I must dissent.

I

The Court's opinion makes plain that certiorari to review these cases should never have been granted. As two Members of today's majority once recognized, "traditional rules governing our decision of constitutional questions and our practice of requiring the exhaustion of available remedies . . . make it appropriate to deny these petitions." *Boumediene v. Bush, 549 U.S. 1328, 1329, 127 S. Ct. 1478, 167 L. Ed. 2d 578 (2007)* (Stevens and Kennedy, JJ., statement respecting denial of certiorari) (citation omitted). Just so. Given the posture in which these cases came to us, the Court should have declined to intervene until the D. C. Circuit had assessed the nature and validity of the congressionally mandated proceedings in a given detainee's case.

The political branches created a two-part, collateral review procedure for testing the legality of the prisoners' detention: It begins with a hearing before a Combatant Status Review Tribunal (CSRT) followed by review in the D. C. Circuit. As part of that review, Congress authorized the D. C. Circuit to decide whether the CSRT proceedings are consistent with "the Constitution and laws of the United States." DTA § 1005(e)(2)(C), 119 Stat. 2742. No petitioner, however, has invoked the D. C. Circuit review the statute specifies. See *375 U.S. App. D.C. 48, 476 F.3d 981, 994, and n 16 (CADC 2007)*; Brief for Federal Respondents 41-43. As a consequence, that court has had no occasion to decide whether the CSRT hearings, followed by review in the Court of Appeals, vindicate whatever constitutional and statutory rights petitioners may possess. See *476 F.3d, at 994*, and n 16.

Remarkably, this Court does not require petitioners to exhaust their remedies under the statute; it does not wait to see whether those remedies will prove sufficient to protect petitioners' rights. Instead, it not only denies the D. C. Circuit the opportunity to assess the statute's remedies, it refuses to do so itself: The majority expressly declines to decide whether the CSRT procedures, coupled with Article III review, satisfy due process. See *ante*, at 785, 171 L. Ed. 2d, at 88.

It is grossly premature to pronounce on the detainees' right to habeas without first assessing whether the remedies the DTA system provides vindicate whatever rights petitioners may claim. The plurality in *Hamdi v. Rumsfeld, 542 U.S. 507, 533, 124 S. Ct. 2633, 159 L. Ed. 2d 578 (2004)*, explained that the Constitution guaranteed an American *citizen* challenging his detention as an enemy combatant the right to "notice of the factual basis for his classification, and a fair opportunity to rebut the Government's factual assertions before a neutral decisionmaker." The plurality specifically stated that constitutionally adequate collateral process could be provided "by an appropriately authorized and properly constituted military tribunal," given the "uncommon potential to burden the Executive at a time of ongoing military conflict." *Id., at 533, 538, 124 S. Ct. 2633, 159 L. Ed. 2d 578*. This point is directly pertinent here, for surely the *Due Process Clause* does not afford *non-citizens* in such circumstances greater protection than citizens are due.

If the CSRT procedures meet the minimal due process requirements outlined in *Hamdi*, and if an Article III court is available to ensure that these procedures are followed in future cases, see *id., at 536, 124 S. Ct. 2633, 159 L. Ed. 2d 578*; *INS v. St. Cyr, 533 U.S. 289, 304, 121 S. Ct. 2271, 150 L. Ed. 2d 347 (2001)*; *Heikkila v. Barber, 345 U.S. 229, 236, 73 S. Ct. 603, 97 L. Ed. 972 (1953)*, there is no need to reach the Suspension Clause question. Detainees will have received all the process the Constitution could possibly require, whether that process is called "habeas" or something else. The question of the writ's reach need not be addressed.

This is why the Court should have required petitioners to exhaust their remedies under the statute. As we explained in *Gusik v. Schilder, 340 U.S. 128, 132, 71 S. Ct. 149, 95 L. Ed. 146 (1950)*: "If an available procedure has not been employed to rectify the alleged error" petitioners complain of, "any interference by [a] federal court may be wholly needless. The procedure established to police the errors of the tribunal whose judgment is challenged may be adequate for the occasion." Because the majority refuses to assess whether the CSRTs comport with the Constitution, it ends up razing a system of collateral review that it admits may in fact satisfy the *Due Process Clause* and be "structurally sound." *Ante*, at 785, 171 L. Ed. 2d, at 89. But if the collateral review procedures Congress has provided --CSRT review coupled with Article III scrutiny--are sound, interference by a federal habeas court may be entirely unnecessary.

The only way to know is to require petitioners to use the alternative procedures Congress designed. Mandating that petitioners exhaust their statutory remedies "is in no sense a suspension of the writ of habeas corpus. It is merely a deferment of resort to the writ until other corrective procedures are shown to be futile." *Gusik, supra, at 132, 71 S. Ct. 149, 95 L. Ed. 146.* So too here, it is not necessary to consider the availability of the writ until the statutory remedies have been shown to be inadequate to protect the detainees' rights. Cf. *28 U.S.C. § 2254(b)(1)(A)* ("An application for a writ of habeas corpus . . . shall not be granted unless it appears that . . . the applicant has exhausted the remedies available in the courts of the State"). Respect for the judgments of Congress --whose Members take the same oath we do to uphold the Constitution --requires no less.

In the absence of any assessment of the DTA's remedies, the question whether detainees are entitled to habeas is an entirely speculative one. Our precedents have long counseled us to avoid deciding such hypothetical questions of constitutional law. See *Spector Motor Service, Inc. v. McLaughlin, 323 U.S. 101, 105, 65 S. Ct. 152, 89 L. Ed. 101 (1944)* ("If there is one doctrine more deeply rooted than any other in the process of constitutional adjudication, it is that we ought not to pass on questions of constitutionality . . . unless such [questions are] unavoidable"); see also *Ashwander v. TVA, 297 U.S. 288, 347, 56 S. Ct. 466, 80 L. Ed. 688 (1936)* (Brandeis, J., concurring) (Constitutional questions should not be decided unless "'absolutely necessary to a decision of the case'" (quoting *Burton v. United States, 196 U.S. 283, 295, 25 S. Ct. 243, 49 L. Ed. 482 (1905)))*. This is a "fundamental rule of judicial restraint." *Three Affiliated Tribes of Fort Berthold Reservation v. Wold Engineering, P. C., 467 U.S. 138, 157, 104 S. Ct. 2267, 81 L. Ed. 2d 113 (1984).*

The Court acknowledges that "the ordinary course" would be not to decide the constitutionality of the DTA at this stage, but abandons that "ordinary course" in light of the "gravity" of the constitutional issues presented and the prospect of additional delay. *Ante, at 772, 171 L. Ed. 2d, at 81.* It is, however, precisely when the issues presented are grave that adherence to the ordinary course is most important. A principle applied only when unimportant is not much of a principle at all, and charges of judicial activism are most effectively rebutted when courts can fairly argue they are following normal practices.

The Court is also concerned that requiring petitioners to pursue "DTA review before proceeding with their habeas corpus actions" could involve additional delay. *Ante, at 794, 171 L. Ed. 2d, at 95.* The nature of the habeas remedy the Court instructs lower courts to craft on remand, however, is far more unsettled than the process Congress provided in the DTA. See *ante, at 798, 171 L. Ed. 2d, at 97* ("[O]ur opinion does not address the content of the law that governs petitioners' detention. That is a matter yet to be determined"). There is no reason to suppose that review according to procedures the Federal Judiciary will design, case by case, will proceed any faster than the DTA process petitioners disdained.

On the contrary, the system the Court has launched (and directs lower courts to elaborate) promises to take longer. The Court assures us that before bringing their habeas petitions, detainees must usually complete the CSRT process. See *ante, at 795, 171 L. Ed. 2d, at 95*. Then they may seek review in federal district court. Either success or failure there will surely result in an appeal to the D. C. Circuit--exactly where judicial review *starts* under Congress's system. The effect of the Court's decision is to add additional layers of quite possibly redundant review. And because nobody knows how these new layers of "habeas" review will operate, or what new procedures they will require, their contours will undoubtedly be subject to fresh bouts of litigation. If the majority were truly concerned about delay, it would have required petitioners to use the DTA process that has been available to them for 2 1/2 years, with its Article III review in the D. C. Circuit. That system might well have provided petitioners all the relief to which they are entitled long before the Court's newly installed habeas review could hope to do so.[1]

The Court's refusal to require petitioners to exhaust the remedies provided by Congress violates the "traditional rules governing our decision of constitutional questions." *Boumediene, 549 U.S., at 1329, 127 S. Ct. 1478, 167 L. Ed. 2d 578* (Stevens and Kennedy, JJ., statement respecting denial of certiorari). The Court's disrespect for these rules makes its decision an awkward business. It rushes to decide the fundamental question of the reach of habeas corpus when the functioning of the DTA may make that decision entirely unnecessary, and it does so with scant idea of how DTA judicial review will actually operate.

II

---

[1] In light of the foregoing, the concurrence is wrong to suggest that I "insufficiently appreciat[e]" the issue of delay in these cases. See *ante, at 799, 171 L. Ed. 2d, at 98* (opinion of Souter, J.). This Court issued its decisions in *Rasul v. Bush, 542 U.S. 466, 124 S. Ct. 2686, 159 L. Ed. 2d 548*, and *Hamdi v. Rumsfeld, 542 U.S. 507, 124 S. Ct. 2633, 159 L. Ed. 2d 578*, in 2004. The concurrence makes it sound as if the political branches have done nothing in the interim. In fact, Congress responded 18 months later by enacting the DTA. Congress cannot be faulted for taking that time to consider how best to accommodate both the detainees' interests and the need to keep the American people safe. Since the DTA became law, petitioners have steadfastly resisted the statute's review mechanisms, preferring to proceed under habeas. It is unfair to complain that the DTA system involves too much delay when petitioners have opted to litigate rather than pursue its procedures. Today's decision obligating district courts to craft new procedures to replace those in the DTA will only prolong the process--and delay relief.

The majority's overreaching is particularly egregious given the weakness of its objections to the DTA. Simply put, the Court's opinion fails on its own terms. The majority strikes down the statute because it is not an "adequate substitute" for habeas review, *ante*, at 772, 171 L. Ed. 2d, at 81, but fails to show what rights the detainees have that cannot be vindicated by the DTA system.

Because the central purpose of habeas corpus is to test the legality of executive detention, the writ requires most fundamentally an Article III court able to hear the prisoner's claims and, when necessary, order release. See *Brown v. Allen*, 344 U.S. 443, 533, 73 S. Ct. 397, 97 L. Ed. 469 (1953) (Jackson, J., concurring in result). Beyond that, the process a given prisoner is entitled to receive depends on the circumstances and the rights of the prisoner. See *Mathews v. Eldridge*, 424 U.S. 319, 335, 96 S. Ct. 893, 47 L. Ed. 2d 18 (1976). After much hemming and hawing, the majority appears to concede that the DTA provides an Article III court competent to order release. See *ante*, at 787-788, 171 L. Ed. 2d, at 92. The only issue in dispute is the process the Guantanamo prisoners are entitled to use to test the legality of their detention. *Hamdi* concluded that American citizens detained as enemy combatants are entitled to only limited process, and that much of that process could be supplied by a military tribunal, with review to follow in an Article III court. That is precisely the system we have here. It is adequate to vindicate whatever due process rights petitioners may have.

A

The Court reaches the opposite conclusion partly because it misreads the statute. The majority appears not to understand how the review system it invalidates actually works--specifically, how CSRT review and review by the D. C. Circuit fit together. After briefly acknowledging in its recitation of the facts that the Government designed the CSRTs "to comply with the due process requirements identified by the plurality in *Hamdi*," *ante*, at 734, 171 L. Ed. 2d, at 57, the Court proceeds to dismiss the tribunal proceedings as no more than a suspect method used by the Executive for determining the status of the detainees in the first instance, see *ante*, at 783, 171 L. Ed. 2d, at 81. This leads the Court to treat the review the DTA provides in the D. C. Circuit as the only opportunity detainees have to challenge their status determination. See *ante*, at 778, 171 L. Ed. 2d, at 85.

The Court attempts to explain its glancing treatment of the CSRTs by arguing that "[w]hether one characterizes the CSRT process as direct review of the Executive's battlefield determination . . . or as the first step in the collateral review of a battlefield determination makes no difference." *Ante*, at 783, 171 L. Ed. 2d, at 88. First of all, the majority is quite wrong to dismiss the Executive's determination of detainee status as no more than a "battlefield" judgment, as if it were somehow provisional and made in great haste. In fact, detainees are designated "enemy combatants" only after "multiple levels of review by military officers and officials of the Department of Defense." Memorandum of the Secretary of the Navy, Implementation of Combatant Status Review Tribunal Procedures for Enemy Combatants Detained at Guantanamo Bay Naval Base (July 29, 2004), App. J to Pet. for Cert. in No. 06-1196, p 150 (hereinafter Implementation Memo).

The majority is equally wrong to characterize the CSRTs as part of that initial determination process. They are instead a means for detainees to *challenge* the Government's determination. The Executive designed the CSRTs to mirror Army Regulation 190-8, see Brief for Federal Respondents 48, the very procedural model the plurality in *Hamdi* said provided the type of process an enemy combatant could expect from a habeas court, see *542 U.S., at 538, 124 S. Ct. 2633, 159 L. Ed. 2d 578* (plurality opinion). The CSRTs operate much as habeas courts would if hearing the detainee's collateral challenge for the first time: They gather evidence, call witnesses, take testimony, and render a decision on the legality of the Government's detention. See Implementation Memo, 153-162. If the CSRT finds a particular detainee has been improperly held, it can order release. See *id.*, at 164.

The majority insists that even if "the CSRTs satisf[ied] due process standards," full habeas review would still be necessary, because habeas is a collateral remedy available even to prisoners "detained pursuant to the most rigorous proceedings imaginable." *Ante, at 785, 171 L. Ed. 2d, at 88, 89.* This comment makes sense only if the CSRTs are incorrectly viewed as a method used by the Executive for determining the prisoners' status, and not as themselves part of the collateral review to test the validity of that determination. See *Gusik, 340 U.S., at 132, 71 S. Ct. 149, 95 L. Ed. 146.* The majority can deprecate the importance of the CSRTs only by treating them as something they are not.

The use of a military tribunal such as the CSRTs to review the aliens' detention should be familiar to this Court in light of the *Hamdi* plurality, which said that the due process rights enjoyed by *American citizens* detained as enemy combatants could be vindicated "by an appropriately authorized and properly constituted military tribunal." *542 U.S., at 538, 124 S. Ct. 2633, 159 L. Ed. 2d 578.* The DTA represents Congress's considered attempt to provide the accused alien combatants detained at Guantanamo a constitutionally adequate opportunity to contest their detentions before just such a tribunal.

But Congress went further in the DTA. CSRT review is just the first tier of collateral review in the DTA system. The statute provides additional review in an Article III court. Given the rationale of today's decision, it is well worth recalling exactly what the DTA provides in this respect. The statute directs the D. C. Circuit to consider whether a particular alien's status determination "was consistent with the standards and procedures specified by the Secretary of Defense" *and* "whether the use of such standards and procedures to make the determination is consistent with the Constitution and laws of the United States." DTA § 1005(e)(2)(C), 119 Stat. 2742. That is, a *court* determines whether the CSRT procedures are constitutional, and a *court* determines whether those procedures were followed in a particular case.

In short, the *Hamdi* plurality concluded that this type of review would be enough to satisfy due process, even for citizens. See *542 U.S., at 538, 124 S. Ct. 2633, 159 L. Ed. 2d 578*. Congress followed the Court's lead, only to find itself the victim of a constitutional bait and switch.

Hamdi merits scant attention from the Court--a remarkable omission, as *Hamdi* bears directly on the issues before us. The majority attempts to dismiss *Hamdi's* relevance by arguing that because the availability of § 2241 federal habeas was never in doubt in that case, "the Court had no occasion to define the necessary scope of habeas review . . . in the context of enemy combatant detentions." *Ante, at 784, 171 L. Ed. 2d, at 89*. Hardly. *Hamdi* was all about the scope of habeas review in the context of enemy combatant detentions. The petitioner, an American citizen held within the United States as an enemy combatant, invoked the writ to challenge his detention. *542 U.S., at 510-511, 124 S. Ct. 2633, 159 L. Ed. 2d 578*. After "a careful examination both of the writ . . . and of the *Due Process Clause*," this Court enunciated the "basic process" the Constitution entitled Hamdi to expect from a habeas court under § 2241. *Id., at 525, 534, 124 S. Ct. 2633, 159 L. Ed. 2d 578*. That process consisted of the right to "receive notice of the factual basis for his classification, and a fair opportunity to rebut the Government's factual assertions before a neutral decisionmaker." *Id., at 533, 124 S. Ct. 2633, 159 L. Ed. 2d 578*. In light of the Government's national security responsibilities, the plurality found the process could be "tailored to alleviate [the] uncommon potential to burden the Executive at a time of ongoing military conflict." *Ibid.* For example, the Government could rely on hearsay and could claim a presumption in favor of its own evidence. See *id., at 533-534, 124 S. Ct. 2633, 159 L. Ed. 2d 578*.

Hamdi further suggested that this "basic process" on collateral review could be provided by a military tribunal. It pointed to prisoner-of-war tribunals as a model that would satisfy the Constitution's requirements. See *id., at 538, 124 S. Ct. 2633, 159 L. Ed. 2d 578*. Only "[i]n the *absence* of such process" before a military tribunal, the Court held, would Article III courts need to conduct full-dress habeas proceedings to "ensure that the minimum requirements of due process are achieved." *Ibid.* (emphasis added). And even then, the petitioner would be entitled to no more process than he would have received from a properly constituted military review panel, given his limited due process rights and the Government's weighty interests. See *id., at 533-534, 538, 124 S. Ct. 2633, 159 L. Ed. 2d 578.*

Contrary to the majority, *Hamdi* is of pressing relevance because it establishes the procedures American *citizens* detained as enemy combatants can expect from a habeas court proceeding under § 2241. The DTA system of military tribunal hearings followed by Article III review looks a lot like the procedure *Hamdi* blessed. If nothing else, it is plain from the design of the DTA that Congress, the President, and this Nation's military leaders have made a good-faith effort to follow our precedent.

The Court, however, will not take "yes" for an answer. The majority contends that "[i]f Congress had envisioned DTA review as coextensive with traditional habeas corpus," it would have granted the D. C. Circuit far broader review authority. *Ante, at 777, 171 L. Ed. 2d, at 84.* Maybe so, but that comment reveals the majority's misunderstanding. "[T]raditional habeas corpus" takes *no* account of what *Hamdi* recognized as the "uncommon potential to burden the Executive at a time of ongoing military conflict." *542 U.S., at 533, 124 S. Ct. 2633, 159 L. Ed. 2d 578.* Besides, Congress and the Executive did not envision "DTA review"--by which I assume the Court means D. C. Circuit review, see *ante, at 777, 171 L. Ed. 2d, at 84*-- as the detainees' only opportunity to challenge their detentions. Instead, the political branches crafted CSRT *and* D. C. Circuit review to operate together, with the goal of providing noncitizen detainees the level of collateral process *Hamdi* said would satisfy the due process rights of American citizens. See Brief for Federal Respondents 48-53.

B

Given the statutory scheme the political branches adopted, and given *Hamdi*, it simply will not do for the majority to dismiss the CSRT procedures as "far more limited" than those used in military trials, and therefore beneath the level of process "that would eliminate the need for habeas corpus review." *Ante, at 767, 171 L. Ed. 2d, at 78.* The question is not how much process the CSRTs provide in comparison to other modes of adjudication. The question is whether the CSRT procedures-- coupled with the judicial review specified by the DTA--provide the "basic process" *Hamdi* said the Constitution affords American citizens detained as enemy combatants. See *542 U.S., at 534, 124 S. Ct. 2633, 159 L. Ed. 2d 578.*

By virtue of its refusal to allow the D. C. Circuit to assess petitioners' statutory remedies, and by virtue of its own refusal to consider, at the outset, the fit between those remedies and due process, the majority now finds itself in the position of evaluating whether the DTA system is an adequate substitute for habeas review without knowing what rights either habeas or the DTA is supposed to protect. The majority attempts to elide this problem by holding that petitioners have a right to habeas corpus and then comparing the DTA against the "historic office" of the writ. *Ante,* at 776, 171 L. Ed. 2d, at 84. But habeas is, as the majority acknowledges, a flexible remedy rather than a substantive right. Its "precise application . . . change[s] depending upon the circumstances." *Ante,* at 779, 171 L. Ed. 2d, at 86. The shape of habeas review ultimately depends on the nature of the rights a petitioner may assert. See, *e.g., Reid v. Covert,* 354 U.S. 1, 75, 77 S. Ct. 1222, 1 L. Ed. 2d 1148 (1957) (Harlan, J., concurring in result) ("[T]he question of which specific safeguards of the Constitution are appropriately to be applied in a particular context . . . can be reduced to the issue of what process is 'due' a defendant in the particular circumstances of a particular case").

The scope of federal habeas review is traditionally more limited in some contexts than in others, depending on the status of the detainee and the rights he may assert. See *St. Cyr,* 533 U.S., at 306, 121 S. Ct. 2271, 150 L. Ed. 2d 347 ("In [immigration cases], other than the question whether there was some evidence to support the [deportation] order, the courts generally did not review factual determinations made by the Executive" (footnote omitted)); *Burns v. Wilson,* 346 U.S. 137, 139, 73 S. Ct. 1045, 97 L. Ed. 1508 (1953) (plurality opinion) ("[I]n military habeas corpus the inquiry, the scope of matters open for review, has always been more narrow than in civil cases"); *In re Yamashita,* 327 U.S. 1, 8, 66 S. Ct. 340, 90 L. Ed. 499 (1946) ("The courts may inquire whether the detention complained of is within the authority of those detaining the petitioner. If the military tribunals have lawful authority to hear, decide and condemn, their action is not subject to judicial review"); *Ex parte Quirin,* 317 U.S. 1, 25, 63 S. Ct. 2, 87 L. Ed. 3 (1942) (federal habeas review of military commission verdict limited to determining commission's jurisdiction).

Declaring that petitioners have a right to habeas in no way excuses the Court from explaining why the DTA does not protect whatever due process or statutory rights petitioners may have. Because if the DTA provides a means for vindicating petitioners' rights, it is necessarily an adequate substitute for habeas corpus. See *Swain v. Pressley,* 430 U.S. 372, 381, 97 S. Ct. 1224, 51 L. Ed. 2d 411 (1977); *United States v. Hayman,* 342 U.S. 205, 223, 72 S. Ct. 263, 96 L. Ed. 232 (1952).

For my part, I will assume that any due process rights petitioners may possess are no greater than those of American citizens detained as enemy combatants. It is worth noting again that the *Hamdi* controlling opinion said the Constitution guarantees citizen detainees only "basic" procedural rights, and that the process for securing those rights can "be tailored to alleviate [the] uncommon potential to burden the Executive at a time of ongoing military conflict." *542 U.S., at 533, 124 S. Ct. 2633, 159 L. Ed. 2d 578.* The majority, however, objects that "the procedural protections afforded to the detainees in the CSRT hearings are ... limited." *Ante, at 767, 171 L. Ed. 2d, at 78.* But the evidentiary and other limitations the Court complains of reflect the nature of the issue in contest, namely, the status of aliens captured by our Armed Forces abroad and alleged to be enemy combatants. Contrary to the repeated suggestions of the majority, DTA review need not parallel the habeas privileges enjoyed by noncombatant American citizens, as set out in *28 U.S.C. § 2241 (2000 ed. and Supp. V).* Cf. *ante, at 777-778, 171 L. Ed. 2d, at 83-84.* It need only provide process adequate for noncitizens detained as alleged combatants.

To what basic process are these detainees due as habeas petitioners? We have said that "at the absolute minimum," the Suspension Clause protects the writ "'as it existed in 1789.'" *St. Cyr, supra, at 301, 121 S. Ct. 2271, 150 L. Ed. 2d 347* (quoting *Felker v. Turpin, 518 U.S. 651, 663-664, 116 S. Ct. 2333, 135 L. Ed. 2d 827 (1996)).* The majority admits that a number of historical authorities suggest that at the time of the Constitution's ratification, "common-law courts abstained altogether from matters involving prisoners of war." *Ante, at 747, 171 L. Ed. 2d, at 66.* If this is accurate, the process provided prisoners under the DTA is plainly more than sufficient--it allows alleged combatants to challenge both the factual and legal bases of their detentions.

Assuming the constitutional baseline is more robust, the DTA still provides adequate process, and by the majority's own standards. Today's Court opines that the Suspension Clause guarantees prisoners such as the detainees "a meaningful opportunity to demonstrate that [they are] being held pursuant to the erroneous application or interpretation of relevant law." *Ante, at 779, 171 L. Ed. 2d, at 85* (internal quotation marks omitted). Further, the Court holds that to be an adequate substitute, any tribunal reviewing the detainees' cases "must have the power to order the conditional release of an individual unlawfully detained." Ibid. The DTA system--CSRT review of the Executive's determination followed by D. C. Circuit review for sufficiency of the evidence and the constitutionality of the CSRT process --meets these criteria.

C

At the CSRT stage, every petitioner has the right to present evidence that he has been wrongfully detained. This includes the right to call witnesses who are reasonably available, question witnesses called by the tribunal, introduce documentary evidence, and testify before the tribunal. See Implementation Memo 154-156, 158-159, 161.

275

While the Court concedes detainees may confront all witnesses called before the tribunal, it suggests this right is "more theoretical than real" because "there are in effect no limits on the admission of hearsay evidence." *Ante, at 784, 171 L. Ed. 2d, at 88.* The Court further complains that petitioners lack "the assistance of counsel," and--given the limits on their access to classified information--"may not be aware of the most critical allegations" against them. *Ante, at 783-784, 171 L. Ed. 2d, at 88.* None of these complaints is persuasive.

Detainees not only have the opportunity to confront any witness who appears before the tribunal, they may call witnesses of their own. The Implementation Memo requires only that detainees' witnesses be "reasonably available," App. J to Pet. for Cert. in No. 06-1196, ¶ F(6), at 155, a requirement drawn from Army Regulation 190-8, ch. 1, § 1-6(*e*)(6), and entirely consistent with the Government's interest in avoiding "a futile search for evidence" that might burden warmaking responsibilities, *Hamdi, supra, at 532, 124 S. Ct. 2633, 159 L. Ed. 2d 578.* The dangerous mission assigned to our forces abroad is to fight terrorists, not serve subpoenas. The Court is correct that some forms of hearsay evidence are admissible before the CSRT, but *Hamdi* expressly approved this use of hearsay by habeas courts. *542 U.S., at 533-534, 124 S. Ct. 2633, 159 L. Ed. 2d 578* ("Hearsay, for example, may need to be accepted as the most reliable available evidence from the Government").

As to classified information, while detainees are not permitted access to it themselves, the Implementation Memo provides each detainee with a "Personal Representative" who may review classified documents and comment on this evidence to the CSRT on the detainee's behalf. Implementation Memo 152, 154-156; Brief for Federal Respondents 54-55. The prisoner's counsel enjoys the same privilege on appeal before the D. C. Circuit. That is more access to classified material for alleged alien enemy combatants than ever before provided. I am not aware of a single instance--and certainly the majority cites none--in which detainees such as petitioners have been provided access to classified material in *any* form. Indeed, prisoners of war who challenge their status determinations under the Geneva Convention are afforded no such access, see Army Regulation 190-8, ch. 1, §§ 1-6(*e*)(3) and (5), and the prisoner-of-war model is the one *Hamdi* cited as consistent with the demands of due process for *citizens*, see *542 U.S., at 538, 124 S. Ct. 2633, 159 L. Ed. 2d 578.*

What alternative does the Court propose? Allow free access to classified information and ignore the risk the prisoner may eventually convey what he learns to parties hostile to this country, with deadly consequences for those who helped apprehend the detainee? If the Court can design a better system for communicating to detainees the substance of any classified information relevant to their cases, without fatally compromising national security interests and sources, the majority should come forward with it. Instead, the majority fobs that vexing question off on district courts to answer down the road.

Prisoners of war are not permitted access to classified information, and neither are they permitted access to counsel, another supposed failing of the CSRT process. And yet the Guantanamo detainees are hardly denied all legal assistance. They are provided a "Personal Representative" who, as previously noted, may access classified information, help the detainee arrange for witnesses, assist the detainee's preparation of his case, and even aid the detainee in presenting his evidence to the tribunal. See Implementation Memo 161. The provision for a personal representative on this order is one of several ways in which the CSRT procedures are *more* generous than those provided prisoners of war under Army Regulation 190-8.

Keep in mind that all this is just at the CSRT stage. Detainees receive additional process before the D. C. Circuit, including full access to appellate counsel and the right to challenge the factual and legal bases of their detentions. DTA § 1005(e)(2)(C) empowers the Court of Appeals to determine not only whether the CSRT observed the "procedures specified by the Secretary of Defense," but also "whether the use of such standards and procedures . . . is consistent with the Constitution and laws of the United States." 119 Stat. 2742. These provisions permit detainees to dispute the sufficiency of the evidence against them. They allow detainees to challenge a CSRT panel's interpretation of any relevant law, and even the constitutionality of the CSRT proceedings themselves. This includes, as the Solicitor General acknowledges, the ability to dispute the Government's right to detain alleged combatants in the first place, and to dispute the Government's definition of "enemy combatant." Brief for Federal Respondents 59. All this before an Article III court--plainly a neutral decisionmaker.

All told, the DTA provides the prisoners held at Guantanamo Bay adequate opportunity to contest the bases of their detentions, which is all habeas corpus need allow. The DTA provides more opportunity and more process, in fact, than that afforded prisoners of war or any other alleged enemy combatants in history.

D

Despite these guarantees, the Court finds the DTA system an inadequate habeas substitute, for one central reason: Detainees are unable to introduce at the appeal stage exculpatory evidence discovered after the conclusion of their CSRT proceedings. See *ante, at 790, 171 L. Ed. 2d, at 90*. The Court hints darkly that the

DTA may suffer from other infirmities, see *ante*, at 792, 171 L. Ed. 2d, at 93 ("We do not imply DTA review would be a constitutionally sufficient replacement for habeas corpus but for these limitations on the detainee's ability to present exculpatory evidence"), but it does not bother to name them, making a response a bit difficult. As it stands, I can only assume the Court regards the supposed defect it did identify as the gravest of the lot.

If this is the most the Court can muster, the ice beneath its feet is thin indeed. As noted, the CSRT procedures provide ample opportunity for detainees to introduce exculpatory evidence--whether documentary in nature or from live witnesses-- before the military tribunals. See *infra*, at 816-817, 171 L. Ed. 2d, at 111-112; Implementation Memo 155-156. And if their ability to introduce such evidence is denied contrary to the Constitution or laws of the United States, the D. C. Circuit has the authority to say so on review.

Nevertheless, the Court asks us to imagine an instance in which evidence is discovered *after* the CSRT panel renders its decision, but *before* the Court of Appeals reviews the detainee's case. This scenario, which of course has not yet come to pass as no review in the D. C. Circuit has occurred, provides no basis for rejecting the DTA as a habeas substitute. While the majority is correct that the DTA does not contemplate the introduction of "newly discovered" evidence before the Court of Appeals, petitioners and the Solicitor General agree that the DTA *does* permit the D. C. Circuit to remand a detainee's case for a new CSRT determination. Brief for Petitioner Boumediene et al. in No. 06-1195, p. 30; Brief for Federal Respondents 60-61. In the event a detainee alleges that he has obtained new and persuasive exculpatory evidence that would have been considered by the tribunal below had it only been available, the D. C. Circuit could readily remand the case to the tribunal to allow that body to consider the evidence in the first instance. The Court of Appeals could later review any new or reinstated decision in light of the supplemented record.

If that sort of procedure sounds familiar, it should. Federal appellate courts reviewing factual determinations follow just such a procedure in a variety of circumstances. See, *e.g., United States v. White, 492 F.3d 380, 413 (CA6 2007)* (remanding new-evidence claim to the district court for a *Brady* evidentiary hearing); *Avila v. Roe, 298 F.3d 750, 754 (CA9 2002)* (remanding habeas claim to the district court for evidentiary hearing to clarify factual record); *United States v. Leone, 215 F.3d 253, 256 (CA2 2000)* (observing that when faced on direct appeal with an underdeveloped claim for ineffective assistance of counsel, the appellate court may remand to the district court for necessary factfinding).

A remand is not the only relief available for detainees caught in the Court's hypothetical conundrum. The DTA expressly directs the Secretary of Defense to "provide for periodic review of any new evidence that may become available relating to the enemy combatant status of a detainee." § 1005(a)(3), 119 Stat. 2741. Regulations issued by the Department of Defense provide that when a detainee puts forward new, material evidence "not previously presented to the detainee's CSRT," the Deputy Secretary of Defense "'will direct that a CSRT convene to reconsider the basis of the detainee's . . . status in light of the new information.'" Office for the Administrative Review of the Detention of Enemy Combatants, Instruction 5421.1, Procedure for Review of "New Evidence" Relating to Enemy Combatant (EC) Status PP 4(a)(1), 5(b) (May 7, 2007); Brief for Federal Respondents 56, n 30. Pursuant to DTA § 1005(e)(2)(A), the resulting CSRT determination is again reviewable in full by the D. C. Circuit.[2]

In addition, DTA § 1005(d)(1) further requires the Department of Defense to conduct a yearly review of the status of each prisoner. See 119 Stat. 2741. The Deputy Secretary of Defense has promulgated concomitant regulations establishing an Administrative Review Board to assess "annually the need to continue to detain each enemy combatant." Deputy Secretary of Defense Order OSD 06942-04 (May 11, 2004), App. K to Pet. for Cert. in No. 06-1196, at 189. In the words of the implementing order, the purpose of this annual review is to afford every detainee the opportunity "to explain why he is no longer a threat to the United States" and should be released. *Ibid.* The Board's findings are forwarded to a presidentially appointed, Senate-confirmed civilian within the Department of Defense whom the Secretary of Defense has designated to administer the review process. This designated civilian official has the authority to order release upon the Board's recommendation. *Id.*, at 201.

The Court's hand wringing over the DTA's treatment of later discovered exculpatory evidence is the most it has to show after a roving search for constitutionally problematic scenarios. But "[t]he delicate power of pronouncing an Act of Congress unconstitutional," we have said, "is not to be exercised with reference to hypothetical cases thus imagined." *United States v. Raines, 362 U.S. 17,*

---

[2] The Court wonders what might happen if the detainee puts forward new material evidence but the Deputy Secretary refuses to convene a new CSRT. See *ante, at 791-792, 171 L. Ed. 2d, at 92-93*. The answer is that the detainee can petition the D. C. Circuit for review. The DTA directs that the procedures for review of new evidence be included among "[t]he procedures submitted under paragraph (1)(A)" governing CSRT review of enemy combatant status. § 1405(a)(3), 119 Stat. 3476. It is undisputed that the D. C. Circuit has statutory authority to review and enforce these procedures. See DTA § 1005(e)(2)(C)(i), *id.*, at 2742.

22, 80 S. Ct. 519, 4 L. Ed. 2d 524 (1960).* The Court today invents a sort of reverse facial challenge and applies it with gusto: If there is *any* scenario in which the statute *might* be constitutionally infirm, the law must be struck down. Cf. *United States v. Salerno,* 481 U.S. 739, 745, 107 S. Ct. 2095, 95 L. Ed. 2d 697 (1987) ("A facial challenge . . . must establish that no set of circumstances exists under which the Act would be valid"); see also *Washington v. Glucksberg,* 521 U.S. 702, 739-740, 117 S. Ct. 2258, 117 S. Ct. 2302, 138 L. Ed. 2d 772, and n 7, *521 U.S. 702, 117 S. Ct. 2258, 117 S. Ct. 2302, 138 L. Ed. 2d 772 (1997)* (Stevens, J., concurring in judgments) (facial challenge must fail where the statute has "'plainly legitimate sweep'" (quoting *Broadrick v. Oklahoma,* 413 U.S. 601, 615, 93 S. Ct. 2908, 37 L. Ed. 2d 830 (1973))). The Court's new method of constitutional adjudication only underscores its failure to follow our usual procedures and require petitioners to demonstrate that *they* have been harmed by the statute they challenge. In the absence of such a concrete showing, the Court is unable to imagine a plausible hypothetical in which the DTA is unconstitutional.

E

The Court's second criterion for an adequate substitute is the "power to order the conditional release of an individual unlawfully detained." *Ante, at 779, 171 L. Ed. 2d, at 85.* As the Court basically admits, the DTA can be read to permit the D. C. Circuit to order release in light of our traditional principles of construing statutes to avoid difficult constitutional issues, when reasonably possible. See *ante, at 787-788, 171 L. Ed. 2d, at 89-90.*

The Solicitor General concedes that remedial authority of some sort must be implied in the statute, given that the DTA--like the general habeas law itself, see *28 U.S.C. § 2243--*provides no express remedy of any kind. Brief for Federal Respondents 60-61. The parties agree that at the least, the DTA empowers the D. C. Circuit to remand a prisoner's case to the CSRT with instructions to perform a new status assessment. Brief for Petitioner Boumediene et al. in No. 06-1195, at 30; Brief for Federal Respondents 60-61. To avoid constitutional infirmity, it is reasonable to imply more, see *Ashwander,* 297 U.S., at 348, 56 S. Ct. 466, 80 L. Ed. 688 (Brandeis, J., concurring) ("When the validity of an act of the Congress is drawn in question . . . it is a cardinal principle that this Court will . . . ascertain whether a construction of the statute is fairly possible by which the [constitutional] question may be avoided" (internal quotation marks omitted)); see also *St. Cyr, 533 U.S., at 299-300, 121 S. Ct. 2271, 150 L. Ed. 2d 347,* especially in view of the Solicitor General's concession at oral argument and in his supplemental brief that authority to release might be read in the statute, see Tr. of Oral Arg. 37; Supplemental Brief for Federal Respondents 9.

The Court grudgingly suggests that "we can assume congressional silence permits a constitutionally required remedy." *Ante, at 788, 171 L. Ed. 2d, at 91.* But the argument in favor of statutorily authorized release is stronger than that. The DTA's parallels to *28 U.S.C. § 2243* on this score are noteworthy. By way of remedy, the general federal habeas statute provides only that the court, having heard and determined the facts, shall "dispose of the matter as law and justice require." *Ibid.* We have long held, and no party here disputes, that this includes the power to order release. See *Wilkinson v. Dotson, 544 U.S. 74, 79, 125 S. Ct. 1242, 161 L. Ed. 2d 253 (2005)* ("[T]he writ's history makes clear that it traditionally has been accepted as the specific instrument to obtain release from [unlawful] confinement" (internal quotation marks omitted)).

The DTA can be similarly read. Because Congress substituted DTA review for habeas corpus and because the "unique purpose" of the writ is "to release the applicant . . . from unlawful confinement," *Allen v. McCurry, 449 U.S. 90, 98, n 12, 101 S. Ct. 411, 66 L. Ed. 2d 308 (1980)*, DTA § 1005(e)(2) can and should be read to confer on the Court of Appeals the authority to order release in appropriate circumstances. Section 1005(e)(2)(D) plainly contemplates release, addressing the effect "release of [an] alien from the custody of the Department of Defense" will have on the jurisdiction of the court. 119 Stat. 2742-2743. This reading avoids serious constitutional difficulty and is consistent with the text of the statute.

The D. C. Circuit can thus order release, the CSRTs can order release, and the head of the Administrative Review Boards can, at the recommendation of those panels, order release. These multiple release provisions within the DTA system more than satisfy the majority's requirement that any tribunal substituting for a habeas court have the authority to release the prisoner.

The basis for the Court's contrary conclusion is summed up in the following sentence near the end of its opinion: "To hold that the detainees at Guantanamo may, under the DTA, challenge the President's legal authority to detain them, contest the CSRT's findings of fact, supplement the record on review with exculpatory evidence, and request an order of release would come close to reinstating the § 2241 habeas corpus process Congress sought to deny them." *Ante, at 792, 171 L. Ed. 2d, at 94.* In other words, any interpretation of the statute that would make it an adequate substitute for habeas must be rejected, because Congress could not possibly have intended to enact an adequate substitute for habeas. The Court could have saved itself a lot of trouble if it had simply announced this **Catch-22** approach at the beginning rather than the end of its opinion.

III

For all its eloquence about the detainees' right to the writ, the Court makes no effort to elaborate how exactly the remedy it prescribes will differ from the procedural protections detainees enjoy under the DTA. The Court objects to the detainees' limited access to witnesses and classified material, but proposes no alternatives of its own. Indeed, it simply ignores the many difficult questions its holding presents. What, for example, will become of the CSRT process? The majority says federal courts should *generally* refrain from entertaining detainee challenges until after the petitioner's CSRT proceeding has finished. See *ante, at 795, 171 L. Ed. 2d, at 95* ("[e]xcept in cases of undue delay"). But to what deference, if any, is that CSRT determination entitled?

There are other problems. Take witness availability. What makes the majority think witnesses will become magically available when the review procedure is labeled "habeas"? Will the location of most of these witnesses change--will they suddenly become easily susceptible to service of process? Or will subpoenas issued by American habeas courts run to Basra? And if they did, how would they be enforced? Speaking of witnesses, will detainees be able to call active-duty military officers as witnesses? If not, why not?

The majority has no answers for these difficulties. What it does say leaves open the distinct possibility that its "habeas" remedy will, when all is said and done, end up looking a great deal like the DTA review it rejects. See *ante, at 796, 171 L. Ed. 2d, at 95* ("We recognize, however, that the Government has a legitimate interest in protecting sources and methods of intelligence gathering; and we expect that the District Court will use its discretion to accommodate this interest to the greatest extent possible"). But "[t]he role of the judiciary is limited to determining whether the procedures meet the essential standard of fairness under the *Due Process Clause* and does not extend to imposing procedures that merely displace congressional choices of policy." *Landon v. Plasencia, 459 U.S. 21, 34-35, 103 S. Ct. 321, 74 L. Ed. 2d 21 (1982).*

The majority rests its decision on abstract and hypothetical concerns. Step back and consider what, in the real world, Congress and the Executive have actually granted aliens captured by our Armed Forces overseas and found to be enemy combatants:

• The right to hear the bases of the charges against them, including a summary of any classified evidence.

• The ability to challenge the bases of their detention before military tribunals modeled after Geneva Convention procedures. Some 38 detainees have been released as a result of this process. Brief for Federal Respondents 57, 60.

• The right, before the CSRT, to testify, introduce evidence, call witnesses, question those the Government calls, and secure release, if and when appropriate.

• The right to the aid of a personal representative in arranging and presenting their cases before a CSRT.

• Before the D C. Circuit, the right to employ counsel, challenge the factual record, contest the lower tribunal's legal determinations, ensure compliance with the Constitution and laws, and secure release, if any errors below establish their entitlement to such relief.

In sum, the DTA satisfies the majority's own criteria for assessing adequacy. This statutory scheme provides the combatants held at Guantanamo greater procedural protections than have ever been afforded alleged enemy detainees--whether citizens or aliens--in our national history.

* * *

So who has won? Not the detainees. The Court's analysis leaves them with only the prospect of further litigation to determine the content of their new habeas right, followed by further litigation to resolve their particular cases, followed by further litigation before the D. C. Circuit--where they could have started had they invoked the DTA procedure. Not Congress, whose attempt to "determine through democratic means how best" to balance the security of the American people with the detainees' liberty interests, see *Hamdan v. Rumsfeld, 548 U.S. 557, 636, 126 S. Ct. 2749, 165 L. Ed. 2d 723 (2006)* (Breyer, J., concurring), has been unceremoniously brushed aside. Not the Great Writ, whose majesty is hardly enhanced by its extension to a jurisdictionally quirky outpost, with no tangible benefit to anyone. Not the rule of law, unless by that is meant the rule of lawyers, who will now arguably have a greater role than military and intelligence officials in shaping policy for alien enemy combatants. And certainly not the American people, who today lose a bit more control over the conduct of this Nation's foreign policy to unelected, politically unaccountable judges.

I respectfully dissent.

JUSTICE SCALIA, with whom CHIEF JUSTICE, JUSTICE THOMAS, and JUSTICE ALITO join, dissenting.

Today, for the first time in our Nation's history, the Court confers a constitutional right to habeas corpus on alien enemies detained abroad by our military forces in the course of an ongoing war. The Chief Justice's dissent, which I join, shows that the procedures prescribed by Congress in the Detainee Treatment Act provide the essential protections that habeas corpus guarantees; there has thus been no suspension of the writ, and no basis exists for judicial intervention beyond what the Act allows. My problem with today's opinion is more fundamental still: The writ of habeas corpus does not, and never has, run in favor of aliens abroad; the Suspension Clause thus has no application, and the Court's intervention in this military matter is entirely *ultra vires*.

I shall devote most of what will be a lengthy opinion to the legal errors contained in the opinion of the Court. Contrary to my usual practice, however, I think it appropriate to begin with a description of the disastrous consequences of what the Court has done today.

I

America is at war with radical Islamists. The enemy began by killing Americans and American allies abroad: 241 at the Marine barracks in Lebanon, 19 at the Khobar Towers in Dhahran, 224 at our embassies in Dar es Salaam and Nairobi, and 17 on the USS Cole in Yemen. See National Commission on Terrorist Attacks Upon the United States, The 9/11 Commission Report, pp 60-61, 70, 190 (2004). On September 11, 2001, the enemy brought the battle to American soil, killing 2,749 at the Twin Towers in New York City, 184 at the Pentagon in Washington, D. C., and 40 in Pennsylvania. See *id.*, at 552, n 188. It has threatened further attacks against our homeland; one need only walk about buttressed and barricaded Washington, or board a plane anywhere in the country, to know that the threat is a serious one. Our Armed Forces are now in the field against the enemy, in Afghanistan and Iraq. Last week, 13 of our countrymen in arms were killed.

The game of bait-and-switch that today's opinion plays upon the Nation's Commander in Chief will make the war harder on us. It will almost certainly cause more Americans to be killed. That consequence would be tolerable if necessary to preserve a time-honored legal principle vital to our constitutional Republic. But it is this Court's blatant *abandonment* of such a principle that produces the decision today. The President relied on our settled precedent in *Johnson v. Eisentrager, 339 U.S. 763, 70 S. Ct. 936, 94 L. Ed. 1255 (1950)*, when he established the prison at

Guantanamo Bay for enemy aliens. Citing that case, the President's Office of Legal Counsel advised him "that the great weight of legal authority indicates that a federal district court could not properly exercise habeas jurisdiction over an alien detained at [Guantanamo Bay]." Memorandum from Patrick F. Philbin and John C. Yoo, Deputy Assistant Attorneys General, Office of Legal Counsel, to William J. Haynes II, General Counsel, Dept. of Defense, p.1 (Dec. 28, 2001). Had the law been otherwise, the military surely would not have transported prisoners there, but would have kept them in Afghanistan, transferred them to another of our foreign military bases, or turned them over to allies for detention. Those other facilities might well have been worse for the detainees themselves.

In the long term, then, the Court's decision today accomplishes little, except perhaps to reduce the well-being of enemy combatants that the Court ostensibly seeks to protect. In the short term, however, the decision is devastating. At least 30 of those prisoners hitherto released from Guantanamo Bay have returned to the battlefield. See S. Rep. No. 110-90, pt. 7, p 13 (2007) (minority views of Sens. Kyl, Sessions, Graham, Cornyn, and Coburn) (hereinafter Minority Report). Some have been captured or killed. See *ibid.;* see also Mintz, Released Detainees Rejoining the Fight, Washington Post, Oct. 22, 2004, ppA1, A12. But others have succeeded in carrying on their atrocities against innocent civilians. In one case, a detainee released from Guantanamo Bay masterminded the kidnaping of two Chinese dam workers, one of whom was later shot to death when used as a human shield against Pakistani commandoes. See Khan & Lancaster, Pakistanis Rescue Hostage; 2nd Dies, Washington Post, Oct. 15, 2004, p A18. Another former detainee promptly resumed his post as a senior Taliban commander and murdered a United Nations engineer and three Afghan soldiers. Mintz, *supra.* Still another murdered an Afghan judge. See Minority Report 13. It was reported only last month that a released detainee carried out a suicide bombing against Iraqi soldiers in Mosul, Iraq. See White, Ex-Guantanamo Detainee Joined Iraq Suicide Attack, Washington Post, May 8, 2008, p A18.

These, mind you, were detainees whom *the military* had concluded were not enemy combatants. Their return to the kill illustrates the incredible difficulty of assessing who is and who is not an enemy combatant in a foreign theater of operations where the environment does not lend itself to rigorous evidence collection. Astoundingly, the Court today raises the bar, requiring military officials to appear before civilian courts and defend their decisions under procedural and evidentiary rules that go beyond what Congress has specified. As The Chief Justice's dissent makes clear, we have no idea what those procedural and evidentiary rules are, but they will be determined by civil courts and (in the Court's contemplation at least) will be more detainee-friendly than those now applied, since otherwise there would no reason to hold the congressionally prescribed procedures unconstitutional. If they impose a higher standard of proof (from foreign battlefields) than the current procedures require, the number of the enemy returned to combat will obviously increase.

But even when the military has evidence that it can bring forward, it is often foolhardy to release that evidence to the attorneys representing our enemies. And one escalation of procedures that the Court *is* clear about is affording the detainees increased access to witnesses (perhaps troops serving in Afghanistan?) and to classified information. See *ante*, at 783-784, 171 L. Ed. 2d, at 88-89. During the 1995 prosecution of Omar Abdel Rahman, federal prosecutors gave the names of 200 unindicted co-conspirators to the "Blind Sheik's" defense lawyers; that information was in the hands of Osama Bin Laden within two weeks. See Minority Report 14-15. In another case, trial testimony revealed to the enemy that the United States had been monitoring their cellular network, whereupon they promptly stopped using it, enabling more of them to evade capture and continue their atrocities. See *id.*, at 15.

And today it is not just the military that the Court elbows aside. A mere two Terms ago in *Hamdan v. Rumsfeld*, 548 U.S. 557, 126 S. Ct. 2749, 165 L. Ed. 2d 723 (2006), when the Court held (quite amazingly) that the Detainee Treatment Act of 2005 had not stripped habeas jurisdiction over Guantanamo petitioners' claims, four Members of today's five-Justice majority joined an opinion saying the following:

> "Nothing prevents the President from returning to Congress to seek the authority [for trial by military commission] he believes necessary.
>
> "Where, as here, no emergency prevents consultation with Congress, judicial insistence upon that consultation does not weaken our Nation's ability to deal with danger. To the contrary, that insistence strengthens the Nation's ability to determine--through democratic means--how best to do so. The Constitution places its faith in those democratic means." *Id.*, at 636, 126 S. Ct. 2749, 165 L. Ed. 2d 723 (Breyer, J., concurring).[1]

---

[1] Even today, the Court cannot resist striking a pose of faux deference to Congress and the President. Citing the above quoted passage, the Court says: "The political branches, consistent with their independent obligations to interpret and uphold the Constitution, can engage in a genuine debate about how best to preserve constitutional values while protecting the Nation from terrorism." *Ante*, at 798, 171 L. Ed. 2d, at 97. Indeed. What the Court apparently means is that the political branches can debate, after which the Third Branch will decide.

Turns out they were just kidding. For in response, Congress, at the President's request, quickly enacted the Military Commissions Act, emphatically reasserting that it did not want these prisoners filing habeas petitions. It is therefore clear that Congress and the Executive--*both* political branches--have determined that limiting the role of civilian courts in adjudicating whether prisoners captured abroad are properly detained is important to success in the war that some 190,000 of our men and women are now fighting. As the Solicitor General argued, "the Military Commissions Act and the Detainee Treatment Act . . . represent an effort by the political branches to strike an appropriate balance between the need to preserve liberty and the need to accommodate the weighty and sensitive governmental interests in ensuring that those who have in fact fought with the enemy during a war do not return to battle against the United States." Brief for Federal Respondents 10-11 (internal quotation marks omitted).

But it does not matter. The Court today decrees that no good reason to accept the judgment of the other two branches is "apparent." *Ante, at 769, 171 L. Ed. 2d, at 79.* "The Government," it declares, "presents no credible arguments that the military mission at Guantanamo would be compromised if habeas corpus courts had jurisdiction to hear the detainees' claims." *Ibid.* What competence does the Court have to second-guess the judgment of Congress and the President on such a point? None whatever. But the Court blunders in nonetheless. Henceforth, as today's opinion makes unnervingly clear, how to handle enemy prisoners in this war will ultimately lie with the branch that knows least about the national security concerns that the subject entails.

II

A

The Suspension Clause of the Constitution provides: "The Privilege of the Writ of Habeas Corpus shall not be suspended, unless when in Cases of Rebellion or Invasion the public Safety may require it." Art. I, § 9, cl. 2. As a court of law operating under a written Constitution, our role is to determine whether there is a conflict between that Clause and the Military Commissions Act. A conflict arises only if the Suspension Clause preserves the privilege of the writ for aliens held by the United States military as enemy combatants at the base in Guantanamo Bay, located within the sovereign territory of Cuba.

We have frequently stated that we owe great deference to Congress's view that a law it has passed is constitutional. See, *e.g., United States Dep't of Labor v. Triplett, 494 U.S. 715, 721, 110 S. Ct. 1428, 108 L. Ed. 2d 701 (1990); United States v. National Dairy Products Corp., 372 U.S. 29, 32, 83 S. Ct. 594, 9 L. Ed. 2d 561 (1963)*; see also

American Communications Ass'n v. Douds, 339 U.S. 382, 435, 70 S. Ct. 674, 94 L. Ed. 925 (1950) (Jackson, J., concurring in part and dissenting in part). That is especially so in the area of foreign and military affairs; "perhaps in no other area has the Court accorded Congress greater deference." *Rostker v. Goldberg*, 453 U.S. 57, 64-65, 101 S. Ct. 2646, 69 L. Ed. 2d 478 (1981). Indeed, we accord great deference even when the President acts alone in this area. See *Dep't of the Navy v. Egan*, 484 U.S. 518, 529-530, 108 S. Ct. 818, 98 L. Ed. 2d 918 (1988); *Regan v. Wald*, 468 U.S. 222, 243, 104 S. Ct. 3026, 82 L. Ed. 2d 171 (1984).

In light of those principles of deference, the Court's conclusion that "the common law [does not] yiel[d] a definite answer to the questions before us," *ante, at 752, 171 L. Ed. 2d, at 68*, leaves it no choice but to affirm the Court of Appeals. The writ as preserved in the Constitution could not possibly extend farther than the common law provided when that Clause was written. See Part III, *infra*. The Court admits that it cannot determine whether the writ historically extended to aliens held abroad, and it concedes (necessarily) that Guantanamo Bay lies outside the sovereign territory of the United States. See *ante, at 752-754, 171 L. Ed. 2d, at 89*; *Rasul v. Bush*, 542 U.S. 466, 500-501, 124 S. Ct. 2686, 159 L. Ed. 2d 548 (2004) (Scalia, J., dissenting). Together, these two concessions establish that it is (in the Court's view) perfectly ambiguous whether the common-law writ would have provided a remedy for these petitioners. If that is so, the Court has no basis to strike down the Military Commissions Act, and must leave undisturbed the considered judgment of the coequal branches.[2]

How, then, does the Court weave a clear constitutional prohibition out of pure interpretive equipoise? The Court resorts to "fundamental separation-of-powers principles" to interpret the Suspension Clause. *Ante, at 755, 171 L. Ed. 2d, at 70*. According to the Court, because "the writ of habeas corpus is itself an indispensable mechanism for monitoring the separation of powers," the test of its

---

[2] The opinion seeks to avoid this straightforward conclusion by saying that the Court has been "careful not to foreclose the possibility that the protections of the Suspension Clause have expanded along with post-1789 developments that define the present scope of the writ." *Ante, at 746, 171 L. Ed. 2d, at 65* (citing *INS v. St. Cyr*, 533 U.S. 289, 300-301, 121 S. Ct. 2271, 150 L. Ed. 2d 347 (2001)). But not foreclosing the possibility that they have expanded is not the same as demonstrating (or at least holding without demonstration, which seems to suffice for today's majority) that they have expanded. The Court must either hold that the Suspension Clause has "expanded" in its application to aliens abroad, or acknowledge that it has no basis to set aside the actions of Congress and the President. It does neither.

extraterritorial reach "must not be subject to manipulation by those whose power it is designed to restrain." *Ante, at 765, 766, 171 L. Ed. 2d, at 77.*

That approach distorts the nature of the separation of powers and its role in the constitutional structure. The "fundamental separation-of-powers principles" that the Constitution embodies are to be derived not from some judicially imagined matrix, but from the sum total of the individual separation-of-powers provisions that the Constitution sets forth. Only by considering them one-by-one does the full shape of the *Constitution's* separation-of-powers principles emerge. It is nonsensical to interpret those provisions themselves in light of some general "separation-of-powers principles" dreamed up by the Court. Rather, they must be interpreted to mean what they were understood to mean when the people ratified them. And if the understood scope of the writ of habeas corpus was "designed to restrain" (as the Court says) the actions of the Executive, the understood *limits* upon that scope were (as the Court seems not to grasp) just as much "designed to restrain" the incursions of the Third Branch. "Manipulation" of the territorial reach of the writ by the Judiciary poses just as much a threat to the proper separation of powers as "manipulation" by the Executive. As I will show below, manipulation is what is afoot here. The understood limits upon the writ deny our jurisdiction over the habeas petitions brought by these enemy aliens, and entrust the President with the crucial wartime determinations about their status and continued confinement.

B

The Court purports to derive from our precedents a "functional" test for the extraterritorial reach of the writ, *ante, at 764, 171 L. Ed. 2d, at 76*, which shows that the Military Commissions Act unconstitutionally restricts the scope of habeas. That is remarkable because the most pertinent of those precedents, *Johnson v. Eisentrager, 339 U.S. 763, 70 S. Ct. 936, 94 L. Ed. 1255*, conclusively establishes the opposite. There we were confronted with the claims of 21 Germans held at Landsberg Prison, an American military facility located in the American zone of occupation in postwar Germany. They had been captured in China, and an American military commission sitting there had convicted them of war crimes --collaborating with the Japanese after Germany's surrender. *Id., at 765-766, 70 S. Ct. 936, 94 L. Ed. 1255.* Like petitioners here, the Germans claimed that their detentions violated the Constitution and international law, and sought a writ of habeas corpus. Writing for the Court, Justice Jackson held that American courts lacked habeas jurisdiction:

> "We are cited to *[sic]* no instance where a court, in this or any other country where the writ is known, has issued it on behalf of an alien enemy who, at no relevant time and in no stage of his captivity, has been within its territorial

289

jurisdiction. Nothing in the text of the Constitution extends such a right, nor does anything in our statutes." *Id.*, *at 768, 70 S. Ct. 936, 94 L. Ed. 1255.*

Justice Jackson then elaborated on the historical scope of the writ:

> "The alien, to whom the United States has been traditionally hospitable, has been accorded a generous and ascending scale of rights as he increases his identity with our society. . . .

> "But, in extending constitutional protections beyond the citizenry, the Court has been at pains to point out that it was the alien's presence within its territorial jurisdiction that gave the Judiciary power to act." *Id., at 770-771, 70 S. Ct. 936, 94 L. Ed. 1255.*

Lest there be any doubt about the primacy of territorial sovereignty in determining the jurisdiction of a habeas court over an alien, Justice Jackson distinguished two cases in which aliens had been permitted to seek habeas relief, on the ground that the prisoners in those cases were in custody within the sovereign territory of the United States. *Id., at 779-780, 70 S. Ct. 936, 94 L. Ed. 1255* (discussing *Ex parte Quirin, 317 U.S. 1, 63 S. Ct. 2, 87 L. Ed. 3 (1942)*, and *In re Yamashita, 327 U.S. 1, 66 S. Ct. 340, 90 L. Ed. 499 (1946)).* "By reason of our sovereignty at that time over [the Philippines]," Jackson wrote, "Yamashita stood much as did Quirin before American courts." *339 U.S., at 780, 70 S. Ct. 936, 94 L. Ed. 1255.*

Eisentrager thus held--*held* beyond any doubt--that the Constitution does not ensure habeas for aliens held by the United States in areas over which our Government is not sovereign.[3]

---

[3] In its failed attempt to distinguish *Eisentrager*, the Court comes up with the notion that "*de jure* sovereignty" is simply an additional factor that can be added to (presumably) "*de facto* sovereignty" (*i.e.*, practical control) to determine the availability of habeas for aliens, but that it is not a necessary factor, whereas *de facto* sovereignty is. It is perhaps in this *de facto* sense, the Court speculates, that *Eisentrager* found "sovereignty" lacking. See *ante, at 755, 763-764, 171 L. Ed. 2d, at 69-70.* If that were so, one would have expected *Eisentrager* to explain in some detail why the United States did not have practical control over the American zone of occupation. It did not (and probably could not). Of course this novel *de facto-de jure* approach does not explain why the writ never issued to Scotland, which was assuredly within the *de facto* control of the English Crown. See *infra, at 846-847, 171 L. Ed. 2d, at 69.* To support its holding that de facto sovereignty is relevant to the reach of habeas corpus, the Court cites our decision in *Fleming v. Page, 50 U.S. 603, 9 How. 603, 13 L. Ed. 276 (1850)*, a case about the application of a customs statute to a foreign port occupied by U. S. forces. See *ante, at 754, 171 L. Ed. 2d, at 70.* The case used the phrase "subject to the sovereignty

The Court would have us believe that *Eisentrager* rested on "[p]ractical considerations," such as the "difficulties of ordering the Government to produce the prisoners in a habeas corpus proceeding." *Ante, at 762, 171 L. Ed. 2d, at 75.* Formal sovereignty, says the Court, is merely one consideration "that bears upon which constitutional guarantees apply" in a given location. *Ante, at 764, 171 L. Ed. 2d, at 76.* This is a sheer rewriting of the case. *Eisentrager* mentioned practical concerns, to be sure--but not for the purpose of determining *under what circumstances* American courts could issue writs of habeas corpus for aliens abroad. It cited them to support *its holding* that the Constitution does not empower courts to issue writs of habeas corpus to aliens abroad *in any circumstances.* As Justice Black accurately said in dissent, "the Court's opinion inescapably denies courts power to afford the least bit of protection for any alien who is subject to our occupation government abroad, even if he is neither enemy nor belligerent and even after peace is officially declared." *339 U.S., at 796, 70 S. Ct. 936, 94 L. Ed. 1255.*

The Court also tries to change *Eisentrager* into a "functional" test by quoting a paragraph that lists the characteristics of the German petitioners:

> "To support [the] assumption [of a constitutional right to habeas corpus] we must hold that a prisoner of our military authorities is constitutionally entitled to the writ, even though he (a) is an enemy alien; (b) has never been or resided in the United States; (c) was captured outside of our territory and there held in military custody as a prisoner of war; (d) was tried and convicted by a Military Commission sitting outside the United States; (e) for offenses against laws of war committed outside the United States; (f) and is at all times imprisoned outside the United States." *Id., at 777, 70 S. Ct. 936, 94 L. Ed. 1255* (quoted in part, *ante, at 777, 171 L. Ed. 2d, at 77*).

But that paragraph is introduced by a sentence stating that "[t]he foregoing demonstrates *how much further we must go* if we are to invest these enemy aliens, resident, captured and imprisoned abroad, with standing to demand access to our courts." *339 U.S., at 777, 70 S. Ct. 936, 94 L. Ed. 1255* (emphasis added). How much further than *what*? Further than the rule set forth in the prior section of the opinion, which said that "in extending constitutional protections beyond the

---

and dominion of the United States" to refer to the United States' practical control over a "foreign country." *9 How., at 614, 13 L. Ed. 276.* But Fleming went on to explain that because the port remained part of the "enemy's country," even though under U. S. military occupation, "its subjugation did not compel the United States, while they held it, to regard it as a part of their dominions, nor to give to it any form of civil government, nor to extend to it our laws." *Id., at 618, 13 L. Ed. 276.* If Fleming is relevant to these cases at all, it undermines the Court's holding.

citizenry, the Court has been at pains to point out that it was the alien's presence within its territorial jurisdiction that gave the Judiciary power to act." *Id., at 771, 70 S. Ct. 936, 94 L. Ed. 1255.* In other words, the characteristics of the German prisoners were set forth, not in application of some "functional" test, but to show that the case before the Court represented an *a fortiori* application of the ordinary rule. That is reaffirmed by the sentences that immediately follow the listing of the Germans' characteristics:

> "We have pointed out that the privilege of litigation has been extended to aliens, whether friendly or enemy, only because permitting their presence in the country implied protection. No such basis can be invoked here, for these prisoners at no relevant time were within any territory over which the United States is sovereign, and the scenes of their offense, their capture, their trial and their punishment were all beyond the territorial jurisdiction of any court of the United States." *Id., at 777-778, 70 S. Ct. 936, 94 L. Ed. 1255.*

Eisentrager nowhere mentions a "functional" test, and the notion that it is based upon such a principle is patently false.[4]

The Court also reasons that *Eisentrager* must be read as a "functional" opinion because of our prior decisions in the Insular Cases. See *ante, at 756-759, 171 L. Ed. 2d, at 71-73.* It cites our statement in *Balzac v. Porto Rico, 258 U.S. 298, 312, 42 S. Ct.*

---

[4] Justice Souter's concurrence relies on our decision four Terms ago in *Rasul v. Bush, 542 U.S. 466, 124 S. Ct. 2686, 159 L. Ed. 2d 548 (2004)*, where the Court interpreted the habeas statute to extend to aliens held at Guantanamo Bay. He thinks that "no one who reads the Court's opinion in *Rasul* could seriously doubt that the jurisdictional question must be answered the same way in purely constitutional cases." *Ante, at 799, 171 L. Ed. 2d, at 97-98.* But *Rasul* was devoted primarily to an explanation of why *Eisentrager*'s statutory holding no longer controlled given our subsequent decision in *Braden v. 30th Judicial Circuit Court of Ky., 410 U.S. 484, 93 S. Ct. 1123, 35 L. Ed. 2d 443 (1973).* See *Rasul, 524 U.S., at 475-479, 124 S. Ct. 2686, 159 L. Ed. 2d 548.* And the opinion of the Court today--which Justice Souter joins--expressly rejects the historical evidence cited in *Rasul* to support its conclusion about the reach of habeas corpus. Compare *id., at 481-482, 124 S. Ct. 2686, 159 L. Ed. 2d 548*, with *ante, at 748, 171 L. Ed. 2d, at 66.* Moreover, even if one were to accept as true what Justice Souter calls *Rasul*'s "well-considered" dictum, that does not explain why *Eisentrager*'s constitutional holding must be overruled or how it can be distinguished. (After all, *Rasul* distinguished *Eisentrager*'s statutory holding on a ground inapplicable to its constitutional holding.) In other words, even if the Court were to conclude that *Eisentrager*'s rule was incorrect as an original matter, the Court would have to explain the justification for departing from that precedent. It therefore cannot possibly be true that *Rasul* controls these cases, as Justice Souter suggests.

343, 66 L. Ed. 627 (1922), that "'the real issue in the *Insular Cases* was not whether the Constitution extended to the Philippines or Porto Rico when we went there, but which of its provisions were applicable by way of limitation upon the exercise of executive and legislative power in dealing with new conditions and requirements.'" *Ante*, at 758, 171 L. Ed. 2d, at 72. But the Court conveniently omits *Balzac*'s predicate to that statement: "The Constitution of the United States is in force in Porto Rico as it is wherever and whenever the *sovereign power* of that government is exerted." *258 U.S., at 312, 42 S. Ct. 343, 66 L. Ed. 627* (emphasis added). The Insular Cases all concerned Trritories acquired by Congress under its Article IV authority and indisputably part of the sovereign territory of the United States. See *United States v. Verdugo-Urquidez, 494 U.S. 259, 268, 110 S. Ct. 1056, 108 L. Ed. 2d 222 (1990); Reid v. Covert, 354 U.S. 1, 13, 77 S. Ct. 1222, 1 L. Ed. 2d 1148 (1957)* (plurality opinion of Black, J.). None of the Insular Cases stands for the proposition that aliens located outside U. S. sovereign territory have constitutional rights, and *Eisentrager* held just the opposite with respect to habeas corpus. As I have said, *Eisentrager* distinguished *Yamashita* on the ground of "our sovereignty [over the Philippines]," *339 U.S., at 780, 70 S. Ct. 936, 94 L. Ed. 1255.*

The Court also relies on the "[p]ractical considerations" that influenced our decision in *Reid v. Covert, supra.* See *ante*, at 759-762, 171 L. Ed. 2d, at 73-75. But all the Justices in the majority except Justice Frankfurter limited their analysis to the rights of *citizens* abroad. See *Reid, 354 U.S., at 5-6, 77 S. Ct. 1222, 1 L. Ed. 2d 1148* (plurality opinion of Black, J.); *id., at 74-75, 77 S. Ct. 1222, 1 L. Ed. 2d 1148* (Harlan, J., concurring in result). (Frankfurter limited his analysis to the even narrower class of civilian dependents of American military personnel abroad, see *id., at 45, 77 S. Ct. 1222, 1 L. Ed. 2d 1148* (opinion concurring in result).) In trying to wring some kind of support out of *Reid* for today's novel holding, the Court resorts to a chain of logic that does not hold. The members of the *Reid* majority, the Court says, were divided over whether *In re Ross, 140 U.S. 453, 11 S. Ct. 897, 35 L. Ed. 581 (1891)*, which had (according to the Court) held that under certain circumstances American citizens abroad do not have indictment and jury-trial rights, should be overruled. In the Court's view, the *Reid* plurality would have overruled *Ross*, but Justices Frankfurter and Harlan preferred to distinguish it. The upshot: "If citizenship had been the only relevant factor in the case, it would have been necessary for the Court to overturn *Ross*, something Justices Harlan and Frankfurter were unwilling to do." *Ante*, at 761-762, 171 L. Ed. 2d, at 74-75. What, exactly, is this point supposed to prove? To say that "practical considerations" determine the precise content of the constitutional protections American citizens enjoy when they are abroad is quite different from saying that "practical considerations" determine whether aliens abroad enjoy any constitutional protections whatever, including habeas. In other words, merely because citizenship is not a *sufficient* factor to extend constitutional rights abroad does not mean that it is not a *necessary* one.

The Court tries to reconcile *Eisentrager* with its holding today by pointing out that in postwar Germany, the United States was "answerable to its Allies" and did not "pla[n] a long-term occupation." *Ante, at 768, 171 L. Ed. 2d, at 78, 79*. Those factors were not mentioned in *Eisentrager*. Worse still, it is impossible to see how they relate to the Court's asserted purpose in creating this "functional" test-- namely, to ensure a judicial inquiry into detention and prevent the political branches from acting with impunity. Can it possibly be that the Court trusts the political branches more when they are beholden to foreign powers than when they act alone?

After transforming the *a fortiori* elements discussed above into a "functional" test, the Court is still left with the difficulty that most of those elements exist here as well with regard to all the detainees. To make the application of the newly crafted "functional" test produce a different result in the present cases, the Court must rely upon factors (d) and (e): The Germans had been tried by a military commission for violations of the laws of war; the present petitioners, by contrast, have been tried by a Combatant Status Review Tribunal (CSRT) whose procedural protections, according to the Court's *ipse dixit*, "fall well short of the procedures and adversarial mechanisms that would eliminate the need for habeas corpus review." *Ante, at 767, 171 L. Ed. 2d, at 78*. But no one looking for "functional" equivalents would put *Eisentrager* and the present cases in the same category, much less place the present cases in a preferred category. The difference between them cries out for lesser procedures in the present cases. The prisoners in *Eisentrager* were *prosecuted* for crimes after the cessation of hostilities; the prisoners here are enemy combatants *detained* during an ongoing conflict. See *Hamdi v. Rumsfeld, 542 U.S. 507, 538, 124 S. Ct. 2633, 159 L. Ed. 2d 578 (2004)* (plurality opinion) (suggesting, as an adequate substitute for habeas corpus, the use of a tribunal akin to a CSRT to authorize the detention of *American citizens* as enemy combatants during the course of the present conflict).

The category of prisoner comparable to these detainees are not the *Eisentrager* criminal defendants, but the more than 400,000 prisoners of war detained in the United States alone during World War II. Not a single one was accorded the right to have his detention validated by a habeas corpus action in federal court--and that despite the fact that they were present on U. S. soil. See Bradley, The Military Commissions Act, Habeas Corpus, and the Geneva Conventions, *101 Am. J. Int'l L. 322, 338 (2007)*. The Court's analysis produces a crazy result: Whereas those convicted and sentenced to death for war crimes are without judicial remedy, all enemy combatants detained during a war, at least insofar as they are confined in an area away from the battlefield over which the United States exercises "absolute and indefinite" control, may seek a writ of habeas corpus in federal court. And, as an even more bizarre implication from the Court's reasoning, those prisoners whom the military plans to try by full-dress Commission at a future date may file habeas petitions and secure release before their trials take place.

There is simply no support for the Court's assertion that constitutional rights extend to aliens held outside U. S. sovereign territory, see *Verdugo-Urquidez, Supra, at 271, 110 S. Ct. 1056, 108 L. Ed. 2d 222*, and *Eisentrager* could not be clearer that the privilege of habeas corpus does not extend to aliens abroad. By blatantly distorting *Eisentrager*, the Court avoids the difficulty of explaining why it should be overruled. See *Planned Parenthood of Southeastern Pa. v. Casey, 505 U.S. 833, 854-855, 112 S. Ct. 2791, 120 L. Ed. 2d 674 (1992)* (identifying *stare decisis* factors). The rule that aliens abroad are not constitutionally entitled to habeas corpus has not proved unworkable in practice; if anything, it is the Court's "functional" test that does not (and never will) provide clear guidance for the future. *Eisentrager* forms a coherent whole with the accepted proposition that aliens abroad have no substantive rights under our Constitution. Since it was announced, no relevant factual premises have changed. It has engendered considerable reliance on the part of our military. And, as the Court acknowledges, text and history do not clearly compel a contrary ruling. It is a sad day for the rule of law when such an important constitutional precedent is discarded without an *apologia*, much less an apology.

C

What drives today's decision is neither the meaning of the Suspension Clause, nor the principles of our precedents, but rather an inflated notion of judicial supremacy. The Court says that if the extraterritorial applicability of the Suspension Clause turned on formal notions of sovereignty, "it would be possible for the political branches to govern without legal constraint" in areas beyond the sovereign territory of the United States. *Ante, at 765, 171 L. Ed. 2d, at 77*. That cannot be, the Court says, because it is the duty of this Court to say what the law is. *Ibid.* It would be difficult to imagine a more question-begging analysis. "The very foundation of the power of the federal courts to declare Acts of Congress unconstitutional lies in the power and duty of those courts to decide cases and controversies *properly before them.*" *United States v. Raines, 362 U.S. 17, 20-21, 80 S. Ct. 519, 4 L. Ed. 2d 524 (1960)* (citing *Marbury v. Madison, 5 U.S. 137, 1 Cranch 137, 2 L. Ed. 60 (1803)*; emphasis added). Our power "to say what the law is" is circumscribed by the limits of our statutorily and constitutionally conferred jurisdiction. See *Lujan v. Defenders of Wildlife, 504 U.S. 555, 573-578, 112 S. Ct. 2130, 119 L. Ed. 2d 351 (1992)*. And that is precisely the question in these cases: whether the Constitution confers habeas jurisdiction on federal courts to decide petitioners' claims. It is both irrational and arrogant to say that the answer must be yes, because otherwise we would not be supreme.

But so long as there are *some* places to which habeas does not run--so long as the Court's new "functional" test will not be satisfied *in every case*--then there will be circumstances in which "it would be possible for the political branches to govern without legal constraint." Or, to put it more impartially, areas in which the legal determinations of the *other* branches will be (shudder!) *supreme*. In other words, judicial supremacy is not really assured by the constitutional rule that the Court creates. The gap between rationale and rule leads me to conclude that the Court's ultimate, unexpressed goal is to preserve the power to review the confinement of enemy prisoners held by the Executive anywhere in the world. The "functional" test usefully evades the precedential landmine of *Eisentrager* but is so inherently subjective that it clears a wide path for the Court to traverse in the years to come.

III

Putting aside the conclusive precedent of *Eisentrager*, it is clear that the original understanding of the Suspension Clause was that habeas corpus was not available to aliens abroad, as Judge Randolph's thorough opinion for the court below detailed. See *375 U.S. App. D.C. 48, 476 F.3d 981, 988-990 (CADC 2007)*.

The Suspension Clause reads: "The Privilege of the Writ of Habeas Corpus shall not be suspended, unless when in Cases of Rebellion or Invasion the public Safety may require it." *U.S. Const., Art. I, § 9, cl. 2*. The proper course of constitutional interpretation is to give the text the meaning it was understood to have at the time of its adoption by the people. See, *e.g., Crawford v. Washington, 541 U.S. 36, 54, 124 S. Ct. 1354, 158 L. Ed. 2d 177 (2004)*. That course is especially demanded when (as here) the Constitution limits the power of Congress to infringe upon a pre-existing common-law right. The nature of the writ of habeas corpus that cannot be suspended must be defined by the common-law writ that was available at the time of the founding. See *McNally v. Hill, 293 U.S. 131, 135-136, 55 S. Ct. 24, 79 L. Ed. 238 (1934)*; see also *INS v. St. Cyr, 533 U.S. 289, 342, 121 S. Ct. 2271, 150 L. Ed. 2d 347 (2001)* (Scalia, J., dissenting); *D'Oench, Duhme & Co. v. FDIC, 315 U.S. 447, 471, n 9, 62 S. Ct. 676, 86 L. Ed. 956 (1942)* (Jackson, J., concurring).

It is entirely clear that, at English common law, the writ of habeas corpus did not extend beyond the sovereign territory of the Crown. To be sure, the writ had an "extraordinary territorial ambit," because it was a so-called "prerogative writ," which, unlike other writs, could extend beyond the realm of England to other places where the Crown was sovereign. R. Sharpe, The Law of Habeas Corpus 188 (2d ed. 1989) (hereinafter Sharpe); see also Note on the Power of the English Courts to Issue the Writ of Habeas to Places Within the Dominions of the Crown, But Out of England, and On the Position of Scotland in Relation to that Power, 8 Jurid. Rev. 157 (1896) (hereinafter Note on Habeas); *King* v. *Cowle*, 2 Burr. 834, 855-856, 97 Eng. Rep. 587, 599 (K. B. 1759).

But prerogative writs could not issue to foreign countries, even for British subjects; they were confined to the King's dominions--those areas over which the Crown was sovereign. See Sharpe 188; 2 R. Chambers, A Course of Lectures on the English Law 1767-1773, pp 7-8 (T. Curley ed. 1986); 3 W. Blackstone, Commentaries on the Laws of England 131 (1768) (hereinafter Blackstone). Thus, the writ has never extended to Scotland, which, although united to England when James I succeeded to the English throne in 1603, was considered a foreign dominion under a different Crown--that of the King of Scotland. Sharpe 191; Note on Habeas 158.[5] That is why Lord Mansfield wrote that "[t]o foreign dominions, which belong to a prince who succeeds to the throne of England, this Court has no power to send any writ of any kind. We cannot send a habeas corpus to Scotland . . . ." *Cowle*, 2 Burr., at 856, 97 Eng. Rep., at 599-600.

The common-law writ was codified by the Habeas Corpus Act of 1679, which "stood alongside Magna Charta and the English Bill of Rights of 1689 as a towering common law lighthouse of liberty--a beacon by which framing lawyers in America consciously steered their course." Amar, Sixth Amendment First Principles, *84 Geo. L. J. 641, 663 (1996)*. The writ was established in the Colonies beginning in the 1690's and at least one colony adopted the 1679 Act almost verbatim. See Dept. of Political Science, Okla. State Univ., Research Reports, No. 1, R. Walker, The American Reception of the Writ of Liberty 12-16 (1961). Section XI of the Act stated where the writ could run. It "may be directed and run into any county palatine, the cinque-ports, or other privileged places within the kingdom of *England*, dominion of *Wales*, or town of *Berwick* upon *Tweed*, and the islands of *Jersey* or *Guernsey*." 31 Car. 2, ch. 2. The cinque-ports and counties palatine were so-called "exempt jurisdictions"--franchises granted by the Crown in which local authorities would manage municipal affairs, including the court system, but over which the Crown maintained ultimate sovereignty. See 3 Blackstone 78-79. The other places listed--Wales, Berwick-upon-Tweed, Jersey, and Guernsey--were territories of the Crown even though not part of England proper. See *Cowle, supra*, at 853-854, 97

---

[5] My dissent in *Rasul v. Bush, 542 U.S. 466, 503, 124 S. Ct. 2686, 159 L. Ed. 2d 548 (2004)*, mistakenly included Scotland among the places to which the writ could run.

Eng. Rep., at 598 (Wales and Berwick-upon-Tweed); 1 Blackstone 104 (Jersey and Guernsey); Sharpe 192 (same).

The Act did not extend the writ elsewhere, even though the existence of other places to which British prisoners could be sent was recognized by the Act. The possibility of evading judicial review through such spiriting-away was eliminated, not by expanding the writ abroad, but by forbidding (in Section XII of the Act) the shipment of prisoners to places where the writ did not run or where its execution would be difficult. See 31 Car. 2, ch. 2; see generally Nutting, The Most Wholesome Law--The Habeas Corpus Act of 1679, 65 Am. Hist. Rev. 527 (1960).

The Habeas Corpus Act, then, confirms the consensus view of scholars and jurists that the writ did not run outside the sovereign territory of the Crown. The Court says that the idea that "jurisdiction followed the King's officers" is an equally credible view. *Ante, at 746, 171 L. Ed. 2d, at 65*. It is not credible at all. The only support the Court cites for it is a page in Boumediene's brief, which in turn cites this Court's dicta in *Rasul, 542 U.S., at 482, 124 S. Ct. 2686, 159 L. Ed. 2d 548*, mischaracterizing Lord Mansfield's statement that the writ ran to any place that was "under the subjection of the Crown," *Cowle, supra,* at 856, 97 Eng. Rep., at 599. It is clear that Lord Mansfield was saying that the writ extended outside the realm of England proper, not outside the sovereign territory of the Crown.[6]

The Court dismisses the example of Scotland on the grounds that Scotland had its own judicial system and that the writ could not, as a practical matter, have been enforced there. *Ante, at 750, 171 L. Ed. 2d, at 67-68*. Those explanations are totally unpersuasive. The existence of a separate court system was never a basis for denying the power of a court to issue the writ. See 9 W. Holdsworth, A History of English Law 124, and n. 6 (3d ed. 1944) (citing *Ex parte Anderson*, 3 El. and El. 487, 121 Eng. Rep. 525 (K. B. 1861)). And as for logistical problems, the same difficulties were present for places like the Channel Islands, where the writ did run. The Court attempts to draw an analogy between the prudential limitations on issuing the writ to such remote areas within the sovereign territory of the Crown and the jurisdictional prohibition on issuing the writ to Scotland. See *ante, at 749-750, 171 L. Ed. 2d, at 67-68*. But the very authority that the Court cites, Lord Mansfield, expressly distinguished between these two concepts, stating that English courts had the "power" to send the writ to places within the Crown's sovereignty, the "only question" being the "propriety," while they had "no power to send any

---

[6] The dicta in *Rasul* also cited *Ex parte Mwenya*, [1960] 1 Q. B. 241 (C. A.), but as I explained in dissent, "[e]ach judge [in *Mwenya*] made clear that the detainee's status as a subject was material to the resolution of the case," *542 U.S., at 504, 124 S. Ct. 2686, 159 L. Ed. 2d 548*.

writ of any kind" to Scotland and other "foreign dominions." *Cowle, supra*, at 856, 97 Eng. Rep., at 599-600. The writ did not run to Scotland because, even after the Union, "Scotland remained a foreign dominion of the prince who succeeded to the English throne," and "union did not extend the prerogative of the English crown to Scotland." Sharpe 191; see also Sir Matthew Hale's The Prerogatives of the King 19 (D. Yale ed. 1976).[7]

In sum, *all* available historical evidence points to the conclusion that the writ would not have been available at common law for aliens captured and held outside the sovereign territory of the Crown. Despite three opening briefs, three reply briefs, and support from a legion of *amici*, petitioners have failed to identify a single case in the history of Anglo-American law that supports their claim to jurisdiction. The Court finds it significant that there is no recorded case *denying* jurisdiction to such prisoners either. See *ante, at 752, 171 L. Ed. 2d, at 68-69*. But a case standing for the remarkable proposition that the writ could issue to a foreign land would surely have been reported, whereas a case denying such a writ for lack of jurisdiction would likely not. At a minimum, the absence of a reported case either way leaves unrefuted the voluminous commentary stating that habeas was confined to the dominions of the Crown.

What history teaches is confirmed by the nature of the limitations that the Constitution places upon suspension of the common-law writ. It can be suspended only "in Cases of Rebellion or Invasion." Art. I, § 9, cl. 2. The latter case (invasion) is plainly limited to the territory of the United States; and while it is conceivable that a rebellion could be mounted by American citizens abroad, surely the overwhelming majority of its occurrences would be domestic. If the extraterritorial scope of habeas turned on flexible, "functional" considerations, as the Court holds, why would the Constitution limit its suspension almost entirely to instances of domestic crisis? Surely there is an even greater justification for suspension in foreign lands where the United States might hold prisoners of war during an ongoing conflict. And correspondingly, there is less threat to liberty when the

---

[7] The Court also argues that the fact that the writ could run to Ireland, even though it was ruled under a "separate" crown, shows that formal sovereignty was not the touchstone of habeas jurisdiction. *Ante, at 751, 171 L. Ed. 2d, at 68*. The passage from Blackstone that the Court cites, however, describes Ireland as "a dependent, subordinate kingdom" that was part of the "king's dominions." 1 Blackstone 98, 100 (internal quotation marks omitted). And Lord Mansfield's opinion in *Cowle* plainly understood Ireland to be "a dominion of the Crown of England," in contrast to the "foreign dominio[n]" of Scotland, and thought that distinction dispositive of the question of habeas jurisdiction. 2 Burr., at 856, 97 Eng. Rep., at 599-600.

Government suspends the writ's (supposed) application in foreign lands, where even on the most extreme view prisoners are entitled to fewer constitutional rights. It makes no sense, therefore, for the Constitution generally to forbid suspension of the writ abroad if indeed the writ has application there.

It may be objected that the foregoing analysis proves too much, since this Court has already suggested that the writ of habeas corpus *does* run abroad for the benefit of United States citizens. "[T]he position that United States citizens throughout the world may be entitled to habeas corpus rights . . . is precisely the position that this Court adopted in *Eisentrager,* see *339 U.S., at 769-770, 70 S. Ct. 936, 94 L. Ed. 1255,* even while holding that aliens abroad did not have habeas corpus rights." *Rasul, Supra,* at *501, 502, 124 S. Ct. 2686, 159 L. Ed. 2d 548* (Scalia, J., dissenting) (emphasis deleted). The reason for that divergence is not difficult to discern. The common-law writ, as received into the law of the new constitutional Republic, took on such changes as were demanded by a system in which rule is derived from the consent of the governed, and in which citizens (not "subjects") are afforded defined protections against the Government. As Justice Story wrote for the Court:

> "The common law of England is not to be taken in all respects to be that of America. Our ancestors brought with them its general principles, and claimed it as their birthright; but they brought with them and adopted only that portion which was applicable to their situation." *Van Ness v. Pacard, 27 U.S. 137, 2 Pet. 137, 144, 7 L. Ed. 374 (1829).*

See also Hall, The Common Law: An Account of its Reception in the United States, 4 Vand. L. Rev. 791 (1951). It accords with that principle to say, as the plurality opinion said in *Reid:* "When the Government reaches out to punish a citizen who is abroad, the shield which the *Bill of Rights* and other parts of the Constitution provide to protect his life and liberty should not be stripped away just because he happens to be in another land." *354 U.S., at 6, 77 S. Ct. 1222, 1 L. Ed. 2d 1148*; see also *Verdugo-Urquidez, 494 U.S., at 269-270, 110 S. Ct. 1056, 108 L. Ed. 2d 222*. On that analysis, "[t]he distinction between citizens and aliens follows from the undoubted proposition that the Constitution does not create, nor do general principles of law create, any juridical relation between our country and some undefined, limitless class of noncitizens who are beyond our territory." *Id., at 275, 110 S. Ct. 1056, 108 L. Ed. 2d 222* (Kennedy, J., concurring).

In sum, because I conclude that the text and history of the Suspension Clause provide no basis for our jurisdiction, I would affirm the Court of Appeals even if *Eisentrager* did not govern these cases.

* * *

Today the Court warps our Constitution in a way that goes beyond the narrow issue of the reach of the Suspension Clause, invoking judicially brainstormed separation-of-powers principles to establish a manipulable "functional" test for the extraterritorial reach of habeas corpus (and, no doubt, for the extraterritorial reach of other constitutional protections as well). It blatantly misdescribes important precedents, most conspicuously Justice Jackson's opinion for the Court in *Johnson* v. *Eisentrager*. It breaks a chain of precedent as old as the common law that prohibits judicial inquiry into detentions of aliens abroad absent statutory authorization. And, most tragically, it sets our military commanders the impossible task of proving to a civilian court, under whatever standards this Court devises in the future, that evidence supports the confinement of each and every enemy prisoner.

The Nation will live to regret what the Court has done today. I dissent.

Crawford v.

Metro. Gov't of Nashville & Davidson County

Supreme Court of the United States

October 8, 2008, Argued

January 26, 2009, Decided

No. 06-1595

555 U.S. 271
129 S. Ct. 846
172 L. Ed. 2d 650

VICKY S. CRAWFORD, Petitioner v. METROPOLITAN GOVERNMENT OF NASHVILLE AND DAVIDSON COUNTY, TENNESSEE

ON WRIT OF CERTIORARI TO THE UNITED STATES COURT OF APPEALS FOR THE SIXTH CIRCUIT.
Crawford v. Metro. Gov't of Nashville & Davidson County, 211 Fed. Appx. 373, 2006 U.S. App. LEXIS 28280 (6th Cir. Tenn., 2006)

Eric Schnapper argued the cause for petitioner. Lisa S. Blatt argued the cause for the United States, as amicus curiae, by special leave of court. Francis H. Young argued the cause for respondent.

SOUTER, J., delivered the opinion of the Court, in which Roberts, C. J., and Stevens, Scalia, Kennedy, Ginsburg, and Breyer, JJ., joined.
ALITO, J., filed an opinion concurring in the judgment, in which Thomas, J., joined.

JUSTICE SOUTER delivered the opinion of the Court.

Title VII of the Civil Rights Act of 1964, 78 Stat. 253, as amended, *42 U.S.C. § 2000e et seq. (2000 ed. and Supp. V)*, forbids retaliation by employers against employees who report workplace race or gender discrimination. The question here is whether this protection extends to an employee who speaks out about discrimination not on her own initiative, but in answering questions during an employer's internal investigation. We hold that it does.

I

In 2002, respondent Metropolitan Government of Nashville and Davidson County, Tennessee (Metro), began looking into rumors of sexual harassment by the Metro School District's employee relations director, Gene Hughes.[1] *211 Fed. Appx. 373, 374 (CA6 2006)*. When Veronica Frazier, a Metro human resources officer, asked petitioner Vicky Crawford, a 30-year Metro employee, whether she had witnessed "inappropriate behavior" on the part of Hughes, *id., at 374-375*, Crawford described several instances of sexually harassing behavior: once, Hughes had answered her greeting, "'Hey Dr. Hughes, [w]hat's up?,'" by grabbing his crotch and saying "'[Y]ou know what's up'"; he had repeatedly "'put his crotch up to [her] window'"; and on one occasion he had entered her office and "'grabbed her head and pulled it to his crotch,'" *id., at 375, and n. 1*. Two other employees also reported being sexually harassed by Hughes. *Id., at 375*. Although Metro took no action against Hughes, it did fire Crawford and the two other accusers soon after finishing the investigation, saying in Crawford's case that it was for embezzlement. *Ibid.* Crawford claimed Metro was retaliating for her report of Hughes's behavior and filed a charge of a Title VII violation with the Equal Employment Opportunity Commission (EEOC), followed by this suit in the United States District Court for the Middle District of Tennessee. *Ibid.*

The Title VII antiretaliation provision has two clauses, making it "an unlawful employment practice for an employer to discriminate against any of his employees . . . because he has opposed any practice made an unlawful employment practice by this subchapter, or because he has made a charge, testified, assisted, or participated in any manner in an investigation, proceeding, or hearing under this

---

[1] Because this case arises out of the District Court's grant of summary judgment for Metro, "we are required to view all facts and draw all reasonable inferences in favor of the nonmoving party, [Crawford]." *Brosseau v. Haugen, 543 U.S. 194, 195, n. 2, 125 S. Ct. 596, 160 L. Ed. 2d 583 (2004) (per curiam)*.

subchapter." *42 U.S.C. § 2000e-3(a)*. The one is known as the "opposition clause," the other as the "participation clause," and Crawford accused Metro of violating both.

The District Court granted summary judgment for Metro. It held that Crawford could not satisfy the opposition clause because she had not "instigated or initiated any complaint," but had "merely answered questions by investigators in an already-pending internal investigatio n, initiated by someone else." Memorandum Opinion, No. 3:03-cv-0996 (MD Tenn., Jan. 6, 2005), App. C to Pet. for Cert. 16a-17a. It concluded that her claim also failed under the participation clause, which Sixth Circuit precedent confined to protecting "'an employee's participation in an employer's internal investigation . . . where that investigation occurs pursuant to a pending EEOC charge'" (not the case here). *Id.*, at 15a (emphasis deleted) (quoting *Abbott v. Crown Motor Co.*, 348 F.3d 537, 543 (CA6 2003)).

The Court of Appeals affirmed on the same grounds, holding that the opposition clause "'demands active, consistent "opposing" activities to warrant . . . protection against retaliation,'" *211 Fed. Appx., at 376* (quoting *Bell v. Safety Grooving & Grinding, LP*, 107 Fed. Appx. 607, 610 (CA6 2004)), whereas Crawford did "not claim to have instigated or initiated any complaint prior to her participation in the investigation, nor did she take any further action following the investigation and prior to her firing," *211 Fed. Appx., at 376*. Again like the trial judge, the Court of Appeals understood that Crawford could show no violation of the participation clause because her "'employer's internal investigation'" was not conducted "'pursuant to a pending EEOC charge.'" *Ibid.* (quoting *Abbott, supra*, at 543).

Because the Sixth Circuit's decision conflicts with those of other Circuits, particularly as to the opposition clause, see, *e.g., McDonnell v. Cisneros*, 84 F.3d 256, 262 (CA7 1996), we granted Crawford's petition for certiorari. *552 U.S. 1162, 128 S. Ct. 1118, 169 L. Ed. 2d 846 (2008)*. We now reverse and remand for further proceedings.

II

The opposition clause makes it "unlawful . . . for an employer to discriminate against any . . . employe[e] . . . because he has opposed any practice made . . . unlawful . . . by this subchapter." *§ 2000e-3(a)*. The term "oppose," being left undefined by the statute, carries its ordinary meaning, *Perrin v. United States*, 444 U.S. 37, 42, 100 S. Ct. 311, 62 L. Ed. 2d 199 (1979): "[t]o resist or antagonize . . .; to contend against; to confront; resist; withstand," Webster's New International Dictionary 1710 (2d ed. 1957). Although these actions entail varying expenditures of energy, "resist frequently implies more active striving than oppose." *Ibid.*; see also Random House Dictionary of the English Language 1359 (2d ed. 1987) (defining "oppose" as ["to be hostile or adverse to, as in opinion"]).

The statement Crawford says she gave to Frazier is thus covered by the opposition clause, as an ostensibly disapproving account of sexually obnoxious behavior toward her by a fellow employee, an answer she says antagonized her employer to the point of sacking her on a false pretense. Crawford's description of the louche goings-on would certainly qualify in the minds of reasonable jurors as "resist[ant]" or "antagoni[stic]" to Hughes's treatment, if for no other reason than [the point argued by the Government and explained by an EEOC guideline: "When an employee communicates to her employer a belief that the employer has engaged in . . . a form of employment discrimination, that communication" virtually always "constitutes the employee's *opposition* to the activity."] Brief for United States as *Amicus Curiae* 9 (citing 2 EEOC Compliance Manual §§ 8-II-B(1), (2), p 614:0003 (Mar. 2003)); see also *Fed. Express Corp. v. Holowecki*, 552 U.S. 389, 399, 128 S. Ct. 1147, 1156, 170 L. Ed. 2d 10 (2008)) (explaining that EEOC compliance manuals "reflect 'a body of experience and informed judgment to which courts and litigants may properly resort for guidance'" (quoting *Bragdon v. Abbott*, 524 U.S. 624, 642, 118 S. Ct. 2196, 141 L. Ed. 2d 540 (1998))). It is true that one can imagine exceptions, like an employee's description of a supervisor's racist joke as hilarious, but these will be eccentric cases, and this is not one of them.[2]

The Sixth Circuit thought answering questions fell short of opposition, taking the view that the clause "'demands active, consistent "opposing" activities to warrant . . . . protection against retaliation,'" 211 Fed. Appx., at 376 (quoting *Bell, supra,* at 610), and that an employee must "instigat[e] or initiat[e]" a complaint to be covered, 211 Fed. Appx., at 376. But though these requirements obviously exemplify opposition as commonly understood, they are not limits of it.

"Oppose" goes beyond "active, consistent" behavior in ordinary discourse, where we would naturally use the word to speak of someone who has taken no action at all to advance a position beyond disclosing it. Countless people were known to "oppose" slavery before Emancipation, or are said to "oppose" capital punishment

---

[2] Metro suggests in passing that it was unclear whether Crawford actually opposed Hughes's behavior because some of her defensive responses were "inappropriate," such as telling Hughes to "bite me" and "flip[ping] him a bird." Brief for Respondent 1-2 (internal quotation marks omitted). This argument fails not only because at the summary judgment stage we must "view all facts and draw all reasonable inferences in [Crawford's] favor," *Brosseau*, 543 U.S., at 195, n. 2, 125 S. Ct. 596, 160 L. Ed. 2d 583, but also because Crawford gave no indication that Hughes's gross clowning was anything but offensive to her.

today, without writing public letters, taking to the streets, or resisting the government. And we would call it "opposition" if an employee took a stand against an employer's discriminatory practices not by "instigating" action, but by standing pat, say, by refusing to follow a supervisor's order to fire a junior worker for discriminatory reasons. Cf. *McDonnell, supra*, at 262 (finding employee covered by Title VII of the Civil Rights Act of 1964 where his employer retaliated against him for failing to prevent his subordinate from filing an EEOC charge). There is, then, no reason to doubt that a person can "oppose" by responding to someone else's question just as surely as by provoking the discussion, and nothing in the statute requires a freakish rule protecting an employee who reports discrimination on her own initiative but not one who reports the same discrimination in the same words when her boss asks a question.

Metro and its *amici* support the Circuit panel's insistence on "active" and "consistent" opposition by arguing that the lower the bar for retaliation claims, the less likely it is that employers will look into what may be happening outside the executive suite. As they see it, if retaliation is an easy charge when things go bad for an employee who responded to enquiries, employers will avoid the headache by refusing to raise questions about possible discrimination.

The argument is unconvincing, for we think it underestimates the incentive to enquire that follows from our decisions in *Burlington Industries, Inc. v. Ellerth*, 524 U.S. 742, 118 S. Ct. 2257, 141 L. Ed. 2d 633 (1998), and *Faragher v. Boca Raton*, 524 U.S. 775, 118 S. Ct. 2275, 141 L. Ed. 2d 662 (1998). *Ellerth* and *Faragher* hold "[a]n employer . . . subject to vicarious liability to a victimized employee for an actionable hostile environment created by a supervisor with . . . authority over the employee." *Ellerth, supra*, at 765, 118 S. Ct. 2257, 141 L. Ed. 2d 633; *Faragher, supra*, at 807, 118 S. Ct. 2275, 141 L. Ed. 2d 662. Although there is no affirmative defense if the hostile environment "culminates in a tangible employment action" against the employee, *Ellerth*, 524 U.S., at 765, 118 S. Ct. 2257, 141 L. Ed. 2d 633, an employer does have a defense "[w]hen no tangible employment action is taken" if it "exercised reasonable care to prevent and correct promptly any" discriminatory conduct and "the plaintiff employee unreasonably failed to take advantage of any preventive or corrective opportunities provided by the employer or to avoid harm otherwise," *ibid*. Employers are thus subject to a strong inducement to ferret out and put a stop to any discriminatory activity in their operations as a way to break the circuit of imputed liability. *Ibid.*; see also Brief for Petitioner 24-28, and nn 31-35 (citing studies demonstrating that *Ellerth* and *Faragher* have prompted many employers to adopt or strengthen procedures for investigating, preventing, and correcting discriminatory conduct). The possibility that an employer might someday want to fire someone who might charge discrimination traceable to an internal investigation does not strike us as likely to diminish the attraction of an *Ellerth-Faragher* affirmative defense.

That aside, we find it hard to see why the Sixth Circuit's rule would not itself largely undermine the *Ellerth-Faragher* scheme, along with the statute's "'primary objective'" of "avoid[ing] harm" to employees. *Faragher, supra, at 806, 118 S. Ct. 2275, 141 L. Ed. 2d 662* (quoting *Albemarle Paper Co. v. Moody, 422 U.S. 405, 417, 95 S. Ct. 2362, 45 L. Ed. 2d 280 (1975)*). If it were clear law that an employee who reported discrimination in answering an employer's questions could be penalized with no remedy, prudent employees would have a good reason to keep quiet about Title VII offenses against themselves or against others. This is no imaginary horrible given the documented indications that "[f]ear of retaliation is the leading reason why people stay silent instead of voicing their concerns about bias and discrimination." Brake, Retaliation, *90 Minn. L. Rev. 18, 20 (2005)*; see also *id., at 37, and n. 58* (compiling studies). The appeals court's rule would thus create a real dilemma for any knowledgeable employee in a hostile work environment if the boss took steps to assure a defense under our cases. If the employee reported discrimination in response to the enquiries, the employer might well be free to penalize her for speaking up. But if she kept quiet about the discrimination and later filed a Title VII claim, the employer might well escape liability, arguing that it "exercised reasonable care to prevent and correct [any discrimination] promptly" but "the plaintiff employee unreasonably failed to take advantage of . . . preventive or corrective opportunities provided by the employer." *Ellerth, supra, at 765, 118 S. Ct. 2257, 141 L. Ed. 2d 633*. Nothing in the statute's text or our precedent supports this ***catch-22***.[3]

---

[3] Metro also argues that "[r]equiring the employee to actually initiate a complaint . . . conforms with the employee's 'obligation of reasonable care to avoid harm' articulated in *Faragher* and *Ellerth*." Brief for Respondent 28 (quoting *Faragher v. Boca Raton, 524 U.S. 775, 807, 118 S. Ct. 2275, 141 L. Ed. 2d 662 (1998)*). But that mitigation requirement only applies to employees who are suffering discrimination and have the opportunity to fix it by "tak[ing] advantage of any preventive or corrective opportunities provided by the employer," *524 U.S., at 807*; it is based on the general principle "that a victim has a duty 'to use such means as are reasonable under the circumstances to avoid or minimize . . . damages,'" *id., at 806, 118 S. Ct. 2275, 141 L. Ed. 2d 662* (quoting *Ford Motor Co. v. EEOC, 458 U.S. 219, 231, n. 15, 102 S. Ct. 3057, 73 L. Ed. 2d 721 (1982)*). We have never suggested that employees have a legal obligation to report discrimination against others to their employer on their own initiative, let alone lose statutory protection by failing to speak. Extending the mitigation requirement so far would make no sense; employees will often face retaliation not for opposing discrimination they themselves face, but for reporting discrimination suffered by

Because Crawford's conduct is covered by the opposition clause, we do not reach her argument that the Sixth Circuit misread the participation clause as well. But that does not mean the end of this case, for Metro's motion for summary judgment raised several defenses to the retaliation charge besides the scope of the two clauses; the District Court never reached these others owing to its ruling on the elements of retaliation, and they remain open on remand.

III

The judgment of the Court of Appeals for the Sixth Circuit is reversed, and the case is remanded for further proceedings consistent with this opinion.

It is so ordered.

---

others. Thus, they are not "victims" of anything until they are retaliated against, and it would be absurd to require them to "mitigate" damages they may be unaware they will suffer.

JUSTICE ALITO, with whom JUSTICE THOMAS joins, concurring in the judgment.

The question in this case is whether Title VII of the Civil Rights Act of 1964, *42 U.S.C. § 2000e et seq. (2000 ed. and Supp. V)*, prohibits retaliation against an employee who testifies in an internal investigation of alleged sexual harassment. I agree with the Court that the "opposition clause" of § 2000e-3(a) (2000 ed.) prohibits retaliation for such conduct. I also agree with the Court's primary reasoning, which is based on "the point argued by the Government and explained by an Equal Employment Opportunity Commission (EEOC) guideline: 'When an employee communicates to her employer a belief that the employer has engaged in . . . a form of employment discrimination, that communication' virtually always 'constitutes the employee's *opposition* to the activity.'" *Ante*, at 276, 172 L. Ed. 2d, at 656. I write separately to emphasize my understanding that the Court's holding does not and should not extend beyond employees who testify in internal investigations or engage in analogous purposive conduct.

As the Court concludes, the term "oppose" does not denote conduct that necessarily rises to the level required by the Sixth Circuit--*i.e.*, conduct that is "'consistent'" and "instigated or initiated" by the employee. *211 Fed. Appx. 373, 376 (2006)*. The primary definitions of the term "oppose" do, however, require conduct that is active and purposive. See Webster's New International Dictionary 1709-1710 (2d ed. 1953); Random House Dictionary of the English Language 1010 (1966) (hereinafter Random Dict.); 10 Oxford English Dictionary 866-867 (2d ed. 1989). For example, the first three definitions of the term in the dictionary upon which the Court principally relies are as follows:

> "1. to act against or provide resistance to; combat. 2. to stand in the way of; hinder; obstruct. 3. to set as an opponent or adversary." Random Dict. 1359 (2d ed. 1987).

In accordance with these definitions, petitioner contends that the statutory term "oppose" means "taking action (including making a statement) to end, prevent, redress, or correct unlawful discrimination." Brief for Petitioner 40.

In order to decide the question that is before us, we have no need to adopt a definition of the term "oppose" that is broader than the definition that petitioner advances. But in dicta, the Court notes that the fourth listed definition in the Random House Dictionary of the English Language goes further, defining "oppose" to mean "'to be hostile or adverse to, *as in opinion*.'" *Ante*, at 276, 172 L. Ed. 2d, at 656 (emphasis added). Thus, this definition embraces silent opposition.

While this is certainly *an* accepted usage of the term "oppose," the term is not always used in this sense, and it is questionable whether silent opposition is covered by the opposition clause of *42 U.S.C. § 2000e-3(a)*. It is noteworthy that all of the other conduct protected by this provision--making a charge, testifying, or assisting or participating in an investigation, proceeding, or hearing--requires active and purposive conduct. "'That several items in a list share an attribute counsels in favor of interpreting the other items as possessing that attribute as well.'" *S. D. Warren Co. v. Maine Bd. of Environmental Protection*, 547 U.S. 370, 378, 126 S. Ct. 1843, 164 L. Ed. 2d 625 (2006) (quoting *Beecham v. United States*, 511 U.S. 368, 371, 114 S. Ct. 1669, 128 L. Ed. 2d 383 (1994)).

An interpretation of the opposition clause that protects conduct that is not active and purposive would have important practical implications. It would open the door to retaliation claims by employees who never expressed a word of opposition to their employers. To be sure, in many cases, such employees would not be able to show that management was aware of their opposition and thus would not be able to show that their opposition caused the adverse actions at issue. But in other cases, such employees might well be able to create a genuine factual issue on the question of causation. Suppose, for example, that an employee alleges that he or she expressed opposition while informally chatting with a co-worker at the proverbial water cooler or in a workplace telephone conversation that was overheard by a co-worker. Or suppose that an employee alleges that such a conversation occurred after work at a restaurant or tavern frequented by co-workers or at a neighborhood picnic attended by a friend or relative of a supervisor.

Some courts hold that an employee asserting a retaliation claim can prove causation simply by showing that the adverse employment action occurred within a short time after the protected conduct. See, *e.g.*, *Clark County School Dist. v. Breeden*, 532 U.S. 268, 273, 121 S. Ct. 1508, 149 L. Ed. 2d 509 (2001) *(per curiam)* (noting that some cases "accept mere temporal proximity between an employer's knowledge of protected activity and an adverse employment action as sufficient evidence of causality to establish a prima facie case"); see also *Gorman-Bakos v. Cornell Cooperative Extension of Schenectady Cty.*, 252 F.3d 545, 554 (CA2 2001); *Conner v. Schnuck Mkts.*, 121 F.3d 1390, 1395 (CA10 1997); *Dey v. Colt Constr. & Development Co.*, 28 F.3d 1446, 1458 (CA7 1994). As a result, an employee claiming retaliation may be able to establish causation simply by showing that, within some time period prior to the adverse action, the employer, by some indirect means, became aware of the views that the employee had expressed. Where the protected conduct consisted of a private conversation, application of this rule would be especially problematic because of uncertainty regarding the point in time when the employer became aware of the employee's private expressions of disapproval.

The number of retaliation claims filed with the EEOC has proliferated in recent years. See U.S. Equal Employment Opportunity Commission, Charge Statistics: FY 1997 Through FY 2007, http://www.eeoc.gov/stats/charges.html; Charge Statistics: FY 1992 Through FY 1996, http://www.eeoc.gov/stats/charges-a.html (as visited Jan. 16, 2009, and available in Clerk of Court's case file) (showing that retaliation charges filed with the EEOC doubled between 1992 and 2007). An expansive interpretation of protected opposition conduct would likely cause this trend to accelerate.

The question whether the opposition clause shields employees who do not communicate their views to their employers through purposive conduct is not before us in this case; the answer to that question is far from clear; and I do not understand the Court's holding to reach that issue here. For present purposes, it is enough to hold that the opposition clause does protect an employee, like petitioner, who testifies about unlawful conduct in an internal investigation.

Shelby County v. Holder

Supreme Court of the United States

February 27, 2013, Argued

June 25, 2013, Decided

No. 12-96

133 S. Ct. 2612
186 L. Ed. 2d 651

SHELBY COUNTY, ALABAMA, Petitioner v. ERIC H. HOLDER, JR., ATTORNEY GENERAL, et al.

ON WRIT OF CERTIORARI TO THE UNITED STATES COURT OF APPEALS FOR THE DISTRICT OF COLUMBIA CIRCUIT
Shelby County v. Holder, 679 F.3d 848, 400 U.S. App. D.C. 367, 2012 U.S. App. LEXIS 10027 (2012)
Perez v. Texas, 2011 U.S. Dist. LEXIS 144735 (W.D. Tex., Nov. 4, 2011)

Bert W. Rein argued the cause for petitioner.

Donald B. Verrilli, Jr. argued the cause for the federal respondent.

Debo P. Adegbile argued the cause for respondents Bobby Pierson, et al.

ROBERTS, C. J., delivered the opinion of the Court, in which Scalia, Kennedy, Thomas, and Alito, JJ., joined.
THOMAS, J., filed a concurring opinion.
GINSBURG, J., filed a dissenting opinion, in which Breyer, Sotomayor, and Kagan, JJ., joined.

CHIEF JUSTICE ROBERTS delivered the opinion of the Court.

The Voting Rights Act of 1965 employed extraordinary measures to address an extraordinary problem. *Section 5* of the Act required States to obtain federal permission before enacting any law related to voting—a drastic departure from basic principles of federalism. And *§4* of the Act applied that requirement only to some States—an equally dramatic departure from the principle that all States enjoy equal sovereignty. This was strong medicine, but Congress determined it was needed to address entrenched racial discrimination in voting, "an insidious and pervasive evil which had been perpetuated in certain parts of our country through unremitting and ingenious defiance of the Constitution." *South Carolina v. Katzenbach, 383 U.S. 301, 309, 86 S. Ct. 803, 15 L. Ed. 2d 769 (1966).* As we explained in upholding the law, "exceptional conditions can justify legislative measures not otherwise appropriate." *Id., at 334, 86 S. Ct. 803, 15 L. Ed. 2d 769.* Reflecting the unprecedented nature of these measures, they were scheduled to expire after five years. See Voting Rights Act of 1965, *§4(a), 79 Stat. 438.*

Nearly 50 years later, they are still in effect; indeed, they have been made more stringent, and are now scheduled to last until 2031. There is no denying, however, that the conditions that originally justified these measures no longer characterize voting in the covered jurisdictions. By 2009, "the racial gap in voter registration and turnout [was] lower in the States originally covered by *§5* than it [was] nationwide." *Northwest Austin Municipal Util. Dist. No. One v. Holder, 557 U.S. 193, 203-204, 129 S. Ct. 2504, 174 L. Ed. 2d 140 (2009).* Since that time, Census Bureau data indicate that African-American voter turnout has come to exceed white voter turnout in five of the six States originally covered by *§5*, with a gap in the sixth State of less than one half of one percent. See Dept. of Commerce, Census Bureau, Re-ported Voting and Registration, by Sex, Race and Hispanic Origin, for States (Nov. 2012) (Table 4b).

At the same time, voting discrimination still exists; no one doubts that. The question is whether the Act's extraordinary measures, including its disparate treatment of the States, continue to satisfy constitutional requirements. As we put it a short time ago, "the Act imposes current burdens and must be justified by current needs." *Northwest Austin, 557 U.S., at 203, 129 S. Ct. 2504, 174 L. Ed. 2d 140.*

I

A

The *Fifteenth Amendment* was ratified in 1870, in the wake of the Civil War. It provides that "[t]he right of citizens of the United States to vote shall not be denied or abridged by the United States or by any State on account of race, color, or previous condition of servitude," and it gives Congress the "power to enforce this article by appropriate legislation."

"The first century of congressional enforcement of the *Amendment*, however, can only be regarded as a failure." *Id., at 197, 129 S. Ct. 2504, 174 L. Ed. 2d 140.* In the 1890s, Alabama, Georgia, Louisiana, Mississippi, North Carolina, South Carolina, and Virginia began to enact literacy tests for voter registration and to employ other methods designed to prevent African-Americans from voting. *Katzenbach, 383 U.S., at 310, 86 S. Ct. 803, 15 L. Ed. 2d 769.* Congress passed statutes outlawing some of these practices and facilitating litigation against them, but litigation remained slow and expensive, and the States came up with new ways to discriminate as soon as existing ones were struck down. Voter registration of African-Americans barely improved. *Id., at 313-314, 86 S. Ct. 803, 15 L. Ed. 2d 769.*

Inspired to action by the civil rights movement, Congress responded in 1965 with the Voting Rights Act. *Section 2* was enacted to forbid, in all 50 States, any "standard, practice, or procedure . . . imposed or applied . . . to deny or abridge the right of any citizen of the United States to vote on account of race or color." *79 Stat. 437.* The current version forbids any "standard, practice, or procedure" that "results in a denial or abridgement of the right of any citizen of the United States to vote on account of race or color." *42 U.S.C. §1973(a).* Both the Federal Government and individuals have sued to enforce §2, see, *e.g., Johnson v. De Grandy, 512 U.S. 997, 114 S. Ct. 2647, 129 L. Ed. 2d 775 (1994),* and injunctive relief is available in appropriate cases to block voting laws from going into effect, see *42 U.S.C. §1973j(d).* Section 2 is permanent, applies nationwide, and is not at issue in this case.

Other sections targeted only some parts of the country. At the time of the Act's passage, these "covered" jurisdictions were those States or political subdivisions that had maintained a test or device as a prerequisite to voting as of November 1, 1964, and had less than 50 percent voter registration or turnout in the 1964 Presidential election. *§4(b), 79 Stat. 438.* Such tests or devices included literacy and knowledge tests, good moral character requirements, the need for vouchers from registered voters, and the like. *§4(c), id., at 438-439.* A covered jurisdiction could "bail out" of coverage if it had not used a test or device in the preceding five years "for the purpose or with the effect of denying or abridging the right to vote on account of race or color." *§4(a), id.,* at 438. In 1965, the covered States included Alabama, Georgia, Louisiana, Mississippi, South Carolina, and Virginia. The additional covered subdivisions included 39 counties in North Carolina and one in Arizona. See *28 CFR pt. 51, App. (2012).*

In those jurisdictions, *§4* of the Act banned all such tests or devices. *§4(a), 79 Stat. 438. Section 5* provided that no change in voting procedures could take effect until it was approved by federal authorities in Washington, D. C.—either the Attorney General or a court of three judges. *Id.,* at 439. A jurisdiction could obtain such "preclearance" only by proving that the change had neither "the purpose [nor] the effect of denying or abridging the right to vote on account of race or color." *Ibid.*

Sections 4 and *5* were intended to be temporary; they were set to expire after five years. See *§4(a), id.,* at 438; *Northwest Austin, supra,* at 199, 129 S. Ct. 2504, 174 L. Ed. 2d 140. In *South Carolina v. Katzenbach,* we upheld the 1965 Act against constitutional challenge, explaining that it was justified to address "voting discrimination where it persists on a pervasive scale." *383 U.S., at 308, 86 S. Ct. 803, 15 L. Ed. 2d 769.*

In 1970, Congress reauthorized the Act for another five years, and extended the coverage formula in *§4(b)* to jurisdictions that had a voting test and less than 50 percent voter registration or turnout as of 1968. Voting Rights Act Amendments of 1970, *§§3-4, 84 Stat. 314.* That swept in several counties in California, New Hampshire, and New York. See *28 CFR pt. 51, App.* Congress also extended the ban in *§4(a)* on tests and devices nationwide. *§6, 84 Stat. 314.*

In 1975, Congress reauthorized the Act for seven more years, and extended its coverage to jurisdictions that had a voting test and less than 50 percent voter registration or turnout as of 1972. Voting Rights Act Amendments of 1975, *§§101, 202, 89 Stat. 400, 401.* Congress also amended the definition of "test or device" to include the practice of providing English-only voting materials in places where over five percent of voting-age citizens spoke a single language other than English. *§203, id.,* at 401-402. As a result of these amendments, the States of Alaska, Arizona, and Texas, as well as several counties in California, Florida, Michigan, New York, North Carolina, and South Dakota, became covered jurisdictions. See *28 CFR pt. 51, App.* Congress correspondingly amended *sections* 2 and 5 to forbid voting discrimination on the basis of membership in a language minority group, in addition to discrimination on the basis of race or color. *§§203, 206, 89 Stat. 400, 402.* Finally, Congress made the nationwide ban on tests and devices permanent. *§102, id.,* at 400.

In 1982, Congress reauthorized the Act for 25 years, but did not alter its coverage formula. See Voting Rights Act Amendments, *96 Stat. 131*. Congress did, however, amend the bailout provisions, allowing political subdivisions of covered jurisdictions to bail out. Among other prerequisites for bailout, jurisdictions and their subdivisions must not have used a forbidden test or device, failed to receive preclearance, or lost a §2 suit, in the ten years prior to seeking bailout. §2, *id.*, at 131-133.

We upheld each of these reauthorizations against constitutional challenge. See *Georgia v. United States*, 411 U.S. 526, 93 S. Ct. 1702, 36 L. Ed. 2d 472 (1973); *City of Rome v. United States*, 446 U.S. 156, 100 S. Ct. 1548, 64 L. Ed. 2d 119 (1980); *Lopez v. Monterey County*, 525 U.S. 266, 119 S. Ct. 693, 142 L. Ed. 2d 728 (1999).

In 2006, Congress again reauthorized the Voting Rights Act for 25 years, again without change to its coverage formula. Fannie Lou Hamer, Rosa Parks, and Coretta Scott King Voting Rights Act Reauthorization and Amendments Act, *120 Stat. 577*. Congress also amended §5 to prohibit more conduct than before. §5, *id.*, at 580-581; see *Reno v. Bossier Parish School Bd.*, 528 U.S. 320, 341, 120 S. Ct. 866, 145 L. Ed. 2d 845 (2000) (*Bossier II*); *Georgia v. Ashcroft*, 539 U.S. 461, 479, 123 S. Ct. 2498, 156 L. Ed. 2d 428 (2003). Section 5 now forbids voting changes with "any discriminatory purpose" as well as voting changes that diminish the ability of citizens, on account of race, color, or language minority status, "to elect their preferred candidates of choice." *42 U.S.C. §§1973c(b)-(d)*.

Shortly after this reauthorization, a Texas utility district brought suit, seeking to bail out from the Act's coverage and, in the alternative, challenging the Act's constitutionality. See *Northwest Austin*, 557 U.S., at 200-201, 129 S. Ct. 2504, 174 L. Ed. 2d 140. A three-judge District Court explained that only a State or political subdivision was eligible to seek bailout under the statute, and concluded that the utility district was not a political subdivision, a term that encompassed only "counties, parishes, and voter-registering subunits." *Northwest Austin Municipal Util. Dist. No. One v. Mukasey*, 573 F. Supp. 2d 221, 232 (DC 2008). The District Court also rejected the constitutional challenge. *Id.*, at 283.

We reversed. We explained that "'normally the Court will not decide a constitutional question if there is some other ground upon which to dispose of the case.'" *Northwest Austin, supra*, at 205, 129 S. Ct. 2504, 174 L. Ed. 2d 140 (quoting *Escambia County v. McMillan*, 466 U.S. 48, 51, 104 S. Ct. 1577, 80 L. Ed. 2d 36 (1984) (*per curiam*)). Concluding that "underlying constitutional concerns," among other things, "compel[led] a broader reading of the bailout provision," we construed the statute to allow the utility district to seek bailout. *Northwest Austin*, 557 U.S., at 207,

129 S. Ct. 2504, 174 L. Ed. 2d 140. In doing so we expressed serious doubts about the Act's continued constitutionality.

We explained that §5 "imposes substantial federalism costs" and "differentiates between the States, despite our historic tradition that all the States enjoy equal sovereignty." *Id., at 202, 203, 129 S. Ct. 2504, 174 L. Ed. 2d 140* (internal quotation marks omitted). We also noted that "[t]hings have changed in the South. Voter turnout and registration rates now approach parity. Blatantly discriminatory evasions of federal decrees are rare. And minority candidates hold office at unprecedented levels." *Id., at 202, 129 S. Ct. 2504, 174 L. Ed. 2d 140*. Finally, we questioned whether the problems that §5 meant to address were still "concentrated in the jurisdictions singled out for preclearance." *Id., at 203, 129 S. Ct. 2504, 174 L. Ed. 2d 140*.

Eight Members of the Court subscribed to these views, and the remaining Member would have held the Act unconstitutional. Ultimately, however, the Court's construction of the bailout provision left the constitutional issues for another day.

B

Shelby County is located in Alabama, a covered jurisdiction. It has not sought bailout, as the Attorney General has recently objected to voting changes proposed from within the county. See App. 87a-92a. Instead, in 2010, the county sued the Attorney General in Federal District Court in Washington, D. C., seeking a declaratory judgment that *sections 4(b)* and *5* of the Voting Rights Act are facially unconstitutional, as well as a permanent injunction against their enforcement. The District Court ruled against the county and upheld the Act. *811 F. Supp. 2d 424, 508 (2011)*. The court found that the evidence before Congress in 2006 was sufficient to justify reauthorizing §5 and continuing the §4(b) coverage formula.

The Court of Appeals for the D. C. Circuit affirmed. In assessing §5, the D. C. Circuit considered six primary categories of evidence: Attorney General objections to voting changes, Attorney General requests for more information regarding voting changes, successful §2 suits in covered jurisdictions, the dispatching of federal observers to monitor elections in covered jurisdictions, §5 preclearance suits involving covered jurisdictions, and the deterrent effect of §5. See *679 F. 3d 848, 862-863, 400 U.S. App. D.C. 367 (2012)*. After extensive analysis of the record, the court accepted Congress's conclusion that §2 litigation remained inadequate in the covered jurisdictions to protect the rights of minority voters, and that §5 was therefore still necessary. *Id., at 873*.

Turning to §4, the D. C. Circuit noted that the evidence for singling out the covered jurisdictions was "less robust" and that the issue presented "a close question." *Id., at 879.* But the court looked to data comparing the number of successful §2 suits in the different parts of the country. Coupling that evidence with the deterrent effect of §5, the court concluded that the statute continued "to single out the jurisdictions in which discrimination is concentrated," and thus held that the coverage formula passed constitutional muster. *Id., at 883.*

Judge Williams dissented. He found "no positive correlation between inclusion in §4(b)'s coverage formula and low black registration or turnout." *Id., at 891.* Rather, to the extent there was any correlation, it actually went the other way: "condemnation under §4(b) is a marker of *higher* black registration and turnout." *Ibid.* (emphasis added). Judge Williams also found that "[c]overed jurisdictions have *far more* black officeholders as a proportion of the black population than do uncovered ones." *Id., at 892.* As to the evidence of successful §2 suits, Judge Williams disaggregated the reported cases by State, and concluded that "[t]he five worst uncovered jurisdictions . . . have worse records than eight of the covered jurisdictions." *Id., at 897.* He also noted that two covered jurisdictions—Arizona and Alaska—had not had any successful reported §2 suit brought against them during the entire 24 years covered by the data. *Ibid.* Judge Williams would have held the coverage formula of §4(b) "irrational" and unconstitutional. *Id., at 885.*

We granted certiorari. *568 U.S. 133 S. Ct. 594, 184 L. Ed. 2d 389 (2012).*

II

In *Northwest Austin*, we stated that "the Act imposes current burdens and must be justified by current needs." *557 U.S., at 203, 129 S. Ct. 2504, 174 L. Ed. 2d 140.* And we concluded that "a departure from the fundamental principle of equal sovereignty requires a showing that a statute's disparate geographic coverage is sufficiently related to the problem that it targets." *Ibid.* These basic principles guide our review of the question before us. [1]

---

[1] Both the *Fourteenth* and *Fifteenth Amendments* were at issue in *Northwest Austin*, see Juris. Statement i, and Brief for Federal Appellee 29-30, in *Northwest Austin Municipal Util. Dist. No. One* v. *Holder*, O. T. 2008, No. 08-322, and accordingly *Northwest Austin* guides our review under both Amendments in this case.

A

The Constitution and laws of the United States are "the supreme Law of the Land." U.S. Const., Art. VI, cl. 2. State legislation may not contravene federal law. The Federal Government does not, however, have a general right to review and veto state enactments before they go into effect. A proposal to grant such authority to "negative" state laws was considered at the Constitutional Convention, but rejected in favor of allowing state laws to take effect, subject to later challenge under the Supremacy Clause. See 1 Records of the Federal Convention of 1787, pp. 21, 164-168 (M. Farrand ed. 1911); 2 *id.*, at 27-29, 390-392.

Outside the strictures of the Supremacy Clause, States retain broad autonomy in structuring their governments and pursuing legislative objectives. Indeed, the Constitution provides that all powers not specifically granted to the Federal Government are reserved to the States or citizens. *Amdt. 10.* This "allocation of powers in our federal system preserves the integrity, dignity, and residual sovereignty of the States." *Bond v. United States, 564 U.S. 131 S. Ct. 2355, 180 L. Ed. 2d 269, 279-280 (2011).* But the federal balance "is not just an end in itself: Rather, federalism secures to citizens the liberties that derive from the diffusion of sovereign power." *Ibid.* (internal quotation marks omitted).

More specifically, "'the Framers of the Constitution intended the States to keep for themselves, as provided in the *Tenth Amendment*, the power to regulate elections.'" *Gregory v. Ashcroft, 501 U.S. 452, 461-462, 111 S. Ct. 2395, 115 L. Ed. 2d 410 (1991)* (quoting *Sugarman v. Dougall, 413 U.S. 634, 647, 93 S. Ct. 2842, 37 L. Ed. 2d 853 (1973)*; some internal quotation marks omitted). Of course, the Federal Government retains significant control over federal elections. For instance, the Constitution authorizes Congress to establish the time and manner for electing Senators and Representatives. Art. I, §4, cl. 1; see also *Arizona v. Inter Tribal Council of Ariz., Inc., ante, at 133 S. Ct. 2247, 186 L. Ed. 2d 239, 2013 U.S. LEXIS 4544, *10.* But States have "broad powers to determine the conditions under which the right of suffrage may be exercised." *Carrington v. Rash, 380 U.S. 89, 91, 85 S. Ct. 775, 13 L. Ed. 2d 675 (1965)* (internal quotation marks omitted); see also *Arizona, ante, at 133 S. Ct. 186 L. Ed. 2d 239, 2013 U.S. LEXIS 4544, *43.* And "[e]ach State has the power to prescribe the qualifications of its officers and the manner in which they shall be chosen." *Boyd v. Nebraska ex rel. Thayer, 143 U.S. 135, 161, 12 S. Ct. 375, 36 L. Ed. 103 (1892).* Drawing lines for congressional districts is likewise "primarily the duty and responsibility of the State." *Perry v. Perez, 565 U.S. 132 S. Ct. 934, 181 L. Ed. 2d 900, 905 (2012) (per curiam)* (internal quotation marks omitted).

Not only do States retain sovereignty under the Constitution, there is also a "fundamental principle of *equal* sovereignty" among the States. *Northwest Austin, supra*, at 203, 129 S. Ct. 2504, 174 L. Ed. 2d 140 (citing *United States v. Louisiana, 363 U.S. 1*, 16, 80 S. Ct. 961, 4 L. Ed. 2d 1025 (1960); *Lessee of Pollard v. Hagan, 44 U.S. 212*, 3 How. 212, 223, 11 L. Ed. 565 (1845); and *Texas v. White, 74 U.S. 700*, 7 Wall. 700, 725-726, 19 L. Ed. 227 (1869); emphasis added). Over a hundred years ago, this Court explained that our Nation "was and is a union of States, equal in power, dignity and authority." *Coyle v. Smith, 221 U.S. 559*, 567, 31 S. Ct. 688, 55 L. Ed. 853 (1911). Indeed, "the constitutional equality of the States is essential to the harmonious operation of the scheme upon which the Republic was organized." *Id., at 580, 31 S. Ct. 688, 55 L. Ed. 853. Coyle* concerned the admission of new States, and *Katzenbach* rejected the notion that the principle operated as a *bar* on differential treatment outside that context. *383 U.S., at 328-329*, 86 S. Ct. 803, 15 L. Ed. 2d 769. At the same time, as we made clear in *Northwest Austin*, the fundamental principle of equal sovereignty remains highly pertinent in assessing subsequent disparate treatment of States. *557 U.S., at 203, 129 S. Ct. 2504, 174 L. Ed. 2d 140.*

The Voting Rights Act sharply departs from these basic principles. It suspends "*all* changes to state election law—however innocuous—until they have been precleared by federal authorities in Washington, D. C." *Id., at 202, 129 S. Ct. 2504, 174 L. Ed. 2d 140*. States must beseech the Federal Government for permission to implement laws that they would otherwise have the right to enact and execute on their own, subject of course to any injunction in a §2 action. The Attorney General has 60 days to object to a preclearance request, longer if he requests more information. See *28 CFR §§51.9, 51.37*. If a State seeks preclearance from a three-judge court, the process can take years.

And despite the tradition of equal sovereignty, the Act applies to only nine States (and several additional counties). While one State waits months or years and expends funds to implement a validly enacted law, its neighbor can typically put the same law into effect immediately, through the normal legislative process. Even if a noncovered jurisdiction is sued, there are important differences between those proceedings and preclearance proceedings; the preclearance proceeding "not only switches the burden of proof to the supplicant jurisdiction, but also applies substantive standards quite different from those governing the rest of the nation." *679 F. 3d, at 884* (Williams, J., dissenting) (case below).

All this explains why, when we first upheld the Act in 1966, we described it as "stringent" and "potent." *Katzenbach, 383 U.S., at 308, 315, 337, 86 S. Ct. 803, 15 L. Ed. 2d 769*. We recognized that it "may have been an uncommon exercise of congressional power," but concluded that "legislative measures not otherwise appropriate" could be justified by "exceptional conditions." *Id., at 334, 86 S. Ct. 803, 15 L. Ed. 2d 769*. We have since noted that the Act "authorizes federal intrusion into sensitive areas of state and local policymaking," *Lopez, 525 U.S., at 282, 119 S. Ct. 693, 142 L. Ed. 2d 728*, and represents an "extraordinary departure from the traditional course of relations between the States and the Federal Government," *Presley v. Etowah County Comm'n, 502 U.S. 491, 500-501, 112 S. Ct. 820, 117 L. Ed. 2d 51 (1992)*. As we reiterated in *Northwest Austin*, the Act constitutes "extraordinary legislation otherwise unfamiliar to our federal system." *557 U.S., at 211, 129 S. Ct. 2504, 174 L. Ed. 2d 140*.

B

In 1966, we found these departures from the basic features of our system of government justified. The "blight of racial discrimination in voting" had "infected the electoral process in parts of our country for nearly a century." *Katzenbach, 383 U.S., at 308, 86 S. Ct. 803, 15 L. Ed. 2d 769*. Several States had enacted a variety of requirements and tests "specifically designed to prevent" African-Americans from voting. *Id., at 310, 86 S. Ct. 803, 15 L. Ed. 2d 769*. Case-by-case litigation had proved inadequate to prevent such racial discrimination in voting, in part because States "merely switched to discriminatory devices not covered by the federal decrees," "enacted difficult new tests," or simply "defied and evaded court orders." *Id., at 314, 86 S. Ct. 803, 15 L. Ed. 2d 769*. Shortly before enactment of the Voting Rights Act, only 19.4 percent of African-Americans of voting age were registered to vote in Alabama, only 31.8 percent in Louisiana, and only 6.4 percent in Mississippi. *Id., at 313, 86 S. Ct. 803, 15 L. Ed. 2d 769*. Those figures were roughly 50 percentage points or more below the figures for whites. *Ibid.*

In short, we concluded that "[u]nder the compulsion of these unique circumstances, Congress responded in a permissibly decisive manner." *Id., at 334, 335, 86 S. Ct. 803, 15 L. Ed. 2d 769*. We also noted then and have emphasized since that this extra-ordinary legislation was intended to be temporary, set to expire after five years. *Id., at 333, 86 S. Ct. 803, 15 L. Ed. 2d 769*; *Northwest Austin, supra, at 199, 129 S. Ct. 2504, 174 L. Ed. 2d 140*.

At the time, the coverage formula—the means of linking the exercise of the unprecedented authority with the problem that warranted it—made sense. We found that "Congress chose to limit its attention to the geographic areas where immediate action seemed necessary." *Katzenbach, 383 U.S., at 328, 86 S. Ct. 803, 15 L. Ed. 2d 769*. The areas where Congress found "evidence of actual voting discrimination" shared two characteristics: "the use of tests and devices for voter registration, and a voting rate in the 1964 presidential election at least 12 points below the national average." *Id., at 330, 86 S. Ct. 803, 15 L. Ed. 2d 769*. We explained that "[t]ests and devices are relevant to voting discrimination because of their long history as a tool for perpetrating the evil; a low voting rate is pertinent for the obvious reason that widespread disenfranchisement must inevitably affect the number of actual voters." *Ibid.* We therefore concluded that "the coverage formula [was] rational in both practice and theory." *Ibid.* It accurately reflected those jurisdictions uniquely characterized by voting discrimination "on a pervasive scale," linking coverage to the devices used to effectuate discrimination and to the resulting disenfranchisement. *Id.,* at 308, 86 S. Ct. 803, 15 L. Ed. 2d 769. The formula ensured that the "stringent remedies [were] aimed at areas where voting discrimination ha[d] been most flagrant." *Id., at 315, 86 S. Ct. 803, 15 L. Ed. 2d 769.*

C

Nearly 50 years later, things have changed dramatically. Shelby County contends that the preclearance requirement, even without regard to its disparate coverage, is now unconstitutional. Its arguments have a good deal of force. In the covered jurisdictions, "[v]oter turnout and registration rates now approach parity. Blatantly discriminatory evasions of federal decrees are rare. And minority candidates hold office at unprecedented levels." *Northwest Austin, 557 U.S.,* at 202, 129 S. Ct. 2504, 174 L. Ed. 2d 140. The tests and devices that blocked access to the ballot have been forbidden nationwide for over 40 years. See §6, 84 Stat. 314; §102, 89 Stat. 400.

Those conclusions are not ours alone. Congress said the same when it reauthorized the Act in 2006, writing that "[s]ignificant progress has been made in eliminating first generation barriers experienced by minority voters, including increased numbers of registered minority voters, minority voter turnout, and minority representation in Congress, State legislatures, and local elected offices." *§2(b)(1), 120 Stat. 577.* The House Report elaborated that "the number of African-Americans who are registered and who turn out to cast ballots has increased significantly over the last 40 years, particularly since 1982," and noted that "[i]n some circumstances, minorities register to vote and cast ballots at levels that surpass those of white voters." H. R. Rep. No. 109-478, p. 12 (2006). That Report also explained that there have been "significant increases in the number of African-Americans serving in elected offices"; more specifically, there has been approximately a 1,000 percent increase since 1965 in the number of African-American elected officials in the six States originally covered by the Voting Rights Act. *Id.,* at 18.

The following chart, compiled from the Senate and House Reports, compares voter registration numbers from 1965 to those from 2004 in the six originally covered States. These are the numbers that were before Congress when it reauthorized the Act in 2006:

	1965			2004		
	White	Black	Gap	White	Black	Gap
Alabama	69.2	19.3	49.9	73.8	72.9	0.9
Georgia	62.	27.4	35.2	63.5	64.2	-0.7
Louisiana	80.5	31.6	48.9	75.1	71.1	4.0
Mississippi	69.9	6.7	63.2	72.3	76.1	-3.8
South Carolina	75.7	37.3	38.4	74.4	71.1	3.3
Virginia	61.1	38.3	22.8	68.2	57.4	10.8

See S. Rep. No. 109-295, p. 11 (2006); H. R. Rep. No. 109-478, at 12. The 2004 figures come from the Census Bureau. Census Bureau data from the most recent election indicate that African-American voter turnout exceeded white voter turnout in five of the six States originally covered by §5, with a gap in the sixth State of less than one half of one percent. See Dept. of Commerce, Census Bureau, Reported Voting and Registration, by Sex, Race and Hispanic Origin, for States (Table 4b). The preclearance statistics are also illuminating. In the first decade after enactment of §5, the Attorney General objected to 14.2 percent of proposed voting changes. H. R Rep. No. 109-478, at 22. In the last decade before reenactment, the Attorney General objected to a mere 0.16 percent. S. Rep. No. 109-295, at 13.

There is no doubt that these improvements are in large part *because of* the Voting Rights Act. The Act has proved immensely successful at redressing racial discrimination and integrating the voting process. See *§2(b)(1), 120 Stat. 577*. During the "Freedom Summer" of 1964, in Philadelphia, Mississippi, three men were murdered while working in the area to register African-American voters. See *United States v. Price, 383 U.S. 787, 790, 86 S. Ct. 1152, 16 L. Ed. 2d 267 (1966)*. On "Bloody Sunday" in 1965, in Selma, Alabama, police beat and used tear gas against hundreds marching in support of African-American enfranchisement. See *Northwest Austin, supra, at 220, n. 3, 129 S. Ct. 2504, 174 L. Ed. 2d 140* (Thomas, J., concurring in judgment in part and dissenting in part). Today both of those towns are governed by African-American mayors. Problems remain in these States and others, but there is no denying that, due to the Voting Rights Act, our Nation has made great strides.

Yet the Act has not eased the restrictions in §5 or narrowed the scope of the coverage formula in §4(b) along the way. Those extraordinary and unprecedented features were reauthorized—as if nothing had changed. In fact, the Act's unusual remedies have grown even stronger. When Congress reauthorized the Act in 2006, it did so for another 25 years on top of the previous 40—a far cry from the initial five-year period. See *42 U.S.C. §1973b(a)(8)*. Congress also expanded the prohibitions in §5. We had previously interpreted §5 to prohibit only those redistricting plans that would have the purpose or effect of worsening the position of minority groups. See *Bossier II, 528 U.S., at 324, 335-336, 120 S. Ct. 866, 145 L. Ed. 2d 845*. In 2006, Congress amended §5 to prohibit laws that could have favored such groups but did not do so because of a discriminatory purpose, see *42 U.S.C. §1973c(c)*, even though we had stated that such broadening of §5 coverage would "exacerbate the substantial federalism costs that the preclearance procedure already exacts, perhaps to the extent of raising concerns about §5's constitutionality," *Bossier II, supra, at 336, 120 S. Ct. 866, 145 L. Ed. 2d 845* (citation and internal quotation marks omitted). In addition, Congress expanded §5 to prohibit any voting law "that has the purpose of or will have the effect of diminishing the ability of any citizens of the United States," on account of race, color, or language minority status, "to elect their preferred candidates of choice." *§1973c(b)*. In light of those two amendments, the bar that covered jurisdictions must clear has been raised even as the conditions justifying that requirement have dramatically improved.

We have also previously highlighted the concern that "the preclearance requirements in one State [might] be unconstitutional in another." *Northwest Austin, 557 U.S., at 203, 129 S. Ct. 2504, 174 L. Ed. 2d 140*; see *Georgia v. Ashcroft, 539 U.S., at 491, 111 S. Ct. 2395, 115 L. Ed. 2d 410* (Kennedy, J., concurring) ("considerations of race that would doom a redistricting plan under the *Fourteenth Amendment* or §2 [of the Voting Rights Act] seem to be what save it under §5"). Nothing has happened since to alleviate this troubling concern about the current application of §5.

Respondents do not deny that there have been improvements on the ground, but argue that much of this can be attributed to the deterrent effect of §5, which dissuades covered jurisdictions from engaging in discrimination that they would resume should §5 be struck down. Under this theory, however, §5 would be effectively immune from scrutiny; no matter how "clean" the record of covered jurisdictions, the argument could always be made that it was deterrence that accounted for the good behavior.

The provisions of §5 apply only to those jurisdictions singled out by §4. We now consider whether that coverage formula is constitutional in light of current conditions.

III

A

When upholding the constitutionality of the coverage formula in 1966, we concluded that it was "rational in both practice and theory." *Katzenbach*, *383 U.S., at 330, 86 S. Ct. 803, 15 L. Ed. 2d 769*. The formula looked to cause (discriminatory tests) and effect (low voter registration and turnout), and tailored the remedy (preclearance) to those jurisdictions exhibiting both.

By 2009, however, we concluded that the "coverage formula raise[d] serious constitutional questions." *Northwest Austin, 557 U.S., at 204, 129 S. Ct. 2504, 174 L. Ed. 2d 140*. As we explained, a statute's "current burdens" must be justified by "current needs," and any "disparate geographic coverage" must be "sufficiently related to the problem that it targets." *Id., at 203, 129 S. Ct. 2504, 174 L. Ed. 2d 140*. The coverage formula met that test in 1965, but no longer does so.

Coverage today is based on decades-old data and eradicated practices. The formula captures States by reference to literacy tests and low voter registration and turnout in the 1960s and early 1970s. But such tests have been banned nationwide for over 40 years. *§6, 84 Stat. 314; §102, 89 Stat. 400*. And voter registration and turnout numbers in the covered States have risen dramatically in the years since. H. R. Rep. No. 109-478, at 12. Racial disparity in those numbers was compelling evidence justifying the preclearance remedy and the coverage formula. See, *e.g.*, *Katzenbach*, supra, at 313, 329-330, 86 S. Ct. 803, 15 L. Ed. 2d 769. There is no longer such a disparity.

In 1965, the States could be divided into two groups: those with a recent history of voting tests and low voter registration and turnout, and those without those characteristics. Congress based its coverage formula on that distinction. Today the Nation is no longer divided along those lines, yet the Voting Rights Act continues to treat it as if it were.

B

The Government's defense of the formula is limited. First, the Government contends that the formula is "reverse-engineered": Congress identified the jurisdictions to be covered and *then* came up with criteria to describe them. Brief for Federal Respondent 48-49. Under that reasoning, there need not be any logical relationship between the criteria in the formula and the reason for coverage; all that

325

is necessary is that the formula happen to capture the jurisdictions Congress wanted to single out.

The Government suggests that *Katzenbach* sanctioned such an approach, but the analysis in *Katzenbach* was quite different. *Katzenbach* reasoned that the coverage formula was rational because the "formula . . . was relevant to the problem": "Tests and devices are relevant to voting discrimination because of their long history as a tool for perpetuating the evil; a low voting rate is pertinent for the obvious reason that widespread disenfranchisement must inevitably affect the number of actual voters." *383 U.S., at 329, 330, 86 S. Ct. 803, 15 L. Ed. 2d 769.*

Here, by contrast, the Government's reverse-engineering argument does not even attempt to demonstrate the continued relevance of the formula to the problem it targets. And in the context of a decision as significant as this one—subjecting a disfavored subset of States to "extraordinary legislation otherwise unfamiliar to our federal system," *Northwest Austin, supra, at 211, 129 S. Ct. 2504, 174 L. Ed. 2d 140*—that failure to establish even relevance is fatal.

The Government falls back to the argument that because the formula was relevant in 1965, its continued use is permissible so long as any discrimination remains in the States Congress identified back then—regardless of how that discrimination compares to discrimination in States unburdened by coverage. Brief for Federal Respondent 49-50. This argument does not look to "current political conditions," *Northwest Austin, supra, at 203, 129 S. Ct. 2504, 174 L. Ed. 2d 140*, but instead relies on a comparison between the States in 1965. That comparison reflected the different histories of the North and South. It was in the South that slavery was upheld by law until uprooted by the Civil War, that the reign of Jim Crow denied African-Americans the most basic freedoms, and that state and local governments worked tirelessly to disenfranchise citizens on the basis of race. The Court invoked that history—rightly so—in sustaining the disparate coverage of the Voting Rights Act in 1966. See *Katzenbach, supra, at 308, 86 S. Ct. 803, 15 L. Ed. 2d 769* ("The constitutional propriety of the Voting Rights Act of 1965 must be judged with reference to the historical experience which it reflects.").

But history did not end in 1965. By the time the Act was reauthorized in 2006, there had been 40 more years of it. In assessing the "current need[ ]" for a preclearance system that treats States differently from one another today, that history cannot be ignored. During that time, largely because of the Voting Rights Act, voting tests were abolished, disparities in voter registration and turnout due to race were erased, and African-Americans attained political office in record numbers. And yet the coverage formula that Congress reauthorized in 2006 ignores these developments, keeping the focus on decades-old data relevant to decades-old problems, rather than current data reflecting current needs.

The *Fifteenth Amendment* commands that the right to vote shall not be denied or abridged on account of race or color, and it gives Congress the power to enforce that command. *The Amendment* is not designed to punish for the past; its purpose is to ensure a better future. See *Rice v. Cayetano, 528 U.S. 495, 512, 120 S. Ct. 1044, 145 L. Ed. 2d 1007 (2000)* ("Consistent with the design of the Constitution, the [Fifteenth] *Amendment* is cast in fundamental terms, terms transcending the particular controversy which was the immediate impetus for its enactment."). To serve that purpose, Congress—if it is to divide the States—must identify those jurisdictions to be singled out on a basis that makes sense in light of current conditions. It cannot rely simply on the past. We made that clear in *Northwest Austin*, and we make it clear again today.

C

In defending the coverage formula, the Government, the intervenors, and the dissent also rely heavily on data from the record that they claim justify disparate coverage. Congress compiled thousands of pages of evidence before reauthorizing the Voting Rights Act. The court below and the parties have debated what that record shows—they have gone back and forth about whether to compare covered to noncovered jurisdictions as blocks, how to disaggregate the data State by State, how to weigh §2 cases as evidence of ongoing discrimination, and whether to consider evidence not before Congress, among other issues. Compare, *e.g., 679 F. 3d, at 873-883* (case below), with *id., at 889-902* (Williams, J., dissenting). Regardless of how to look at the record, however, no one can fairly say that it shows anything approaching the "pervasive," "flagrant," "widespread," and "rampant" discrimination that faced Congress in 1965, and that clearly distinguished the covered jurisdictions from the rest of the Nation at that time. *Katzenbach, supra, at 308, 315, 331, 86 S. Ct. 803, 15 L. Ed. 2d 769*; *Northwest Austin, 557 U.S., at 201, 129 S. Ct. 2504, 174 L. Ed. 2d 140* .

But a more fundamental problem remains: Congress did not use the record it compiled to shape a coverage formula grounded in current conditions. It instead reenacted a formula based on 40-year-old facts having no logical relation to the present day. The dissent relies on "second-generation barriers," which are not impediments to the casting of ballots, but rather electoral arrangements that affect the weight of minority votes. That does not cure the problem. Viewing the preclearance requirements as targeting such efforts simply highlights the irrationality of continued reliance on the §4 coverage formula, which is based on voting tests and access to the ballot, not vote dilution. We cannot pretend that we are reviewing an updated statute, or try our hand at updating the statute ourselves, based on the new record compiled by Congress. Contrary to the dissent's contention, see *post, at 186 L. Ed. 2d, at 687*, we are not ignoring the record; we are simply recognizing that it played no role in shaping the statutory formula before us today.

The dissent also turns to the record to argue that, in light of voting discrimination in Shelby County, the county cannot complain about the provisions that subject it to preclearance. *Post, at 186 L. Ed. 2d, at 688-692*. But that is like saying that a driver pulled over pursuant to a policy of stopping all redheads cannot complain about that policy, if it turns out his license has expired. Shelby County's claim is that the coverage formula here is unconstitutional in all its applications, because of how it selects the jurisdictions subjected to preclearance. The county was selected based on that formula, and may challenge it in court.

D

The dissent proceeds from a flawed premise. It quotes the famous sentence from *McCulloch v. Maryland, 17 U.S. 316, 4 Wheat. 316, 421, 4 L. Ed. 579 (1819)*, with the following emphasis: "Let the end be legitimate, let it be within the scope of the constitution, and *all means which are appropriate, which are plainly adapted to that end, which are not prohibited, but consist with the letter and spirit of the constitution, are constitutional.*" *Post, at 186 L. Ed. 2d, at 679* (emphasis in dissent). But this case is about a part of the sentence that the dissent does not emphasize—the part that asks whether a legislative means is "consist[ent] with the letter and spirit of the constitution." The dissent states that "[i]t cannot tenably be maintained" that this is an issue with regard to the Voting Rights Act, *post, at 186 L. Ed. 2d, at 679*, but four years ago, in an opinion joined by two of today's dissenters, the Court expressly stated that "[t]he Act's preclearance requirement and its coverage formula raise serious constitutional questions." *Northwest Austin, supra, at 204, 129 S. Ct. 2504, 174 L. Ed. 2d 140*. The dissent does not explain how those "serious constitutional questions" became untenable in four short years.

The dissent treats the Act as if it were just like any other piece of legislation, but this Court has made clear from the beginning that the Voting Rights Act is far from ordinary. At the risk of repetition, *Katzenbach* indicated that the Act was "uncommon" and "not otherwise appropriate," but was justified by "exceptional" and "unique" conditions. *383 U.S., at 334, 335, 86 S. Ct. 803, 15 L. Ed. 2d 769*. Multiple decisions since have reaffirmed the Act's "extraordinary" nature. See, *e.g., Northwest Austin, supra, at 211, 129 S. Ct. 2504, 174 L. Ed. 2d 140*. Yet the dissent goes so far as to suggest instead that the preclearance requirement and disparate treatment of the States should be upheld into the future "unless there [is] no or almost no evidence of unconstitutional action by States." *Post, at 186 L. Ed. 2d, at 693.*

In other ways as well, the dissent analyzes the question presented as if our decision in *Northwest Austin* never happened. For example, the dissent refuses to consider the principle of equal sovereignty, despite *Northwest Austin*'s emphasis on its significance. *Northwest Austin* also emphasized the "dramatic" progress since 1965, *557 U.S., at 201, 129 S. Ct. 2504, 174 L. Ed. 2d 140*, but the dissent describes current levels of discrimination as "flagrant," "widespread," and "pervasive," *post, at 186 L. Ed. 2d, at 678, 684* (internal quotation marks omitted). Despite the fact that *Northwest Austin* requires an Act's "disparate geographic coverage" to be "sufficiently related" to its targeted problems, *557 U.S., at 203, 129 S. Ct. 2504, 174 L. Ed. 2d 140*, the dissent maintains that an Act's limited coverage actually eases Congress's burdens, and suggests that a fortuitous relationship should suffice. Although *Northwest Austin* stated definitively that "current burdens" must be justified by "current needs," *ibid.*, the dissent argues that the coverage formula can be justified by history, and that the required showing can be weaker on reenactment than when the law was first passed.

There is no valid reason to insulate the coverage formula from review merely because it was previously enacted 40 years ago. If Congress had started from scratch in 2006, it plainly could not have enacted the present coverage formula. It would have been irrational for Congress to distinguish between States in such a fundamental way based on 40-year-old data, when today's statistics tell an entirely different story. And it would have been irrational to base coverage on the use of voting tests 40 years ago, when such tests have been illegal since that time. But that is exactly what Congress has done.

***

Striking down an Act of Congress "is the gravest and most delicate duty that this Court is called on to perform." *Blodgett v. Holden, 275 U.S. 142, 148, 48 S. Ct. 105, 72 L. Ed. 206, 1928-1 C.B. 324 (1927)* (Holmes, J., concurring). We do not do so lightly. That is why, in 2009, we took care to avoid ruling on the constitutionality of the Voting Rights Act when asked to do so, and instead resolved the case then before us on statutory grounds. But in issuing that decision, we expressed our broader concerns about the constitutionality of the Act. Congress could have updated the coverage formula at that time, but did not do so. Its failure to act leaves us today with no choice but to declare §4(b) unconstitutional. The formula in that section can no longer be used as a basis for subjecting jurisdictions to preclearance.

Our decision in no way affects the permanent, nationwide ban on racial discrimination in voting found in §2. We issue no holding on §5 itself, only on the coverage formula. Congress may draft another formula based on current conditions. Such a formula is an initial prerequisite to a determination that exceptional conditions still exist justifying such an "extraordinary departure from the traditional course of relations between the States and the Federal Government." *Presley, 502 U.S., at 500-501, 112 S. Ct. 820, 117 L. Ed. 2d 51.* Our country has changed, and while any racial discrimination in voting is too much, Congress must ensure that the legislation it passes to remedy that problem speaks to current conditions.

The judgment of the Court of Appeals is reversed.

It is so ordered.

JUSTICE THOMAS, concurring.

I join the Court's opinion in full but write separately to explain that I would find §5 of the Voting Rights Act unconstitutional as well. The Court's opinion sets forth the reasons.

"The Voting Rights Act of 1965 employed extraordinary measures to address an extraordinary problem." *Ante, at 186 L. Ed. 2d, at 659.* In the face of "unremitting and ingenious defiance" of citizens' constitutionally protected right to vote, §5 was necessary to give effect to the *Fifteenth Amendment* in particular regions of the country. *South Carolina v. Katzenbach,* 383 U.S. 301, 309, 86 S. Ct. 803, 15 L. Ed. 2d 769 (1966). Though §5's preclearance requirement represented a "shar[p] depart[ure]" from "basic principles" of federalism and the equal sovereignty of the States, *ante, at 186 L. Ed. 2d, at 663, 665,* the Court upheld the measure against early constitutional challenges because it was necessary at the time to address "voting discrimination where it persist[ed] on a pervasive scale." *Katzenbach, supra,* at 308, 86 S. Ct. 803, 15 L. Ed. 2d 769.

Today, our Nation has changed. "[T]he conditions that originally justified [§5] no longer characterize voting in the covered jurisdictions." *Ante, at 186 L. Ed. 2d, at 659.* As the Court explains: "'[V]oter turnout and registration rates now approach parity. Blatantly discriminatory evasions of federal decrees are rare. And minority candidates hold office at unprecedented levels.'" *Ante, at 186 L. Ed. 2d, at 667* (quoting *Northwest Austin Municipal Util. Dist. No. One v. Holder,* 557 U.S. 193, 202, 129 S. Ct. 2504, 174 L. Ed. 2d 140 (2009)).

In spite of these improvements, however, Congress *increased* the already significant burdens of §5. Following its reenactment in 2006, the Voting Rights Act was amended to "prohibit more conduct than before." *Ante, at 186 L. Ed. 2d, at 662.* "*Section 5* now forbids voting changes with 'any discriminatory purpose' as well as voting changes that diminish the ability of citizens, on account of race, color, or language minority status, 'to elect their preferred candidates of choice.'" *Ante, at 186 L. Ed. 2d, at 662.* While the pre-2006 version of the Act went well beyond protection guaranteed under the Constitution, see *Reno v. Bossier Parish School Bd.,* 520 U.S. 471, 480-482, 117 S. Ct. 1491, 137 L. Ed. 2d 730 (1997), it now goes even further.

It is, thus, quite fitting that the Court repeatedly points out that this legislation is "extraordinary" and "unprecedented" and recognizes the significant constitutional problems created by Congress' decision to raise "the bar that covered jurisdictions must clear," even as "the conditions justifying that requirement have dramatically improved." *Ante, at 186 L. Ed. 2d, at 668*. However one aggregates the data compiled by Congress, it cannot justify the considerable burdens created by §5. As the Court aptly notes: "[N]o one can fairly say that [the record] shows anything approaching the 'pervasive,' 'flagrant,' 'widespread,' and 'rampant' discrimination that faced Congress in 1965, and that clearly distinguished the covered jurisdictions from the rest of the Nation at that time." *Ante, at 186 L. Ed. 2d, at 671*. Indeed, circumstances in the covered jurisdictions can no longer be characterized as "exceptional" or "unique." "The extensive pattern of discrimination that led the Court to previously uphold §5 as enforcing the *Fifteenth Amendment* no longer exists." *Northwest Austin, supra, at 226, 129 S. Ct. 2504, 174 L. Ed. 2d 140* (Thomas, J., concurring in judgment in part and dissenting in part). *Section 5* is, thus, unconstitutional.

While the Court claims to "issue no holding on §5 itself," *ante, at 186 L. Ed. 2d, at 673*, its own opinion compellingly demonstrates that Congress has failed to justify "'current burdens'" with a record demonstrating "'current needs.'" See *ante, at 186 L. Ed. 2d, at 663* (quoting *Northwest Austin, supra, at 203, 129 S. Ct. 2504, 174 L. Ed. 2d 140*). By leaving the inevitable conclusion unstated, the Court needlessly prolongs the demise of that provision. For the reasons stated in the Court's opinion, I would find §5 unconstitutional.

JUSTICE GINSBURG, with whom JUSTICE BREYER, JUSTICE SOTOMAYOR, and JUSTICE KAGAN join, dissenting.

In the Court's view, the very success of §5 of the Voting Rights Act demands its dormancy. Congress was of another mind. Recognizing that large progress has been made, Congress determined, based on a voluminous record, that the scourge of discrimination was not yet extirpated. The question this case presents is who decides whether, as currently operative, §5 remains justifiable, [1] this Court, or a Congress charged with the obligation to enforce the post-Civil War Amendments "by appropriate legislation." With overwhelming support in both Houses, Congress concluded that, for two prime reasons, §5 should continue in force, unabated. First, continuance would facilitate completion of the impressive gains thus far made; and second, continuance would guard against backsliding. Those assessments were well within Congress' province to make and should elicit this Court's unstinting approbation.

I

"[V]oting discrimination still exists; no one doubts that." *Ante, at 186 L. Ed. 2d, at 659.* But the Court today terminates the remedy that proved to be best suited to block that discrimination. The Voting Rights Act of 1965 (VRA) has worked to combat voting discrimination where other remedies had been tried and failed. Particularly effective is the VRA's requirement of federal preclearance for all changes to voting laws in the regions of the country with the most aggravated records of rank discrimination against minority voting rights.

A century after the *Fourteenth* and *Fifteenth Amendments* guaranteed citizens the right to vote free of discrimination on the basis of race, the "blight of racial discrimination in voting" continued to "infec[t] the electoral process in parts of our country." *South Carolina v. Katzenbach, 383 U.S. 301, 308, 86 S. Ct. 803, 15 L. Ed. 2d 769 (1966).* Early attempts to cope with this vile infection resembled battling the Hydra. Whenever one form of voting discrimination was identified and prohibited, others sprang up in its place. This Court repeatedly encountered the remarkable "variety and persistence" of laws disenfranchising minority citizens. *Id., at 311, 86 S. Ct. 803, 15 L. Ed. 2d 769.* To take just one example, the Court, in 1927, held unconstitutional a Texas law barring black voters from participating in primary elections, *Nixon v. Herndon, 273 U.S. 536, 541, 47 S. Ct. 446, 71 L. Ed. 759*; in 1944,

---

[1] The Court purports to declare unconstitutional only the coverage formula set out in §4(b). See *ante, at 186 L. Ed. 2d, at 673.* But without that formula, §5 is immobilized.

the Court struck down a "reenacted" and slightly altered version of the same law, *Smith v. Allwright, 321 U.S. 649, 658, 64 S. Ct. 757, 88 L. Ed. 987*; and in 1953, the Court once again confronted an attempt by Texas to "circumven[t]" the *Fifteenth Amendment* by adopting yet another variant of the all-white primary, *Terry v. Adams, 345 U.S. 461, 469, 73 S. Ct. 809, 97 L. Ed. 1152*.

During this era, the Court recognized that discrimination against minority voters was a quintessentially political problem requiring a political solution. As Justice Holmes explained: If "the great mass of the white population intends to keep the blacks from voting," "relief from [that] great political wrong, if done, as alleged, by the people of a State and the State itself, must be given by them or by the legislative and political department of the government of the United States." *Giles v. Harris, 189 U.S. 475, 488, 23 S. Ct. 639, 47 L. Ed. 909 (1903)*.

Congress learned from experience that laws targeting particular electoral practices or enabling case-by-case litigation were inadequate to the task. In the Civil Rights Acts of 1957, 1960, and 1964, Congress authorized and then expanded the power of "the Attorney General to seek injunctions against public and private interference with the right to vote on racial grounds." *Katzenbach, 383 U.S., at 313, 86 S. Ct. 803, 15 L. Ed. 2d 769*. But circumstances reduced the ameliorative potential of these legislative Acts:

> "Voting suits are unusually onerous to prepare, sometimes requiring as many as 6,000 man-hours spent combing through registration records in preparation for trial. Litigation has been exceedingly slow, in part because of the ample opportunities for delay afforded voting officials and others involved in the proceedings. Even when favorable decisions have finally been obtained, some of the States affected have merely switched to discriminatory devices not covered by the federal decrees or have enacted difficult new tests designed to prolong the existing disparity between white and Negro registration. Alternatively, certain local officials have defied and evaded court orders or have simply closed their registration offices to freeze the voting rolls." *Id., at 314, 86 S. Ct. 803, 15 L. Ed. 2d 769* (footnote omitted).

Patently, a new approach was needed.

Answering that need, the Voting Rights Act became one of the most consequential, efficacious, and amply justified exercises of federal legislative power in our Nation's his-tory. Requiring federal preclearance of changes in voting laws in the covered jurisdictions—those States and localities where opposition to the Constitution's commands were most virulent—the VRA provided a fit solution for minority voters as well as for States. Under the preclearance regime established by *§5 of the*

VRA, covered jurisdictions must submit proposed changes in voting laws or procedures to the Department of Justice (DOJ), which has 60 days to respond to the changes. 79 Stat. 439, codified at *42 U.S.C. §1973c(a)*. A change will be approved unless DOJ finds it has "the purpose [or] . . . the effect of denying or abridging the right to vote on account of race or color." *Ibid.* In the alternative, the covered jurisdiction may seek approval by a three-judge District Court in the District of Columbia.

After a century's failure to fulfill the promise of the *Fourteenth* and *Fifteenth Amendments*, passage of the VRA finally led to signal improvement on this front. "The Justice Department estimated that in the five years after [the VRA's] passage, almost as many blacks registered [to vote] in Alabama, Mississippi, Georgia, Louisiana, North Carolina, and South Carolina as in the entire century before 1965." Davidson, The Voting Rights Act: A Brief History, in Controversies in Minority Voting 7, 21 (B. Grofman & C. Davidson eds. 1992). And in assessing the overall effects of the VRA in 2006, Congress found that "[s]ignificant progress has been made in eliminating first generation barriers experienced by minority voters, including increased numbers of registered minority voters, minority voter turnout, and minority representation in Congress, State legislatures, and local elected offices. This progress is the direct result of the Voting Rights Act of 1965." Fannie Lou Hamer, Rosa Parks, and Coretta Scott King Voting Rights Act Reauthorization and Amendments Act of 2006 (hereinafter 2006 Reauthorization), *§2(b)(1), 120 Stat. 577*. On that matter of cause and effects there can be no genuine doubt.

Although the VRA wrought dramatic changes in the realization of minority voting rights, the Act, to date, surely has not eliminated all vestiges of discrimination against the exercise of the franchise by minority citizens. Jurisdictions covered by the preclearance requirement continued to submit, in large numbers, proposed changes to voting laws that the Attorney General declined to approve, auguring that barriers to minority voting would quickly resurface were the preclearance remedy eliminated. *City of Rome v. United States, 446 U.S. 156, 181, 100 S. Ct. 1548, 64 L. Ed. 2d 119 (1980)*. Congress also found that as "registration and voting of minority citizens increas[ed], other measures may be resorted to which would dilute increasing minority voting strength." *Ibid.* (quoting H. R. Rep. No. 94-196, p. 10 (1975)). See also *Shaw v. Reno, 509 U.S. 630, 640, 113 S. Ct. 2816, 125 L. Ed. 2d 511 (1993)* ("[I]t soon became apparent that guaranteeing equal access to the polls would not suffice to root out other racially discriminatory voting practices" such as voting dilution). Efforts to reduce the impact of minority votes, in contrast to direct attempts to block access to the ballot, are aptly described as "second-generation barriers" to minority voting.

Second-generation barriers come in various forms. One of the blockages is racial gerrymandering, the redrawing of legislative districts in an "effort to segregate the races for purposes of voting." *Id., at 642, 113 S. Ct. 2816, 125 L. Ed. 2d 511*. Another is adoption of a system of at-large voting in lieu of district-by-district voting in a city with a sizable black minority. By switching to at-large voting, the overall majority could control the election of each city council member, effectively eliminating the potency of the minority's votes. Grofman & Davidson, The Effect of Municipal Election Structure on Black Representation in Eight Southern States, in Quiet Revolution in the South 301, 319 (C. Davidson & B. Grofman eds. 1994) (hereinafter Quiet Revolution). A similar effect could be achieved if the city engaged in discriminatory annexation by incorporating majority-white areas into city limits, thereby decreasing the effect of VRA-occasioned increases in black voting. Whatever the device employed, this Court has long recognized that vote dilution, when adopted with a discriminatory purpose, cuts down the right to vote as certainly as denial of access to the ballot. *Shaw, 509 U.S., at 640-641, 113 S. Ct. 2816, 125 L. Ed. 2d 511; Allen v. State Bd. of Elections, 393 U.S. 544, 569, 89 S. Ct. 817, 22 L. Ed. 2d 1 (1969); Reynolds v. Sims, 377 U.S. 533, 555, 84 S. Ct. 1362, 12 L. Ed. 2d 506 (1964)*. See also H. R. Rep. No. 109-478, p. 6 (2006) (although "[d]iscrimination today is more subtle than the visible methods used in 1965," "the effect and results are the same, namely a diminishing of the minority community's ability to fully participate in the electoral process and to elect their preferred candidates").

In response to evidence of these substituted barriers, Congress reauthorized the VRA for five years in 1970, for seven years in 1975, and for 25 years in 1982. *Ante, at 186 L. Ed. 2d, at 661*. Each time, this Court upheld the reauthorization as a valid exercise of congressional power. *Ante, at 186 L. Ed. 2d, at 661*. As the 1982 reauthorization approached its 2007 expiration date, Congress again considered whether the VRA's preclearance mechanism remained an appropriate response to the problem of voting discrimination in covered jurisdictions.

Congress did not take this task lightly. Quite the opposite. The 109th Congress that took responsibility for the renewal started early and conscientiously. In October 2005, the House began extensive hearings, which continued into November and resumed in March 2006. S. Rep. No. 109-295, p. 2 (2006). In April 2006, the Senate followed suit, with hearings of its own. *Ibid*. In May 2006, the bills that became the VRA's reauthorization were introduced in both Houses. *Ibid*. The House held further hearings of considerable length, as did the Senate, which continued to hold hearings into June and July. H. R. Rep. 109-478, at 5; S. Rep. 109-295, at 3-4. In mid-July, the House considered and rejected four amendments, then passed the reauthorization by a vote of 390 yeas to 33 nays. 152 Cong. Rec. H5207 (July 13,

2006); Persily, The Promise and Pitfalls of the New Voting Rights Act, *117 Yale L. J. 174, 182-183 (2007)* (hereinafter Persily). The bill was read and debated in the Senate, where it passed by a vote of 98 to 0. 152 Cong. Rec. S8012 (July 20, 2006). President Bush signed it a week later, on July 27, 2006, recognizing the need for "further work . . . in the fight against injustice," and calling the reauthorization "an example of our continued commitment to a united America where every person is valued and treated with dignity and respect." 152 Cong. Rec. S8781 (Aug. 3, 2006).

In the long course of the legislative process, Congress "amassed a sizable record." *Northwest Austin Municipal Util. Dist. No. One v. Holder, 557 U.S. 193, 205, 129 S. Ct. 2504, 174 L. Ed. 2d 140 (2009).* See also *679 F. 3d 848, 865-873, 400 U.S. App. D.C. 367 (CADC 2012)* (describing the "extensive record" supporting Congress' determination that "serious and widespread intentional discrimination persisted in covered jurisdictions"). The House and Senate Judiciary Committees held 21 hearings, heard from scores of witnesses, received a number of investigative reports and other written documentation of continuing discrimination in covered jurisdictions. In all, the legislative record Congress compiled filled more than 15,000 pages. H. R. Rep. 109-478, at 5, 11-12; S. Rep. 109-295, at 2-4, 15. The compilation presents countless "examples of flagrant racial discrimination" since the last reauthorization; Congress also brought to light systematic evidence that "intentional racial discrimination in voting remains so serious and widespread in covered jurisdictions that section 5 preclearance is still needed." *679 F. 3d, at 866.*

After considering the full legislative record, Congress made the following findings: The VRA has directly caused significant progress in eliminating first-generation barriers to ballot access, leading to a marked increase in minority voter registration and turnout and the number of minority elected officials. 2006 Reauthorization §2(b)(1). But despite this progress, "second generation barriers constructed to prevent minority voters from fully participating in the electoral process" continued to exist, as well as racially polarized voting in the covered jurisdictions, which increased the political vulnerability of racial and language minorities in those jurisdictions. §§2(b)(2)-(3), *120 Stat. 577.* Extensive "[e]vidence of continued discrimination," Congress concluded, "clearly show[ed] the continued need for Federal oversight" in covered jurisdictions. §§2(b)(4)-(5), *id.,* at 577-578. The overall record demonstrated to the federal lawmakers that, "without the continuation of the Voting Rights Act of 1965 protections, racial and language minority citizens will be deprived of the opportunity to exercise their right to vote, or will have their votes diluted, undermining the significant gains made by minorities in the last 40 years." §2(b)(9), *id.,* at 578.

Based on these findings, Congress reauthorized preclearance for another 25 years, while also undertaking to reconsider the extension after 15 years to ensure that the provision was still necessary and effective. 42 U.S.C. §1973b(a)(7), (8) (2006 ed., Supp. V). The question before the Court is whether Congress had the authority under the Constitution to act as it did.

II

In answering this question, the Court does not write on a clean slate. It is well established that Congress' judgment regarding exercise of its power to enforce the *Fourteenth* and *Fifteenth Amendments* warrants substantial deference. The VRA addresses the combination of race discrimination and the right to vote, which is "preservative of all rights." *Yick Wo v. Hopkins, 118 U.S. 356, 370, 6 S. Ct. 1064, 30 L. Ed. 220 (1886).* When confronting the most constitutionally invidious form of discrimination, and the most fundamental right in our democratic system, Congress' power to act is at its height.

The basis for this deference is firmly rooted in both constitutional text and precedent. The *Fifteenth Amendment*, which targets precisely and only racial discrimination in voting rights, states that, in this domain, "Congress shall have power to enforce this article by appropriate legislation." [2] In choosing this language, the Amendment's framers invoked Chief Justice Marshall's formulation of the scope of Congress' powers under the Necessary and Proper Clause:

> "Let the end be legitimate, let it be within the scope of the constitution, and *all means which are appropriate, which are plainly adapted to that end,* which are not prohibited, but consist with the letter and spirit of the constitution, are constitutional." *McCulloch v. Maryland, 17 U.S. 316, 4 Wheat. 316, 421, 4 L. Ed. 579 (1819)* (emphasis added).

---

[2] The Constitution uses the words "right to vote" in five separate places: the *Fourteenth, Fifteenth, Nineteenth, Twenty-Fourth,* and *Twenty-Sixth Amendments.* Each of these Amendments contains the same broad empowerment of Congress to enact "appropriate legislation" to enforce the protected right. The implication is unmistakable: Under our constitutional structure, Congress holds the lead rein in making the right to vote equally real for all U.S. citizens. These Amendments are in line with the special role assigned to Congress in protecting the integrity of the democratic process in federal elections. U.S. Const., Art. I, §4 ("[T]he Congress may at any time by Law make or alter" regulations concerning the "Times, Places and Manner of holding Elections for Senators and Representatives."); *Arizona v. Inter Tribal Council of Ariz., Inc., ante,* at ___ - 133 S. Ct. 186 L. Ed. 2d 239, 2013 U.S. LEXIS 4544, *10.

It cannot tenably be maintained that the VRA, an Act of Congress adopted to shield the right to vote from racial discrimination, is inconsistent with the letter or spirit of the *Fifteenth Amendment*, or any provision of the Constitution read in light of the Civil War Amendments. Nowhere in today's opinion, or in *Northwest Austin*,[3] is there clear recognition of the transformative effect the *Fifteenth Amendment* aimed to achieve. Notably, "the Founders' first successful amendment told Congress that it could 'make no law' over a certain domain"; in contrast, the Civil War Amendments used "language [that] authorized transformative new federal statutes to uproot all vestiges of unfreedom and inequality" and provided "sweeping enforcement powers . . . to enact 'appropriate' legislation targeting state abuses." A. Amar, America's Constitution: A Biography 361, 363, 399 (2005). See also McConnell, Institutions and Interpretation: A Critique of *City of Boerne* v. *Flores*, *111 Harv. L. Rev. 153, 182 (1997)* (quoting Civil War-era framer that "the remedy for the violation of the *fourteenth* and *fifteenth amendments* was expressly not left to the courts. The remedy was legislative.").

The stated purpose of the Civil War Amendments was to arm Congress with the power and authority to protect all persons within the Nation from violations of their rights by the States. In exercising that power, then, Congress may use "all means which are appropriate, which are plainly adapted" to the constitutional ends declared by these Amendments. *McCulloch, 17 U.S. 316, 4 Wheat., at 421, 4 L. Ed. 579.* So when Congress acts to enforce the right to vote free from racial discrimination, we ask not whether Congress has chosen the means most wise, but whether Congress has rationally selected means appropriate to a legitimate end. "It is not for us to review the congressional resolution of [the need for its chosen remedy]. It is enough that we be able to perceive a basis upon which the Congress might resolve the conflict as it did." *Katzenbach v. Morgan, 384 U.S. 641, 653, 86 S. Ct. 1717, 16 L. Ed. 2d 828 (1966).*

Until today, in considering the constitutionality of the VRA, the Court has accorded Congress the full measure of respect its judgments in this domain should garner. *South Carolina* v. *Katzenbach* supplies the standard of review: "As against the reserved powers of the States, Congress may use any rational means to effectuate the constitutional prohibition of racial discrimination in voting." *383 U.S., at 324, 86 S. Ct. 803, 15 L. Ed. 2d 769.* Faced with subsequent reauthorizations of the VRA, the Court has reaffirmed this standard. *E.g., City of Rome, 446 U.S., at 178,*

---

[3] Acknowledging the existence of "serious constitutional questions," see *ante, at 186 L. Ed. 2d, at 672* (internal quotation marks omitted), does not suggest how those questions should be answered.

100 S. Ct. 1548, 64 L. Ed. 2d 119. Today's Court does not purport to alter settled precedent establishing that the dispositive question is whether Congress has employed "rational means."

For three reasons, legislation *re*authorizing an existing statute is especially likely to satisfy the minimal requirements of the rational-basis test. First, when reauthorization is at issue, Congress has already assembled a legislative record justifying the initial legislation. Congress is en-titled to consider that preexisting record as well as the record before it at the time of the vote on reauthorization. This is especially true where, as here, the Court has repeatedly affirmed the statute's constitutionality and Congress has adhered to the very model the Court has upheld. See *id.*, *at 174, 100 S. Ct. 1548, 64 L. Ed. 2d 119* ("The appellants are asking us to do nothing less than overrule our decision in *South Carolina v. Katzenbach* . . ., in which we upheld the constitutionality of the Act."); *Lopez v. Monterey County, 525 U.S. 266, 283, 119 S. Ct. 693, 142 L. Ed. 2d 728 (1999)* (similar).

Second, the very fact that reauthorization is necessary arises because Congress has built a temporal limitation into the Act. It has pledged to review, after a span of years (first 15, then 25) and in light of contemporary evidence, the continued need for the VRA. Cf. *Grutter v. Bollinger, 539 U.S. 306, 343, 123 S. Ct. 2325, 156 L. Ed. 2d 304 (2003)* (anticipating, but not guaranteeing, that, in 25 years, "the use of racial preferences [in higher education] will no longer be necessary").

Third, a reviewing court should expect the record supporting reauthorization to be less stark than the record originally made. Demand for a record of violations equivalent to the one earlier made would expose Congress to a **catch-22**. If the statute was working, there would be less evidence of discrimination, so opponents might argue that Congress should not be allowed to renew the statute. In contrast, if the statute was not working, there would be plenty of evidence of discrimination, but scant reason to renew a failed regulatory regime. See *Persily 193-194*.

This is not to suggest that congressional power in this area is limitless. It is this Court's responsibility to ensure that Congress has used appropriate means. The question meet for judicial review is whether the chosen means are "adapted to carry out the objects the amendments have in view." *Ex parte Virginia, 100 U.S. 339, 346, 25 L. Ed. 676 (1880)*. The Court's role, then, is not to substitute its judgment for that of Congress, but to determine whether the legislative record sufficed to show that "Congress could rationally have determined that [its chosen] provisions were appropriate methods." *City of Rome, 446 U.S., at 176-177, 100 S. Ct. 1548, 64 L. Ed. 2d 119*.

In summary, the Constitution vests broad power in Congress to protect the right to vote, and in particular to combat racial discrimination in voting. This Court has repeatedly reaffirmed Congress' prerogative to use any rational means in exercise of its power in this area. And both precedent and logic dictate that the rational-means test should be easier to satisfy, and the burden on the statute's challenger should be higher, when what is at issue is the reauthorization of a remedy that the Court has previously affirmed, and that Congress found, from contemporary evidence, to be working to advance the legislature's legitimate objective.

III

The 2006 reauthorization of the Voting Rights Act fully satisfies the standard stated in *McCulloch*, *17 U.S. 316, 4 Wheat., at 421, 4 L. Ed. 579*: Congress may choose any means "appropriate" and "plainly adapted to" a legitimate constitutional end. As we shall see, it is implausible to suggest otherwise.

A

I begin with the evidence on which Congress based its decision to continue the preclearance remedy. The surest way to evaluate whether that remedy remains in order is to see if preclearance is still effectively preventing discriminatory changes to voting laws. See *City of Rome, 446 U.S., at 181, 100 S. Ct. 1548, 64 L. Ed. 2d 119* (identifying "information on the number and types of submissions made by covered jurisdictions and the number and nature of objections interposed by the Attorney General" as a primary basis for upholding the 1975 reauthorization). On that score, the record before Congress was huge. In fact, Congress found there were *more* DOJ objections between 1982 and 2004 (626) than there were between 1965 and the 1982 reauthorization (490). 1 Voting Rights Act: Evidence of Continued Need, Hearing before the Subcommittee on the Constitution of the House Committee on the Judiciary, 109th Cong., 2d Sess., p. 172 (2006) (hereinafter Evidence of Continued Need).

All told, between 1982 and 2006, DOJ objections blocked over 700 voting changes based on a determination that the changes were discriminatory. H. R. Rep. No. 109-478, at 21. Congress found that the majority of DOJ objections included findings of discriminatory intent, see *679 F. 3d, at 867*, and that the changes blocked by preclearance were "calculated decisions to keep minority voters from fully participating in the political process." H. R. Rep. 109-478, at 21. On top of that, over the same time period the DOJ and private plaintiffs succeeded in more than 100 actions to enforce the §5 preclearance requirements. 1 Evidence of Continued Need 186, 250.

In addition to blocking proposed voting changes through preclearance, DOJ may request more information from a jurisdiction proposing a change. In turn, the jurisdiction may modify or withdraw the proposed change. The number of such modifications or withdrawals provides an indication of how many discriminatory proposals are deterred without need for formal objection. Congress received evidence that more than 800 proposed changes were altered or withdrawn since the last reauthorization in 1982. H. R. Rep. No. 109-478, at 40-41. [4] Congress also received empirical studies finding that DOJ's requests for more information had a significant effect on the degree to which covered jurisdictions "compl[ied] with their obligatio[n]" to protect minority voting rights. 2 Evidence of Continued Need 2555.

Congress also received evidence that litigation under §2 of the *VRA* was an inadequate substitute for preclearance in the covered jurisdictions. Litigation occurs only after the fact, when the illegal voting scheme has already been put in place and individuals have been elected pursuant to it, thereby gaining the advantages of incumbency. 1 Evidence of Continued Need 97. An illegal scheme might be in place for several election cycles before a §2 plaintiff can gather sufficient evidence to challenge it. 1 Voting Rights Act: *Section 5* of the Act—History, Scope, and Purpose: Hearing before the Subcommittee on the Constitution of the House Committee on the Judiciary, 109th Cong., 1st Sess., p. 92 (2005) (hereinafter Section 5 Hearing). And litigation places a heavy financial burden on minority voters. See *id.,* at 84. Congress also received evidence that preclearance lessened the litigation burden on covered jurisdictions themselves, because the preclearance process is far less costly than defending against a §2 claim, and clearance by DOJ substantially reduces the likelihood that a §2 claim will be mounted. Reauthorizing the Voting Rights Act's Temporary Provisions: Policy Perspectives and Views From the Field: Hearing before the Subcommittee on the Constitution, Civil Rights and Property Rights of the Senate Committee on the Judiciary, 109th Cong., 2d Sess., pp. 13, 120-121 (2006). See also Brief for States of New York, California,

---

[4] This number includes only changes actually proposed. Congress also received evidence that many covered jurisdictions engaged in an "informal consultation process" with DOJ before formally submitting a proposal, so that the deterrent effect of preclearance was far broader than the formal submissions alone suggest. The Continuing Need for Section 5 Pre-Clearance: Hearing before the Senate Committee on the Judiciary, 109th Cong., 2d Sess., pp. 53-54 (2006). All agree that an unsupported assertion about "deterrence" would not be sufficient to justify keeping a remedy in place in perpetuity. See *ante,* at *186 L. Ed. 2d, at 669*. But it was certainly reasonable for Congress to consider the testimony of witnesses who had worked with officials in covered jurisdictions and observed a real-world deterrent effect.

Mississippi, and North Carolina as *Amici Curiae* 8-9 (*Section 5* "reduc[es] the likelihood that a jurisdiction will face costly and protracted Section 2 litigation").

The number of discriminatory changes blocked or deterred by the preclearance requirement suggests that the state of voting rights in the covered jurisdictions would have been significantly different absent this remedy. Surveying the type of changes stopped by the preclearance procedure conveys a sense of the extent to which §5 continues to protect minority voting rights. Set out below are characteristic examples of changes blocked in the years leading up to the 2006 reauthorization:

- In 1995, Mississippi sought to reenact a dual voter registration system, "which was initially enacted in 1892 to disenfranchise Black voters," and for that reason, was struck down by a federal court in 1987. H. R. Rep. No. 109-478, at 39.

- Following the 2000 census, the City of Albany, Georgia, proposed a redistricting plan that DOJ found to be "designed with the purpose to limit and retrogress the increased black voting strength . . . in the city as a whole." *Id.*, at 37 (internal quotation marks omitted).

- In 2001, the mayor and all-white five-member Board of Aldermen of Kilmichael, Mississippi, abruptly canceled the town's election after "an unprecedented number" of African-American candidates announced they were running for office. DOJ required an election, and the town elected its first black mayor and three black aldermen. *Id.,* at 36-37.

- In 2006, this Court found that Texas' attempt to redraw a congressional district to reduce the strength of Latino voters bore "the mark of intentional discrimination that could give rise to an equal protection violation," and ordered the district redrawn in compliance with the VRA. *League of United Latin American Citizens v. Perry*, 548 U.S. 399, 440, 126 S. Ct. 2594, 165 L. Ed. 2d 609 (2006). In response, Texas sought to undermine this Court's order by curtailing early voting in the district, but was blocked by an action to enforce the §5 preclearance requirement. See Order in *League of United Latin American Citizens* v. *Texas*, No. 06-cv-1046 (WD Tex.), Doc. 8.

- In 2003, after African-Americans won a majority of the seats on the school board for the first time in history, Charleston County, South Carolina, proposed an at-large voting mechanism for the board. The proposal, made without consulting any of the African-American members of the school board, was found to be an "'exact replica'" of an earlier voting scheme that, a federal court had determined, violated the VRA. *811 F. Supp. 2d 424, 483 (DDC 2011).* See also S. Rep. No. 109-295, at 309. DOJ invoked §5 to block the proposal.

- In 1993, the City of Millen, Georgia, proposed to delay the election in a majority-black district by two years, leaving that district without representation on the city council while the neighboring majority-white district would have three representatives. 1 Section 5 Hearing 744. DOJ blocked the proposal. The county then sought to move a polling place from a predominantly black neighborhood in the city to an inaccessible location in a predominantly white neighborhood outside city limits. *Id.,* at 816.

- In 2004, Waller County, Texas, threatened to prosecute two black students after they announced their intention to run for office. The county then attempted to reduce the availability of early voting in that election at polling places near a historically black university. *679 F. 3d, at 865-866.*

- In 1990, Dallas County, Alabama, whose county seat is the City of Selma, sought to purge its voter rolls of many black voters. DOJ rejected the purge as discriminatory, noting that it would have disqualified many citizens from voting "simply because they failed to pick up or return a voter update form, when there was no valid requirement that they do so." 1 Section 5 Hearing 356.

These examples, and scores more like them, fill the pages of the legislative record. The evidence was indeed sufficient to support Congress' conclusion that "racial discrimination in voting in covered jurisdictions [remained] serious and pervasive." *679 F. 3d, at 865.* [5]

---

[5] For an illustration postdating the 2006 reauthorization, see *South Carolina v. United States, 898 F. Supp. 2d 30 (DC 2012),* which involved a South Carolina voter-identification law enacted in 2011. Concerned that the law would burden minority voters, DOJ brought a §5 enforcement action to block the law's implementation. In the course of the litigation, South Carolina officials agreed to binding interpretations that made it "far easier than some might have expected or feared" for South Carolina citizens to vote. *Id., at 37.* A three-judge panel precleared the law after adopting both interpretations as an express "condition of preclearance." *Id., at 37-38.* Two of the judges commented that the case demonstrated "the continuing utility of *Section 5* of the Voting Rights Act in deterring problematic, and hence encouraging non-discriminatory, changes in state and local voting laws." *Id., at 54* (opinion of Bates, J.).

Congress further received evidence indicating that formal requests of the kind set out above represented only the tip of the iceberg. There was what one commentator described as an "avalanche of case studies of voting rights violations in the covered jurisdictions," ranging from "outright intimidation and violence against minority voters" to "more subtle forms of voting rights deprivations." *Persily 202* (footnote omitted). This evidence gave Congress ever more reason to conclude that the time had not yet come for relaxed vigilance against the scourge of race discrimination in voting.

True, conditions in the South have impressively improved since passage of the Voting Rights Act. Congress noted this improvement and found that the VRA was the driving force behind it. 2006 Reauthorization §2(b)(1). But Congress also found that voting discrimination had evolved into subtler second-generation barriers, and that eliminating preclearance would risk loss of the gains that had been made. §§2(b)(2), (9). Concerns of this order, the Court previously found, gave Congress adequate cause to reauthorize the VRA. *City of Rome, 446 U.S., at 180-182, 100 S. Ct. 1548, 64 L. Ed. 2d 119* (congressional reauthorization of the preclearance requirement was justified based on "the number and nature of objections interposed by the Attorney General" since the prior reauthorization; extension] was "necessary to pre-serve the limited and fragile achievements of the Act and to promote further amelioration of voting discrimination") (internal quotation marks omitted). Facing such evidence then, the Court expressly rejected the argument that disparities in voter turnout and number of elected officials were the only metrics capable of justifying reauthorization of the VRA. *Ibid.*

B

I turn next to the evidence on which Congress based its decision to reauthorize the coverage formula in §4(b). Because Congress did not alter the coverage formula, the same jurisdictions previously subject to preclearance continue to be covered by this remedy. The evidence just described, of preclearance's continuing efficacy in blocking constitutional violations in the covered jurisdictions, itself grounded Congress' conclusion that the remedy should be retained for those jurisdictions.

There is no question, moreover, that the covered jurisdictions have a unique history of problems with racial discrimination in voting. *Ante, at 186 L. Ed. 2d, at 666.* Consideration of this long history, still in living memory, was altogether appropriate. The Court criticizes Congress for failing to recognize that "history did not end in 1965." *Ante, at 186 L. Ed. 2d, at 670.* But the Court ignores that "what's past is prologue." W. Shakespeare, The Tempest, act 2, sc. 1. And "[t]hose who cannot remember the past are condemned to repeat it." 1 G. Santayana, The Life of Reason 284 (1905). Congress was especially mindful of the need to reinforce the gains already made and to prevent backsliding. 2006 Reauthorization §2(b)(9).

Of particular importance, even after 40 years and thousands of discriminatory changes blocked by preclearance, conditions in the covered jurisdictions demonstrated that the formula was still justified by "current needs." *Northwest Austin*, 557 U.S., at 203, 129 S. Ct. 2504, 174 L. Ed. 2d 140.

Congress learned of these conditions through a report, known as the Katz study, that looked at §2 suits between 1982 and 2004. To Examine the Impact and Effectiveness of the Voting Rights Act: Hearing before the Subcommittee on the Constitution of the House Committee on the Judiciary, 109th Cong., 1st Sess., pp. 964-1124 (2005) (hereinafter Impact and Effectiveness). Because the private right of action authorized by *§2 of the VRA* applies nationwide, a comparison of §2 lawsuits in covered and noncovered jurisdictions provides an appropriate yardstick for measuring differences between covered and noncovered jurisdictions. If differences in the risk of voting discrimination between covered and noncovered jurisdictions had disappeared, one would expect that the rate of successful §2 lawsuits would be roughly the same in both areas. [6] The study's findings, however, indicated that racial discrimination in voting remains "concentrated in the jurisdictions singled out for preclearance." *Northwest Austin*, 557 U.S., at 203, 129 S. Ct. 2504, 174 L. Ed. 2d 140.

Although covered jurisdictions account for less than 25 percent of the country's population, the Katz study revealed that they accounted for 56 percent of successful §2 litigation since 1982. Impact and Effectiveness 974. Controlling for population, there were nearly *four* times as many successful §2 cases in covered jurisdictions as there were in noncovered jurisdictions. *679 F. 3d, at 874*. The Katz study further found that §2 lawsuits are more likely to succeed when they are filed in covered jurisdictions than in noncovered jurisdictions. Impact and Effectiveness 974. From these findings—ignored by the Court—Congress reasonably concluded that the coverage formula continues to identify the jurisdictions of greatest concern.

The evidence before Congress, furthermore, indicated that voting in the covered jurisdictions was more racially polarized than elsewhere in the country. H. R. Rep.

---

[6] Because preclearance occurs only in covered jurisdictions and can be expected to stop the most obviously objectionable measures, one would expect a *lower* rate of successful §2 lawsuits in those jurisdictions if the risk of voting discrimination there were the same as elsewhere in the country.

No. 109-478, at 34-35. While racially polarized voting alone does not signal a constitutional violation, it is a factor that increases the vulnerability of racial minorities to discriminatory changes in voting law. The reason is twofold. First, racial polarization means that racial minorities are at risk of being systematically outvoted and having their interests underrepresented in legislatures. Second, "when political preferences fall along racial lines, the natural inclinations of incumbents and ruling parties to entrench themselves have predictable racial effects. Under circumstances of severe racial polarization, efforts to gain political advantage translate into race-specific disadvantages." Ansolabehere, Persily, & Stewart, Regional Differences in Racial Polarization in the 2012 Presidential Election: Implications for the Constitutionality of Section 5 of the Voting Rights Act, *126 Harv. L. Rev. Forum 205, 209 (2013).*

In other words, a governing political coalition has an incentive to prevent changes in the existing balance of voting power. When voting is racially polarized, efforts by the ruling party to pursue that incentive "will inevitably discriminate against a racial group." *Ibid.* Just as buildings in California have a greater need to be earthquake-proofed, places where there is greater racial polarization in voting have a greater need for prophylactic measures to prevent purposeful race discrimination. This point was understood by Congress and is well recognized in the academic literature. See 2006 Reauthorization *§2(b)(3), 120 Stat. 577* ("The continued evidence of racially polarized voting in each of the jurisdictions covered by the [preclearance requirement] demonstrates that racial and language minorities remain politically vulnerable"); H. R. Rep. No. 109-478, at 35; Davidson, The Recent Evolution of Voting Rights Law Affecting Racial and Language Minorities, in Quiet Revolution 21, 22.

The case for retaining a coverage formula that met needs on the ground was therefore solid. Congress might have been charged with rigidity had it afforded covered jurisdictions no way out or ignored jurisdictions that needed superintendence. Congress, however, responded to this concern. Critical components of the congressional design are the statutory provisions allowing jurisdictions to "bail out" of preclearance, and for court-ordered "bail ins." See *Northwest Austin, 557 U.S., at 199, 129 S. Ct. 2504, 174 L. Ed. 2d 140.* The VRA permits a jurisdiction to bail out by showing that it has complied with the Act for ten years, and has engaged in efforts to eliminate intimidation and harassment of voters. *42 U.S.C. §1973b(a) (2006 ed. and Supp. V).* It also authorizes a court to subject a noncovered jurisdiction to federal preclearance upon finding that violations of the *Fourteenth* and *Fifteenth Amendments* have occurred there. *§1973a(c) (2006 ed.).*

Congress was satisfied that the VRA's bailout mechanism provided an effective means of adjusting the VRA's coverage over time. H. R. Rep. No. 109-478, at 25 (the success of bailout "illustrates that: (1) covered status is neither permanent nor over-broad; and (2) covered status has been and continues to be within the control of the jurisdiction such that those jurisdictions that have a genuinely clean record and want to terminate coverage have the ability to do so"). Nearly 200 jurisdictions have successfully bailed out of the preclearance requirement, and DOJ has consented to every bailout application filed by an eligible jurisdiction since the current bailout procedure became effective in 1984. Brief for Federal Respondent 54. The bail-in mechanism has also worked. Several jurisdictions have been subject to federal preclearance by court orders, including the States of New Mexico and Arkansas. App. to Brief for Federal Respondent 1a-3a.

This experience exposes the inaccuracy of the Court's portrayal of the Act as static, unchanged since 1965. Congress designed the VRA to be a dynamic statute, capable of adjusting to changing conditions. True, many covered jurisdictions have not been able to bail out due to recent acts of noncompliance with the VRA, but that truth reinforces the congressional judgment that these jurisdictions were rightfully subject to preclearance, and ought to remain under that regime.

IV

Congress approached the 2006 reauthorization of the VRA with great care and seriousness. The same cannot be said of the Court's opinion today. The Court makes no genuine attempt to engage with the massive legislative record that Congress assembled. Instead, it relies on increases in voter registration and turnout as if that were the whole story. See *supra, at 186 L. Ed. 2d, at 684-685*. Without even identifying a standard of review, the Court dismissively brushes off arguments based on "data from the record," and declines to enter the "debat[e about] what [the] record shows." *Ante, at 186 L. Ed. 2d, at 671*. One would expect more from an opinion striking at the heart of the Nation's signal piece of civil-rights legislation.

I note the most disturbing lapses. First, by what right, given its usual restraint, does the Court even address Shelby County's facial challenge to the VRA? Second, the Court veers away from controlling precedent regarding the "equal sovereignty" doctrine without even acknowledging that it is doing so. Third, hardly showing the respect ordinarily paid when Congress acts to implement the Civil War Amendments, and as just stressed, the Court does not even deign to grapple with the legislative record.

A

Shelby County launched a purely facial challenge to the VRA's 2006 reauthorization. "A facial challenge to a legislative Act," the Court has other times said, "is, of course, the most difficult challenge to mount successfully, since the challenger must establish that no set of circumstances exists under which the Act would be valid." *United States v. Salerno, 481 U.S. 739, 745, 107 S. Ct. 2095, 95 L. Ed. 2d 697 (1987).*

"[U]nder our constitutional system[,] courts are not roving commissions assigned to pass judgment on the validity of the Nation's laws." *Broadrick v. Oklahoma, 413 U.S. 601, 610-611, 93 S. Ct. 2908, 37 L. Ed. 2d 830 (1973).* Instead, the "judicial Power" is limited to deciding particular "Cases" and "Controversies." U.S. Const., Art. III, §2. "Embedded in the traditional rules governing constitutional adjudication is the principle that a person to whom a statute may constitutionally be applied will not be heard to challenge that statute on the ground that it may conceivably be applied unconstitutionally to others, in other situations not before the Court." *Broadrick, 413 U.S., at 610, 93 S. Ct. 2908, 37 L. Ed. 2d 830.* Yet the Court's opinion in this case contains not a word explaining why Congress lacks the power to subject to preclearance the particular plaintiff that initiated this lawsuit—Shelby County, Alabama. The reason for the Court's silence is apparent, for as applied to Shelby County, the VRA's preclearance requirement is hardly contestable.

Alabama is home to Selma, site of the "Bloody Sunday" beatings of civil-rights demonstrators that served as the catalyst for the VRA's enactment. Following those events, Martin Luther King, Jr., led a march from Selma to Montgomery, Alabama's capital, where he called for passage of the VRA. If the Act passed, he foresaw, progress could be made even in Alabama, but there had to be a steadfast national commitment to see the task through to completion. In King's words, "the arc of the moral universe is long, but it bends toward justice." G. May, Bending Toward Justice: The Voting Rights Act and the Transformation of American Democracy 144 (2013).

History has proved King right. Although circumstances in Alabama have changed, serious concerns remain. Between 1982 and 2005, Alabama had one of the highest rates of successful §2 suits, second only to its VRA-covered neighbor Mississippi. *679 F. 3d, at 897* (Williams, J., dissenting). In other words, even while subject to the restraining effect of §5, Alabama was found to have "deni[ed] or abridge[d]" voting rights "on account of race or color" more frequently than nearly all other States in the Union. *42 U.S.C. §1973(a).* This fact prompted the dissenting judge below to concede that "a more narrowly tailored coverage formula" capturing Alabama and a handful of other jurisdictions with an established track record of racial discrimination in voting "might be defensible." *679 F. 3d, at 897* (opinion of Williams, J.). That is an understatement. Alabama's sorry history of §2 violations alone provides sufficient justification for Congress' determination in 2006 that the State should remain subject to §5's preclearance requirement.[7]

A few examples suffice to demonstrate that, at least in Alabama, the "current burdens" imposed by §5's preclearance requirement are "justified by current needs." *Northwest Austin, 557 U.S., at 203, 129 S. Ct. 2504, 174 L. Ed. 2d 140.* In the interim between the VRA's 1982 and 2006 reauthorizations, this Court twice confronted purposeful racial discrimination in Alabama. In *Pleasant Grove v. United States, 479 U.S. 462, 107 S. Ct. 794, 93 L. Ed. 2d 866 (1987),* the Court held that Pleasant Grove—a city in Jefferson County, Shelby County's neighbor—engaged in purposeful discrimination by annexing all-white areas while rejecting the annexation request of an adjacent black neighborhood. The city had "shown unambiguous opposition to racial integration, both before and after the passage of the federal civil rights laws," and its strategic annexations appeared to be an attempt "to provide for the growth of a monolithic white voting block" for "the impermissible purpose of minimizing future black voting strength." *Id., at 465, 471-472, 107 S. Ct. 794, 93 L. Ed. 2d 866.*

Two years before Pleasant Grove, the Court in *Hunter v. Underwood, 471 U.S. 222, 105 S. Ct. 1916, 85 L. Ed. 2d 222 (1985),* struck down a provision of the Alabama Constitution that prohibited individuals convicted of misdemeanor offenses "involving moral turpitude" from voting. *Id., at 223, 105 S. Ct. 1916, 85 L. Ed. 2d 222* (internal quotation marks omitted). The provision violated the *Fourteenth Amendment*'s *Equal Protection Clause*, the Court unanimously concluded, because "its original enactment was motivated by a desire to discriminate against blacks on account of race[,] and the [provision] continues to this day to have that effect." *Id., at 233, 105 S. Ct. 1916, 85 L. Ed. 2d 222.*

---

[7] This lawsuit was filed by Shelby County, a political subdivision of Alabama, rather than by the State itself. Nevertheless, it is appropriate to judge Shelby County's constitutional challenge in light of instances of discrimination statewide because Shelby County is subject to §5's preclearance requirement by virtue of *Alabama's* designation as a covered jurisdiction under *§4(b) of the VRA.* See *ante, at 186 L. Ed. 2d, at 662.* In any event, Shelby County's recent record of employing an at-large electoral system tainted by intentional racial discrimination is by itself sufficient to justify subjecting the county to §5's preclearance mandate. See *infra, at 186 L. Ed. 2d, at 689.*

Pleasant Grove and *Hunter* were not anomalies. In 1986, a Federal District Judge concluded that the at-large election systems in several Alabama counties violated §2. *Dillard v. Crenshaw Cty.*, 640 F. Supp. 1347, 1354-1363 (MD Ala. 1986). Summarizing its findings, the court stated that "[f]rom the late 1800's through the present, [Alabama] has consistently erected barriers to keep black persons from full and equal participation in the social, economic, and political life of the state." *Id.*, at 1360.

The *Dillard* litigation ultimately expanded to include 183 cities, counties, and school boards employing discriminatory at-large election systems. *Dillard v. Baldwin Cty. Bd. of Ed.*, 686 F. Supp. 1459, 1461 (MD Ala. 1988). One of those defendants was Shelby County, which eventually signed a consent decree to resolve the claims against it. See *Dillard v. Crenshaw Cty.*, 748 F. Supp. 819 (MD Ala. 1990).

Although the *Dillard* litigation resulted in overhauls of numerous electoral systems tainted by racial discrimination, concerns about backsliding persist. In 2008, for example, the city of Calera, located in Shelby County, requested preclearance of a redistricting plan that "would have eliminated the city's sole majority-black district, which had been created pursuant to the consent decree in *Dillard*." 811 F. Supp. 2d 424, 443 (DC 2011). Although DOJ objected to the plan, Calera forged ahead with elections based on the unprecleared voting changes, resulting in the defeat of the incumbent African-American councilman who represented the former majority-black district. *Ibid.* The city's defiance required DOJ to bring a §5 enforcement action that ultimately yielded appropriate redress, including restoration of the majority-black district. *Ibid.*; Brief for Respondent-Intervenors Earl Cunningham et al. 20.

A recent FBI investigation provides a further window into the persistence of racial discrimination in state politics. See *United States v. McGregor*, 824 F. Supp. 2d 1339, 1344-1348 (MD Ala. 2011). Recording devices worn by state legislators cooperating with the FBI's investigation captured conversations between members of the state legislature and their political allies. The recorded conversations are shocking. Members of the state Senate derisively refer to African-Americans as "Aborigines" and talk openly of their aim to quash a particular gambling-related referendum because the referendum, if placed on the ballot, might increase African-American voter turnout. *Id.*, at 1345-1346 (internal quotation marks omitted). See also *id.*, at 13 45 (legislators and their allies expressed concern that if the referendum were placed on the ballot, "'[e]very black, every illiterate' would be 'bused [to the polls] on HUD financed buses'"). These conversations occurred not in the 1870's, or even in the 1960's, they took place in 2010. *Id.*, at 1344-1345. The District Judge presiding over the criminal trial at which the recorded conversations were

351

introduced commented that the "recordings represent compelling evidence that political exclusion through racism remains a real and enduring problem" in Alabama. *Id., at 1347.* Racist sentiments, the judge observed, "remain regrettably entrenched in the high echelons of state government." *Ibid.*

These recent episodes forcefully demonstrate that §5's preclearance requirement is constitutional as applied to Alabama and its political subdivisions. [8] And under our case law, that conclusion should suffice to resolve this case. See *United States v. Raines,* 362 U.S. 17, 24-25, 80 S. Ct. 519, 4 L. Ed. 2d 524 (1960) ("[I]f the complaint here called for an application of the statute clearly constitutional under the *Fifteenth Amendment,* that should have been an end to the question of constitutionality."). See also *Nev. Dep't of Human Res. v. Hibbs,* 538 U.S. 721, 743, 123 S. Ct. 1972, 155 L. Ed. 2d 953 (2003) (Scalia, J., dissenting) (where, as here, a state or local government raises a facial challenge to a federal statute on the ground that it exceeds Congress' enforcement powers under the Civil War Amendments, the challenge fails if the opposing party is able to show that the statute "could constitutionally be applied to *some* jurisdictions").

This Court has consistently rejected constitutional challenges to legislation enacted pursuant to Congress' enforcement powers under the Civil War Amendments upon finding that the legislation was constitutional as applied to the particular set of circumstances before the Court. See *United States v. Georgia,* 546 U.S. 151, 159, 126 S. Ct. 877, 163 L. Ed. 2d 650 (2006) (Title II of the *Americans with Disabilities Act of 1990* (ADA) validly abrogates state sovereign immunity "insofar as [it] creates a private cause of action . . . for conduct that *actually* violates the *Fourteenth Amendment*"); *Tennessee v. Lane,* 541 U.S. 509, 530-534, 124 S. Ct. 1978, 158 L. Ed. 2d 820 (2004) (Title II of the ADA is constitutional "as it applies to the class of cases implicating the fundamental right of access to the courts"); *Raines,* 362 U.S., at 24-26, 80 S. Ct. 519, 4 L. Ed. 2d 524 (federal statute proscribing deprivations of the right to vote based on race was constitutional as applied to the state officials before the Court, even if it could not constitutionally be applied to other parties). A similar approach is warranted here. [9]

---

[8] Congress continued preclearance over Alabama, including Shelby County, *after* considering evidence of current barriers there to minority voting clout. Shelby County, thus, is no "redhead" caught up in an arbitrary scheme. See *ante, at* 186 L. Ed. 2d, at 671.

[9] The Court does not contest that Alabama's history of racial discrimination provides a sufficient basis for Congress to require Alabama and its political subdivisions to preclear electoral changes. Nevertheless, the Court asserts that Shelby County may prevail on its facial challenge to §4's coverage formula because it is subject to §5's preclearance

The VRA's exceptionally broad severability provision makes it particularly inappropriate for the Court to allow Shelby County to mount a facial challenge to §§4(b) and 5 of the VRA, even though application of those provisions to the county falls well within the bounds of Congress' legislative authority. The severability provision states:

> "If any provision of [this Act] or the application thereof to any person or circumstances is held invalid, the remainder of [the Act] and the application of the provision to other persons not similarly situated or to other circumstances shall not be affected thereby." *42 U.S.C. §1973p.*

In other words, even if the VRA could not constitutionally be applied to certain States—*e.g.*, Arizona and Alaska, see *ante*, at 186 L. Ed. 2d, at 663—§1973p calls for those unconstitutional applications to be severed, leaving the Act in place for jurisdictions as to which its application does not transgress constitutional limits.

Nevertheless, the Court suggests that limiting the jurisdictional scope of the VRA in an appropriate case would be "to try our hand at updating the statute." *Ante, at 186 L. Ed. 2d, at 671.* Just last Term, however, the Court rejected this very argument when addressing a materially identical severability provision, explaining that such a provision is "Congress' explicit textual instruction to leave unaffected the remainder of [the Act]" if any particular "application is unconstitutional." *National Federation of Independent Business v. Sebelius*, 567 U.S. ___, ___, 132 S. Ct. 2566, 183 L. Ed. 2d 450, 497 (2012) (plurality opinion) (internal quotation marks omitted); *id.*, at ___, 132 S. Ct. 2566, 183 L. Ed. 2d 450, 499 (Ginsburg, J., concurring in part, concurring in judgment in part, and dissenting in part) (agreeing with the plurality's severability analysis). See also *Raines*, 362 U.S., at 23, 80 S. Ct. 519, 4 L. Ed. 2d 524 (a statute capable of some constitutional applications may nonetheless be susceptible to a facial challenge only in "that rarest of cases where this Court can justifiably think itself able confidently to discern that Congress would not have desired its legislation to stand at all unless it could validly stand in its every application"). Leaping to resolve Shelby County's facial challenge without considering whether application of the VRA to Shelby County is constitutional, or even addressing the VRA's severability provision, the Court's opinion can hardly be described as an exemplar of restrained and moderate decisionmaking. Quite the opposite. Hubris is a fit word for today's demolition of the VRA.

---

requirement by virtue of that formula. See *ante, at 186 L. Ed. 2d, at 671* ("The county was selected [for preclearance] based on th[e] [coverage] formula."). This misses the reality that Congress decided to subject Alabama to preclearance based on evidence of continuing constitutional violations in that State. See *supra*, at n. 8, 186 L. Ed. 2d, at 690.

B

The Court stops any application of §5 by holding that §4(b)'s coverage formula is unconstitutional. It pins this result, in large measure, to "the fundamental principle of equal sovereignty." *Ante, at 186 L. Ed. 2d, at 664-665, 672.* In *Katzenbach*, however, the Court held, in no uncertain terms, that the principle "*applies only to the terms upon which States are admitted to the Union*, and not to the remedies for local evils which have subsequently appeared." *383 U.S., at 328-329, 86 S. Ct. 803, 15 L. Ed. 2d 769* (emphasis added).

Katzenbach, the Court acknowledges, "rejected the notion that the [equal sovereignty] principle operate[s] as a bar on differential treatment outside [the] context [of the admission of new States]." *Ante, at 186 L. Ed. 2d, at 665* (citing *383 U.S., at 328-329, 86 S. Ct. 803, 15 L. Ed. 2d 769*) (emphasis omitted). But the Court clouds that once clear understanding by citing dictum from *Northwest Austin* to convey that the principle of equal sovereignty "remains highly pertinent in assessing subsequent disparate treatment of States." *Ante, at 186 L. Ed. 2d, at 665* (citing *557 U.S., at 203, 129 S. Ct. 2504, 174 L. Ed. 2d 140*). See also *ante, at 186 L. Ed. 2d, at 672* (relying on *Northwest Austin*'s "emphasis on [the] significance" of the equal-sovereignty principle). If the Court is suggesting that dictum in *Northwest Austin* silently overruled *Katzenbach*'s limitation of the equal sovereignty doctrine to "the admission of new States," the suggestion is untenable. *Northwest Austin* cited *Katzenbach*'s holding in the course of *declining to decide* whether the VRA was constitutional or even what standard of review applied to the question. *557 U.S., at 203-204, 129 S. Ct. 2504, 174 L. Ed. 2d 140*. In today's decision, the Court ratchets up what was pure dictum in *Northwest Austin*, attributing breadth to the equal sovereignty principle in flat contradiction of *Katzenbach*. The Court does so with nary an explanation of why it finds *Katzenbach* wrong, let alone any discussion of whether *stare decisis* nonetheless counsels adherence to *Katzenbach*'s ruling on the limited "significance" of the equal sovereignty principle.

Today's unprecedented extension of the equal sovereignty principle outside its proper domain—the admission of new States—is capable of much mischief. Federal statutes that treat States disparately are hardly novelties. See, *e.g., 28 U.S.C. §3704* (no State may operate or permit a sports-related gambling scheme, unless that State conducted such a scheme "at any time during the period beginning January 1, 1976, and ending August 31, 1990"); *26 U.S.C. §142(l)* (EPA required to locate green building project in a State meeting specified population criteria); *42 U.S.C. §3796bb* (at least 50 percent of rural drug enforcement assistance funding must be allocated to States with "a population density of fifty-two or fewer persons per square mile or a State in which the largest county has fewer than one hundred and fifty thousand people, based on the decennial census of 1990 through fiscal year 1997"); §§13925, 13971 (similar population criteria for funding to combat rural domestic violence); §10136 (specifying rules applicable to Nevada's Yucca Mountain nuclear waste site, and providing that "[n]o State, other than the State of Nevada, may receive financial assistance under this subsection after December 22, 1987"). Do such provisions remain safe given the Court's expansion of equal sovereignty's sway?

Of gravest concern, Congress relied on our pathmarking *Katzenbach* decision in each reauthorization of the VRA. It had every reason to believe that the Act's limited geographical scope would weigh in favor of, not against, the Act's constitutionality. See, *e.g., United States v. Morrison, 529 U.S. 598, 626-627, 120 S. Ct. 1740, 146 L. Ed. 2d 658 (2000)* (confining preclearance regime to States with a record of discrimination bolstered the VRA's constitutionality). Congress could hardly have foreseen that the VRA's limited geographic reach would render the Act constitutionally suspect. See *Persily 195* ("[S]upporters of the Act sought to develop an evidentiary record for the principal purpose of explaining why the covered jurisdictions should remain covered, rather than justifying the coverage of certain jurisdictions but not others.").

In the Court's conception, it appears, defenders of the VRA could not prevail upon showing what the record overwhelmingly bears out, *i.e.,* that there is a need for continuing the preclearance regime in covered States. In addition, the defenders would have to disprove the existence of a comparable need elsewhere. See Tr. of Oral Arg. 61-62 (suggesting that proof of egregious episodes of racial discrimination in covered jurisdictions would not suffice to carry the day for the VRA, unless such episodes are shown to be absent elsewhere). I am aware of no precedent for imposing such a double burden on defenders of legislation.

C

The Court has time and again declined to upset legislation of this genre unless there was no or almost no evidence of unconstitutional action by States. See, *e.g., City of Boerne v. Flores, 521 U.S. 507, 530, 117 S. Ct. 2157, 138 L. Ed. 2d 624 (1997)* (legislative record "mention[ed] no episodes [of the kind the legislation aimed to check] occurring in the past 40 years"). No such claim can be made about the congressional record for the 2006 VRA reauthorization. Given a record replete with examples of denial or abridgment of a paramount federal right, the Court should have left the matter where it belongs: in Congress' bailiwick.

Instead, the Court strikes §4(b)'s coverage provision because, in its view, the provision is not based on "current conditions." *Ante, at 186 L. Ed. 2d, at 669*. It discounts, however, that one such condition was the preclearance remedy in place in the covered jurisdictions, a remedy Congress designed both to catch discrimination before it causes harm, and to guard against return to old ways. 2006 Reauthorization §2(b)(3), (9). Volumes of evidence supported Congress' determination that the prospect of retrogression was real. Throwing out preclearance when it has worked and is continuing to work to stop discriminatory changes is like throwing away your umbrella in a rainstorm because you are not getting wet.

But, the Court insists, the coverage formula is no good; it is based on "decades-old data and eradicated practices." *Ante, at 186 L. Ed. 2d, at 669*. Even if the legislative record shows, as engaging with it would reveal, that the formula accurately identifies the jurisdictions with the worst conditions of voting discrimination, that is of no moment, as the Court sees it. Congress, the Court decrees, must "star[t] from scratch." *Ante, at 186 L. Ed. 2d, at 672*. I do not see why that should be so.

Congress' chore was different in 1965 than it was in 2006. In 1965, there were a "small number of States . . . which in most instances were familiar to Congress by name," on which Congress fixed its attention. *Katzenbach, 383 U.S., at 328, 86 S. Ct. 803, 15 L. Ed. 2d 769*. In drafting the coverage formula, "Congress began work with reliable evidence of actual voting discrimination in a great majority of the States" it sought to target. *Id., at 329, 86 S. Ct. 803, 15 L. Ed. 2d 769*. "The formula [Congress] eventually evolved to describe these areas" also captured a few States that had not been the subject of congressional factfinding. *Ibid.* Nevertheless, the Court upheld the formula in its entirety, finding it fair "to infer a significant danger of the evil" in all places the formula covered. *Ibid.*

The situation Congress faced in 2006, when it took up *re*authorization of the coverage formula, was not the same. By then, the formula had been in effect for many years, and *all* of the jurisdictions covered by it were "familiar to Congress by name." *Id., at 328, 86 S. Ct. 803, 15 L. Ed. 2d 769*. The question before Congress: Was there still a sufficient basis to support continued application of the preclearance remedy in each of those already-identified places? There was at that point no chance that the formula might inadvertently sweep in new areas that were not the subject of congressional findings. And Congress could determine from the record whether the jurisdictions captured by the coverage formula still belonged under the preclearance regime. If they did, there was no need to alter the formula. That is why the Court, in addressing prior reauthorizations of the VRA, did not question the continuing "relevance" of the formula.

Consider once again the components of the record before Congress in 2006. The coverage provision identified a known list of places with an undisputed history of serious problems with racial discrimination in voting. Recent evidence relating to

Alabama and its counties was there for all to see. Multiple Supreme Court decisions had upheld the coverage provision, most recently in 1999. There was extensive evidence that, due to the preclearance mechanism, conditions in the covered jurisdictions had notably improved. And there was evidence that preclearance was still having a substantial real-world effect, having stopped hundreds of discriminatory voting changes in the covered jurisdictions since the last reauthorization. In addition, there was evidence that racial polarization in voting was higher in covered jurisdictions than elsewhere, increasing the vulnerability of minority citizens in those jurisdictions. And countless witnesses, reports, and case studies documented continuing problems with voting discrimination in those jurisdictions. In light of this record, Congress had more than a reasonable basis to conclude that the existing coverage formula was not out of sync with conditions on the ground in covered areas. And certainly Shelby County was no candidate for release through the mechanism Congress provided. See *supra, at 186 L. Ed. 2d, at 687, 689-690.*

The Court holds §4(b) invalid on the ground that it is "irrational to base coverage on the use of voting tests 40 years ago, when such tests have been illegal since that time." *Ante, at 186 L. Ed. 2d, at 673.* But the Court disregards what Congress set about to do in enacting the VRA. That extraordinary legislation scarcely stopped at the particular tests and devices that happened to exist in 1965. The grand aim of the Act is to secure to all in our polity equal citizenship stature, a voice in our democracy undiluted by race. As the record for the 2006 reauthorization makes abundantly clear, second-generation barriers to minority voting rights have emerged in the covered jurisdictions as attempted *substitutes* for the first-generation barriers that originally triggered preclearance in those jurisdictions. See *supra, at 186 L. Ed. 2d, at 677-678, 678, 683-684.*

The sad irony of today's decision lies in its utter failure to grasp why the VRA has proven effective. The Court appears to believe that the VRA's success in eliminating the specific devices extant in 1965 means that preclearance is no longer needed. *Ante, at 186 L. Ed. 2d, at 671, 672-673.* With that belief, and the argument derived from it, history repeats itself. The same assumption—that the problem could be solved when particular methods of voting discrimination are identified and eliminated—was indulged and proved wrong repeatedly prior to the VRA's enactment. Unlike prior statutes, which singled out particular tests or devices, the VRA is grounded in Congress' recognition of the "variety and persistence" of measures designed to impair minority voting rights. *Katzenbach, 383 U.S., at 311, 86 S. Ct. 803, 15 L. Ed. 2d 769*; *supra, at 186 L. Ed. 2d, at 675.* In truth, the evolution of voting discrimination into more subtle second-generation barriers is powerful evidence that a remedy as effective as preclearance remains vital to protect minority voting rights and prevent backsliding.

Beyond question, the VRA is no ordinary legislation. It is extraordinary because Congress embarked on a mission long delayed and of extraordinary importance: to realize the purpose and promise of the *Fifteenth Amendment*. For a half century, a concerted effort has been made to end racial discrimination in voting. Thanks to the Voting Rights Act, progress once the subject of a dream has been achieved and continues to be made.

The record supporting the 2006 reauthorization of the VRA is also extraordinary. It was described by the Chairman of the House Judiciary Committee as "one of the most extensive considerations of any piece of legislation that the United States Congress has dealt with in the 27½ years" he had served in the House. 152 Cong. Rec. H5143 (July 13, 2006) (statement of Rep. Sensenbrenner). After exhaustive evidence-gathering and deliberative process, Congress reauthorized the VRA, including the coverage provision, with overwhelming bipartisan support. It was the judgment of Congress that "40 years has not been a sufficient amount of time to eliminate the vestiges of discrimination following nearly 100 years of disregard for the dictates of the *15th amendment* and to ensure that the right of all citizens to vote is protected as guaranteed by the Constitution." 2006 Reauthorization *§2(b)(7), 120 Stat. 577*. That determination of the body empowered to enforce the Civil War Amendments "by appropriate legislation" merits this Court's utmost respect. In my judgment, the Court errs egregiously by overriding Congress' decision.
***

For the reasons stated, I would affirm the judgment of the Court of Appeals.

CONCLUSION

Catch-22 has appeared in the judicial opinions of nine U.S. Supreme Court cases. The Supreme Court of the United States is an important American institution. Its works are the high art of American law. The word catch-22 appears in both majority opinions and dissents, and on both sides of the political spectrum. Justices Stewart, Brennan, Rehnquist, Blackmun, Souter, Roberts, and Ginsburg, have each used the word and have incorporated what was a fictional book, into the American legal lexicon.

This book is published to coincide with the start of the October Term 2016. It begins this week with an eight member court, two of whom (Roberts and Ginsburg) have used catch-22 in recent dissent. Will they use it again? Is it relevant, or just a very long version of taps? And who wrote that law journal note that Justice Stewart cited? Would the word have entered the Court's vocabulary without that journal article? What words will enter this year?

Meanwhile, Judge Merrick Garland was nominated by President Obama on March 16, 2016. The Senate has continued to refuse a confirmation hearing. This obstruction is unprecedented. Was the Garland nomination a sort of catch-22 bind on Senate Republicans? Or, is the Supreme Court itself the catch-22 of constitutional democracy? A political body forced to bind itself outside of politics; a political will without its own political arms.

From a dissenting position, any majority rule might appear to be a vague paradoxical catch, so, perhaps it's better if the court must try to decide by wider majorities. The Garland gambit may be just what the Court needs to depolarize, and pursue the Chief Justice's dream of narrower holdings with wider consensus, or else they will fall into the catch 4-4.

Happy October Term 2016.

LAW OF THE HORSE

This book is part of a series entitled *Law of the Horse*. The phrase was coined by Gerhard Casper and adopted in argument by Judge Easterbrook to decry the development of cyberlaw as a specialized area of legal study. However, in April 1997, Lawrence Lessig, then professor at Harvard Law School, responded to Easterbrook and argued for the burgeoning field in "The Law of the Horse: What Cyberlaw Might Teach." Use of this phrase for this series of case law books is a sort of parody of the controversy and a use of computer technology to collect case law about popular topics.

<u>Currently available:</u>

Werewolf in the Federal Courts
Red Herring in the Supreme Court
Mad Scientist in the Federal Courts
Cocker Spaniel in the Federal Courts
Dachshund in the Federal Courts
Zombie in the Federal Courts
Valentines Day in the Federal Courts *(short format)
Creativity in the Supreme Court
Undead in the Federal Courts
Labrador Retriever in the Federal Courts
Catch-22 in the Supreme Court

More coming soon

ABOUT THE EDITOR

Joshua Warren is an artist, educator, scientist, and practicing attorney, with an interest in politics, language and creativity.

Other artwork by Joshua Warren can be found at:
warrbo.com

www.ingramcontent.com/pod-product-compliance
Lightning Source LLC
Chambersburg PA
CBHW021419170526
45164CB00001B/15